THE 2010–2011 COMPENSATION HANDBOOK FOR CHURCH STAFF

Richard R. Hammar, J.D., LL.M., CPA

YOUR CHURCH

CHRISTIANITY TODAY
INTERNATIONAL

The 2010-2011 Compensation Handbook for Church Staff

ISBN-10: 0-917463-55-2

ISBN-13: 978-0-917463-55-6

Published by Your Church Resources
Christianity Today International
465 Gundersen Drive
Carol Stream, IL 60188
(630) 260-6200
www.ChristianityToday.com
www.YourChurch.net

Data compiled and interpreted by the Market Research team at Christianity Today International.

CREDITS

Edited by: Marian V. Liautaud

Cover design: Ryan Hamm

Interior design: Mary Bellus

10 9 8 7 6 5 4 3 2 1   11 10 09

Printed in the United States of America

TABLE OF CONTENTS

1

BEFORE
YOU BEGIN

If you've ever had questions or needed guidance when it comes to compensation planning for your church staff, you've picked up the right resource. Welcome to the *2010-2011 Compensation Handbook for Church Staff*. As you read through this introductory chapter, you'll learn about the many ways you can use this book to meet your compensation planning needs.

The *Compensation Handbook* was developed to provide church leaders and employees with a current and reliable picture of compensation practices across a broad spectrum of American churches. It presents survey data from nearly 5,000 churches representing more than 10,000 staff members. The survey data was obtained in February and March 2009 from subscribers of one or more of the following publications: *Church Law & Tax Report, Church Finance Today, Leadership Journal*, and various Christianity Today International e-newsletters and web channels.

The information included can play an important role in determining equitable compensation packages for church staff members. The *Compensation Handbook* can help you:

* **Determine appropriate compensation levels** for 13 key pastoral, professional, and support staff positions, both full-time and part-time. (Note: Eleven of these positions have information for both full-time and part-time individuals. For seven of the ten positions, we've provided an expanded part-time section given the level of response. Two positions are unique: Executive or Administrative Pastor has information for full-time individuals only, while Musician/Vocalist has information for part-time individuals only.)

* **Develop effective compensation packages** with guidelines given in the Special Section to help you maximize net income while remaining in compliance with federal tax laws.

* **Provide church workers with a statistical framework** for evaluating their present compensation packages. Comparisons can be made regarding church size, budget, setting, and other important variables.

* **Establish an objective standard** for evaluating requests for raises and changes in benefits.

* **Promote equitable and fair compensation practices** by assisting denominational offices and other ecclesiastical organizations in understanding and guiding churches' financial practices.

* **Better understand** the nature of church compensation planning.

How to Make the Best Use of this Book

Compensation planning is a multi-faceted process. This book is one tool you can use to measure appropriate levels of compensation, but it is not a complete guide. Many factors go into determining compensation planning, and this book attempts to help you explore those aspects knowledgeably.

Informative charts are featured throughout the book. You can find the background information you need to use the data in these tables with ease and accuracy in Chapter 2: *Using the Compensation Tables*. Included in this chapter is an example that illustrates how to determine the compensation range for a senior pastor. You can use the same process to examine all staff positions.

Chapter 3 provides comparisons among the overall averages for each of the thirteen staff positions included in this study. Table 3-1 provides a comparative listing of each position.

Chapters 4 through 14 provide detailed information on each individual staff position. Each chapter begins by providing an employment profile for each staff position. Natural curiosity will pull most church staff members immediately to the chapter on their positions. Remember, though, understanding chapters 2 and 3 is critical to using this book effectively.

Chapter 17 provides a statistical abstract of the churches participating in this study. This data is useful for learning more about the churches that are contributing information. The participating church profile includes the percentage of church budgets devoted to salaries, the percentage of churches that contribute to their Senior Pastor's or Solo Pastor's Social Security, the percentage that reimburse professional expenses, and more. It also includes church attendance and financial condition over the past year by worship attendance and region.

The *Special Section: Tax Law & Compensation Planning* by Richard Hammar provides critical information for completing the compensation planning process. Anyone engaged in this type of planning for church staff members must become familiar with some basic federal tax laws, since the structure of a compensation package can either help or hurt a church staff member. This special section explores in detail the major (and often hard-to-understand) laws that affect compensation planning. It also provides tax saving tips that can benefit everyone. Additional resources are also listed in this section.

Background Information

The results in the charts that follow represent the positions that were reported among those participating in the survey. The sampling population used represents the positions reported from subscribers to *Church Law & Tax Report, Church Finance Today, Leadership Journal,* and various Christianity Today International e-newsletters and web channels. Therefore, certain church sizes, budget sizes, and denominations have a stronger representation than others. To the extent possible, we have attempted to organize the data in ways that avoid small samples. At times, however, a small sample simply reflects a reality—such as rural churches with attendance over 1,000, or churches smaller than 100 with a full-time bookkeeper. Nevertheless, sample size should be taken into account when considering the value of any particular finding.

Here are a few additional facts to help clarify the data analyses which follow.

* **Averages, medians, and quartiles** (*Lowest 25%* and *Highest 25%*) are based on individuals receiving the item in the compensation and/or benefit packages. Zeros are not included in calculations.

* **Wide gaps** between averages and medians are due to a wider range of data reported.

* **A footnote that says** "Not enough responses to provide meaningful data" means either one or both of these:

  • There are less than eight people responding.

  • There are relatively few responses (maybe more than eight) with a very wide gap between the lowest and highest values.

* **Blanks** (no response) and zeros are treated similarly and are not part of the compensation median, quartile, and average calculations.

* **Figures** that appeared unrealistic or fell outside the normal distribution were eliminated to avoid skewing the results.

* **Total Compensation includes** base salary, housing allowance, and parsonage amount. Given that many individuals do not receive both housing and parsonage, Total Compensation as presented is not calculated by adding base salary, housing, and parsonage. Rather, the Total Compensation figures are calculated for each individual and reported in aggregate. As a result, in some instances, the Total Compensation figure is less than individual entries of base salary, housing, and parsonage added together.

* **This is also true in regard to *Total Benefits*.** Given that many individuals do not receive all or some of the following benefits—health, life, and disability insurance as well as retirement or continuing education—Total Benefits figures are not calculated by adding each benefit together. Rather, the Total Benefits figures are calculated for each individual and reported in aggregate.

✳ **Please note:** in some instances total insurance premium was reported without the breakdown of individual premiums for health, life, and disability insurance. In these situations, the total insurance premium was included in the Total Benefits figure, as it is unknown how to distribute the total premiums across each category.

✳ **Hourly Rate** is provided across part-time positions. Hourly Rate is calculated by taking the base salary divided by (the number of hours per week compensated for multiplied by 52 weeks). In other words: base salary divided by (# weekly hours x 52) = hourly rate. Housing, parsonage, and benefits are not included in this calculation.

✳ **Some percentages** may not always add up to 100% due to rounding. This particularly refers to the data found at the beginning of each section titled *Employment Profile*.

✳ **For reporting purposes,** Adult Ministry and Christian Education Pastor/Director positions were combined due to the overlap in the job descriptions and the similarities in the findings.

Explanation of Data Distribution

In the charts that follow, averages, medians, and quartiles (noted as *Lowest 25%* and *Highest 25%*) are used to represent survey findings.

The *average*, also called the mean, is a value that depends equally on all of the data. It is calculated by taking the sum of all the data values, dividing by the total number of data values. Please keep in mind that the averages, as presented, are not the averages of the highest and lowest quartiles, but an average of the overall data.

The *median* is a value that divides the higher half of the data set from the lower half of the data set. When sorting the data set from lowest to highest, the median is the middle value.

A *quartile* is one of three values that divide sorted data from a particular table into quarters. The first quartile, called *Lowest 25%* in this handbook, is the value that separates the lowest 25% of the sorted data from the highest 75%. The third quartile, called *Highest 25%* in this handbook, is the value that separates the highest 25 % of the sorted data from the lowest 75%. The second quartile, called *median* in this handbook, is the middle value among the data, i.e. 50% of the data is higher than the median and 50% of the data is lower.

For example, in tables showing compensation ranges for a specific position, the *Lowest 25%* value (first quartile) means that 25% of respondents reported lower compensation amounts than this first quartile value while 75% of respondents reported higher compensation amounts.

The same is true with the third quartile, or the upper quartile, which cuts off highest 25% of the data. This actually means that the number shown represents a number that exceeds 1–75% of the people in the population represented in the report. The upper quartile is reported as *Highest 25%* by church income among each position.

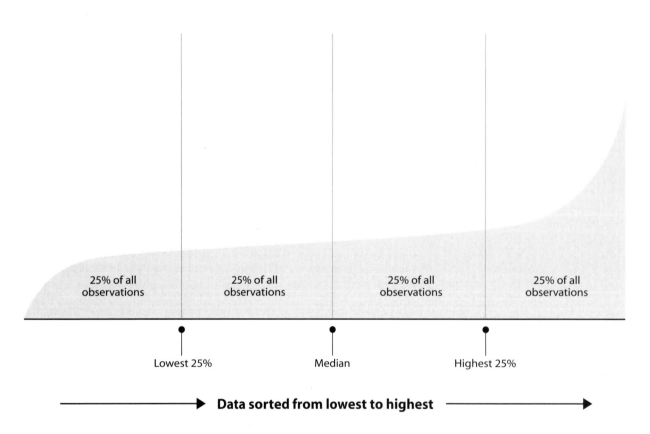

25% of all observations   25% of all observations   25% of all observations   25% of all observations

Lowest 25%   Median   Highest 25%

Data sorted from lowest to highest

2

USING THE COMPENSATION TABLES

The following chapters present compensation patterns for 13 major positions within the local church. These profiles are the statistical heart of the *Compensation Handbook*. This chapter is designed to help you interpret the tables and maximize your use of the information in this book.

Each staff position has its own chapter, including both compensation tables and a discussion of the findings. The tables are for full-time staff members, except for the last tables in each chapter, which provide data for part-time staff members. Note, however, that due to the low incidence of part-time Executive or Administrative Pastors, data is not reported. On the other hand, Musicians/Accompanists/Vocalists tables are for part-time only, due to the low incidence of full-timers in this position.

A comparative summary of all the positions is presented in Chapter 3.

Interpreting the Tables

Each chapter contains tables that portray compensation averages according to several key identifiers, grouped according to the most meaningful breaks. They include the following:

* **Church income (from all sources).** Question asked: "Approximately what is your total annual church budget this past year?"

* **Worship attendance (weekend).** Question asked: "Approximately how many people, including children, attend all weekend worship services?"

* **Church setting.** Question asked: "Which of the following best describes the setting in which your church is located?"

* **Region.** Question asked: "In what state is your church located?" (Regional breakout by state is included in the appendix.)

* **Education.** Question asked: "What is this person's highest level of education?"

* **Years employed (in current position).** Question asked: "How long has this person been in this position?"

* **Denomination.** Question asked: "What is your church's denomination or fellowship?"

* **Gender.** Question asked: "What is this person's gender?"

Each table provides key characteristics that include:

* **Average weekend worship attendance.** Question asked: "Approximately how many people, including children, attend all weekend worship services?"

* **Average church income.** Question asked: "Approximately what was your total annual church budget this past year?"

✳ **Average number of years employed.** Question asked: "How long has this person been in this position?"

✳ **Average number of paid vacation days.** Question asked: "How many paid vacation days does this person receive?"

✳ **Percentage that are college graduates or higher.** Question asked: "What is this person's highest level of education?"

✳ **Percentage who receive automobile reimbursement.** Question asked: "Does the church help with this person's automobile expenses?"

✳ **Percentage that are ordained.** Question asked: "Is this person ordained, licensed, or commissioned?"

✳ **Percentage that supervise one or more people.** Question asked: "Does this person supervise one or more people?"

✳ **Average percentage salary increase this year.** Question asked: "What was this person's salary increase in the past year?"

In addition, each table provides several columns of data for these compensation and benefit items (Compensation and Benefits are listed separately):

Compensation

✳ **Base Salary:** annual base salary

✳ **Housing allowance***

✳ **Parsonage:** rental value of parsonage plus allowance*

Benefits

✳ **Pension/retirement contribution**

✳ **Continuing Education**

✳ **Insurance Premiums:** amount paid to insurance companies for:

  • Health Insurance

  • Life Insurance

  • Disability Insurance

The data shown in the first table for each full-time position is Annual Compensation by Church Income. Since Church Income is an important variable in compensation, we've provided expanded data for your reference by including the *Highest 25%* and *Lowest 25%* data in addition to the *Median* and *Average* as presented in the rest of the tables.

*In gathering data, we allowed respondents to use their own judgment in determining the definition of housing and parsonage

The number listed after *Lowest 25%* represents a number that exceeds the base salary of 1–25% of the people in the population represented in the report. Similarly, the number following *Highest 25%* represents a number that exceeds the base salary of 1–75% of the people in the population represented in the report. For more information, please see section titled "Explanation of Data Distribution" in the Chapter 1.

To illustrate, consider this example for a Senior Pastor position:

	Data Distribution*	CHURCH INCOME				
		$250k & Under	$251K-$500K	$501K-$750K	$751K-$1M	Over $1 Million
COMPENSATION						
Base Salary	Highest 25%	$39,300	$50,000	$61,086	$62,800	$88,796
	Median	$30,000	$40,000	$50,000	$50,075	$65,913
	Lowest 25%	$23,000	$30,000	$40,278	$40,000	$52,498
	Average	$31,573	$41,217	$51,859	$53,174	$71,742
Housing	Highest 25%	$25,000	$30,000	$35,000	$36,000	$45,000
	Median	$18,000	$24,000	$25,900	$27,050	$33,000
	Lowest 25%	$12,000	$17,500	$19,468	$20,550	$25,000
	Average	$18,756	$24,702	$27,011	$29,091	$36,061
Parsonage	Highest 25%	$14,400	$18,000	$20,000	$22,000	$37,500
	Median	$9,600	$11,800	$15,000	$15,500	$21,150
	Lowest 25%	$5,740	$7,900	$9,600	$12,342	$12,000
	Average	$11,122	$13,208	$17,359	$19,868	$27,205
Total Compensation	**Highest 25%**	**$56,044**	**$70,000**	**$86,000**	**$87,000**	**$117,700**
	Median	**$47,040**	**$61,568**	**$74,200**	**$77,855**	**$97,000**
	Lowest 25%	**$36,000**	**$52,446**	**$65,000**	**$69,100**	**$83,538**
	Average	**$46,980**	**$63,465**	**$76,506**	**$79,637**	**$104,298**

Notice that within the first column Base Salary, figures are shown in four categories: *Highest 25%, Median, Lowest 25%,* and *Average*. After *Highest 25%*, the number $39,300 appears. This means that 25% of all Senior Pastors serving a church with an income of *$250,000 and under* make $39,300 or more in Base Salary. Another way to say this is that 75% of Senior Pastors in a church with an income of *$250,000 and under* make less than $39,300 in Base Salary.

Next is the *Median* where the number $30,000 appears. This number is the value that divides the higher half of the data set from the lower half of the data set. This means that 50% of all Senior Pastors serving a church with an income of *$250,000 and under* make $30,000 or more in Base Salary. Another way to say this is that 50% of Senior Pastors in a church with an income of *$250,000 and under* make less than $30,000 in Base Salary.

Following the category *Lowest 25%* the number $23,000 appears, which indicates that 25% of all Senior Pastors in a church with an income of *$250,000 and under* make $23,000 or less. Again, another way to say this is that 75% of Senior Pastors in a church with an income of *$250,000 and under* make more than $23,000.

After the category *Average*, the number $31,573 is listed. This number represents the average amount of the salaries for all Senior Pastors in a church with an income of *$250,000 and under.*

Also, all calculated figures, including the sub-categories *Highest 25%, Median, Lowest 25%* and *Average* are based on individuals receiving the specific items in the Compensation chart (the same is true of the Benefits chart).

Medians and averages are provided for each full-time position by the following data breaks in addition to Church Income for your reference.

* **Worship attendance**
* **Church setting**
* **Region**
* **Education**
* **Years employed (in current position)**
* **Denomination**
* **Gender**

Total Compensation plus Benefits Comparisons

At the bottom of each compensation chart is a category that lists Total Compensation. These numbers include base salary, housing allowance, and parsonage allowance. Likewise, at the bottom of each Benefits chart is a category that lists Total Benefits. These numbers include health insurance, life insurance, disability insurance, retirement, and continuing education benefits. A separate box in the table, titled Total Compensation Plus Benefits includes all of the Compensation and Benefits items. Note: Totals are the key figures for compensation analysis.

Rounding errors may exist in some of the data in this study. They do not, however, impact the final results in any significant way.

In general, church income, attendance, education, geographical setting, and years of service play some role in almost every church—as they increase, compensation increases. Yet, the correlation between these variables and employee compensation accounts for only part of the variation in compensation figures by position. These factors, while important, must be viewed in the context of other factors, the combination of which ultimately determines compensation and benefits.

As an example, theology may play a significant role in some churches in the determination of compensation. In churches that promote financial prosperity as a sign of God's blessing, the pastor may receive a disproportionate amount of the church's total income. A building program may be the controlling factor somewhere else. In general, education, geographical setting, and years of service play some role in almost every church.

Using the Tables to Plan Compensation

The most important use of this handbook is for compensation planning. The following example illustrates one approach of how this book can be used.

EXAMPLE: PLANNING THE COMPENSATION OF A SENIOR PASTOR

Pastor Jones has served as First Church Senior Pastor for the past five years. First Church is a small-town congregation in the West-South Central region with an average worship attendance of 365, and an annual budget of $375,000. Pastor Jones has a Master of Divinity degree.

The above example provides us with relevant data that can be used in coordination with the tables in this book. Variables we will look at include the church's income ($375,000), worship attendance (365), the pastor's length of service (five years) and educational background (Master's degree), plus the geographical setting of the church (in this case small town) and region (West-South Central).

KEY POINT

The goal is not to come up with a single compensation number, but rather to identify a *compensation range*. Once that range is determined, a variety of factors will affect the final choice of a specific level of compensation.

STEP 1

Since Church income is one of the most important variables, the first step is to use Table 4-1: *Annual Compensation of Full-time Senior Pastor by Church Income* in Chapter 4 to provide us with some working boundaries on both the upper and lower limits. We can examine the range of the middle 50% of respondents by looking at the *Lowest 25%* and the *Highest 25%* numbers across church income levels. The main data we are interested in is found at the bottom of each table in the box labeled *Total Compensation Plus Benefits*. Since Pastor Jones's church income is $375,000, we will look at the second level *($251,000-$500,000)*. The following is the range of the middle 50% *(Lowest 25% – Highest 25%)* of senior pastors' compensation plus benefits at the *$251,000-$500,000* level from Table 4-1.

$62,700 on the low end – $88,000 on the high end

The median for this distribution is $74,000.

These figures serve as a broad range of average compensation plus benefits for senior pastors in churches with incomes between $250,000 and $500,000. This means that 25% of senior pastors in this church income level make less than $62,700 while 25% of them make more than $88,000.

STEP 2

For a narrower, more relevant range, we will identify median compensation plus benefits in other comparable settings. We will examine each of the following variables: *church income* (Table 4-1), *worship attendance* (Table 4-2), *church setting* (Table 4-3), *region* (Table 4-4), *education* (Table 4-5), and *years employed* (Table 4-6). The main data we are interested in is found at the bottom of each table in the box labeled *Total Compensation Plus Benefits*.

Data for Example	Pastor Jones' Data	Median compensation plus benefits from this study
Table 4-1 Church Income: $25IK-$500K	$375,000	$74,000
Table 4-2 Worship Attendance: 301-500	365	**$86,071**
Table 4-3 Church Setting: Small town or rural city	Small town	**$70,680**
Table 4-4 Region: West-South Central	W-S Central	$74,540
Table 4-5 Education: Master	Master's Degree	$78,300
Table 4-6 Years Employed: Less than 6 years	5 years	$74,000

The above table enables us to establish a median compensation plus benefit range. This is based on the data shown above. The following is the range of median compensation plus benefits:

$70,680 on the low end – $86,071 on the high end

STEP 3

After establishing a relevant base compensation plus benefits range in Step 2, the next step is to determine if Pastor Jones's final compensation plus benefits should fit within that range, and if so, where, or if the compensation plus benefits should go beyond or below that range based upon key variables, and if so, how much above or below.

Since church income and worship attendance are two important factors in determining compensation, we will start by looking at these factors across each of the factors in the table above. If church income or attendance skews higher compared to the averages across the key factors, it might suggest moving toward or above the higher end of the range determined in Step 2. While, if church income or attendance skews lower compared to the averages, it might suggest moving toward or below the lower end of the range.

Data for Example	Median compensation plus benefits from this study	Average church income	Average worship attendance
Pastor Jones at First Church	To be determined	$375,000	365
Table 4-1 Church Income: $251K-$500K	$74,000	**$369,247**	**240**
Table 4-2 Worship Attendance: 301-500	$86,071	$742,427	406
Table 4-3 Church Setting: Small town or rural city	$70,680	$551,329	350
Table 4-4 Region: West-South Central	$74,540	**$920,683**	**480**
Table 4-5 Education: Master	$78,300	$631,744	389

The above table shows that the average church income across Pastor Jones's key data ranges from $369,247 - $920,683. The average worship attendance ranges from 240-480. In this case, since Pastor Jones's church income ($375,000) and worship attendance (365) are on the lower end of the averages of other church income levels based on this pastor's specific characteristics, it would be a variable that might suggest moving toward or below the lower end of the range.

STEP 4

The next step is to examine additional variables that might impact compensation plus benefits such as years of service, education, and church setting. They are helpful in deciding whether an individual is in the upper or lower part of the range identified in Step 2.

In general, as years of service and education increase, compensation plus benefits will also increase. Also, senior pastors serving at churches located in metropolitan and suburban settings tend to earn more than those located in small towns or rural settings.

STEP 5

The fifth step is to take into account the unique circumstances that define each individual situation. One factor is the cost of living for your area. Is it higher or lower than the national average? Your local Chamber of Commerce or a real estate agency can help you obtain that information. Other factors such as denominational affiliation (see Table 4-7), theological beliefs, pastoral performance, financial needs, goodwill, the local economy, personal motivation, congregational goals, internal church politics, and many other considerations will also contribute to the final decision. For some churches that may mean a final compensation package much lower or much higher than the projected range listed in Step 2.

How that compensation will be divided up will vary greatly from one church to another, and even from one individual staff member to another. Care should be given, however, to avoid gender discrimination. This is a widespread problem involving many churches (see Table 4-8). In addition, a large disparity between the pastor's compensation and that of other staff members can have an impact on the rate of increase that the pastor may experience in future years. Often, once a staff member has reached the upper limits of his or her compensation range, future raises may be somewhat smaller in order to better compensate other staff members.

The final determination of compensation plus benefits is unique to every congregation. It would not be surprising to see a range of compensation for Pastor Jones somewhere between the broader range of $70,680-$86,071. Higher compensation levels are possible, and could be argued to be reasonable. It would be unlikely, however, for Pastor Jones to exceed $100,000, which would fall outside the limits of the *Highest 25%* range for churches similar to First Church. Such a compensation level would require independent justification to avoid the possibility of intermediate sanctions (see the *Special Section* for a discussion of intermediate sanctions). Also, remember that a crucial step in this decision-making process must involve an awareness of tax law found in the *Special Section*.

The detailed process above can be used for each of the twelve full-time staff positions found in this handbook.

3

COMPENSATION PROFILES: GENERAL COMPARISONS

This chapter provides comparisons of the average compensations for the 12 full-time staff positions and the 11 part-time staff positions included in this study. A summary table exists for each of the variables examined. More detailed analysis can be found in the individual chapter for each staff position.

Note: Eleven positions have information for both full-time and part-time staff. For seven positions, we've provided an expanded part-time section given the high level of response. Two positions are unique: Executive/Administrative Pastor has information for full-timers only, while Musician/Vocalist has information for part-timers only.

Senior Pastors and Executive/Administrative Pastors rank at the top in total compensation plus benefits. Music/Choir/Worship Pastors/Directors and Associate Pastors receive the next highest compensation amount followed generally by Adult Ministry/Christian Education Pastors/ Directors, Administrators, and Solo Pastors. The tables presented later in this chapter provide compensation comparisons according to the averages for each position.

General Trends

As stated earlier, in general, church income, attendance, education, geographical setting and years of service play some role in almost every church's compensation plans. Church income proved the biggest factor affecting compensation and benefits in this study.

Please note this about gender differences: female staff members consistently receive significantly lower compensation than their male counterparts in all positions except Solo Pastor and Secretary/ Administrative Assistant. On average, females earned approximately 80% of the compensation of males. Or, in other words, males earned about 30% more than females. Some of the difference can be explained on the basis of demographic factors such as education.

Benefits vary significantly from one position to the next. This is especially true for health insurance and retirement programs. The numbers of church staff receiving health insurance varied from 45% to 76%, depending on position. A similar gap is seen among those reported receiving retirement benefits (46% to 76%). Part-time staff members receive fewer fringe benefits.

This study examined the "rate of increase" with respect to compensation plus benefits and church income, and compensation plus benefits and church attendance. In this context, "rate of increase" refers to the percent change in compensation with respect to size of church budget or church attendance.

For all staff positions, except Children's/Preschool Pastor/Director, compensation plus benefits increased at every budget level. Generally, the greatest increases across positions are seen at the lowest levels (from *$250,000 & Under* to *$251,000-$500,000*) and then at the highest levels (from *$751,000-$1,000,000* to *Over $1,000,000*). Increases averaged about 20% at every budget level, ranging from a 6% increase to a 41% increase across budget levels. Similar trends could be seen based upon church attendance as well.

The following tables provide comparisons of compensation and benefit packages.

Table 3-1: Percentages of Full-Time Staff Receiving and Reporting Compensation Plus Benefits

	Senior Pastors	Solo Pastors	Executive or Administrative Pastors	Associate Pastors	Adult Ministry/ Christian Education Pastors/ Directors	Youth Pastors/ Directors
TOTAL REPORTING	1902	1304	233	697	251	552
Base Salary	99%	97%	99%	99%	99%	99%
Housing	82%	71%	71%	75%	48%	60%
Parsonage	14%	25%	3%	5%	3%	5%
Health Insurance*	69%	59%	71%	65%	63%	68%
Life Insurance*	25%	16%	38%	24%	34%	24%
Disability Insurance*	21%	17%	40%	23%	32%	20%
Retirement	70%	64%	64%	64%	60%	54%
Continuing Education	39%	41%	27%	35%	35%	30%
Received salary increase	53%	51%	52%	57%	59%	56%
Received paid vacation	97%	94%	96%	96%	96%	96%
Received auto reimbursement/allowance	66%	69%	52%	61%	52%	58%

	Children's/ Preschool Pastors/ Directors	Music/ Choir/ Worship Pastors/ Directors	Administrators	Bookkeepers/ Accountants	Secretaries/ Administrative Assistants	Custodians
TOTAL REPORTING	264	314	257	170	552	251
Base Salary	100%	99%	100%	100%	100%	100%
Housing	38%	58%	13%	2%	1%	1%
Parsonage	1%	2%	1%	0%	0%	2%
Health Insurance*	57%	63%	60%	54%	41%	55%
Life Insurance*	30%	25%	31%	26%	16%	26%
Disability Insurance*	24%	19%	24%	21%	14%	20%
Retirement	53%	60%	56%	56%	40%	45%
Continuing Education	23%	29%	23%	12%	8%	4%
Received salary increase	58%	58%	57%	58%	59%	60%
Received paid vacation	96%	95%	97%	97%	95%	98%
Received auto reimbursement/allowance	45%	49%	39%	24%	18%	18%

*Only those reporting individual insurance premiums for Health, Life, or Disability (not total insurance premiums) are included.

Table 3-2: Percentages of Part-Time Staff Receiving and Reporting Compensation Plus Benefits

	Senior Pastors	Solo Pastors	Associate Pastors	Adult Ministry/ Christian Education Pastors/ Directors	Youth Pastors/ Directors	Children's/ Preschool Pastors/ Directors
TOTAL REPORTING	71	245	201	165	233	224
Base Salary	77%	78%	83%	95%	94%	97%
Housing	64%	58%	38%	13%	16%	5%
Parsonage	8%	10%	2%	0%	5%	0%
Health Insurance*	15%	18%	13%	6%	6%	5%
Life Insurance*	6%	9%	3%	5%	1%	3%
Disability Insurance*	1%	6%	3%	2%	1%	5%
Retirement	23%	33%	13%	12%	5%	8%
Continuing Education	13%	27%	18%	16%	12%	11%
Received salary increase	23%	31%	30%	42%	36%	40%
Received paid vacation	60%	69%	47%	48%	46%	46%
Received auto reimbursement/allowance	26%	43%	48%	27%	36%	25%

	Music/ Choir/ Worship Pastors/ Directors	Admin-istrators	Book-keepers/ Account-ants	Secretaries/A dmin-istrative Assistants	Custodians	Musicians/ Vocalists
TOTAL REPORTING	448	84	232	744	526	273
Base Salary	96%	99%	100%	100%	100%	99%
Housing	6%	3%	0%	0%	1%	1%
Parsonage	1%	0%	0%	0%	0%	0%
Health Insurance*	3%	8%	4%	4%	2%	1%
Life Insurance*	1%	5%	2%	1%	1%	0%
Disability Insurance*	2%	3%	2%	2%	2%	1%
Retirement	5%	14%	9%	8%	2%	2%
Continuing Education	10%	7%	2%	4%	0%	4%
Received salary increase	45%	51%	53%	50%	41%	38%
Received paid vacation	46%	71%	39%	57%	27%	33%
Received auto reimbursement/allowance	9%	19%	11%	11%	6%	3%

*Only those reporting individual insurance premiums for Health, Life, or Disability (not total insurance premiums) are included.

Table 3-3: Annual Compensation Plus Benefits Averages for Full-Time Church Staff

	Average Compensation	Range as determined by Lowest 25% quartile - Highest 25% quartile (50%)
Solo Pastors	$56,189	$41,636 - $69,650
Senior Pastors	$80,745	$58,629 - $98,055
Associate Pastors	$62,024	$46,800 - $75,025
Youth Pastors/Directors	$50,540	$39,542 - $60,170
Adult Ministry/Christian Education Pastors/Directors	$58,877	$42,400 - $71,500
Children's/Preschool Pastors/Directors	$50,782	$37,000 - $60,278
Music/Choir/Worship Pastors/Directors	$61,754	$46,991 - $74,606
Administrators	$56,637	$40,799 - $70,230
Bookkeepers/Accountants	$38,809	$30,170 - $43,302
Secretaries/Administrative Assistants	$30,727	$23,849 - $36,326
Custodians	$35,425	$25,365 - $42,777
Executive or Administrative Pastors	$77,972	$60,000 - $93,522

Table 3-4: Annual Compensation Plus Benefits Averages for Full-Time Church Staff by Church Income

	CHURCH INCOME				
	$250K & Under	$251-$500K	$501-$750K	$751K-$1M	Over $1 Million
Solo Pastors	$52,427	$76,064	$86,645	-	-
Senior Pastors	$54,419	$77,021	$91,117	$94,686	$123,225
Associate Pastors	$37,917	$52,241	$63,201	$69,393	$71,786
Youth Pastors/Directors	$41,003	$44,719	$47,597	$52,056	$58,532
Adult Ministry/Christian Education Pastors/Directors	$37,680	$48,628	$44,098	$55,756	$67,460
Children's/Preschool Pastors/Directors	-	$40,342	$42,505	$47,276	$55,448
Music/Choir/Worship Pastors/Directors	$42,995	$45,412	$53,790	$59,719	$73,283
Administrators	$40,043	$41,364	$44,028	$53,914	$66,681
Bookkeepers/Accountants	-	$30,478	$33,689	$35,252	$43,028
Secretaries/Administrative Assistants	$22,614	$27,816	$30,526	$31,056	$35,486
Custodians	-	$24,781	$33,452	$32,991	$39,451
Executive or Administrative Pastors	$49,887	$58,883	$67,090	$69,044	$88,296

- Not enough response to provide meaningful data.

Table 3-5: Annual Compensation Plus Benefits Averages for Full-Time Church Staff by Worship Attendance

	WORSHIP ATTENDANCE					
	100 or less	101-300	301-500	501-750	751-1,000	Over 1,000
Solo Pastors	$48,851	$66,739	$78,425	-	-	-
Senior Pastors	$47,742	$72,983	$90,374	$98,154	$112,705	$133,504
Associate Pastors	$36,436	$50,929	$65,068	$68,805	$61,618	$73,804
Youth Pastors/Directors	$39,721	$44,295	$49,553	$54,236	$56,991	$60,660
Adult Ministry/Christian Education Pastors/Directors	-	$44,470	$56,209	$57,408	$61,385	$68,982
Children's/Preschool Pastors/Directors	-	$38,882	$47,554	$49,743	$49,873	$59,792
Music/Choir/Worship Pastors/Directors	-	$48,476	$57,963	$60,430	$70,694	$79,623
Administrators	-	$41,371	$50,535	$57,398	$62,553	$71,329
Bookkeepers/Accountants	-	$31,601	$35,383	$38,067	$40,052	$49,634
Secretaries/Administrative Assistants	$21,086	$26,952	$30,679	$32,665	$35,952	$35,877
Custodians	-	$30,577	$32,081	$34,997	$38,776	$43,547
Executive or Administrative Pastors	-	$59,169	$64,391	$76,548	$84,251	$92,213

- Not enough response to provide meaningful data.

Table 3-6: Annual Compensation Plus Benefits Averages for Full-Time Church Staff by Church Setting

	CHURCH SETTING			
	Metropolitan city	Suburb of large city	Small town or rural city	Farming area
Solo Pastors	$61,578	$63,516	$53,620	$48,802
Senior Pastors	$85,572	$89,332	$73,876	$55,223
Associate Pastors	$66,056	$66,223	$55,632	$43,300
Youth Pastors/Directors	$53,156	$53,670	$46,718	$45,541
Adult Ministry/Christian Education Pastors/Directors	$63,233	$61,195	$51,956	-
Children's/Preschool Pastors/Directors	$55,556	$52,518	$46,668	-
Music/Choir/Worship Pastors/Directors	$62,253	$64,048	$59,357	-
Administrators	$62,473	$56,238	$53,625	-
Bookkeepers/Accountants	$42,280	$42,070	$33,884	-
Secretaries/Administrative Assistants	$33,102	$33,250	$27,903	$25,116
Custodians	$36,138	$38,130	$33,030	-
Executive or Administrative Pastors	$82,979	$80,873	$70,780	-

- Not enough response to provide meaningful data.

Table 3-7: Annual Compensation Plus Benefits Averages for Full-Time Church Staff by Region

	REGION								
	New England	Middle Atlantic	South Atlantic	E-N Central	E-S Central	W-N Central	W-S Central	Mountain	Pacific
Solo Pastors	$62,577	$61,059	$57,587	$54,298	$55,422	$51,958	$47,976	$58,182	$59,438
Senior Pastors	$84,118	$81,182	$84,699	$77,117	$74,093	$77,632	$83,794	$74,687	$83,467
Associate Pastors	$67,256	$61,979	$63,034	$59,562	$61,732	$62,070	$59,768	$62,341	$64,213
Youth Pastors/Directors	$46,989	$50,642	$51,445	$50,213	$47,910	$45,914	$50,192	$51,529	$54,676
Adult Ministry/Christian Education Pastors/Directors	-	$60,550	$58,986	$55,112	$60,785	$50,385	$64,465	$57,876	$61,479
Children's/Preschool Pastors/Directors	-	$50,385	$47,727	$53,056	$47,021	$50,493	$54,540	$48,021	$51,423
Music/Choir/Worship Pastors/Directors	-	$67,696	$65,824	$52,541	$58,898	$56,899	$65,403	$62,128	$61,761
Administrators	-	$53,219	$53,370	$53,396	$63,232	$61,504	$58,025	$58,367	$60,082
Bookkeepers/Accountants	-	-	$36,222	$39,007	$34,433	$50,368	$38,336	$41,179	$46,351
Secretaries/Administrative Assistants	$31,050	$31,834	$32,359	$30,173	$27,620	$28,524	$29,704	$28,748	$34,513
Custodians	-	$35,659	$35,965	$36,946	$32,777	$36,381	$31,613	$30,102	$41,829
Executive or Administrative Pastors	-	$76,126	$72,662	$74,754	$82,180	$83,265	$74,707	$80,330	$84,816

- Not enough response to provide meaningful data.

Table 3-8: Annual Compensation Plus Benefits Averages for Full-Time Church Staff by Education

	EDUCATION			
	Less than Bachelor	Bachelor	Master	Doctorate
Solo Pastors	$42,620	$49,025	$59,589	$63,988
Senior Pastors	$58,426	$70,846	$81,927	$94,552
Associate Pastors	$44,982	$58,216	$66,827	$75,976
Youth Pastors/Directors	$45,735	$49,325	$55,571	-
Adult Ministry/Christian Education Pastors/Directors	$41,973	$58,872	$63,278	$76,425
Children's/Preschool Pastors/Directors	$42,927	$50,684	$55,684	-
Music/Choir/Worship Pastors/Directors	$51,481	$60,750	$66,476	$65,160
Administrators	$48,337	$57,733	$70,095	-
Bookkeepers/Accountants	$35,744	$41,351	$51,100	-
Secretaries/Administrative Assistants	$29,569	$33,311	$30,979	-
Custodians	$34,210	$42,484	-	-
Executive or Administrative Pastors	$66,039	$73,910	$79,531	$93,850

- Not enough response to provide meaningful data.

Table 3-9: Annual Compensation Plus Benefits Averages for Full-Time Church Staff by Years Employed

	YEARS EMPLOYED			
	Less than 6 years	6-10 years	11-15 years	Over 15 years
Solo Pastors	$55,807	$55,272	$54,777	$59,630
Senior Pastors	$77,463	$79,153	$83,012	$87,432
Associate Pastors	$58,191	$65,148	$70,467	$74,153
Youth Pastors/Directors	$49,427	$52,720	$63,164	-
Adult Ministry/Christian Education Pastors/Directors	$58,199	$55,832	$60,260	$71,074
Children's/Preschool Pastors/Directors	$48,816	$52,603	$59,012	-
Music/Choir/Worship Pastors/Directors	$59,051	$63,349	$68,780	$64,505
Administrators	$56,890	$57,378	$58,409	$54,235
Bookkeepers/Accountants	$38,755	$40,448	$38,726	$37,738
Secretaries/Administrative Assistants	$29,190	$32,733	$32,906	$32,117
Custodians	$32,384	$37,170	$38,429	$38,713
Executive or Administrative Pastors	$75,012	$78,372	$90,410	$82,648

- Not enough response to provide meaningful data.

Table 3-10: Annual Compensation Plus Benefits Averages for Full-Time Church Staff by Denomination

	DENOMINATION					
	Assemblies of God	Baptist	Independent/ Nondenom	Lutheran	Methodist	Presbyte-rian
Solo Pastors	$43,158	$50,844	$54,409	$67,981	$64,877	$68,289
Senior Pastors	$73,496	$79,075	$80,742	$97,190	$93,683	$101,798
Associate Pastors	$49,363	$60,635	$62,946	$66,381	$62,353	$72,648
Youth Pastors/Directors	$49,098	$52,925	$52,607	$42,814	$40,795	$50,110
Adult Ministry/Christian Education Pastors/Directors	$44,213	$65,878	$62,783	$52,934	$44,781	$56,989
Children's/Preschool Pastors/Directors	$49,302	$52,542	$52,326	-	$38,845	$46,048
Music/Choir/Worship Pastors/Directors	$57,242	$64,152	$67,101	$51,960	$57,451	$58,306
Administrators	$51,115	$58,852	$54,003	$60,296	$52,158	$57,014
Bookkeepers/Accountants	$34,568	$36,152	$42,622	-	$36,628	-
Secretaries/Administrative Assistants	$27,908	$30,069	$30,947	$34,282	$28,723	$35,993
Custodians	$35,162	$31,259	$38,941	$44,934	$32,246	$35,548
Executive or Administrative Pastors	$68,715	$80,621	$77,305	-	$63,634	-

- Not enough response to provide meaningful data.

Table 3-11: Annual Compensation Plus Benefits Averages for Full-Time Church Staff by Gender

	GENDER	
	Male	Female
Solo Pastors	$56,240	$55,775
Senior Pastors	$81,134	$60,798
Associate Pastors	$62,884	$55,644
Youth Pastors/Directors	$51,616	$40,021
Adult Ministry/Christian Education Pastors/Directors	$65,882	$45,673
Children's/Preschool Pastors/Directors	$60,201	$46,974
Music/Choir/Worship Pastors/Directors	$63,690	$49,915
Administrators	$67,313	$46,498
Bookkeepers/Accountants	$45,268	$38,327
Secretaries/Administrative Assistants	$43,605	$30,447
Custodians	$37,068	$27,754
Executive or Administrative Pastors	$80,371	$60,198

- Not enough response to provide meaningful data.

Table 3-12: Annual Compensation Plus Benefits Averages for Part-Time Church Staff by Church Income

	CHURCH INCOME				
	$250K & Under	$251-$500K	$501-$750K	$751K-$1M	Over 1 Million
Solo Pastors	$23,538	-	-	-	-
Senior Pastor	$19,802	-	-	-	-
Associate Pastors	$13,415	$17,597	$24,533	$23,769	$20,954
Youth Pastors/Directors	$11,313	$15,664	$18,705	$19,037	$17,132
Adult Ministry/Christian Education Pastors/Directors	$10,427	$15,977	$15,624	$18,218	$19,159
Children's/Preschool Pastors/Directors	$10,971	$12,362	$16,203	$17,290	$18,967
Music/Choir/Worship Pastors/Directors	$9,548	$13,353	$16,868	$18,925	$19,704
Administrators	$16,661	$19,665	$25,617	-	$29,910
Bookkeepers/Accountants	$6,608	$10,062	$14,201	$17,437	$22,093
Secretaries/Administrative Assistants	$10,446	$14,798	$14,952	$16,293	$16,544
Custodians	$6,068	$10,894	$12,880	$13,496	$12,304
Musicians/Vocalists	$5,814	$7,924	$8,202	$11,039	$11,553

- Not enough response to provide meaningful data.

4

SENIOR PASTORS

Employment Profile

With 1,902 positions reported, Senior Pastors provided a significant number of responses to this survey. Senior Pastors are defined as the lead pastor in a church where there are multiple paid pastoral ministry positions. As expected, this group is quite diverse.

Nearly all Senior Pastors responding to this survey are ordained (99%) and male (98%). About three-quarters of full-time (71%) and almost half of part-time (46%) Senior Pastors have a graduate degree. About nine in ten full-time Senior Pastors are employed by the church. Part-time Senior Pastors are almost evenly split between being a church employee (57%) and self-employed (43%).

The following chart provides a demographic profile of this sample:

	Full-Time	Part-Time
Number of respondents	1902	71
Ordained	99%	100%
Average years employed	10	9
Male	98%	96%
Female	2%	4%
Self-employed (receives 1099)	13%	43%
Church employee (receives W-2)	87%	57%
High school diploma	4%	14%
Associate Degree	4%	11%
Bachelor's Degree	21%	28%
Master's Degree	48%	32%
Doctoral Degree	23%	14%

Total Compensation plus Benefits Package Analysis

The analyses on the next page are based on the data in the tables that you will find in the remainder of the chapter. The tables show compensation plus benefits data for Senior Pastors who serve full-time and are presented according to church income, church attendance, church setting, region, education, years employed, denomination, and gender. In this way, the Senior Pastor's compensation plus benefit can be analyzed and compared from a variety of useful perspectives.

There is also a table showing compensation plus benefit data for Senior Pastors who serve part-time presented by church income.

The total compensation plus benefits amount includes the base salary, housing allowance and/or parsonage amount, health, life, and disability insurance payments, retirement contribution, and educational funds.

The Senior Pastor is one of the most highly paid positions in the local church with the most comprehensive benefit packages. A strong majority of Senior Pastors receive housing allowance, but a slim percentage, a little more than one in ten, live in church-provided parsonages. About seven in ten full-time Senior Pastors receive health insurance benefits, and a similar percentage receive retirement benefits.

Compensation Plus Benefits	Full-Time	Part-Time
Base Salary	99%	77%
Housing	82%	64%
Parsonage	14%	8%
Health Insurance	69%	15%
Life Insurance	25%	6%
Disability Insurance	21%	1%
Retirement	70%	23%
Continuing Education	39%	13%
Received Salary Increase	53%	23%
Received Paid Vacation	97%	60%
Received Auto Reimbursement/ Allowance	66%	26%

KEY POINTS

* About six in ten full-time Senior Pastors who responded serve churches with an income of $500,000 or less and a worship attendance of 300 or less.

* In general, as church income, worship attendance, the minister's education level, and years employed increase, average compensation and benefits for Senior Pastors also increase.

* Slightly less than half of Senior Pastors surveyed (43%) serve churches in a small town/rural city setting. Contributing to the difference is the fact that church income in metropolitan and suburban settings is higher than that in small town or farming areas.

✳ Senior Pastors serving churches in suburban or metropolitan settings have the highest compensation and benefits packages. Contributing to the difference is the fact that church income in metropolitan and suburban settings is higher than that in small town or farming areas.

✳ Among regional differences noted: lowest average compensation and benefits packages are in East-South Central and Mountain regions.

Compensation & Benefits: National Averages for Full-Time Senior Pastors*

	Full-Time	Part-Time
	Senior Pastor data only	Combined Solo and Senior Pastor data*
2000		$66,096
2001		$69,543
2002		$71,232
2003		$73,230
2004		$74,969
2005		$77,096
2006	$87,284	$78,339
2007	$81,067	$70,789
2008	$81,113	$72,519
2009	$80,745**	$70,806**

*National averages for Senior Pastors from 1998-2005 include data for both Senior and Solo Pastors. Beginning in 2006, we are able to provide detailed data for each position. Refer to Chapter 5 for Solo Pastors' data.

**The above trend is made available for your reference only. In addition to looking at this overall data, please refer to the detailed tables using your church's income, attendance, setting, region, and denomination as well as the person's education, gender, and years employed for guidance in compensating this position.

Table 4-1: Annual Compensation of Full-Time Senior Pastors by Church Income

CHARACTERISTICS	Data Distribution*	$250K & Under	$251-$500K	$501-$750K	$751K-$1M	Over 1 Million
			CHURCH INCOME			
Average weekend worship attendance		137	240	396	525	1,174
Average church income		$164,568	$369,247	$628,936	$884,501	$2,202,721
Average # of years employed		9	9	10	11	12
Average # of paid vacation days		20	23	24	23	23
% College graduate or higher		86%	95%	95%	92%	97%
% Who receive auto reimbursement/allowance		60%	68%	72%	73%	69%
% Ordained		99%	99%	100%	99%	99%
% Supervise one or more people		93%	98%	99%	97%	99%
Average % salary increase (for those who had an increase) this year		6.0%	4.4%	4.7%	4.2%	4.0%
COMPENSATION						
Base Salary	Highest 25%	$39,300	$50,000	$61,086	$62,800	$88,796
	Median	$30,000	$40,000	$50,000	$50,075	$65,913
	Lowest 25%	$23,000	$30,000	$40,278	$40,000	$52,498
	Average	$31,573	$41,217	$51,859	$53,174	$71,742
Housing	Highest 25%	$25,000	$30,000	$35,000	$36,000	$45,000
	Median	$18,000	$24,000	$25,900	$27,050	$33,000
	Lowest 25%	$12,000	$17,500	$19,468	$20,550	$25,000
	Average	$18,756	$24,702	$27,011	$29,091	$36,061
Parsonage	Highest 25%	$14,400	$18,000	$20,000	$22,000	$37,500
	Median	$9,600	$11,800	$15,000	$15,500	$21,150
	Lowest 25%	$5,740	$7,900	$9,600	$12,342	$12,000
	Average	$11,122	$13,208	$17,359	$19,868	$27,205
Total Compensation	**Highest 25%**	**$56,044**	**$70,000**	**$86,000**	**$87,000**	**$117,700**
	Median	**$47,040**	**$61,568**	**$74,200**	**$77,855**	**$97,000**
	Lowest 25%	**$36,000**	**$52,446**	**$65,000**	**$69,100**	**$83,538**
	Average	**$46,980**	**$63,465**	**$76,506**	**$79,637**	**$104,298**
BENEFITS						
Health Insurance	Highest 25%	$11,500	$13,100	$13,943	$14,000	$14,000
	Median	$7,200	$9,618	$10,646	$10,047	$10,600
	Lowest 25%	$4,560	$6,000	$6,000	$7,550	$7,200
	Average	$8,111	$10,544	$11,287	$10,711	$11,183
Life Insurance	Highest 25%	$1,000	$1,200	$1,200	$1,597	$1,280
	Median	$600	$500	$677	$766	$525
	Lowest 25%	$350	$300	$292	$250	$200
	Average	$931	$1,077	$1,028	$1,387	$1,377
Disability Insurance	Highest 25%	$1,200	$1,200	$2,100	$1,000	$1,200
	Median	$500	$506	$700	$525	$606
	Lowest 25%	$300	$257	$380	$278	$389
	Average	$783	$838	$1,413	$822	$1,182
Retirement	Highest 25%	$6,000	$7,500	$9,311	$8,935	$12,000
	Median	$3,193	$4,838	$5,819	$5,500	$8,343
	Lowest 25%	$1,578	$2,500	$3,500	$3,700	$4,900
	Average	$4,118	$5,980	$7,108	$6,849	$9,635
Continuing Education	Highest 25%	$1,500	$2,000	$2,500	$2,000	$2,500
	Median	$1,000	$1,000	$1,500	$1,500	$2,000
	Lowest 25%	$500	$720	$1,000	$1,000	$1,000
	Average	$1,437	$1,545	$1,984	$1,970	$2,281
Total Benefits	**Highest 25%**	**$13,900**	**$18,972**	**$22,050**	**$20,850**	**$24,500**
	Median	**$8,416**	**$12,702**	**$13,900**	**$15,088**	**$17,730**
	Lowest 25%	**$3,870**	**$7,400**	**$7,596**	**$10,491**	**$11,581**
	Average	**$9,754**	**$14,416**	**$15,818**	**$16,001**	**$19,594**
TOTAL COMPENSATION PLUS BENEFITS	**Highest 25%**	**$66,872**	**$88,000**	**$102,753**	**$104,998**	**$139,300**
	Median	**$55,000**	**$74,000**	**$87,679**	**$90,537**	**$116,800**
	Lowest 25%	**$40,800**	**$62,700**	**$76,555**	**$82,075**	**$97,600**
	Average	**$54,419**	**$77,021**	**$91,117**	**$94,686**	**$123,225**
Number of Respondents		594	570	236	168	323

- Not enough response to provide meaningful data.

* For detailed description and definitions of Data Distribution (Highest 25%, Median, Lowest 25% and Average), see Chapter 1's "Explanation of Data Distribution"

Table 4-2: Annual Compensation of Full-Time Senior Pastors by Worship Attendance

	Data Distribution*	WORSHIP ATTENDANCE					
		100 or less	101-300	301-500	501-750	751-1,000	Over 1,000
CHARACTERISTICS							
Average weekend worship attendance		76	198	406	617	887	2,052
Average church income		$201,974	$350,015	$742,427	$1,034,646	$1,507,203	$3,056,469
Average # of years employed		8	9	11	11	13	14
Average # of paid vacation days		20	22	24	23	23	23
% College graduate or higher		83%	93%	94%	96%	94%	96%
% Who receive auto reimbursement/allowance		56%	67%	73%	68%	68%	62%
% Ordained		100%	99%	100%	99%	100%	99%
% Supervise one or more people		89%	97%	98%	98%	99%	99%
Average % salary increase (for those who had an increase) this year		6.0%	4.9%	4.4%	3.9%	4.2%	4.6%
COMPENSATION							
Base Salary	Median	$26,500	$38,400	$49,000	$53,100	$61,117	$79,300
	Average	$27,410	$39,744	$51,476	$56,705	$65,329	$81,063
Housing	Median	$17,700	$22,000	$25,000	$28,000	$31,300	$35,000
	Average	$18,904	$23,417	$27,272	$28,241	$34,225	$38,505
Parsonage	Median	$7,200	$12,000	$12,063	$12,684	-	-
	Average	$9,508	$14,276	$16,013	$14,435	-	-
Total Compensation	**Median**	**$40,420**	**$59,873**	**$73,000**	**$80,000**	**$94,284**	**$107,000**
	Average	**$41,624**	**$61,049**	**$75,701**	**$82,109**	**$96,183**	**$113,810**
BENEFITS							
Health Insurance	Median	$7,000	$8,800	$10,000	$11,450	$10,462	$9,600
	Average	$7,820	$9,882	$10,783	$11,219	$10,284	$11,223
Life Insurance	Median	$650	$600	$600	$499	$603	$500
	Average	$935	$1,015	$973	$1,464	$1,552	$1,259
Disability	Median	$503	$611	$500	$585	$605	$600
	Average	$695	$1,003	$878	$1,024	$1,150	$1,307
Retirement	Median	$2,450	$4,800	$6,000	$5,927	$7,300	$8,700
	Average	$3,783	$5,820	$7,129	$7,285	$8,186	$9,902
Continuing Education	Median	$1,000	$1,000	$1,500	$1,500	$1,500	$2,000
	Average	$1,431	$1,519	$1,969	$2,109	$2,376	$2,680
Total Benefits	**Median**	**$8,965**	**$11,600**	**$13,814**	**$15,325**	**$15,600**	**$18,000**
	Average	**$9,143**	**$13,257**	**$15,651**	**$17,135**	**$17,382**	**$20,355**
TOTAL COMPENSATION PLUS BENEFITS	**Median**	**$47,478**	**$70,230**	**$86,071**	**$93,400**	**$110,462**	**$126,044**
	Average	**$47,742**	**$72,983**	**$90,374**	**$98,154**	**$112,705**	**$133,504**
Number of Respondents		266	922	320	173	101	123

- Not enough response to provide meaningful data.

* For detailed description and definitions of Data Distribution (Median and Average), see Chapter 1's "Explanation of Data Distribution."

Table 4-3: Annual Compensation of Full-Time Senior Pastors by Church Setting

CHARACTERISTICS	Data Distribution*	Metro-politan city	Suburb of large city	Small town or rural city	Farming area
Average weekend worship attendance		475	475	350	210
Average church income		$882,276	$827,432	$551,329	$283,510
Average # of years employed		10	10	10	10
Average # of paid vacation days		22	23	22	20
% College graduate or higher		93%	93%	92%	83%
% Who receive auto reimbursement/allowance		60%	66%	68%	77%
% Ordained		100%	100%	99%	99%
% Supervise one or more people		97%	98%	97%	90%
Average % salary increase (for those who had an increase) this year		4.4%	4.6%	4.9%	5.2%
COMPENSATION					
Base Salary	Median	$44,600	$45,385	$40,000	$31,200
	Average	$48,407	$49,104	$43,198	$33,034
Housing	Median	$25,000	$26,400	$20,000	$16,000
	Average	$28,086	$29,377	$21,676	$16,243
Parsonage	Median	$15,000	$14,400	$10,000	$5,540
	Average	$18,935	$18,268	$12,291	$6,688
Total Compensation	**Median**	**$67,899**	**$70,240**	**$59,600**	**$46,694**
	Average	**$72,614**	**$75,166**	**$62,169**	**$46,158**
BENEFITS					
Health Insurance	Median	$8,828	$10,700	$9,000	$7,800
	Average	$9,723	$10,883	$9,684	$8,811
Life Insurance	Median	$728	$595	$600	$450
	Average	$1,572	$1,045	$1,121	$954
Disability Insurance	Median	$600	$600	$545	$470
	Average	$1,149	$1,006	$988	$869
Retirement	Median	$5,732	$6,000	$4,800	$4,100
	Average	$7,037	$7,032	$5,925	$4,111
Continuing Education	Median	$1,200	$1,500	$1,000	$1,000
	Average	$1,627	$2,083	$1,543	$1,509
Total Benefits	**Median**	**$12,000**	**$14,126**	**$12,000**	**$11,200**
	Average	**$14,538**	**$15,720**	**$13,329**	**$11,591**
TOTAL COMPENSATION PLUS BENEFITS	**Median**	**$80,064**	**$84,375**	**$70,680**	**$57,850**
	Average	**$85,572**	**$89,332**	**$73,876**	**$55,223**
Number of Respondents		322	698	814	78

- Not enough response to provide meaningful data.

* For detailed description and definitions of Data Distribution (Median and Average), see Chapter 1's "Explanation of Data Distribution."

Table 4-4: Annual Compensation of Full-Time Senior Pastors by Region

	Data Distribution*	New England	Middle Atlantic	South Atlantic	E-N Central	E-S Central	W-N Central	W-S Central	Mountain	Pacific
CHARACTERISTICS										
Average weekend worship attendance		285	349	396	389	382	413	480	407	464
Average church income		$458,705	$516,842	$718,995	$625,362	$702,232	$638,509	$920,683	$583,806	$775,649
Average # of years employed		12	10	10	10	8	10	9	10	10
Average # of paid vacation days		23	24	21	24	19	22	19	23	24
% College graduate or higher		93%	91%	93%	92%	88%	90%	92%	94%	94%
% Who receive auto reimbursement/allowance		63%	70%	70%	70%	60%	72%	61%	56%	61%
% Ordained		100%	100%	100%	99%	98%	99%	99%	100%	100%
% Supervise one or more people		95%	96%	98%	96%	94%	98%	97%	96%	97%
Average % salary increase (for those who had an increase) this year		3.7%	4.9%	4.9%	5.2%	4.4%	3.9%	5.4%	4.2%	4.3%
COMPENSATION										
Base Salary	Median	$35,500	$41,550	$42,920	$44,000	$42,240	$42,230	$44,974	$40,000	$40,000
	Average	$40,902	$44,392	$48,006	$45,342	$45,553	$44,080	$50,133	$41,012	$43,870
Housing	Median	$31,603	$21,000	$24,000	$21,228	$20,000	$20,750	$24,000	$27,000	$30,000
	Average	$29,608	$25,179	$26,248	$22,630	$20,700	$22,920	$25,757	$26,484	$31,299
Parsonage	Median	$13,500	$11,000	$10,800	$10,800	$12,000	$11,200	$10,800	$10,800	$14,700
	Average	$15,340	$13,018	$16,280	$11,298	$10,761	$12,522	$14,539	$12,210	$18,467
Total Compensation	**Median**	**$63,000**	**$62,075**	**$67,902**	**$62,468**	**$61,000**	**$62,000**	**$64,500**	**$65,000**	**$65,888**
	Average	**$63,650**	**$66,805**	**$71,530**	**$64,401**	**$63,548**	**$64,538**	**$72,319**	**$63,914**	**$71,099**
BENEFITS										
Health Insurance	Median	$12,000	$11,650	$9,500	$10,000	$8,160	$8,800	$7,648	$8,502	$9,600
	Average	$14,534	$11,007	$10,326	$10,341	$9,175	$10,023	$8,845	$8,702	$10,084
Life Insurance	Median	$1,000	$600	$650	$500	$971	$425	$700	$445	$500
	Average	$1,005	$979	$1,140	$1,048	$1,708	$919	$1,569	$1,075	$1,046
Disability Insurance	Median	$800	$325	$645	$503	$600	$712	$835	$425	$500
	Average	$1,129	$767	$1,296	$904	$773	$976	$1,225	$680	$1,105
Retirement	Median	$6,313	$4,961	$5,270	$5,000	$4,200	$5,000	$4,900	$4,800	$5,750
	Average	$10,806	$6,020	$6,964	$6,256	$5,471	$5,973	$6,831	$5,625	$6,324
Continuing Education	Median	$1,100	$1,000	$1,500	$1,000	$2,000	$1,000	$1,500	$1,200	$1,500
	Average	$2,559	$1,509	$1,957	$1,566	$2,650	$1,273	$1,898	$1,699	$1,881
Total Benefits	**Median**	**$15,900**	**$13,919**	**$12,680**	**$13,050**	**$10,750**	**$12,065**	**$11,875**	**$10,917**	**$13,000**
	Average	**$21,466**	**$15,125**	**$14,861**	**$14,353**	**$13,156**	**$14,395**	**$13,556**	**$12,119**	**$13,994**
TOTAL COMPENSATION PLUS BENEFITS	**Median**	**$79,073**	**$75,611**	**$80,000**	**$74,953**	**$70,000**	**$74,709**	**$74,540**	**$74,000**	**$78,600**
	Average	**$84,118**	**$81,182**	**$84,699**	**$77,117**	**$74,093**	**$77,632**	**$83,794**	**$74,687**	**$83,467**
Number of Respondents		43	162	413	368	131	177	241	99	284

- Not enough response to provide meaningful data.

* For detailed description and definitions of Data Distribution (Median and Average), see Chapter 1's "Explanation of Data Distribution."

Table 4-5: Annual Compensation of Full-Time Senior Pastors by Education

	Data Distribution*	EDUCATION			
		Less than Bachelor	Bachelor	Master	Doctorate
CHARACTERISTICS					
Average weekend worship attendance		289	368	389	529
Average church income		$439,862	$562,681	$631,744	$1,019,307
Average # of years employed		11	10	9	11
Average # of paid vacation days		19	20	23	24
% College graduate or higher		0%	100%	100%	100%
% Who receive auto reimbursement/allowance		51%	61%	68%	73%
% Ordained		97%	100%	100%	100%
% Supervise one or more people		88%	95%	98%	98%
Average % salary increase (for those who had an increase) this year		6.8%	5.5%	4.7%	3.9%
COMPENSATION					
Base Salary	Median	$32,000	$37,000	$42,844	$47,270
	Average	$34,404	$41,747	$46,114	$51,805
Housing	Median	$19,406	$22,050	$24,000	$26,375
	Average	$20,512	$23,047	$25,798	$29,095
Parsonage	Median	$10,800	$9,600	$11,000	$12,000
	Average	$12,358	$11,097	$14,454	$15,725
Total Compensation	**Median**	**$47,000**	**$58,129**	**$65,280**	**$72,280**
	Average	**$51,874**	**$61,345**	**$68,579**	**$78,109**
BENEFITS					
Health Insurance	Median	$7,800	$8,186	$10,000	$10,000
	Average	$8,177	$8,436	$10,578	$11,058
Life Insurance	Median	$640	$720	$475	$766
	Average	$1,295	$1,417	$843	$1,479
Disability Insurance	Median	$316	$769	$503	$700
	Average	$555	$1,313	$931	$1,117
Retirement	Median	$2,520	$3,423	$5,000	$7,040
	Average	$3,640	$4,620	$6,305	$8,490
Continuing Education	Median	$1,000	$1,200	$1,000	$1,500
	Average	$1,400	$1,738	$1,633	$2,084
Total Benefits	**Median**	**$7,200**	**$10,200**	**$13,100**	**$16,000**
	Average	**$9,298**	**$10,971**	**$14,757**	**$17,827**
TOTAL COMPENSATION PLUS BENEFITS	**Median**	**$52,000**	**$67,840**	**$78,300**	**$89,750**
	Average	**$58,426**	**$70,846**	**$81,927**	**$94,552**
Number of Respondents		149	403	911	438

- Not enough response to provide meaningful data.

* For detailed description and definitions of Data Distribution (Median and Average), see Chapter 1's "Explanation of Data Distribution."

Table 4-6: Annual Compensation of Full-Time Senior Pastors by Years Employed

	Data Distribution*	YEARS EMPLOYED			
		Less than 6 years	6-10 years	11-15 years	Over 15 years
CHARACTERISTICS					
Average weekend worship attendance		317	406	492	535
Average church income		$587,907	$636,385	$803,308	$893,259
Average # of years employed		3	8	13	23
Average # of paid vacation days		20	23	24	25
% College graduate or higher		92%	93%	94%	90%
% Who receive auto reimbursement/allowance		63%	64%	70%	71%
% Ordained		99%	100%	99%	99%
% Supervise one or more people		96%	97%	97%	98%
Average % salary increase (for those who had an increase) this year		5.1%	5.2%	4.1%	3.9%
COMPENSATION					
Base Salary	Median	$40,000	$42,000	$42,000	$46,939
	Average	$44,139	$45,275	$45,924	$49,394
Housing	Median	$24,000	$23,650	$24,000	$24,740
	Average	$25,193	$24,716	$26,671	$26,610
Parsonage	Median	$12,000	$12,000	$10,500	$10,400
	Average	$14,204	$13,022	$13,285	$16,224
Total Compensation	**Median**	**$62,500**	**$63,865**	**$64,600**	**$69,576**
	Average	**$65,744**	**$66,274**	**$69,330**	**$73,733**
BENEFITS					
Health Insurance	Median	$9,116	$9,600	$9,600	$9,532
	Average	$10,094	$9,748	$10,453	$10,327
Life Insurance	Median	$500	$700	$500	$766
	Average	$773	$1,300	$828	$1,664
Disability Insurance	Median	$659	$600	$549	$500
	Average	$981	$981	$1,022	$1,112
Retirement	Median	$5,000	$5,000	$5,592	$5,462
	Average	$6,293	$6,116	$6,730	$6,914
Continuing Education	Median	$1,200	$1,200	$1,000	$1,200
	Average	$1,816	$1,691	$1,782	$1,772
Total Benefits	**Median**	**$12,000**	**$13,050**	**$13,000**	**$13,000**
	Average	**$13,789**	**$14,234**	**$14,888**	**$15,226**
TOTAL COMPENSATION PLUS BENEFITS	**Median**	**$74,000**	**$75,800**	**$76,764**	**$81,980**
	Average	**$77,463**	**$79,153**	**$83,012**	**$87,432**
Number of Respondents		746	462	284	409

- Not enough response to provide meaningful data.

* For detailed description and definitions of Data Distribution (Median and Average), see Chapter 1's "Explanation of Data Distribution."

Table 4-7: Annual Compensation of Full-Time Senior Pastors by Denomination

	Data Distribution*	Assemblies of God	Baptist	Independent/ Nondenom.	Lutheran	Methodist	Presby- terian
CHARACTERISTICS							
Average weekend worship attendance		351	398	521	449	420	377
Average church income		$612,249	$734,190	$778,140	$846,922	$854,514	$802,960
Average # of years employed		10	9	11	11	8	9
Average # of paid vacation days		20	21	21	27	24	27
% College graduate or higher		81%	96%	85%	100%	100%	100%
% Who receive auto reimbursement/allowance		55%	70%	53%	83%	78%	85%
% Ordained		98%	100%	99%	100%	100%	100%
% Supervise one or more people		97%	98%	96%	100%	99%	99%
Average % salary increase (for those who had an increase) this year		6.7%	4.8%	6.1%	2.9%	5.4%	4.2%
COMPENSATION							
Base Salary	Median	$34,083	$40,000	$42,821	$50,833	$57,820	$43,876
	Average	$40,459	$44,136	$46,924	$54,245	$58,513	$49,279
Housing	Median	$23,730	$24,000	$25,000	$28,500	$18,000	$30,000
	Average	$24,185	$24,756	$28,113	$30,322	$18,486	$33,535
Parsonage	Median	$12,000	$9,500	$10,800	-	$12,000	$9,450
	Average	$14,108	$12,739	$14,519	-	$14,154	$11,485
Total Compensation	**Median**	**$59,389**	**$61,072**	**$66,231**	**$80,000**	**$71,807**	**$74,600**
	Average	**$63,054**	**$66,416**	**$70,445**	**$80,077**	**$74,817**	**$80,336**
BENEFITS							
Health Insurance	Median	$8,400	$9,069	$8,733	$12,552	$11,000	$14,000
	Average	$9,179	$10,414	$9,347	$11,946	$11,282	$12,809
Life Insurance	Median	$650	$642	$600	$200	$425	$677
	Average	$1,467	$1,293	$1,257	$518	$1,017	$1,399
Disability Insurance	Median	$2,000	$500	$505	$1,731	$1,864	$763
	Average	$1,806	$875	$1,129	$1,591	$1,913	$794
Retirement	Median	$2,620	$4,800	$3,884	$7,275	$8,000	$9,438
	Average	$4,692	$5,796	$5,307	$8,035	$8,511	$12,810
Continuing Education	Median	$2,000	$1,200	$1,500	$1,000	$1,200	$1,800
	Average	$1,708	$1,888	$2,146	$1,278	$2,015	$1,878
Total Benefits	**Median**	**$10,238**	**$12,490**	**$11,653**	**$18,750**	**$19,000**	**$22,487**
	Average	**$11,624**	**$14,137**	**$12,530**	**$18,135**	**$19,131**	**$22,472**
TOTAL COMPENSATION PLUS BENEFITS	**Median**	**$68,650**	**$72,749**	**$76,436**	**$93,500**	**$91,010**	**$95,930**
	Average	**$73,496**	**$79,075**	**$80,742**	**$97,190**	**$93,683**	**$101,798**
Number of Respondents		118	526	348	71	144	89

- Not enough response to provide meaningful data.

* For detailed description and definitions of Data Distribution (Median and Average), see Chapter 1's "Explanation of Data Distribution."

Table 4-8: Annual Compensation of Full-Time Senior Pastors by Gender

	Data Distribution*	GENDER	
		Male	Female
CHARACTERISTICS			
Average weekend worship attendance		415	173
Average church income		$703,366	$313,994
Average # of years employed		10	7
Average # of paid vacation days		22	26
% College graduate or higher		92%	95%
% Who receive auto reimbursement/allowance		66%	66%
% Ordained		99%	100%
% Supervise one or more people		97%	100%
Average % salary increase (for those who had an increase) this year		4.7%	7.4%
COMPENSATION			
Base Salary	Median	$42,000	$34,000
	Average	$45,940	$34,904
Housing	Median	$24,000	$15,000
	Average	$25,693	$18,711
Parsonage	Median	$12,000	-
	Average	$14,097	-
Total Compensation	**Median**	**$65,000**	**$49,000**
	Average	**$68,333**	**$50,667**
BENEFITS			
Health Insurance	Median	$9,600	$9,600
	Average	$10,167	$7,683
Life Insurance	Median	$600	-
	Average	$1,168	-
Disability Insurance	Median	$596	-
	Average	$1,012	-
Retirement	Median	$5,000	$7,456
	Average	$6,467	$6,520
Continuing Education	Median	$1,200	$1,350
	Average	$1,770	$1,714
Total Benefits	**Median**	**$12,785**	**$10,780**
	Average	**$14,454**	**$11,868**
TOTAL COMPENSATION PLUS BENEFITS	**Median**	**$76,508**	**$63,300**
	Average	**$81,134**	**$60,798**
Number of Respondents		1863	41

- Not enough response to provide meaningful data.

* For detailed description and definitions of Data Distribution (Median and Average), see Chapter 1's "Explanation of Data Distribution."

Table 4-9: Annual Compensation of Part-Time Senior Pastors by Church Income

	Data Distribution*	CHURCH INCOME				
		$250K & Under	$251-$500K	$501-$750K	$751K-$1M	Over 1 Million
CHARACTERISTICS						
Average weekend worship attendance		72	-	-	-	-
Average church income		$83,111	-	-	-	-
Average # of years employed		8	-	-	-	-
Average # of paid vacation days		14	-	-	-	-
% College graduate or higher		73%	-	-	-	-
% Who receive auto reimbursement/allowance		22%	-	-	-	-
% Ordained		100%	-	-	-	-
% Supervise one or more people		76%	-	-	-	-
Average % salary increase (for those who had an increase) this year		13.3%	-	-	-	-
HOURLY RATE						
Base Rate	Average	$17	-	-	-	-
COMPENSATION						
Base Salary	Median	$12,000	-	-	-	-
	Average	$13,925	-	-	-	-
Housing	Median	$10,200	-	-	-	-
	Average	$11,942	-	-	-	-
Parsonage	Median	-	-	-	-	-
	Average	-	-	-	-	-
Total Compensation	**Median**	**$15,600**	-	-	-	-
	Average	**$18,678**	-	-	-	-
BENEFITS			-			
Health Insurance	Median	$2,400	-	-	-	-
	Average	$4,625	-	-	-	-
Life Insurance	Median	-	-	-	-	-
	Average	-	-	-	-	-
Disability Insurance	Median	-	-	-	-	-
	Average	-	-	-	-	-
Retirement	Median	$1,800	-	-	-	-
	Average	$2,312	-	-	-	-
Continuing Education	Median	$650	-	-	-	-
	Average	$581	-	-	-	-
Total Benefits	**Median**	**$1,500**	-	-	-	-
	Average	**$3,038**	-	-	-	-
TOTAL COMPENSATION PLUS BENEFITS	**Median**	**$16,200**	-	-	-	-
	Average	**$19,802**	-	-	-	-
Number of Respondents		73	10	1	0	0

- Not enough response to provide meaningful data.

* For detailed description and definitions of Data Distribution (Median and Average), see Chapter 1's "Explanation of Data Distribution."

5

SOLO
PASTORS

Employment Profile

Solo Pastors are a unique group of church staff members. Solo Pastors are set apart from the previous group of Senior Pastors in that they are the only ministerial staff serving their congregation. The church may employ non-pastoral staff, such as Church Secretary or Custodian. With 1,304 full-time positions reported in this survey, these participants provided significant information for study.

Nearly all Solo Pastors are ordained; about nine in ten are male. On average, full-time Solo Pastors have been in their current positions for eight years, while part-time Solo Pastors have been in their positions for six years. Most of those working full-time are church employees, rather than self-employed. About seven in ten of them have graduate degrees.

The following chart provides a demographic profile of this sample:

	Full-Time	Part-Time
Number of respondents	1304	245
Ordained	99%	97%
Average years employed	8	6
Male	92%	88%
Female	8%	12%
Self-employed (receives 1099)	18%	39%
Church employee (receives W-2)	82%	61%
High school diploma	4%	5%
Associate Degree	6%	8%
Bachelor's Degree	22%	33%
Master's Degree	55%	44%
Doctoral Degree	13%	9%

Total Compensation plus Benefits Package Analysis

The analyses on the next page are based on the data in the tables that you will find in the remainder of the chapter. The tables show compensation plus benefits data for full-time and part-time Solo Pastors and are presented according to church income, church attendance, church setting, region, education, years employed, denomination, and gender. In this way, the Solo Pastor's compensation plus benefits can be analyzed and compared from a variety of useful perspectives.

The total compensation plus benefits amount includes the base salary, housing allowance and/or parsonage amount, health, life, and disability insurance payments, retirement contribution, and educational funds.

The average compensation for a full-time Solo Pastor is about 30% lower than that of a full-time Senior Pastor who has additional pastoral staff. The compensation difference is most likely related to the fact that Solo Pastors serve in smaller churches.

About six in ten full-time Solo Pastors receive health insurance, and nearly two-thirds of them receive retirement benefits.

Compensation Plus Benefits	Full-Time	Part-Time
Base Salary	97%	78%
Housing	71%	58%
Parsonage	25%	10%
Health Insurance	59%	18%
Life Insurance	16%	9%
Disability Insurance	17%	6%
Retirement	64%	33%
Continuing Education	41%	27%
Received Salary Increase	51%	31%
Received Paid Vacation	94%	69%
Received Auto Reimbursement/ Allowance	69%	43%

KEY POINTS

✳ **Nearly all full-time Solo Pastors serve in churches with an income of $500,000 or less and a worship attendance of 300 or less.**

✳ **In general, as church income, worship attendance, and the minister's education level increase, compensation and benefits for full-time Solo Pastors also increase.**

✳ **Years of service has little impact on the compensation and benefits package of the full-time Solo Pastor.**

✳ **Generally, full-time Solo Pastors serving churches in a metropolitan city or a suburban setting have the highest compensation and benefits packages compared to those who serve in small town or farming areas. Church income in these settings is also higher, which greatly impacts overall compensation.**

✳ **Some regional differences emerge across average compensation and benefits packages for full-time Solo Pastors. The lowest packages are found in the Central regions, while the highest are found in New England and Middle Atlantic.**

Compensation & Benefits: National Averages for Full-Time Solo Pastors*

2000	
2001	
2002	
2003	
2004	
2005	
2006	$59,852
2007	$56,797
2008	$60,162
2009	$56,189**

National averages for Senior Pastors from 1998-2005 include data for both Senior and Solo Pastors. Beginning in 2006, we are able to provide detailed data for each position. Refer to Chapter 5 for Solo Pastors' data.

**The above trend is made available for your reference only. In addition to looking at this overall data, please refer to the detailed tables using your church's income, attendance, setting, region, and denomination as well as the person's education, gender, and years employed for guidance in compensating this position.*

Table 5-1: Annual Compensation of Full-Time Solo Pastors by Church Income

CHARACTERISTICS	Data Distribution*	CHURCH INCOME				
		$250K & Under	$251-$500K	$501-$750K	$751K-$1M	Over 1 Million
Average weekend worship attendance		90	201	296	-	-
Average church income		$128,437	$331,115	$615,442	-	-
Average # of years employed		7	8	10	-	-
Average # of paid vacation days		21	23	23	-	-
% College graduate or higher		89%	92%	-	-	-
% Who receive auto reimbursement/allowance		68%	81%	84%	-	-
% Ordained		99%	99%	100%	-	-
% Supervise one or more people		67%	95%	96%	-	-
Average % salary increase (for those who had an increase) this year		5.4%	4.5%	4.0%	-	-
COMPENSATION						
Base Salary	Highest 25%	$38,000	$52,912	$60,000	-	-
	Median	$30,000	$42,000	$43,000	-	-
	Lowest 25%	$22,000	$30,000	$37,000	-	-
	Average	$30,266	$41,514	$47,849	-	-
Housing	Highest 25%	$22,500	$28,000	$32,967	-	-
	Median	$15,980	$22,000	$25,000	-	-
	Lowest 25%	$10,000	$15,600	$16,000	-	-
	Average	$16,624	$21,427	$25,143	-	-
Parsonage	Highest 25%	$12,000	$18,000	-	-	-
	Median	$9,000	$14,000	-	-	-
	Lowest 25%	$5,400	$8,000	-	-	-
	Average	$10,232	$13,576	-	-	-
Total Compensation	**Highest 25%**	**$53,120**	**$72,000**	**$82,000**	-	-
	Median	**$42,760**	**$59,978**	**$69,757**	-	-
	Lowest 25%	**$34,000**	**$50,800**	**$57,300**	-	-
	Average	**$43,645**	**$60,961**	**$71,426**	-	-
BENEFITS						
Health Insurance	Highest 25%	$12,000	$13,000	$13,750	-	-
	Median	$8,331	$9,600	$10,925	-	-
	Lowest 25%	$5,000	$6,200	$8,400	-	-
	Average	$8,792	$10,172	$11,040	-	-
Life Insurance	Highest 25%	$1,000	$1,077	$1,400	-	-
	Median	$590	$800	$551	-	-
	Lowest 25%	$272	$385	$306	-	-
	Average	$831	$967	$975	-	-
Disability Insurance	Highest 25%	$1,000	$1,560	-	-	-
	Median	$600	$925	-	-	-
	Lowest 25%	$300	$500	-	-	-
	Average	$927	$1,253	-	-	-
Retirement	Highest 25%	$6,300	$8,800	$9,603	-	-
	Median	$4,400	$5,756	$7,700	-	-
	Lowest 25%	$2,288	$3,300	$3,600	-	-
	Average	$5,078	$7,871	$7,905	-	-
Continuing Education	Highest 25%	$1,200	$1,800	-	-	-
	Median	$800	$1,159	-	-	-
	Lowest 25%	$500	$750	-	-	-
	Average	$1,152	$1,383	-	-	-
Total Benefits	**Highest 25%**	**$15,842**	**$21,302**	**$22,959**	-	-
	Median	**$10,000**	**$15,100**	**$16,616**	-	-
	Lowest 25%	**$4,658**	**$9,138**	**$3,880**	-	-
	Average	**$11,149**	**$16,189**	**$15,854**	-	-
TOTAL COMPENSATION PLUS BENEFITS	**Highest 25%**	**$64,276**	**$87,364**	**$103,937**	-	-
	Median	**$52,247**	**$75,491**	**$82,440**	-	-
	Lowest 25%	**$40,000**	**$61,918**	**$69,863**	-	-
	Average	**$52,427**	**$76,064**	**$86,645**	-	-
Number of Respondents		1074	164	25	8	9

- Not enough response to provide meaningful data.

* For detailed description and definitions of Data Distribution (Median and Average), see Chapter 1's "Explanation of Data Distribution."

Table 5-2: Annual Compensation of Full-Time Solo Pastors by Worship Attendance

	Data Distribution*	WORSHIP ATTENDANCE					
		100 or less	101-300	301-500	501-750	751-1,000	Over 1,000
CHARACTERISTICS							
Average weekend worship attendance		66	160	390	-	-	-
Average church income		$144,269	$242,003	$541,304	-	-	-
Average # of years employed		7	8	9	-	-	-
Average # of paid vacation days		21	22	22	-	-	-
% College graduate or higher		89%	91%	91%	-	-	-
% Who receive auto reimbursement/allowance		65%	76%	83%	-	-	-
% Ordained		99%	100%	100%	-	-	-
% Supervise one or more people		61%	87%	96%	-	-	-
Average % salary increase (for those who had an increase) this year		5.6%	4.8%	5.3%	-	-	-
COMPENSATION							
Base Salary	Median	$27,750	$36,000	$49,466	-	-	-
	Average	$28,140	$37,714	$47,063	-	-	-
Housing	Median	$15,000	$20,000	$22,000	-	-	-
	Average	$16,102	$19,514	$22,420	-	-	-
Parsonage	Median	$8,683	$10,800	-	-	-	-
	Average	$9,681	$12,855	-	-	-	-
Total Compensation	**Median**	**$40,000**	**$54,000**	**$63,221**	-	-	-
	Average	**$40,560**	**$54,917**	**$64,689**	-	-	-
BENEFITS							
Health Insurance	Median	$8,000	$9,600	$7,800	-	-	-
	Average	$8,810	$9,550	$8,676	-	-	-
Life Insurance	Median	$500	$702	-	-	-	-
	Average	$647	$995	-	-	-	-
Disability	Median	$600	$700	-	-	-	-
	Average	$948	$1,041	-	-	-	-
Retirement	Median	$4,100	$5,361	$6,188	-	-	-
	Average	$4,956	$6,353	$6,200	-	-	-
Continuing Education	Median	$750	$1,000	$1,500	-	-	-
	Average	$1,067	$1,327	$1,871	-	-	-
Total Benefits	**Median**	**$9,658**	**$12,250**	**$14,150**	-	-	-
	Average	**$10,883**	**$13,530**	**$14,333**	-	-	-
TOTAL COMPENSATION PLUS BENEFITS	**Median**	**$48,776**	**$64,600**	**$77,945**	-	-	-
	Average	**$48,851**	**$66,739**	**$78,425**	-	-	-
Number of Respondents		785	483	24	7	0	3

- Not enough response to provide meaningful data.

* For detailed description and definitions of Data Distribution (Median and Average), see Chapter 1's "Explanation of Data Distribution."

Table 5-3: Annual Compensation of Full-Time Solo Pastors by Church Setting

	Data Distribution*	CHURCH SETTING			
		Metro-politan city	Suburb of large city	Small town or rural city	Farming area
CHARACTERISTICS					
Average weekend worship attendance		130	116	111	97
Average church income		$232,912	$283,362	$182,074	$125,910
Average # of years employed		8	8	8	6
Average # of paid vacation days		21	22	21	19
% College graduate or higher		88%	92%	89%	87%
% Who receive auto reimbursement/allowance		65%	66%	71%	73%
% Ordained		99%	100%	99%	97%
% Supervise one or more people		78%	78%	72%	54%
Average % salary increase (for those who had an increase) this year		5.3%	4.7%	5.2%	5.9%
COMPENSATION					
Base Salary	Median	$33,566	$34,000	$30,000	$30,000
	Average	$35,017	$34,830	$30,971	$30,242
Housing	Median	$20,000	$21,000	$15,188	$10,000
	Average	$20,477	$21,263	$16,092	$12,875
Parsonage	Median	$12,000	$12,000	$8,300	$7,200
	Average	$17,540	$12,787	$9,631	$9,132
Total Compensation	**Median**	**$51,000**	**$52,788**	**$43,000**	**$39,000**
	Average	**$51,843**	**$52,773**	**$43,884**	**$40,687**
BENEFITS					
Health Insurance	Median	$8,730	$9,500	$8,388	$8,453
	Average	$8,657	$9,592	$9,133	$8,594
Life Insurance	Median	$571	$600	$563	$500
	Average	$1,121	$891	$778	$749
Disability Insurance	Median	$635	$700	$600	$600
	Average	$1,191	$1,200	$917	$791
Retirement	Median	$4,260	$5,500	$4,800	$3,800
	Average	$5,943	$6,519	$5,469	$4,196
Continuing Education	Median	$1,000	$1,000	$850	$700
	Average	$1,940	$1,159	$1,172	$842
Total Benefits	**Median**	**$11,000**	**$11,500**	**$10,556**	**$9,300**
	Average	**$12,742**	**$13,016**	**$11,934**	**$10,190**
TOTAL COMPENSATION PLUS BENEFITS	**Median**	**$60,760**	**$61,726**	**$53,000**	**$46,760**
	Average	**$61,578**	**$63,516**	**$53,620**	**$48,802**
Number of Respondents		161	292	679	16

- Not enough response to provide meaningful data.

* For detailed description and definitions of Data Distribution (Median and Average), see Chapter 1's "Explanation of Data Distribution."

Table 5-4: Annual Compensation of Full-Time Solo Pastors by Region

	Data Distribution*	REGION								
		New England	Middle Atlantic	South Atlantic	E-N Central	E-S Central	W-N Central	W-S Central	Mountain	Pacific
CHARACTERISTICS										
Average weekend worship attendance		93	111	127	106	136	116	112	109	105
Average church income		$166,511	$177,156	$242,181	$203,862	$231,221	$225,683	$211,264	$164,493	$177,043
Average # of years employed		8	9	7	7	7	7	8	8	8
Average # of paid vacation days		24	24	20	21	18	22	18	20	21
% College graduate or higher		92%	90%	89%	88%	94%	93%	84%	96%	87%
% Who receive auto reimbursement/allowance		79%	76%	66%	74%	64%	75%	50%	69%	64%
% Ordained		100%	100%	99%	98%	97%	98%	100%	100%	100%
% Supervise one or more people		76%	65%	77%	70%	76%	60%	75%	72%	81%
Average % salary increase (for those who had an increase) this year		6.4%	4.7%	6.1%	4.8%	4.8%	4.4%	5.8%	6.9%	5.3%
COMPENSATION										
Base Salary	Median	$34,828	$34,000	$31,800	$30,000	$32,000	$30,300	$29,829	$29,163	$30,000
	Average	$34,861	$34,331	$33,452	$31,094	$32,842	$30,383	$31,303	$31,760	$31,687
Housing	Median	$19,000	$18,875	$18,000	$15,000	$15,000	$14,400	$12,500	$21,800	$22,000
	Average	$21,618	$19,234	$18,331	$15,562	$15,483	$14,789	$14,136	$21,819	$21,042
Parsonage	Median	$12,000	$9,920	$10,000	$8,000	$10,000	$6,000	$6,000	$10,750	$13,910
	Average	$13,003	$11,147	$11,860	$9,734	$19,169	$7,358	$7,150	$10,683	$15,088
Total Compensation	**Median**	**$49,000**	**$46,848**	**$46,800**	**$43,297**	**$46,133**	**$41,000**	**$38,800**	**$51,082**	**$48,960**
	Average	**$51,621**	**$48,742**	**$48,493**	**$44,223**	**$48,113**	**$41,727**	**$41,279**	**$50,758**	**$49,238**
BENEFITS										
Health Insurance	Median	$10,840	$10,260	$7,440	$9,000	$7,800	$8,000	$6,000	$7,300	$9,600
	Average	$10,410	$10,740	$8,935	$9,375	$7,720	$8,202	$7,275	$7,736	$9,474
Life Insurance	Median	$650	$703	$489	$450	-	$900	$580	$600	$540
	Average	$686	$887	$709	$678	-	$1,153	$769	$1,038	$1,145
Disability Insurance	Median	$800	$500	$563	$560	-	$635	-	$1,027	$1,000
	Average	$834	$1,377	$1,187	$774	-	$883	-	$976	$1,240
Retirement	Median	$3,600	$5,149	$4,576	$4,800	$5,000	$4,180	$4,500	$4,260	$4,400
	Average	$5,148	$5,948	$5,478	$5,494	$4,754	$5,468	$5,388	$4,396	$6,750
Continuing Education	Median	$1,000	$1,000	$1,000	$800	$750	$900	$1,000	$600	$1,000
	Average	$1,105	$1,180	$1,143	$1,073	$1,574	$1,184	$1,694	$943	$1,474
Total Benefits	**Median**	**$11,000**	**$15,040**	**$10,000**	**$11,335**	**$9,648**	**$10,103**	**$7,050**	**$8,700**	**$12,000**
	Average	**$12,521**	**$14,764**	**$11,497**	**$12,380**	**$9,798**	**$11,645**	**$9,124**	**$9,117**	**$13,511**
TOTAL COMPENSATION PLUS BENEFITS	**Median**	**$59,450**	**$62,000**	**$53,676**	**$54,204**	**$53,350**	**$51,600**	**$46,700**	**$57,450**	**$58,593**
	Average	**$62,577**	**$61,059**	**$57,587**	**$54,298**	**$55,422**	**$51,958**	**$47,976**	**$58,182**	**$59,438**
Number of Respondents		72	175	201	290	63	173	109	70	151

- Not enough response to provide meaningful data.

* For detailed description and definitions of Data Distribution (Median and Average), see Chapter 1's "Explanation of Data Distribution."

Table 5-5: Annual Compensation of Full-Time Solo Pastors by Education

	Data Distribution*	EDUCATION			
		Less than Bachelor	Bachelor	Master	Doctorate
CHARACTERISTICS					
Average weekend worship attendance		113	104	109	142
Average church income		$138,736	$203,017	$173,739	$388,122
Average # of years employed		9	7	7	8
Average # of paid vacation days		16	18	23	23
% College graduate or higher		0%	100%	100%	100%
% Who receive auto reimbursement/allowance		45%	66%	75%	71%
% Ordained		99%	99%	99%	100%
% Supervise one or more people		71%	63%	73%	81
Average % salary increase (for those who had an increase) this year		7.0%	6.7%	4.7%	4.9%
COMPENSATION					
Base Salary	Median	$25,000	$28,000	$32,744	$33,391
	Average	$26,389	$29,496	$33,497	$34,915
Housing	Median	$13,100	$17,000	$18,000	$20,000
	Average	$15,847	$16,914	$17,844	$19,460
Parsonage	Median	$8,500	$7,500	$9,600	$12,000
	Average	$9,075	$8,176	$10,759	$16,515
Total Compensation	**Median**	**$36,000**	**$42,200**	**$46,474**	**$50,000**
	Average	**$37,942**	**$42,316**	**$48,364**	**$51,490**
BENEFITS					
Health Insurance	Median	$7,200	$7,032	$9,093	$9,000
	Average	$8,155	$8,146	$9,358	$9,643
Life Insurance	Median	$550	$600	$500	$1,000
	Average	$649	$1,161	$764	$1,028
Disability Insurance	Median	$850	$800	$600	$600
	Average	$1,398	$856	$986	$1,108
Retirement	Median	$2,000	$3,000	$5,000	$5,700
	Average	$2,791	$4,140	$5,934	$6,770
Continuing Education	Median	$1,000	$800	$900	$1,000
	Average	$1,538	$1,510	$1,072	$1,403
Total Benefits	**Median**	**$7,400**	**$7,200**	**$11,600**	**$13,971**
	Average	**$8,140**	**$9,345**	**$12,824**	**$14,656**
TOTAL COMPENSATION PLUS BENEFITS	**Median**	**$40,110**	**$46,998**	**$58,882**	**$61,668**
	Average	**$42,620**	**$49,025**	**$59,589**	**$63,988**
Number of Respondents		134	280	714	163

- Not enough response to provide meaningful data.

* For detailed description and definitions of Data Distribution (Median and Average), see Chapter 1's "Explanation of Data Distribution."

Table 5-6: Annual Compensation of Full-Time Solo Pastors by Years Employed

	Data Distribution*	YEARS EMPLOYED			
		Less than 6 years	6-10 years	11-15 years	Over 15 years
CHARACTERISTICS					
Average weekend worship attendance		106	122	118	117
Average church income		$168,173	$263,201	$181,143	$256,065
Average # of years employed		3	8	13	23
Average # of paid vacation days		20	22	22	24
% College graduate or higher		90%	90%	91%	86%
% Who receive auto reimbursement/allowance		68%	71%	73%	67%
% Ordained		99%	99%	99%	98%
% Supervise one or more people		72%	70%	74%	70%
Average % salary increase (for those who had an increase) this year		5.9%	4.0%	4.7%	5.5%
COMPENSATION					
Base Salary	Median	$30,300	$32,000	$29,000	$32,958
	Average	$32,315	$32,098	$30,767	$32,721
Housing	Median	$17,350	$17,000	$15,000	$17,000
	Average	$17,940	$17,353	$15,925	$18,165
Parsonage	Median	$9,000	$9,000	$8,700	$12,000
	Average	$10,444	$9,168	$9,661	$14,519
Total Compensation	**Median**	**$45,000**	**$44,000**	**$44,576**	**$49,378**
	Average	**$46,416**	**$45,804**	**$44,218**	**$48,830**
BENEFITS					
Health Insurance	Median	$8,346	$8,400	$9,600	$9,500
	Average	$8,608	$9,286	$9,352	$10,331
Life Insurance	Median	$576	$522	-	$600
	Average	$786	$715	-	$994
Disability Insurance	Median	$610	$500	-	$909
	Average	$1,002	$923	-	$1,109
Retirement	Median	$5,000	$4,000	$5,000	$4,450
	Average	$5,824	$4,731	$6,618	$5,184
Continuing Education	Median	$1,000	$800	$800	$1,000
	Average	$1,260	$1,149	$1,040	$1,138
Total Benefits	**Median**	**$10,750**	**$9,578**	**$12,050**	**$11,627**
	Average	**$11,822**	**$11,135**	**$13,643**	**$13,021**
TOTAL COMPENSATION PLUS BENEFITS	**Median**	**$54,941**	**$53,339**	**$54,921**	**$59,424**
	Average	**$55,807**	**$55,272**	**$54,777**	**$59,630**
Number of Respondents		676	294	146	170

- Not enough response to provide meaningful data.

* For detailed description and definitions of Data Distribution (Median and Average), see Chapter 1's "Explanation of Data Distribution."

Table 5-7: Annual Compensation of Full-Time Solo Pastors by Denomination

	Data Distribution*	DENOMINATION					
		Assemblies of God	Baptist	Independent/ Nondenom.	Lutheran	Methodist	Presby- terian
CHARACTERISTICS							
Average weekend worship attendance		101	115	117	121	121	125
Average church income		$137,949	$184,822	$170,149	$199,154	$284,398	$237,742
Average # of years employed		8	8	9	9	5	7
Average # of paid vacation days		15	19	19	25	23	26
% College graduate or higher		74%	88%	82%	99%	94%	99%
% Who receive auto reimbursement/allowance		45%	67%	52%	89%	68%	89%
% Ordained		100%	100%	99%	100%	99%	100%
% Supervise one or more people		59%	72%	71%	77%	83%	83%
Average % salary increase (for those who had an increase) this year		7.8%	5.9%	6.4%	4.5%	4.1%	4.5%
COMPENSATION							
Base Salary	Median	$26,500	$27,288	$29,200	$35,120	$39,850	$33,275
	Average	$26,710	$28,465	$30,594	$37,118	$39,843	$34,425
Housing	Median	$15,250	$16,190	$20,000	$22,127	$11,000	$20,000
	Average	$16,052	$16,865	$20,596	$21,170	$11,505	$19,689
Parsonage	Median	$9,600	$10,000	$7,800	$7,800	$10,000	$11,000
	Average	$9,000	$10,015	$13,012	$8,254	$11,719	$12,338
Total Compensation	**Median**	**$39,400**	**$41,910**	**$45,658**	**$52,265**	**$48,960**	**$49,000**
	Average	**$38,418**	**$42,461**	**$48,126**	**$54,034**	**$49,718**	**$52,852**
BENEFITS							
Health Insurance	Median	$5,555	$8,358	$8,000	$10,292	$10,000	$9,141
	Average	$6,717	$9,296	$8,040	$10,581	$10,752	$9,792
Life Insurance	Median	-	$700	$550	$575	$600	$636
	Average	-	$985	$545	$624	$1,054	$731
Disability Insurance	Median	-	$500	$800	$1,000	$1,658	$538
	Average	-	$841	$1,110	$1,220	$1,716	$1,183
Retirement	Median	$1,450	$3,600	$3,000	$4,649	$6,000	$6,200
	Average	$1,733	$4,477	$3,933	$6,540	$6,647	$9,415
Continuing Education	Median	-	$800	$1,200	$750	$750	$1,000
	Average	-	$1,133	$1,495	$903	$1,223	$1,191
Total Benefits	**Median**	**$6,318**	**$9,709**	**$8,200**	**$12,878**	**$16,200**	**$15,105**
	Average	**$7,292**	**$10,830**	**$9,025**	**$14,308**	**$15,911**	**$16,087**
TOTAL COMPENSATION PLUS BENEFITS	**Median**	**$40,525**	**$50,387**	**$54,171**	**$66,000**	**$64,509**	**$64,600**
	Average	**$43,158**	**$50,844**	**$54,409**	**$67,981**	**$64,877**	**$68,289**
Number of Respondents		40	292	158	119	127	99

- Not enough response to provide meaningful data.

* For detailed description and definitions of Data Distribution (Median and Average), see Chapter 1's "Explanation of Data Distribution."

Table 5-8: Annual Compensation of Full-Time Solo Pastors by Gender

	Data Distribution*	GENDER	
		Male	Female
CHARACTERISTICS			
Average weekend worship attendance		114	95
Average church income		$197,083	$287,441
Average # of years employed		8	5
Average # of paid vacation days		21	25
% College graduate or higher		89%	95%
% Who receive auto reimbursement/allowance		69%	75%
% Ordained		99%	99%
% Supervise one or more people		71%	85%
Average % salary increase (for those who had an increase) this year		5.4%	3.9%
COMPENSATION			
Base Salary	Median	$30,723	$32,778
	Average	$32,298	$31,134
Housing	Median	$17,081	$15,000
	Average	$17,727	$16,530
Parsonage	Median	$9,000	$8,842
	Average	$10,787	$8,942
Total Compensation	**Median**	**$45,000**	**$45,000**
	Average	**$46,648**	**$43,962**
BENEFITS			
Health Insurance	Median	$8,760	$8,286
	Average	$9,179	$8,342
Life Insurance	Median	$600	$636
	Average	$867	$770
Disability Insurance	Median	$627	$540
	Average	$1,027	$766
Retirement	Median	$4,500	$5,665
	Average	$5,459	$6,661
Continuing Education	Median	$900	$900
	Average	$1,178	$1,359
Total Benefits	**Median**	**$10,581**	**$11,700**
	Average	**$12,030**	**$12,449**
TOTAL COMPENSATION PLUS BENEFITS	**Median**	**$54,841**	**$58,640**
	Average	**$56,240**	**$55,775**
Number of Respondents		1204	98

- Not enough response to provide meaningful data.

* For detailed description and definitions of Data Distribution (Median and Average), see Chapter 1's "Explanation of Data Distribution."

Table 5-9: Annual Compensation of Part-Time Solo Pastors by Church Income

	Data Distribution*	CHURCH INCOME				
		$250K & Under	$251-$500K	$501-$750K	$751K-$1M	Over 1 Million
CHARACTERISTICS						
Average weekend worship attendance		54	-	-	-	-
Average church income		$67,025	-	-	-	-
Average # of years employed		6	-	-	-	-
Average # of paid vacation days		16	-	-	-	-
% College graduate or higher		87%	-	-	-	-
% Who receive auto reimbursement/allowance		44%	-	-	-	-
% Ordained		97%	-	-	-	-
% Supervise one or more people		44%	-	-	-	-
Average % salary increase (for those who had an increase) this year		9.2%	-	-	-	-
HOURLY RATE						
Base Rate	Average	$18	-	-	-	-
COMPENSATION						
Base Salary	Median	$13,500	-	-	-	-
	Average	$16,064	-	-	-	-
Housing	Median	$12,000	-	-	-	-
	Average	$12,487	-	-	-	-
Parsonage	Median	$9,100	-	-	-	-
	Average	$8,700	-	-	-	-
Total Compensation	**Median**	**$18,860**	-	-	-	-
	Average	**$20,970**	-	-	-	-
BENEFITS						
Health Insurance	Median	$6,000	-	-	-	-
	Average	$5,539	-	-	-	-
Life Insurance	Median	$613	-	-	-	-
	Average	$1,043	-	-	-	-
Disability Insurance	Median	$318	-	-	-	-
	Average	$478	-	-	-	-
Retirement	Median	$2,560	-	-	-	-
	Average	$3,669	-	-	-	-
Continuing Education	Median	$525	-	-	-	-
	Average	$870	-	-	-	-
Total Benefits	**Median**	**$3,500**	-	-	-	-
	Average	**$4,922**	-	-	-	-
TOTAL COMPENSATION PLUS BENEFITS	**Median**	**$20,900**	-	-	-	-
	Average	**$23,538**	-	-	-	-
Number of Respondents		228	6	1	1	1

- Not enough response to provide meaningful data.

* For detailed description and definitions of Data Distribution (Median and Average), see Chapter 1's "Explanation of Data Distribution."

Table 5-10: Annual Compensation of Part-Time Solo Pastors by Worship Attendance

	Data Distribution*	WORSHIP ATTENDANCE					
		100 or less	101-300	301-500	501-750	751-1,000	Over 1,000
CHARACTERISTICS							
Average weekend worship attendance		47	155	-	-	-	-
Average church income		$75,466	$196,778	-	-	-	-
Average # of years employed		6	7	-	-	-	-
Average # of paid vacation days		16	18	-	-	-	-
% College graduate or higher		86%	89%	-	-	-	-
% Who receive auto reimbursement/allowance		41%	71%	-	-	-	-
% Ordained		97%	100%	-	-	-	-
% Supervise one or more people		42%	81%	-	-	-	-
Average % salary increase (for those who had an increase) this year		9.3%	6.2%	-	-	-	-
HOURLY RATE							
Base Rate	Average	$17	$21	-	-	-	-
COMPENSATION							
Base Salary	Median	$12,845	$28,600	-	-	-	-
	Average	$15,015	$25,866	-	-	-	-
Housing	Median	$12,000	$15,340	-	-	-	-
	Average	$11,994	$16,360	-	-	-	-
Parsonage	Median	$10,100	-	-	-	-	-
	Average	$9,177	-	-	-	-	-
Total Compensation	**Median**	**$18,000**	**$39,200**	-	-	-	-
	Average	**$19,266**	**$37,636**	-	-	-	-
BENEFITS							
Health Insurance	Median	$5,085	$6,300	-	-	-	-
	Average	$5,390	$6,050	-	-	-	-
Life Insurance	Median	$600	-	-	-	-	-
	Average	$986	-	-	-	-	-
Disability	Median	$279	-	-	-	-	-
	Average	$461	-	-	-	-	-
Retirement	Median	$2,500	$4,250	-	-	-	-
	Average	$3,562	$5,138	-	-	-	-
Continuing Education	Median	$563	$625	-	-	-	-
	Average	$875	$719	-	-	-	-
Total Benefits	**Median**	**$3,160**	**$7,100**	-	-	-	-
	Average	**$4,767**	**$7,496**	-	-	-	-
TOTAL COMPENSATION PLUS BENEFITS	**Median**	**$18,850**	**$42,950**	-	-	-	-
	Average	**$21,618**	**$43,050**	-	-	-	-
Number of Respondents		225	18	0	0	0	0

- Not enough response to provide meaningful data.

* For detailed description and definitions of Data Distribution (Median and Average), see Chapter 1's "Explanation of Data Distribution."

Table 5-11: Annual Compensation of Part-Time Solo Pastors by Church Setting

	Data Distribution*	CHURCH SETTING			
		Metro-politan city	Suburb of large city	Small town or rural city	Farming area
CHARACTERISTICS					
Average weekend worship attendance		63	77	53	42
Average church income		$87,408	$122,982	$89,288	$47,085
Average # of years employed		6	6	6	5
Average # of paid vacation days		18	17	16	13
% College graduate or higher		84%	90%	87%	84%
% Who receive auto reimbursement/allowance		42%	37%	44%	47%
% Ordained		100%	100%	97%	95%
% Supervise one or more people		68%	53%	50%	18%
Average % salary increase (for those who had an increase) this year		-	7.0%	8.3%	7.6%
HOURLY RATE					
Base Rate	Average	$18	$17	$18	$16
COMPENSATION					
Base Salary	Median	$16,000	$18,180	$14,000	$10,000
	Average	$17,016	$18,301	$16,068	$13,801
Housing	Median	$19,062	$14,700	$11,750	$7,500
	Average	$18,576	$14,321	$12,008	$9,295
Parsonage	Median	-	-	$7,000	-
	Average	-	-	$7,399	-
Total Compensation	**Median**	**$23,800**	**$26,300**	**$18,000**	**$13,415**
	Average	**$25,165**	**$26,029**	**$20,185**	**$16,658**
BENEFITS					
Health Insurance	Median	-	-	$6,000	$3,835
	Average	-	-	$5,755	$4,358
Life Insurance	Median	-	-	$724	-
	Average	-	-	$1,068	-
Disability Insurance	Median	-	-	$328	-
	Average	-	-	$639	-
Retirement	Median	$3,341	$2,400	$2,604	$1,200
	Average	$4,830	$4,159	$3,981	$1,902
Continuing Education	Median	-	$750	$700	$500
	Average	-	$733	$829	$1,184
Total Benefits	**Median**	**$3,200**	**$2,900**	**$5,172**	**$1,600**
	Average	**$4,100**	**$5,063**	**$5,896**	**$3,394**
TOTAL COMPENSATION PLUS BENEFITS	**Median**	**$26,000**	**$28,000**	**$20,100**	**$13,534**
	Average	**$27,971**	**$29,405**	**$22,993**	**$18,179**
Number of Respondents		19	39	126	58

- Not enough response to provide meaningful data.

* For detailed description and definitions of Data Distribution (Median and Average), see Chapter 1's "Explanation of Data Distribution."

Table 5-12: Annual Compensation of Part-Time Solo Pastors by Region

	Data Distribution*	REGION								
		New England	Middle Atlantic	South Atlantic	E-N Central	E-S Central	W-N Central	W-S Central	Mountain	Pacific
CHARACTERISTICS										
Average weekend worship attendance		51	54	66	59	44	55	47	58	43
Average church income		$78,820	$97,659	$88,861	$72,310	$152,766	$63,914	$61,102	$66,065	$102,557
Average # of years employed		5	5	6	7	5	7	8	6	5
Average # of paid vacation days		19	15	14	17	7	17	16	15	19
% College graduate or higher		88%	79%	92%	87%	71%	86%	86%	82%	92%
% Who receive auto reimbursement/allowance		36%	61%	40%	49%	38%	34%	38%	36%	42%
% Ordained		88%	100%	98%	98%	93%	100%	95%	100%	96%
% Supervise one or more people		38%	43%	49%	32%	31%	63%	50%	45%	50%
Average % salary increase (for those who had an increase) this year		-	4.2%	9.6%	9.6%	-	6.2%	-	-	-
HOURLY RATE										
Base Rate	Average	$18	$17	$19	$16	$21	$15	$19	-	$16
COMPENSATION										
Base Salary	Median	$15,500	$18,500	$15,840	$14,000	$15,500	$11,250	$6,200	-	$9,550
	Average	$17,951	$18,952	$16,986	$16,244	$13,658	$15,339	$12,080	-	$12,878
Housing	Median	$13,724	$13,000	$10,250	$10,800	-	$11,088	-	$11,500	$14,000
	Average	$13,665	$13,727	$11,055	$11,072	-	$12,645	-	$10,659	$15,275
Parsonage	Median	-	-	-	-	-	-	-	-	-
	Average	-	-	-	-	-	-	-	-	-
Total Compensation	**Median**	**$25,100**	**$20,400**	**$19,000**	**$18,000**	**$17,000**	**$17,500**	**$14,400**	**$14,410**	**$21,900**
	Average	**$25,556**	**$23,826**	**$20,305**	**$21,184**	**$17,093**	**$20,674**	**$16,677**	**$19,488**	**$18,859**
BENEFITS										
Health Insurance	Median	-	-	-	$3,640	-	-	-	-	-
	Average	-	-	-	$3,552	-	-	-	$6,360	-
Life Insurance	Median	-	-	-	-	-	-	-	-	-
	Average	-	-	-	-	-	-	-	-	-
Disability Insurance	Median	-	-	-	-	-	-	-	-	-
	Average	-	-	-	-	-	-	-	-	-
Retirement	Median	-	$4,866	$2,500	$2,130	-	$3,780	-	-	-
	Average	-	$4,562	$3,224	$3,200	-	$4,086	-	-	-
Continuing Education	Median	-	$525	$1,000	$550	-	$650	-	-	-
	Average	-	$738	$1,300	$879	-	$681	-	-	-
Total Benefits	**Median**	-	**$3,768**	**$3,120**	**$4,920**	-	**$8,900**	-	-	**$3,302**
	Average	-	**$4,688**	**$4,002**	**$4,850**	-	**$6,979**	-	-	**$5,685**
TOTAL COMPENSATION PLUS BENEFITS	**Median**	**$25,300**	**$23,100**	**$20,800**	**$21,230**	**$17,600**	**$18,850**	**$14,400**	**$18,825**	**$24,203**
	Average	**$29,120**	**$27,059**	**$22,344**	**$24,347**	**$18,664**	**$24,284**	**$17,318**	**$22,217**	**$21,045**
Number of Respondents		16	29	53	46	14	29	21	11	26

- Not enough response to provide meaningful data.

* For detailed description and definitions of Data Distribution (Median and Average), see Chapter 1's "Explanation of Data Distribution."

Table 5-13: Annual Compensation of Part-Time Solo Pastors by Education

	Data Distribution*	EDUCATION			
		Less than Bachelor	Bachelor	Master	Doctorate
CHARACTERISTICS					
Average weekend worship attendance		54	46	60	64
Average church income		$105,330	$59,063	$93,702	$92,159
Average # of years employed		7	6	6	4
Average # of paid vacation days		12	13	19	17
% College graduate or higher		0%	100%	100%	100%
% Who receive auto reimbursement/allowance		38%	39%	46%	52%
% Ordained		100%	96%	96%	100%
% Supervise one or more people		45%	42%	45%	55%
Average % salary increase (for those who had an increase) this year		9.2%	8.6%	9.2%	-
HOURLY RATE					
Base Rate	Average	$15	$20	$17	$16
COMPENSATION					
Base Salary	Median	$12,400	$11,000	$15,915	$12,750
	Average	$13,111	$15,244	$17,042	$17,304
Housing	Median	$13,500	$11,000	$12,180	$14,650
	Average	$12,345	$11,718	$12,603	$14,124
Parsonage	Median	-	-	$7,236	-
	Average	-	-	$8,422	-
Total Compensation	**Median**	**$20,200**	**$16,218**	**$20,000**	**$20,800**
	Average	**$19,343**	**$18,942**	**$21,615**	**$23,242**
BENEFITS					
Health Insurance	Median	-	$5,500	$6,106	-
	Average	-	$4,553	$5,523	-
Life Insurance	Median	-	-	$468	-
	Average	-	-	$914	-
Disability Insurance	Median	-	-	$237	-
	Average	-	-	$442	-
Retirement	Median	$1,260	$1,600	$2,800	-
	Average	$1,492	$2,164	$3,947	-
Continuing Education	Median	$875	$300	$525	-
	Average	$1,246	$733	$843	-
Total Benefits	**Median**	**$1,480**	**$1,500**	**$4,325**	**$10,635**
	Average	**$3,283**	**$3,131**	**$5,677**	**$9,990**
TOTAL COMPENSATION PLUS BENEFITS	**Median**	**$21,944**	**$17,184**	**$21,500**	**$21,300**
	Average	**$21,133**	**$20,234**	**$25,000**	**$27,586**
Number of Respondents		33	80	109	23

- Not enough response to provide meaningful data.

* For detailed description and definitions of Data Distribution (Median and Average), see Chapter 1's "Explanation of Data Distribution."

Table 5-14: Annual Compensation of Part-Time Solo Pastors by Years Employed

	Data Distribution*	YEARS EMPLOYED			
		Less than 6 years	6-10 years	11-15 years	Over 15 years
CHARACTERISTICS					
Average weekend worship attendance		54	54	48	74
Average church income		$81,652	$65,677	$157,190	$80,475
Average # of years employed		2	8	12	21
Average # of paid vacation days		15	17	17	19
% College graduate or higher		88%	83%	76%	90%
% Who receive auto reimbursement/allowance		43%	43%	38%	50%
% Ordained		96%	98%	100%	100%
% Supervise one or more people		45%	51%	48%	35%
Average % salary increase (for those who had an increase) this year		9.7%	5.7%	-	6.0%
HOURLY RATE					
Base Rate	Average	$18	$15	$16	$17
COMPENSATION					
Base Salary	Median	$13,000	$14,000	$15,300	$15,000
	Average	$15,660	$17,016	$16,049	$16,232
Housing	Median	$12,000	$14,628	$10,000	$11,284
	Average	$12,388	$13,605	$11,359	$10,854
Parsonage	Median	$8,218	-	-	-
	Average	$9,676	-	-	-
Total Compensation	**Median**	**$18,000**	**$23,673**	**$17,500**	**$18,000**
	Average	**$19,787**	**$23,109**	**$20,680**	**$21,152**
BENEFITS					
Health Insurance	Median	$5,500	$6,556	-	-
	Average	$4,643	$6,861	-	-
Life Insurance	Median	$335	-	-	-
	Average	$604	-	-	-
Disability Insurance	Median	$220	-	-	-
	Average	$389	-	-	-
Retirement	Median	$2,460	$2,800	$1,350	-
	Average	$3,972	$4,048	$1,916	-
Continuing Education	Median	$525	$850	-	-
	Average	$895	$843	-	-
Total Benefits	**Median**	**$3,500**	**$5,322**	**$1,425**	**$4,700**
	Average	**$4,735**	**$5,860**	**$2,781**	**$7,577**
TOTAL COMPENSATION PLUS BENEFITS	**Median**	**$18,500**	**$24,500**	**$21,300**	**$21,160**
	Average	**$22,013**	**$26,600**	**$22,534**	**$25,482**
Number of Respondents		151	47	21	21

- Not enough response to provide meaningful data.

* For detailed description and definitions of Data Distribution (Median and Average), see Chapter 1's "Explanation of Data Distribution."

Table 5-15: Annual Compensation of Part-Time Solo Pastors by Denomination

	Data Distribution*	DENOMINATION					
		Assemblies of God	Baptist	Independent/ Nondenom.	Lutheran	Methodist	Presby-terian
CHARACTERISTICS							
Average weekend worship attendance		-	61	57	54	48	43
Average church income		-	$101,065	$83,317	$81,538	$69,971	$66,780
Average # of years employed		-	6	8	5	4	5
Average # of paid vacation days		-	13	13	22	20	20
% College graduate or higher		-	81%	93%	100%	83%	94%
% Who receive auto reimbursement/allowance		-	30%	34%	67%	49%	65%
% Ordained		-	100%	93%	100%	91%	100%
% Supervise one or more people		-	48%	59%	56%	32%	41%
Average % salary increase (for those who had an increase) this year		-	13.4%	14.1%	-	6.4%	-
HOURLY RATE							
Base Rate	Average	-	$19	$20	$17	$17	$19
COMPENSATION							
Base Salary	Median	-	$10,800	$11,700	$16,369	$15,215	$14,000
	Average	-	$13,732	$15,163	$18,535	$17,714	$13,079
Housing	Median	-	$11,150	$12,000	-	$9,050	$14,100
	Average	-	$12,079	$13,908	-	$8,979	$15,433
Parsonage	Median	-	-	-	-	-	-
	Average	-	-	-	-	-	-
Total Compensation	**Median**	-	**$18,500**	**$17,950**	**$21,000**	**$20,244**	**$23,673**
	Average	-	**$18,835**	**$19,763**	**$26,431**	**$20,644**	**$19,340**
BENEFITS							
Health Insurance	Median	-	-	-	-	-	-
	Average	-	-	-	-	-	-
Life Insurance	Median	-	-	-	-	-	-
	Average	-	-	-	-	-	-
Disability Insurance	Median	-	-	-	-	-	-
	Average	-	-	-	-	-	-
Retirement	Median	-	$1,280	-	-	$2,610	-
	Average	-	$3,572	-	-	$2,811	-
Continuing Education	Median	-	$1,400	-	-	$500	$550
	Average	-	$1,975	-	-	$635	$607
Total Benefits	**Median**	-	**$3,000**	**$1,120**	-	**$1,900**	**$9,888**
	Average	-	**$5,062**	**$2,434**	-	**$3,327**	**$8,413**
TOTAL COMPENSATION PLUS BENEFITS	**Median**	-	**$18,825**	**$18,300**	**$30,000**	**$20,456**	**$26,900**
	Average	-	**$20,763**	**$20,574**	**$31,164**	**$23,021**	**$24,288**
Number of Respondents		6	63	30	9	35	17

- Not enough response to provide meaningful data.

* For detailed description and definitions of Data Distribution (Median and Average), see Chapter 1's "Explanation of Data Distribution."

Table 5-16: Annual Compensation of Part-Time Solo Pastors by Gender

	Data Distribution*	GENDER	
		Male	Female
CHARACTERISTICS			
Average weekend worship attendance		55	54
Average church income		$85,954	$72,494
Average # of years employed		6	4
Average # of paid vacation days		16	16
% College graduate or higher		87%	80%
% Who receive auto reimbursement/allowance		41%	57%
% Ordained		98%	93%
% Supervise one or more people		44%	48%
Average % salary increase (for those who had an increase) this year		8.1%	12.4%
HOURLY RATE			
Base Rate	Average	$18	$15
COMPENSATION			
Base Salary	Median	$13,000	$17,491
	Average	$15,595	$17,924
Housing	Median	$12,000	$10,000
	Average	$12,732	$9,637
Parsonage	Median	$10,100	-
	Average	$8,918	-
Total Compensation	**Median**	**$18,000**	**$22,200**
	Average	**$20,305**	**$22,622**
BENEFITS			
Health Insurance	Median	$6,000	$3,420
	Average	$5,797	$4,219
Life Insurance	Median	$675	-
	Average	$1,118	-
Disability Insurance	Median	$318	-
	Average	$538	-
Retirement	Median	$2,160	$2,800
	Average	$3,822	$3,227
Continuing Education	Median	$600	$500
	Average	$939	$774
Total Benefits	**Median**	**$3,341**	**$4,440**
	Average	**$5,065**	**$4,769**
TOTAL COMPENSATION PLUS BENEFITS	**Median**	**$20,400**	**$25,770**
	Average	**$22,731**	**$26,278**
Number of Respondents		215	30

- Not enough response to provide meaningful data.

* For detailed description and definitions of Data Distribution (Median and Average), see Chapter 1's "Explanation of Data Distribution."

6

EXECUTIVE OR ADMINISTRATIVE PASTORS

Employment Profile

Executive or Administrative Pastors are those pastors who handle ministry staff supervision, management, and development. Nearly all of the Executive or Administrative Pastors who responded to our survey serve full-time.

About nine in ten Executive or Administrative Pastors are ordained, male, and employed by the church. On average, they've been in their current positions for seven years. Six in ten have graduate degrees.

The following provides a profile of the demographic data reported for this position:

	Full-Time	Part-Time
Number of respondents	233	14
Ordained	90%	-
Average years employed	7	-
Male	88%	-
Female	12%	-
Self-employed (receives 1099)	12%	-
Church employee (receives W-2)	88%	-
High school diploma	5%	-
Associate Degree	6%	-
Bachelor's Degree	28%	-
Master's Degree	50%	-
Doctoral Degree	10%	-

Total Compensation plus Benefits Package Analysis

The analyses on the next page are based on the data in the tables that you will find in the remainder of the chapter. The tables show compensation plus benefits data for Executive or Administrative Pastors who serve full time and are presented according to church income, church attendance, church setting, region, education, years employed, denomination, and gender. In this way, Executive or Administrative Pastors' compensation plus benefits can be analyzed and compared from a variety of useful perspectives.

The total compensation plus benefits amount includes the base salary, housing allowance and/or parsonage amount, health, life, and disability insurance payments, retirement contribution, and educational funds.

Similar to full-time Senior Pastors, the full-time Executive or Administrative Pastor is one of the highest paid positions with comprehensive benefits packages in the local church. Seven in ten Executive or Administrative Pastors receive housing allowances; most, however, do not live in church-provided parsonages. Seven in ten also receive health insurance, and about two-thirds receive retirement benefits.

The following is a profile of the demographics reported for this position:

Compensation Plus Benefits	Full-Time	Part-Time
Base Salary	99%	-
Housing	71%	-
Parsonage	3%	-
Health Insurance	71%	-
Life Insurance	38%	-
Disability Insurance	40%	-
Retirement	64%	-
Continuing Education	27%	-
Received Salary Increase	52%	-
Received Paid Vacation	96%	-
Received Auto Reimbursement/ Allowance	52%	-

KEY POINTS

✳ **More than six in ten full-time Executive or Administrative Pastors serve in churches with income over $1,000,000. Nearly four in ten serve in churches with worship attendance over 1,000.**

✳ **In general, as church income, worship attendance, and the minister's education level increase, compensation and benefits for full-time Executive or Administrative Pastors also increase.**

✳ **Half of full-time Executive or Administrative Pastors serve in churches set in a suburb of a large city. Those serving in churches in metropolitan and suburban settings receive higher compensation compared to those who serve in small towns.**

Compensation & Benefits: National Averages for Full-Time Executive or Administrative Pastors*

2000	
2001	
2002	
2003	
2004	
2005	
2006	
2007	$81,279
2008	$79,625
2009	$77,972**

No historical data available before 2007.

**The above trend is made available for your reference only. In addition to looking at this overall data, please refer to the detailed tables using your church's income, attendance, setting, region, and denomination as well as the person's education, gender, and years employed for guidance in compensating this position.*

Table 6-1: Annual Compensation of Full-Time Executive or Administrative Pastors by Church Income

CHARACTERISTICS	Data Distribution*	CHURCH INCOME				
		$250K & Under	$251-$500K	$501-$750K	$751K-$1M	Over 1 Million
Average weekend worship attendance		170	257	409	524	1,541
Average church income		$161,738	$382,125	$649,672	$904,706	$2,513,951
Average # of years employed		8	9	7	9	8
Average # of paid vacation days		15	15	17	17	18
% College graduate or higher		27%	41%	47%	57%	74%
% Who receive auto reimbursement/allowance		47%	33%	22%	36%	45%
% Ordained		21%	18%	15%	20%	24%
% Supervise one or more people		80%	85%	85%	96%	95%
Average % salary increase (for those who had an increase) this year		4.7%	4.1%	5.3%	4.1%	4.5%
COMPENSATION						
Base Salary	Highest 25%	$42,000	$41,900	$39,728	$50,000	$64,394
	Median	$24,600	$34,500	$35,158	$45,000	$51,798
	Lowest 25%	$20,800	$30,672	$32,211	$37,346	$40,854
	Average	$34,002	$36,950	$35,757	$44,957	$53,134
Housing	Highest 25%	-	-	-	-	$38,520
	Median	-	-	-	-	$29,736
	Lowest 25%	-	-	-	-	$22,200
	Average	-	-	-	-	$30,249
Parsonage	Highest 25%	-	-	-	-	-
	Median	-	-	-	-	-
	Lowest 25%	-	-	-	-	-
	Average	-	-	-	-	-
Total Compensation	**Highest 25%**	**$42,000**	**$43,850**	**$43,500**	**$51,184**	**$68,000**
	Median	**$27,200**	**$34,500**	**$36,228**	**$46,275**	**$59,007**
	Lowest 25%	**$20,800**	**$30,672**	**$33,075**	**$38,198**	**$45,000**
	Average	**$34,602**	**$37,480**	**$39,454**	**$47,411**	**$57,757**
BENEFITS						
Health Insurance	Highest 25%	-	$7,500	$9,310	$11,227	$10,274
	Median	-	$5,568	$7,320	$5,000	$6,600
	Lowest 25%	-	$2,400	$4,100	$2,031	$4,703
	Average	-	$5,939	$6,938	$6,501	$7,899
Life Insurance	Highest 25%	-	-	-	-	$340
	Median	-	-	-	-	$159
	Lowest 25%	-	-	-	-	$100
	Average	-	-	-	-	$296
Disability Insurance	Highest 25%	-	-	-	-	$586
	Median	-	-	-	-	$300
	Lowest 25%	-	-	-	-	$200
	Average	-	-	-	524	$513
Retirement	Highest 25%	-	$3,698	$3,720	$3,750	$6,000
	Median	-	$2,450	$3,095	$3,078	$3,119
	Lowest 25%	-	$1,260	$1,978	$1,884	$2,220
	Average	-	$2,467	$3,375	$3,218	$4,155
Continuing Education	Highest 25%	-	-	-	-	$1,500
	Median	-	-	-	-	$1,000
	Lowest 25%	-	-	-	-	$600
	Average	-	-	-	-	$1,363
Total Benefits	**Highest 25%**	**$11,605**	**$8,750**	**$10,904**	**$10,850**	**$13,926**
	Median	**$7,195**	**$4,845**	**$4,300**	**$6,693**	**$9,575**
	Lowest 25%	**$863**	**$2,075**	**$2,530**	**$1,890**	**$4,800**
	Average	**$8,162**	**$6,003**	**$6,654**	**$7,872**	**$10,084**
TOTAL COMPENSATION PLUS BENEFITS	**Highest 25%**	**$50,000**	**$47,491**	**$50,928**	**$64,174**	**$79,154**
	Median	**$39,000**	**$40,000**	**$41,418**	**$51,070**	**$65,357**
	Lowest 25%	**$24,192**	**$31,800**	**$37,225**	**$41,227**	**$52,800**
	Average	**$40,043**	**$41,364**	**$44,028**	**$53,914**	**$66,681**
Number of Respondents		15	34	32	46	139

- Not enough response to provide meaningful data.

* For detailed description and definitions of Data Distribution (Median and Average), see Chapter 1's "Explanation of Data Distribution."

Table 6-2: Annual Compensation of Full-Time Executive or Administrative Pastors by Worship Attendance

	Data Distribution*	WORSHIP ATTENDANCE					
		100 or less	101-300	301-500	501-750	751-1,000	Over 1,000
CHARACTERISTICS							
Average weekend worship attendance	-		228	415	631	887	2,297
Average church income	-		$518,105	$705,631	$1,150,004	$1,701,690	$3,302,334
Average # of years employed	-		6	5	7	7	8
Average # of paid vacation days	-		18	20	19	19	20
% College graduate or higher	-		81%	89%	92%	97%	89%
% Who receive auto reimbursement/allowance	-		50%	54%	49%	47%	57%
% Ordained	-		91%	85%	89%	95%	92%
% Supervise one or more people	-		97%	93%	97%	97%	98%
Average % salary increase (for those who had an increase) this year	-		5.0%	4.3%	3.7%	3.4%	4.5%
COMPENSATION							
Base Salary	Median	-	$34,200	$42,000	$42,240	$44,683	$52,000
	Average	-	$35,821	$43,426	$43,280	$49,301	$56,431
Housing	Median	-	$24,000	$20,000	$25,000	$28,000	$30,000
	Average	-	$26,266	$20,384	$26,860	$30,432	$31,125
Parsonage	Median	-	-	-	-	-	-
	Average	-	-	-	-	-	-
Total Compensation	**Median**	-	**$53,750**	**$55,000**	**$64,800**	**$68,000**	**$73,796**
	Average	-	**$53,884**	**$57,016**	**$64,657**	**$72,381**	**$79,510**
BENEFITS							
Health Insurance	Median	-	$6,000	$7,248	$7,200	$11,023	$9,569
	Average	-	$6,188	$8,134	$8,748	$10,454	$9,026
Life Insurance	Median	-	-	$542	$288	$600	$328
	Average	-	-	$609	$407	$1,265	$602
Disability	Median	-	-	-	$344	$678	$402
	Average	-	-	-	$398	$833	$776
Retirement	Median	-	$4,210	$2,000	$4,784	$3,950	$4,500
	Average	-	$3,465	$2,900	$4,910	$4,675	$5,696
Continuing Education	Median	-	$1,100	-	$1,000	$1,500	$2,000
	Average	-	$1,750	-	$1,604	$1,982	$2,095
Total Benefits	**Median**	-	**$6,400**	**$7,832**	**$13,548**	**$14,433**	**$13,578**
	Average	-	**$7,610**	**$9,052**	**$12,570**	**$12,183**	**$13,166**
TOTAL COMPENSATION PLUS BENEFITS	**Median**	-	**$57,463**	**$62,596**	**$75,785**	**$82,540**	**$88,543**
	Average	-	**$59,169**	**$64,391**	**$76,548**	**$84,251**	**$92,213**
Number of Respondents		8	36	27	37	39	85

- Not enough response to provide meaningful data.

* For detailed description and definitions of Data Distribution (Median and Average), see Chapter 1's "Explanation of Data Distribution."

Table 6-3: Annual Compensation of Full-Time Executive or Administrative Pastors by Church Setting

	Data Distribution*	CHURCH SETTING			
		Metro-politan city	Suburb of large city	Small town or rural city	Farming area
CHARACTERISTICS					
Average weekend worship attendance		1,657	1,236	798	-
Average church income		$2,396,533	$2,042,963	$1,227,813	-
Average # of years employed		7	7	6	-
Average # of paid vacation days		20	20	18	-
% College graduate or higher		91%	95%	78%	-
% Who receive auto reimbursement/allowance		43%	51%	62%	-
% Ordained		98%	89%	86%	-
% Supervise one or more people		100%	97%	94%	-
Average % salary increase (for those who had an increase) this year		4.0%	4.0%	4.5%	-
COMPENSATION					
Base Salary	Median	$45,000	$46,780	$42,500	-
	Average	$51,400	$49,466	$42,325	-
Housing	Median	$25,000	$28,811	$26,000	-
	Average	$27,791	$28,528	$26,153	-
Parsonage	Median	-	-	-	-
	Average	-	-	-	-
Total Compensation	**Median**	**$69,125**	**$68,715**	**$60,435**	**-**
	Average	**$71,941**	**$70,076**	**$61,298**	**-**
BENEFITS					
Health Insurance	Median	$10,000	$8,894	$7,200	-
	Average	$9,486	$8,649	$8,514	-
Life Insurance	Median	$470	$268	$275	-
	Average	$1,259	$530	$543	-
Disability Insurance	Median	$494	$450	$585	-
	Average	$544	$806	$648	-
Retirement	Median	$4,900	$3,950	$3,900	-
	Average	$6,003	$4,539	$4,581	-
Continuing Education	Median	$2,250	$1,300	$1,100	-
	Average	$2,267	$1,839	$1,456	-
Total Benefits	**Median**	**$13,343**	**$12,296**	**$9,500**	**-**
	Average	**$12,693**	**$11,596**	**$11,311**	**-**
TOTAL COMPENSATION PLUS BENEFITS	**Median**	**$84,138**	**$80,173**	**$69,000**	**-**
	Average	**$82,979**	**$80,873**	**$70,780**	**-**
Number of Respondents		46	116	68	2

- Not enough response to provide meaningful data.

* For detailed description and definitions of Data Distribution (Median and Average), see Chapter 1's "Explanation of Data Distribution."

Table 6-4: Annual Compensation of Full-Time Executive or Administrative Pastors by Region

CHARACTERISTICS	Data Distribution*	New England	Middle Atlantic	South Atlantic	E-N Central	E-S Central	W-N Central	W-S Central	Mountain	Pacific
						REGION				
Average weekend worship attendance	-		713	834	984	1,058	853	865	846	1,505
Average church income	-		$1,394,442	$1,441,551	$1,660,346	$2,019,347	$1,322,945	$1,751,803	$1,245,092	$1,957,651
Average # of years employed	-		6	8	6	9	7	10	9	9
Average # of paid vacation days	-		18	17	17	16	18	18	18	17
% College graduate or higher	-		52%	63%	72%	67%	59%	63%	67%	46%
% Who receive auto reimbursement/allowance	-		24%	43%	40%	47%	38%	45%	40%	33%
% Ordained	-		28%	24%	14%	27%	24%	24%	19%	18%
% Supervise one or more people	-		92%	93%	98%	93%	95%	84%	100%	82%
Average % salary increase (for those who had an increase) this year	-		6.3%	3.3%	4.7%	3.7%	4.2%	5.5%	5.5%	4.2%
COMPENSATION										
Base Salary	Median	-	$37,250	$41,490	$43,285	$52,522	$46,157	$48,200	$45,000	$46,182
	Average	-	$42,748	$41,747	$47,128	$50,254	$51,132	$45,786	$46,271	$50,489
Housing	Median	-	-	$28,000	-	-	-	-	-	-
	Average	-	-	$26,960	-	-	-	-	-	-
Parsonage	Median	-	-	-	-	-	-	-	-	-
	Average	-	-	-	-	-	-	-	-	-
Total Compensation	**Median**	-	**$40,000**	**$45,000**	**$43,500**	**$60,312**	**$48,000**	**$52,298**	**$48,800**	**$48,988**
	Average	-	**$45,388**	**$45,661**	**$47,686**	**$55,342**	**$53,923**	**$51,849**	**$51,138**	**$52,772**
BENEFITS										
Health Insurance	Median	-	$9,600	$6,800	$6,582	$4,800	$5,202	$5,760	$5,784	$6,000
	Average	-	$8,913	$8,221	$7,636	$6,461	$7,086	$6,941	$6,859	$6,648
Life Insurance	Median	-	-	$240	$163	-	-	$120	$130	-
	Average	-	-	$505	$281	-	-	$288	$314	-
Disability Insurance	Median	-	-	$391	$456	-	-	$284	$401	-
	Average	-	-	$402	$570	-	-	$332	$487	-
Retirement	Median	-	$2,400	$3,088	$2,588	$3,100	$2,800	$2,525	$3,539	$3,454
	Average	-	$3,472	$3,872	$3,166	$3,665	$3,369	$3,684	$3,772	$4,458
Continuing Education	Median	-	$900	$1,250	$600	-	-	$800	-	-
	Average	-	$1,256	$1,357	$944	-	-	$1,063	-	-
Total Benefits	**Median**	-	**$9,665**	**$8,209**	**$7,303**	**$9,203**	**$9,138**	**$7,402**	**$8,307**	**$7,695**
	Average	-	**$9,788**	**$9,958**	**$7,221**	**$9,863**	**$9,266**	**$7,570**	**$8,930**	**$8,934**
TOTAL COMPENSATION PLUS BENEFITS	**Median**	-	**$47,100**	**$53,468**	**$45,825**	**$67,952**	**$60,282**	**$57,351**	**$54,172**	**$55,812**
	Average	-	**$53,219**	**$53,370**	**$53,396**	**$63,232**	**$61,504**	**$58,025**	**$58,367**	**$60,082**
Number of Respondents		1	25	62	43	15	22	38	21	44

- Not enough response to provide meaningful data.

* For detailed description and definitions of Data Distribution (Median and Average), see Chapter 1's "Explanation of Data Distribution."

Table 6-5: Annual Compensation of Full-Time Executive or Administrative Pastors by Education

	Data Distribution*	EDUCATION			
		Less than Bachelor	Bachelor	Master	Doctorate
CHARACTERISTICS					
Average weekend worship attendance		790	1,054	1,175	1,931
Average church income		$1,292,344	$1,824,909	$1,862,326	$2,501,867
Average # of years employed		7	6	7	7
Average # of paid vacation days		16	19	20	21
% College graduate or higher		0%	100%	100%	100%
% Who receive auto reimbursement/allowance		54%	45%	55%	58%
% Ordained		92%	85%	92%	96%
% Supervise one or more people		96%	97%	97%	100%
Average % salary increase (for those who had an increase) this year		5.0%	4.2%	4.1%	3.5%
COMPENSATION					
Base Salary	Median	$36,400	$44,000	$46,365	$47,500
	Average	$41,369	$45,068	$48,658	$54,769
Housing	Median	$22,000	$28,926	$26,200	$29,300
	Average	$22,112	$31,101	$27,169	$29,612
Parsonage	Median	-	-	-	-
	Average	-	-	-	-
Total Compensation	**Median**	**$52,000**	**$65,750**	**$67,000**	**$77,835**
	Average	**$57,005**	**$65,379**	**$68,418**	**$80,779**
BENEFITS					
Health Insurance	Median	$8,755	$9,116	$9,585	$6,000
	Average	$9,970	$8,495	$8,956	$7,160
Life Insurance	Median	-	$300	$390	$365
	Average	-	$790	$507	$1,105
Disability Insurance	Median	-	$528	$500	$450
	Average	-	$585	$702	$1,129
Retirement	Median	$2,340	$3,300	$4,584	$6,774
	Average	$2,793	$3,643	$4,958	$7,303
Continuing Education	Median	-	$1,300	$2,000	$1,100
	Average	-	$2,391	$2,007	$1,320
Total Benefits	**Median**	**$9,400**	**$10,033**	**$13,274**	**$12,394**
	Average	**$11,293**	**$10,425**	**$12,039**	**$13,071**
TOTAL COMPENSATION PLUS BENEFITS	**Median**	**$61,680**	**$74,977**	**$79,168**	**$89,522**
	Average	**$66,039**	**$73,910**	**$79,531**	**$93,850**
Number of Respondents		25	66	117	24

- Not enough response to provide meaningful data.

* For detailed description and definitions of Data Distribution (Median and Average), see Chapter 1's "Explanation of Data Distribution."

Table 6-6: Annual Compensation of Full-Time Executive or Administrative Pastors by Years Employed

CHARACTERISTICS	Data Distribution*	Less than 6 years	6-10 years	11-15 years	Over 15 years
		YEARS EMPLOYED			
Average weekend worship attendance		945	1,282	1,386	2,059
Average church income		$1,688,585	$1,684,737	$2,488,966	$2,794,394
Average # of years employed		3	8	13	21
Average # of paid vacation days		18	19	21	24
% College graduate or higher		88%	95%	90%	80%
% Who receive auto reimbursement/allowance		44%	54%	62%	75%
% Ordained		90%	89%	100%	95%
% Supervise one or more people		98%	95%	95%	100%
Average % salary increase (for those who had an increase) this year		5.0%	3.4%	2.7%	4.5%
COMPENSATION					
Base Salary	Median	$45,348	$42,000	$52,500	$45,000
	Average	$47,668	$43,612	$52,551	$54,881
Housing	Median	$26,000	$28,026	$30,000	$22,000
	Average	$27,724	$29,055	$30,464	$23,781
Parsonage	Median	-	-	-	-
	Average	-	-	-	-
Total Compensation	**Median**	**$65,616**	**$66,765**	**$79,000**	**$62,900**
	Average	**$65,154**	**$67,102**	**$80,187**	**$72,128**
BENEFITS					
Health Insurance	Median	$8,900	$9,530	$8,510	$7,350
	Average	$8,735	$8,830	$8,020	$8,599
Life Insurance	Median	$400	$309	$200	-
	Average	$606	$950	$285	-
Disability Insurance	Median	$500	$345	$500	-
	Average	$613	$587	$1,075	-
Retirement	Median	$3,850	$5,024	$3,943	$3,426
	Average	$4,429	$5,674	$4,285	$5,194
Continuing Education	Median	$1,300	$1,200	-	-
	Average	$1,682	$1,805	-	-
Total Benefits	**Median**	**$10,855**	**$12,893**	**$10,172**	**$14,530**
	Average	**$11,184**	**$12,376**	**$10,733**	**$13,151**
TOTAL COMPENSATION PLUS BENEFITS	**Median**	**$75,360**	**$79,590**	**$87,458**	**$73,125**
	Average	**$75,012**	**$78,372**	**$90,410**	**$82,648**
Number of Respondents		118	67	21	20

- Not enough response to provide meaningful data.

* For detailed description and definitions of Data Distribution (Median and Average), see Chapter 1's "Explanation of Data Distribution."

Table 6-7: Annual Compensation of Full-Time Executive or Administrative Pastors by Denomination

	Data Distribution*	DENOMINATION					
		Assemblies of God	Baptist	Independent/ Nondenom.	Lutheran	Methodist	Presby-terian
CHARACTERISTICS							
Average weekend worship attendance		1,032	1,005	1,225	-	754	-
Average church income		$1,564,128	$1,752,414	$1,954,079	-	$1,446,231	-
Average # of years employed		7	6	7	-	3	-
Average # of paid vacation days		16	19	20	-	18	-
% College graduate or higher		71%	93%	85%	-	92%	-
% Who receive auto reimbursement/allowance		69%	55%	37%	-	54%	-
% Ordained		100%	93%	89%	-	85%	-
% Supervise one or more people		100%	98%	97%	-	100%	-
Average % salary increase (for those who had an increase) this year		5.3%	4.3%	4.9%	-	3.8%	-
COMPENSATION							
Base Salary	Median	$32,000	$44,600	$44,500	-	$50,000	-
	Average	$31,979	$47,104	$47,005	-	$48,798	-
Housing	Median	$30,000	$25,000	$29,000	-	-	-
	Average	$29,417	$28,822	$28,206	-	-	-
Parsonage	Median	-	-	-	-	-	-
	Average	-	-	-	-	-	-
Total Compensation	**Median**	**$55,394**	**$68,125**	**$66,805**	**-**	**$57,240**	**-**
	Average	**$57,193**	**$70,077**	**$67,550**	**-**	**$56,487**	**-**
BENEFITS							
Health Insurance	Median	$12,228	$7,888	$9,350	-	-	-
	Average	$11,512	$7,893	$8,910	-	-	-
Life Insurance	Median	-	$500	$356	-	-	-
	Average	-	$867	$698	-	-	-
Disability Insurance	Median	-	$550	$535	-	-	-
	Average	-	$637	$851	-	-	-
Retirement	Median	-	$6,000	$2,430	-	$5,000	-
	Average	-	$5,162	$3,350	-	$4,901	-
Continuing Education	Median	-	$1,200	$2,500	-	$875	-
	Average	-	$1,600	$2,863	-	$1,088	-
Total Benefits	**Median**	**$16,000**	**$11,580**	**$10,833**	**-**	**$7,200**	**-**
	Average	**$13,442**	**$11,469**	**$11,055**	**-**	**$7,743**	**-**
TOTAL COMPENSATION PLUS BENEFITS	**Median**	**$67,450**	**$77,230**	**$78,728**	**-**	**$69,544**	**-**
	Average	**$68,715**	**$80,621**	**$77,305**	**-**	**$63,634**	**-**
Number of Respondents		14	62	68	4	13	-

- Not enough response to provide meaningful data.

* For detailed description and definitions of Data Distribution (Median and Average), see Chapter 1's "Explanation of Data Distribution."

Table 6-8: Annual Compensation of Full-Time Executive or Administrative Pastors by Gender

	Data Distribution*	GENDER	
		Male	Female
CHARACTERISTICS			
Average weekend worship attendance		1,220	857
Average church income		$1,895,384	$1,520,481
Average # of years employed		7	7
Average # of paid vacation days		19	19
% College graduate or higher		90%	81%
% Who receive auto reimbursement/allowance		55%	38%
% Ordained		93%	74%
% Supervise one or more people		97%	96%
Average % salary increase (for those who had an increase) this year		4.1%	4.3%
COMPENSATION			
Base Salary	Median	$45,000	$45,000
	Average	$48,027	$43,731
Housing	Median	$27,852	$19,200
	Average	$28,661	$18,883
Parsonage	Median	-	-
	Average	-	-
Total Compensation	**Median**	**$68,000**	**$54,000**
	Average	**$69,794**	**$51,281**
BENEFITS			
Health Insurance	Median	$9,231	$5,880
	Average	$8,901	$7,383
Life Insurance	Median	$378	$300
	Average	$683	$729
Disability Insurance	Median	$494	-
	Average	$652	-
Retirement	Median	$4,000	$3,900
	Average	$4,820	$4,711
Continuing Education	Median	$1,300	$2,000
	Average	$1,846	$2,117
Total Benefits	**Median**	**$12,269**	**$7,860**
	Average	**$11,913**	**$10,029**
TOTAL COMPENSATION PLUS BENEFITS	**Median**	**$79,590**	**$60,160**
	Average	**$80,371**	**$60,198**
Number of Respondents		205	2

- Not enough response to provide meaningful data.

* For detailed description and definitions of Data Distribution (Median and Average), see Chapter 1's "Explanation of Data Distribution."

7

ASSOCIATE PASTORS

Employment Profile

The roles and duties of the Associate Pastor are quite diverse depending upon the church. For this survey, an Associate or Assistant Pastor is any paid pastor who assists the Senior Pastor in general or specific ministries other than those specifically listed in the survey. (This excludes Executive, Education, Music, Youth, and Children's pastors, who were surveyed and reported separately.)

Associate Pastor may include positions or responsibilities such as Assimilation Pastor, Congregational Care Pastor, Counseling Pastor, Disabilities Ministry Pastor, Ethnic Ministries Pastor, Evangelism Pastor, Family Life Pastor, Lay Pastor, Membership Pastor, Missions Pastor, Outreach Pastor, Prayer Pastor, Teaching/Preaching Pastor, Visitation Pastor, etc.

About nine in ten full-time Associate Pastors are ordained males who are employed by the church, rather than self-employed. The majority have a graduate degree.

Almost one-quarter of the Associate Pastors in this survey serve on a part-time basis. More than seven in ten part-time Associate Pastors are ordained males.

The statistical profile of Associate Pastors is as follows:

	Full-Time	Part-Time
Number of respondents	697	201
Ordained	91%	79%
Average years employed	6	6
Male	87%	72%
Female	13%	28%
Self-employed (receives 1099)	7%	17%
Church employee (receives W-2)	93%	83%
High school diploma	6%	14%
Associate Degree	4%	7%
Bachelor's Degree	34%	35%
Master's Degree	50%	38%
Doctoral Degree	6%	6%

Total Compensation plus Benefits Package Analysis

The analyses on the next page are based on the data in the tables that you will find in the remainder of the chapter. The tables show compensation plus benefits data for full-time and part-time Associate Pastors and are presented according to church income, church attendance, church setting, region, education, years employed, denomination, and gender. In this way, Associate Pastors' compensation plus benefits can be analyzed and compared from a variety of useful perspectives.

The total compensation plus benefits amount includes the base salary, housing allowance and/or parsonage amount, health, life, and disability insurance payments, retirement contribution, and educational funds.

Full-time Associate Pastors receive approximately the same benefits as Senior or Solo Pastors, except Senior and Solo Pastors are more likely to live in a church-owned parsonage. On average, Associate Pastors tend to receive a compensation of about 75% of that of Senior Pastors, but about 10% higher than that of Solo Pastors. Two-thirds of full-time Associate Pastors receive health insurance and retirement benefits.

Compensation Plus Benefits	Full-Time	Part-Time
Base Salary	99%	83%
Housing	75%	38%
Parsonage	5%	2%
Health Insurance	65%	13%
Life Insurance	24%	3%
Disability Insurance	23%	3%
Retirement	64%	13%
Continuing Education	35%	18%
Received Salary Increase	57%	30%
Received Paid Vacation	96%	47%
Received Auto Reimbursement/ Allowance	61%	48%

KEY POINTS

✳ **Almost four in ten full-time Associate Pastors serve in churches with income higher than $1,000,000.**

✳ **In general, as church income, the minister's education and years employed increase, average compensation and benefits for full-time Associate Pastors also increase.**

✳ **Full-time Associate Pastors serving churches in a suburban setting or a metropolitan city have higher compensation and benefits packages compared to those serving churches in a small town/rural city or a farming area.**

✳ **About six in ten part-time Associate Pastors serve in churches with income of $500,000 or less.**

Compensation & Benefits: National Averages for Full-Time Associate Pastors*

2000	$51,973
2001	$54,729
2002	$58,072
2003	$59,742
2004	$61,263
2005	$64,034
2006	$66,310
2007	$64,842
2008	$64,775
2009	$62,024*

The above trend is made available for your reference only. In addition to looking at this overall data, please refer to the detailed tables using your church's income, attendance, setting, region, and denomination as well as the person's education, gender, and years employed for guidance in compensating this position.

Table 7-1: Annual Compensation of Full-Time Associate Pastors by Church Income

CHARACTERISTICS	Data Distribution*	CHURCH INCOME				
		$250K & Under	$251-$500K	$501-$750K	$751K-$1M	Over 1 Million
Average weekend worship attendance		306	268	392	537	1,296
Average church income		$184,222	$393,712	$641,699	$883,935	$2,311,731
Average # of years employed		5	5	7	6	7
Average # of paid vacation days		14	17	20	18	19
% College graduate or higher		71%	90%	90%	93%	94%
% Who receive auto reimbursement/allowance		54%	58%	67%	67%	61%
% Ordained		89%	90%	97%	91%	91%
% Supervise one or more people		51%	55%	64%	78%	73%
Average % salary increase (for those who had an increase) this year		6.8%	5.9%	3.4%	4.3%	4.1%
COMPENSATION						
Base Salary	Highest 25%	$28,902	$39,000	$45,000	$45,000	$49,325
	Median	$21,200	$30,000	$35,000	$35,000	$38,000
	Lowest 25%	$14,000	$22,033	$26,572	$29,295	$28,000
	Average	$22,708	$30,965	$35,496	$37,122	$39,652
Housing	Highest 25%	$19,500	$21,748	$25,000	$30,000	$32,000
	Median	$14,200	$19,000	$20,000	$24,000	$25,000
	Lowest 25%	$10,000	$14,000	$15,000	$19,500	$20,000
	Average	$15,618	$19,173	$20,786	$25,036	$26,582
Parsonage	Highest 25%	-	-	$21,500	-	$18,000
	Median	-	-	$11,500	-	$12,000
	Lowest 25%	-	-	$6,300	-	$9,900
	Average	-	-	$13,406	-	$12,825
Total Compensation	**Highest 25%**	**$43,750**	**$51,300**	**$60,195**	**$66,000**	**$69,250**
	Median	**$33,769**	**$43,801**	**$51,700**	**$55,000**	**$60,000**
	Lowest 25%	**$24,300**	**$36,282**	**$42,998**	**$49,544**	**$51,325**
	Average	**$33,693**	**$44,223**	**$52,794**	**$58,554**	**$60,169**
BENEFITS						
Health Insurance	Highest 25%	$7,200	$12,000	$12,600	$13,836	$12,553
	Median	$5,100	$8,200	$10,352	$9,129	$9,000
	Lowest 25%	$3,115	$4,388	$6,250	$6,549	$4,986
	Average	$5,546	$8,644	$9,730	$10,385	$9,636
Life Insurance	Highest 25%	-	$600	$384	$1,014	$505
	Median	-	$400	$200	$500	$220
	Lowest 25%	-	$300	$118	$175	$129
	Average	-	$437	$324	$691	$471
Disability Insurance	Highest 25%	-	$552	$902	$595	$680
	Median	-	$392	$416	$360	$400
	Lowest 25%	-	$246	$200	$206	$250
	Average	-	$420	$834	$447	$506
Retirement	Highest 25%	$4,046	$4,750	$5,663	$6,000	$7,000
	Median	$1,320	$3,000	$3,276	$3,600	$4,762
	Lowest 25%	$767	$1,440	$1,784	$2,597	$2,500
	Average	$2,599	$3,381	$4,060	$4,574	$5,199
Continuing Education	Highest 25%	-	$1,650	$1,500	$2,000	$2,000
	Median	-	$1,000	$1,000	$1,500	$1,200
	Lowest 25%	-	$775	$500	$1,000	$750
	Average	-	$1,484	$1,153	$1,587	$1,686
Total Benefits	**Highest 25%**	**$9,770**	**$14,870**	**$15,600**	**$17,789**	**$18,079**
	Median	**$5,585**	**$9,145**	**$11,366**	**$11,000**	**$12,084**
	Lowest 25%	**$3,325**	**$4,892**	**$6,306**	**$5,175**	**$6,200**
	Average	**$6,511**	**$9,874**	**$11,574**	**$12,084**	**$12,492**
TOTAL COMPENSATION PLUS BENEFITS	**Highest 25%**	**$47,575**	**$61,600**	**$73,500**	**$83,000**	**$83,936**
	Median	**$38,710**	**$51,700**	**$62,800**	**$67,583**	**$71,100**
	Lowest 25%	**$27,540**	**$42,500**	**$52,900**	**$56,681**	**$60,300**
	Average	**$37,917**	**$52,241**	**$63,201**	**$69,393**	**$71,786**
Number of Respondents		74	133	119	97	257

- Not enough response to provide meaningful data.

* For detailed description and definitions of Data Distribution (Median and Average), see Chapter 1's "Explanation of Data Distribution."

Table 7-2: Annual Compensation of Full-Time Associate Pastors by Worship Attendance

	Data Distribution*	WORSHIP ATTENDANCE					
		100 or less	101-300	301-500	501-750	751-1,000	Over 1,000
CHARACTERISTICS							
Average weekend worship attendance		78	218	412	629	889	2,112
Average church income		$219,239	$414,911	$793,764	$1,150,454	$1,488,146	$3,071,415
Average # of years employed		4	5	6	6	7	8
Average # of paid vacation days		17	17	20	20	16	18
% College graduate or higher		63%	89%	90%	90%	86%	96%
% Who receive auto reimbursement/allowance		26%	58%	71%	63%	57%	60%
% Ordained		79%	91%	92%	94%	92%	90%
% Supervise one or more people		63%	55%	67%	71%	65%	80%
Average % salary increase (for those who had an increase) this year		5.3%	5.0%	4.8%	3.8%	4.3%	4.2%
COMPENSATION							
Base Salary	Median	$18,000	$28,851	$33,850	$39,800	$35,000	$39,309
	Average	$25,905	$30,054	$34,598	$39,876	$35,835	$39,805
Housing	Median	$14,000	$19,000	$21,000	$23,961	$21,667	$26,500
	Average	$15,257	$18,822	$22,899	$24,338	$22,183	$28,277
Parsonage	Median	-	$11,500	$6,600	-	-	-
	Average	-	$13,164	$7,764	-	-	-
Total Compensation	**Median**	**$32,000**	**$44,000**	**$52,100**	**$57,500**	**$54,172**	**$60,033**
	Average	**$33,867**	**$43,513**	**$53,687**	**$58,376**	**$53,422**	**$61,992**
BENEFITS							
Health Insurance	Median	-	$7,500	$10,745	$8,425	$7,100	$9,244
	Average	-	$7,841	$10,740	$9,697	$8,050	$9,579
Life Insurance	Median	-	$250	$430	$475	$118	$220
	Average	-	$329	$545	$735	$521	$443
Disability	Median	-	$400	$400	$459	$374	$337
	Average	-	$591	$644	$538	$442	$497
Retirement	Median	-	$3,000	$4,653	$4,900	$3,200	$3,694
	Average	-	$3,626	$5,147	$4,979	$3,796	$4,345
Continuing Education	Median	-	$1,000	$1,000	$1,000	$1,060	$1,500
	Average	-	$1,406	$1,278	$1,880	$1,386	$1,678
Total Benefits	**Median**	-	**$9,396**	**$12,000**	**$9,716**	**$7,107**	**$13,257**
	Average	-	**$9,543**	**$12,335**	**$12,115**	**$9,518**	**$12,626**
TOTAL COMPENSATION PLUS BENEFITS	**Median**	**$32,000**	**$50,850**	**$65,436**	**$67,025**	**$60,419**	**$72,680**
	Average	**$36,436**	**$50,929**	**$65,068**	**$68,805**	**$61,618**	**$73,804**
Number of Respondents		19	193	168	115	72	124

- Not enough response to provide meaningful data.

* For detailed description and definitions of Data Distribution (Median and Average), see Chapter 1's "Explanation of Data Distribution."

Table 7-3: Annual Compensation of Full-Time Associate Pastors by Church Setting

	Data Distribution*	CHURCH SETTING			
		Metro-politan city	Suburb of large city	Small town or rural city	Farming area
CHARACTERISTICS					
Average weekend worship attendance		764	842	624	392
Average church income		$1,318,547	$1,496,521	$838,627	$528,709
Average # of years employed		6	6	7	5
Average # of paid vacation days		18	19	18	17
% College graduate or higher		91%	93%	85%	82%
% Who receive auto reimbursement/allowance		57%	59%	65%	64%
% Ordained		92%	90%	93%	82%
% Supervise one or more people		62%	71%	61%	82%
Average % salary increase (for those who had an increase) this year		5.0%	4.7%	4.2%	3.5%
COMPENSATION					
Base Salary	Median	$39,900	$35,000	$30,900	$30,000
	Average	$37,651	$36,512	$32,196	$25,689
Housing	Median	$21,263	$24,000	$19,000	$14,400
	Average	$24,006	$25,151	$19,600	$14,044
Parsonage	Median	$9,675	$12,000	$9,600	-
	Average	$9,964	$14,945	$10,718	-
Total Compensation	**Median**	**$54,000**	**$55,030**	**$45,060**	**$38,800**
	Average	**$55,370**	**$55,976**	**$47,125**	**$37,617**
BENEFITS					
Health Insurance	Median	$9,500	$9,400	$7,200	-
	Average	$9,180	$10,202	$8,015	-
Life Insurance	Median	$400	$220	$220	-
	Average	$694	$399	$531	-
Disability Insurance	Median	$276	$500	$309	-
	Average	$375	$599	$528	-
Retirement	Median	$3,705	$4,000	$3,500	-
	Average	$4,530	$4,727	$3,981	-
Continuing Education	Median	$1,160	$1,200	$1,000	-
	Average	$1,585	$1,525	$1,436	-
Total Benefits	**Median**	**$12,529**	**$11,400**	**$9,029**	**-**
	Average	**$11,844**	**$12,231**	**$9,965**	**-**
TOTAL COMPENSATION PLUS BENEFITS	**Median**	**$65,672**	**$66,240**	**$54,499**	**$42,000**
	Average	**$66,056**	**$66,223**	**$55,632**	**$43,300**
Number of Respondents		133	302	246	11

- Not enough response to provide meaningful data.

* For detailed description and definitions of Data Distribution (Median and Average), see Chapter 1's "Explanation of Data Distribution."

Table 7-4: Annual Compensation of Full-Time Associate Pastors by Region

CHARACTERISTICS	Data Distribution*	New England	Middle Atlantic	South Atlantic	E-N Central	E-S Central	W-N Central	W-S Central	Mountain	Pacific
Average weekend worship attendance		480	633	719	715	710	753	907	873	738
Average church income		$983,357	$939,956	$1,148,074	$1,137,635	$1,118,558	$1,216,809	$1,657,430	$1,510,783	$1,223,766
Average # of years employed		6	6	7	6	6	6	6	6	7
Average # of paid vacation days		18	20	18	19	15	19	16	18	19
% College graduate or higher		100%	92%	90%	90%	91%	93%	80%	84%	92%
% Who receive auto reimbursement/allowance		50%	59%	70%	59%	64%	63%	66%	39%	59%
% Ordained		93%	97%	91%	88%	98%	90%	87%	93%	92%
% Supervise one or more people		71%	75%	59%	66%	61%	66%	67%	72%	72%
Average % salary increase (for those who had an increase) this year		5.0%	4.4%	4.6%	4.6%	4.4%	4.8%	5.5%	3.8%	4.1%
COMPENSATION										
Base Salary	Median	$42,150	$31,850	$35,000	$34,000	$33,000	$35,000	$32,500	$34,425	$32,000
	Average	$42,096	$32,631	$36,094	$34,250	$33,997	$36,456	$34,619	$36,567	$33,742
Housing	Median	$22,450	$20,500	$20,000	$20,000	$20,000	$21,000	$20,000	$24,800	$28,800
	Average	$25,601	$22,235	$22,124	$20,957	$21,972	$21,346	$20,281	$25,369	$27,703
Parsonage	Median	-	-	-	-	-	$6,000	-	-	-
	Average	-	-	-	-	-	$7,111	-	-	-
Total Compensation	Median	**$58,000**	**$51,250**	**$51,875**	**$49,000**	**$52,000**	**$53,537**	**$51,657**	**$52,400**	**$54,490**
	Average	**$57,376**	**$50,360**	**$52,463**	**$49,825**	**$53,861**	**$52,761**	**$51,058**	**$53,112**	**$55,745**
BENEFITS										
Health Insurance	Median	$12,000	$10,700	$8,714	$10,171	$6,594	$6,720	$7,764	$11,208	$8,100
	Average	$10,497	$10,382	$9,431	$9,832	$8,051	$7,620	$8,061	$10,390	$8,870
Life Insurance	Median	-	$600	$364	$250	$374	$159	$217	$180	$295
	Average	-	$574	$579	$305	$750	$304	$492	$231	$714
Disability Insurance	Median	-	$300	$500	$314	-	$500	$240	$579	$280
	Average	-	$366	$624	$620	-	$610	$291	$679	$335
Retirement	Median	-	$2,788	$4,977	$3,120	$3,600	$4,427	$4,000	$2,825	$4,000
	Average	-	$3,846	$5,243	$3,744	$4,405	$4,846	$4,347	$3,513	$4,409
Continuing Education	Median	-	$1,500	$1,000	$1,200	-	$1,163	$1,150	$1,000	$1,000
	Average	-	$2,204	$1,377	$1,529	-	$1,403	$1,775	$1,409	$1,130
Total Benefits	Median	**$13,000**	**$13,050**	**$10,320**	**$10,845**	**$7,623**	**$9,800**	**$9,894**	**$12,804**	**$8,800**
	Average	**$12,575**	**$12,435**	**$11,950**	**$10,809**	**$9,838**	**$10,579**	**$11,199**	**$12,130**	**$10,686**
TOTAL COMPENSATION PLUS BENEFITS	Median	**$68,352**	**$65,000**	**$63,366**	**$59,750**	**$60,198**	**$65,475**	**$62,800**	**$63,350**	**$62,809**
	Average	**$67,256**	**$61,979**	**$63,034**	**$59,562**	**$61,732**	**$62,070**	**$59,768**	**$62,341**	**$64,213**
Number of Respondents		14	61	156	131	45	75	63	46	106

- Not enough response to provide meaningful data.

* For detailed description and definitions of Data Distribution (Median and Average), see Chapter 1's "Explanation of Data Distribution."

Table 7-5: Annual Compensation of Full-Time Associate Pastors by Education

	Data Distribution*	EDUCATION			
		Less than Bachelor	Bachelor	Master	Doctorate
CHARACTERISTICS					
Average weekend worship attendance		495	910	678	736
Average church income		$801,965	$1,318,372	$1,187,651	$1,456,455
Average # of years employed		7	7	6	7
Average # of paid vacation days		16	16	19	22
% College graduate or higher		0%	100%	100%	100%
% Who receive auto reimbursement/allowance		50%	52%	68%	68%
% Ordained		84%	87%	95%	97%
% Supervise one or more people		73%	58%	69%	83%
Average % salary increase (for those who had an increase) this year		7.3%	4.1%	4.6%	4.4%
COMPENSATION					
Base Salary	Median	$24,800	$32,080	$34,705	$39,000
	Average	$27,795	$34,472	$36,256	$38,113
Housing	Median	$16,750	$20,000	$21,500	$28,002
	Average	$18,302	$22,348	$23,305	$27,037
Parsonage	Median	-	$9,675	$12,000	-
	Average	-	$9,506	$13,482	-
Total Compensation	**Median**	**$40,000**	**$50,000**	**$54,000**	**$65,000**
	Average	**$39,908**	**$50,058**	**$55,403**	**$64,271**
BENEFITS					
Health Insurance	Median	$6,075	$8,625	$9,724	$9,905
	Average	$6,314	$8,685	$10,106	$9,197
Life Insurance	Median	$113	$200	$320	$335
	Average	$260	$443	$543	$544
Disability Insurance	Median	$321	$318	$432	$377
	Average	$380	$551	$562	$458
Retirement	Median	$2,105	$2,950	$4,300	$5,000
	Average	$2,273	$3,525	$4,971	$5,553
Continuing Education	Median	$1,000	$1,200	$1,000	$1,300
	Average	$1,456	$1,404	$1,539	$1,441
Total Benefits	**Median**	**$6,386**	**$10,060**	**$12,260**	**$13,415**
	Average	**$7,104**	**$9,881**	**$12,689**	**$13,331**
TOTAL COMPENSATION PLUS BENEFITS	**Median**	**$43,025**	**$57,400**	**$65,800**	**$78,000**
	Average	**$44,982**	**$58,216**	**$66,827**	**$75,976**
Number of Respondents		70	235	341	41

- Not enough response to provide meaningful data.

* For detailed description and definitions of Data Distribution (Median and Average), see Chapter 1's "Explanation of Data Distribution."

Table 7-6: Annual Compensation of Full-Time Associate Pastors by Years Employed

	Data Distribution*	Less than 6 years	6-10 years	11-15 years	Over 15 years
CHARACTERISTICS					
Average weekend worship attendance		673	811	929	981
Average church income		$1,144,973	$1,257,153	$1,284,454	$1,644,029
Average # of years employed		3	8	13	21
Average # of paid vacation days		17	19	21	24
% College graduate or higher		90%	89%	91%	89%
% Who receive auto reimbursement/allowance		59%	61%	66%	66%
% Ordained		89%	96%	98%	93%
% Supervise one or more people		62%	75%	82%	72%
Average % salary increase (for those who had an increase) this year		4.9%	4.0%	5.2%	3.1%
COMPENSATION					
Base Salary	Median	$31,958	$34,736	$39,809	$40,000
	Average	$32,980	$36,403	$40,084	$41,013
Housing	Median	$20,000	$20,400	$22,000	$25,500
	Average	$22,059	$24,162	$22,711	$25,951
Parsonage	Median	$12,000	$8,450	-	-
	Average	$13,314	$8,288	-	-
Total Compensation	**Median**	**$48,900**	**$55,000**	**$56,996**	**$61,500**
	Average	**$49,390**	**$54,845**	**$58,207**	**$62,769**
BENEFITS					
Health Insurance	Median	$8,450	$9,600	$10,747	$7,350
	Average	$8,885	$9,326	$10,300	$9,224
Life Insurance	Median	$240	$200	$205	$338
	Average	$420	$519	$307	$613
Disability Insurance	Median	$416	$278	$400	$500
	Average	$554	$452	$487	$480
Retirement	Median	$3,600	$3,637	$4,000	$3,550
	Average	$4,419	$3,967	$4,538	$5,234
Continuing Education	Median	$1,200	$1,000	$1,350	$1,160
	Average	$1,648	$1,409	$1,589	$1,112
Total Benefits	**Median**	**$9,894**	**$10,800**	**$13,200**	**$10,110**
	Average	**$10,778**	**$11,448**	**$13,462**	**$11,973**
TOTAL COMPENSATION PLUS BENEFITS	**Median**	**$57,450**	**$66,447**	**$69,969**	**$73,000**
	Average	**$58,191**	**$65,148**	**$70,467**	**$74,153**
Number of Respondents		398	130	56	61

- Not enough response to provide meaningful data.

* For detailed description and definitions of Data Distribution (Median and Average), see Chapter 1's "Explanation of Data Distribution."

Table 7-7: Annual Compensation of Full-Time Associate Pastors by Denomination

	Data Distribution*	Assemblies of God	Baptist	Independent/ Nondenom.	Lutheran	Methodist	Presby-terian
CHARACTERISTICS							
Average weekend worship attendance		804	795	939	608	592	677
Average church income		$1,363,745	$1,198,902	$1,355,255	$1,212,597	$1,227,870	$1,441,394
Average # of years employed		5	7	8	5	4	4
Average # of paid vacation days		17	17	18	22	19	23
% College graduate or higher		64%	92%	85%	100%	98%	96%
% Who receive auto reimbursement/allowance		42%	67%	49%	87%	77%	64%
% Ordained		100%	92%	90%	93%	94%	87%
% Supervise one or more people		62%	63%	75%	77%	65%	65%
Average % salary increase (for those who had an increase) this year		7.0%	5.2%	5.3%	3.7%	3.4%	3.9%
COMPENSATION							
Base Salary	Median	$22,518	$32,000	$34,850	$35,000	$38,598	$36,955
	Average	$26,106	$33,948	$36,446	$35,998	$37,420	$38,813
Housing	Median	$20,000	$20,000	$22,500	$25,000	$15,000	$26,000
	Average	$20,584	$22,109	$24,940	$24,395	$14,552	$26,172
Parsonage	Median	-	-	-	-	$12,000	-
	Average	-	-	-	-	$12,133	-
Total Compensation	**Median**	**$41,889**	**$50,230**	**$53,849**	**$52,850**	**$50,000**	**$56,814**
	Average	**$42,171**	**$50,927**	**$54,075**	**$54,700**	**$49,852**	**$59,312**
BENEFITS							
Health Insurance	Median	$10,900	$8,000	$10,500	$6,000	$9,818	$11,250
	Average	$9,268	$8,802	$9,868	$7,954	$9,898	$10,709
Life Insurance	Median	-	$328	$187	-	-	$320
	Average	-	$488	$491	-	-	$429
Disability Insurance	Median	-	$377	$416	$1,050	-	$431
	Average	-	$462	$513	$1,007	-	$553
Retirement	Median	$2,300	$3,600	$2,600	$4,725	$6,500	$6,000
	Average	$2,566	$4,001	$3,077	$4,473	$6,465	$7,165
Continuing Education	Median	-	$1,160	$1,250	$850	$1,020	$1,200
	Average	-	$1,574	$2,080	$1,102	$1,695	$1,424
Total Benefits	**Median**	**$9,894**	**$9,129**	**$11,168**	**$11,525**	**$13,000**	**$15,495**
	Average	**$8,905**	**$10,936**	**$11,222**	**$12,084**	**$13,044**	**$15,282**
TOTAL COMPENSATION PLUS BENEFITS	**Median**	**$50,420**	**$61,558**	**$64,000**	**$68,196**	**$64,062**	**$70,503**
	Average	**$49,363**	**$60,635**	**$62,946**	**$66,381**	**$62,353**	**$72,648**
Number of Respondents		26	196	148	30	48	55

- Not enough response to provide meaningful data.

* For detailed description and definitions of Data Distribution (Median and Average), see Chapter 1's "Explanation of Data Distribution."

Table 7-8: Annual Compensation of Full-Time Associate Pastors by Gender

	Data Distribution*	GENDER	
		Male	Female
CHARACTERISTICS			
Average weekend worship attendance		735	769
Average church income		$1,173,079	$1,461,517
Average # of years employed		6	6
Average # of paid vacation days		18	20
% College graduate or higher		90%	87%
% Who receive auto reimbursement/allowance		62%	56%
% Ordained		93%	79%
% Supervise one or more people		65%	77%
Average % salary increase (for those who had an increase) this year		4.6%	4.1%
COMPENSATION			
Base Salary	Median	$33,768	$34,000
	Average	$35,166	$33,876
Housing	Median	$20,508	$20,788
	Average	$22,823	$22,012
Parsonage	Median	$12,000	-
	Average	$11,866	-
Total Compensation	**Median**	**$52,126**	**$45,237**
	Average	**$53,186**	**$46,813**
BENEFITS			
Health Insurance	Median	$9,000	$7,250
	Average	$9,395	$7,338
Life Insurance	Median	$245	$263
	Average	$479	$520
Disability Insurance	Median	$400	$418
	Average	$543	$495
Retirement	Median	$3,600	$5,395
	Average	$4,201	$5,571
Continuing Education	Median	$1,000	$1,125
	Average	$1,494	$1,499
Total Benefits	**Median**	**$10,414**	**$9,450**
	Average	**$11,397**	**$10,303**
TOTAL COMPENSATION PLUS BENEFITS	**Median**	**$62,660**	**$58,369**
	Average	**$62,884**	**$55,644**
Number of Respondents		604	91

- Not enough response to provide meaningful data.

* For detailed description and definitions of Data Distribution (Median and Average), see Chapter 1's "Explanation of Data Distribution."

Table 7-9: Annual Compensation of Part-Time Associate Pastors by Church Income

	Data Distribution*	CHURCH INCOME				
		$250K & Under	$251-$500K	$501-$750K	$751K-$1M	Over 1 Million
CHARACTERISTICS						
Average weekend worship attendance		141	250	437	566	939
Average church income		$172,010	$394,172	$647,083	$932,325	$1,717,822
Average # of years employed		4	6	7	8	6
Average # of paid vacation days		17	15	16	16	17
% College graduate or higher		73%	78%	84%	82%	90%
% Who receive auto reimbursement/allowance		35%	54%	65%	41%	61%
% Ordained		79%	80%	90%	88%	68%
% Supervise one or more people		45%	26%	26%	24%	53%
Average % salary increase (for those who had an increase) this year		16.1%	13.2%	5.2%	-	-
HOURLY RATE						
Base Rate	Average	$15	$16	$17	$19	$19
COMPENSATION						
Base Salary	Median	$10,400	$12,000	$15,000	$15,500	$15,298
	Average	$11,975	$14,033	$15,775	$17,458	$17,036
Housing	Median	$7,500	$12,500	$14,747	-	$10,020
	Average	$8,806	$11,783	$15,464	-	$12,986
Parsonage	Median	-	-	-	-	-
	Average	-	-	-	-	-
Total Compensation	**Median**	**$10,350**	**$14,600**	**$23,584**	**$18,998**	**$18,146**
	Average	**$12,786**	**$16,461**	**$21,731**	**$21,557**	**$19,370**
BENEFITS						
Health Insurance	Median	-	$2,500	-	-	-
	Average	-	$3,326	-	-	-
Life Insurance	Median	-	-	-	-	-
	Average	-	-	-	-	-
Disability Insurance	Median	-	-	-	-	-
	Average	-	-	-	-	-
Retirement	Median	-	-	$2,300	-	-
	Average	-	-	$4,191	-	-
Continuing Education	Median	$575	$975	$1,000	-	$531
	Average	$588	$1,748	$910	-	$608
Total Benefits	**Median**	**$1,350**	**$3,000**	**$2,000**	**-**	**$2,539**
	Average	**$2,592**	**$3,712**	**$5,790**	**-**	**$4,224**
TOTAL COMPENSATION PLUS BENEFITS	**Median**	**$10,600**	**$14,600**	**$25,992**	**$25,680**	**$18,146**
	Average	**$13,415**	**$17,597**	**$24,533**	**$23,769**	**$20,954**
Number of Respondents		66	49	31	17	32

- Not enough response to provide meaningful data.

* For detailed description and definitions of Data Distribution (Median and Average), see Chapter 1's "Explanation of Data Distribution."

Table 7-10: Annual Compensation of Part-Time Associate Pastors by Worship Attendance

	Data Distribution*	WORSHIP ATTENDANCE					
		100 or less	101-300	301-500	501-750	751-1,000	Over 1,000
CHARACTERISTICS							
Average weekend worship attendance		79	196	403	640	823	1,606
Average church income		$158,148	$337,725	$690,468	$994,819	$1,639,154	$1,925,111
Average # of years employed		4	5	8	6	6	6
Average # of paid vacation days		19	16	16	16	15	16
% College graduate or higher		76%	76%	81%	86%	91%	78%
% Who receive auto reimbursement/allowance		27%	44%	69%	43%	54%	100%
% Ordained		83%	77%	87%	79%	77%	67%
% Supervise one or more people		48%	36%	25%	34%	46%	56%
Average % salary increase (for those who had an increase) this year		-	12.6%	3.5%	5.5%	-	-
HOURLY RATE							
Base Rate	Average	$14	$16	$17	$20	$16	-
COMPENSATION							
Base Salary	Median	$10,140	$12,000	$12,312	$17,792	$11,350	$17,500
	Average	$11,611	$13,282	$14,795	$18,349	$14,015	$20,919
Housing	Median	$6,750	$12,000	$13,624	$13,000	-	-
	Average	$7,661	$11,977	$14,739	$13,191	-	-
Parsonage	Median	-	-	-	-	-	-
	Average	-	-	-	-	-	-
Total Compensation	**Median**	**$9,000**	**$12,740**	**$18,597**	**$18,500**	**$12,000**	**$19,000**
	Average	**$12,740**	**$15,655**	**$18,909**	**$19,457**	**$18,543**	**$23,044**
BENEFITS							
Health Insurance	Median	-	$4,834	-	-	-	-
	Average	-	$4,816	-	-	-	-
Life Insurance	Median	-	-	-	-	-	-
	Average	-	-	-	-	-	-
Disability	Median	-	-	-	-	-	-
	Average	-	-	-	-	-	-
Retirement	Median	-	$2,800	-	-	-	-
	Average	-	$4,651	-	-	-	-
Continuing Education	Median	-	$650	-	$531	-	-
	Average	-	$1,115	-	$602	-	-
Total Benefits	**Median**	**-**	**$2,000**	**$2,000**	**$4,109**	**-**	**-**
	Average	**-**	**$4,323**	**$2,971**	**$6,919**	**-**	**-**
TOTAL COMPENSATION PLUS BENEFITS	**Median**	**$9,000**	**$13,100**	**$18,597**	**$20,000**	**$12,000**	**$19,000**
	Average	**$13,344**	**$16,883**	**$19,930**	**$22,320**	**$19,216**	**$25,453**
Number of Respondents		30	88	32	29	13	9

- Not enough response to provide meaningful data.

* For detailed description and definitions of Data Distribution (Median and Average), see Chapter 1's "Explanation of Data Distribution."

Table 7-11: Annual Compensation of Part-Time Associate Pastors by Church Setting

	Data Distribution*	CHURCH SETTING			
		Metro-politan city	Suburb of large city	Small town or rural city	Farming area
CHARACTERISTICS					
Average weekend worship attendance		356	443	368	216
Average church income		$653,634	$807,549	$495,191	$339,250
Average # of years employed		6	5	6	7
Average # of paid vacation days		19	16	15	18
% College graduate or higher		85%	88%	71%	60%
% Who receive auto reimbursement/allowance		48%	44%	52%	67%
% Ordained		78%	82%	81%	58%
% Supervise one or more people		54%	39%	28%	33%
Average % salary increase (for those who had an increase) this year		9.5%	5.0%	11.3%	-
HOURLY RATE					
Base Rate	Average	$19	$17	$15	$18
COMPENSATION					
Base Salary	Median	$15,000	$12,000	$11,487	$14,925
	Average	$15,933	$14,454	$13,372	$16,460
Housing	Median	$7,000	$12,006	$10,000	-
	Average	$10,596	$13,189	$11,332	-
Parsonage	Median	-	-	-	-
	Average	-	-	-	-
Total Compensation	**Median**	**$15,298**	**$15,457**	**$13,055**	**$13,963**
	Average	**$17,122**	**$17,262**	**$16,536**	**$17,472**
BENEFITS					
Health Insurance	Median	-	-	$3,600	-
	Average	-	-	$5,011	-
Life Insurance	Median	-	-	-	-
	Average	-	-	-	-
Disability Insurance	Median	-	-	-	-
	Average	-	-	-	-
Retirement	Median	-	$1,565	$2,300	-
	Average	-	$3,514	$2,963	-
Continuing Education	Median	$1,000	$875	$575	-
	Average	$994	$1,405	$628	-
Total Benefits	**Median**	**$6,000**	**$2,000**	**$1,435**	**-**
	Average	**$6,874**	**$4,276**	**$4,226**	**-**
TOTAL COMPENSATION PLUS BENEFITS	**Median**	**$15,688**	**$16,573**	**$13,055**	**$14,238**
	Average	**$19,013**	**$18,456**	**$17,815**	**$18,910**
Number of Respondents		40	68	76	12

- Not enough response to provide meaningful data.

* For detailed description and definitions of Data Distribution (Median and Average), see Chapter 1's "Explanation of Data Distribution."

Table 7-12: Annual Compensation of Part-Time Associate Pastors by Region

	Data Distribution*	REGION								
		New England	Middle Atlantic	South Atlantic	E-N Central	E-S Central	W-N Central	W-S Central	Mountain	Pacific
CHARACTERISTICS										
Average weekend worship attendance		185	300	488	389	454	394	287	535	294
Average church income		$327,667	$646,144	$862,974	$584,889	$734,836	$676,860	$509,906	$697,203	$472,917
Average # of years employed		4	7	6	7	4	4	5	5	5
Average # of paid vacation days		19	17	16	17	13	21	12	16	18
% College graduate or higher		88%	86%	81%	90%	75%	89%	53%	50%	83%
% Who receive auto reimbursement/allowance		38%	60%	38%	61%	50%	78%	21%	39%	40%
% Ordained		88%	81%	66%	79%	83%	83%	85%	76%	83%
% Supervise one or more people		57%	45%	37%	35%	25%	24%	40%	39%	43%
Average % salary increase (for those who had an increase) this year		-	6.1%	-	10.3%	-	3.4%	-	-	-
HOURLY RATE										
Base Rate	Average	-	$14	$15	$20	-	-	$19	$17	$14
COMPENSATION										
Base Salary	Median	-	$11,150	$11,469	$15,000	$10,000	$15,000	$12,840	$13,300	$12,000
	Average	-	$13,247	$11,426	$16,230	$10,338	$17,433	$15,685	$16,070	$14,784
Housing	Median	-	-	-	$10,510	-	$12,500	-	-	$14,000
	Average	-	-	-	$12,997	-	$11,729	-	-	$12,354
Parsonage	Median	-	-	-	-	-	-	-	-	-
	Average	-	-	-	-	-	-	-	-	-
Total Compensation	**Median**	$12,000	$12,000	$11,918	$16,116	$11,050	$15,000	$14,318	$14,584	$16,853
	Average	$13,426	$15,907	$13,387	$19,065	$13,506	$18,455	$16,407	$18,930	$17,754
BENEFITS										
Health Insurance	Median	-	-	-	-	-	-	-	-	-
	Average	-	-	-	-	-	-	-	-	-
Life Insurance	Median	-	-	-	-	-	-	-	-	-
	Average	-	-	-	-	-	-	-	-	-
Disability Insurance	Median	-	-	-	-	-	-	-	-	-
	Average	-	-	-	-	-	-	-	-	-
Retirement	Median	-	-	-	-	-	-	-	-	-
	Average	-	-	-	-	-	-	-	-	-
Continuing Education	Median	-	-	-	$1,000	-	-	-	-	-
	Average	-	-	-	$768	-	-	-	-	-
Total Benefits	**Median**	-	$2,400	-	$1,393	-	$4,494	-	-	$1,791
	Average	-	$4,426	-	$4,041	-	$5,861	-	-	$4,751
TOTAL COMPENSATION PLUS BENEFITS	**Median**	$13,000	$12,000	$11,918	$18,616	$11,050	$19,014	$14,318	$14,584	$16,853
	Average	$15,003	$17,804	$13,857	$20,718	$14,545	$21,711	$16,607	$19,773	$19,180
Number of Respondents		8	21	30	44	12	18	20	18	30

- Not enough response to provide meaningful data.

* For detailed description and definitions of Data Distribution (Median and Average), see Chapter 1's "Explanation of Data Distribution."

Table 7-13: Annual Compensation of Part-Time Associate Pastors by Education

	Data Distribution*	EDUCATION			
		Less than Bachelor	Bachelor	Master	Doctorate
CHARACTERISTICS					
Average weekend worship attendance		381	419	332	406
Average church income		$487,467	$744,867	$522,448	$841,489
Average # of years employed		6	5	5	6
Average # of paid vacation days		13	15	17	24
% College graduate or higher		0%	100%	100%	100%
% Who receive auto reimbursement/allowance		41%	47%	51%	55%
% Ordained		73%	72%	90%	83%
% Supervise one or more people		48%	43%	31%	33%
Average % salary increase (for those who had an increase) this year		-	14.7%	4.4%	-
HOURLY RATE					
Base Rate	Average	$16	$18	$17	$17
COMPENSATION					
Base Salary	Median	$10,200	$14,925	$13,900	$12,624
	Average	$11,950	$15,277	$15,385	$15,527
Housing	Median	$6,930	$12,000	$10,000	-
	Average	$10,299	$12,616	$10,925	-
Parsonage	Median	-	-	-	-
	Average	-	-	-	-
Total Compensation	**Median**	**$10,000**	**$16,051**	**$15,300**	**$17,712**
	Average	**$13,785**	**$17,695**	**$17,825**	**$19,382**
BENEFITS					
Health Insurance	Median	-	$1,396	$4,834	-
	Average	-	$4,112	$5,542	-
Life Insurance	Median	-	-	-	-
	Average	-	-	-	-
Disability Insurance	Median	-	-	-	-
	Average	-	-	-	-
Retirement	Median	-	$1,440	$2,150	-
	Average	-	$1,958	$3,459	-
Continuing Education	Median	-	$950	$650	-
	Average	-	$745	$1,112	-
Total Benefits	**Median**	-	**$1,350**	**$3,000**	-
	Average	-	**$3,192**	**$4,712**	-
TOTAL COMPENSATION PLUS BENEFITS	**Median**	**$10,000**	**$17,169**	**$15,417**	**$17,712**
	Average	**$14,721**	**$18,681**	**$19,799**	**$20,950**
Number of Respondents		41	68	74	12

- Not enough response to provide meaningful data.

* For detailed description and definitions of Data Distribution (Median and Average), see Chapter 1's "Explanation of Data Distribution."

Table 7-14: Annual Compensation of Part-Time Associate Pastors by Years Employed

	Data Distribution*	YEARS EMPLOYED			
		Less than 6 years	6-10 years	11-15 years	Over 15 years
CHARACTERISTICS					
Average weekend worship attendance		370	377	404	518
Average church income		$596,901	$756,229	$497,861	$785,583
Average # of years employed		2	8	13	22
Average # of paid vacation days		16	16	13	20
% College graduate or higher		79%	81%	82%	70%
% Who receive auto reimbursement/allowance		49%	46%	55%	55%
% Ordained		74%	91%	100%	100%
% Supervise one or more people		39%	39%	45%	42%
Average % salary increase (for those who had an increase) this year		7.9%	13.8%	-	-
HOURLY RATE					
Base Rate	Average	$16	$18	$16	-
COMPENSATION					
Base Salary	Median	$12,000	$11,551	$16,253	$16,750
	Average	$13,668	$14,398	$18,568	$21,185
Housing	Median	$10,000	$10,050	-	-
	Average	$11,381	$10,142	-	-
Parsonage	Median	-	-	-	-
	Average	-	-	-	-
Total Compensation	**Median**	**$14,000**	**$15,593**	**$23,621**	**$24,250**
	Average	**$16,250**	**$15,512**	**$24,063**	**$25,218**
BENEFITS					
Health Insurance	Median	$5,000	-	-	-
	Average	$5,721	-	-	-
Life Insurance	Median	-	-	-	-
	Average	-	-	-	-
Disability Insurance	Median	-	-	-	-
	Average	-	-	-	-
Retirement	Median	$2,000	-	-	-
	Average	$3,221	-	-	-
Continuing Education	Median	$700	$500	-	-
	Average	$675	$883	-	-
Total Benefits	**Median**	**$2,096**	**$2,000**	**-**	**-**
	Average	**$4,854**	**$1,782**	**-**	**-**
TOTAL COMPENSATION PLUS BENEFITS	**Median**	**$14,000**	**$15,593**	**$26,338**	**$29,000**
	Average	**$17,770**	**$16,041**	**$25,554**	**$29,093**
Number of Respondents		115	37	11	12

- Not enough response to provide meaningful data.

* For detailed description and definitions of Data Distribution (Median and Average), see Chapter 1's "Explanation of Data Distribution."

Table 7-15: Annual Compensation of Part-Time Associate Pastors by Denomination

	Data Distribution*	DENOMINATION					
		Assemblies of God	Baptist	Independent/ Nondenom.	Lutheran	Methodist	Presby-terian
CHARACTERISTICS							
Average weekend worship attendance		472	368	454	364	393	354
Average church income		$880,265	$606,854	$682,635	$652,927	$718,960	$715,789
Average # of years employed		6	5	9	5	5	4
Average # of paid vacation days		11	15	16	21	17	22
% College graduate or higher		64%	78%	75%	100%	96%	100%
% Who receive auto reimbursement/allowance		43%	44%	34%	100%	63%	60%
% Ordained		93%	75%	91%	86%	76%	89%
% Supervise one or more people		38%	35%	59%	63%	17%	25%
Average % salary increase (for those who had an increase) this year		-	3.4%	-	-	3.7%	-
HOURLY RATE							
Base Rate	Average	-	$15	$18	-	$16	$17
COMPENSATION							
Base Salary	Median	$10,070	$12,000	$15,000	-	$12,000	$12,612
	Average	$11,968	$12,861	$17,867	-	$13,682	$15,744
Housing	Median	-	$12,000	$10,080	-	-	-
	Average	-	$12,375	$12,117	-	-	-
Parsonage	Median	-	-	-	-	-	-
	Average	-	-	-	-	-	-
Total Compensation	**Median**	**$10,350**	**$13,295**	**$18,500**	**$22,021**	**$12,000**	**$20,822**
	Average	**$15,671**	**$15,509**	**$20,954**	**$22,724**	**$14,308**	**$20,680**
BENEFITS							
Health Insurance	Median	-	-	-	-	-	=
	Average	-	-	-	-	-	-
Life Insurance	Median	-	-	-	-	-	-
	Average	-	-	-	-	-	-
Disability Insurance	Median	-	-	-	-	-	-
	Average	-	-	-	-	-	-
Retirement	Median	-	-	-	-	-	-
	Average	-	-	-	-	-	-
Continuing Education	Median	-	$500	-	-	-	-
	Average	-	$572	-	-	-	-
Total Benefits	**Median**	-	**$2,900**	**$5,800**	-	**$2,500**	-
	Average	-	**$3,532**	**$6,788**	-	**$4,523**	-
TOTAL COMPENSATION PLUS BENEFITS	**Median**	**$10,350**	**$14,055**	**$21,500**	**$25,573**	**$12,000**	**$20,822**
	Average	**$15,928**	**$16,425**	**$22,651**	**$27,074**	**$16,479**	**$22,824**
Number of Respondents		14	54	32	8	25	20

- Not enough response to provide meaningful data.

* For detailed description and definitions of Data Distribution (Median and Average), see Chapter 1's "Explanation of Data Distribution."

Table 7-16: Annual Compensation of Part-Time Associate Pastors by Gender

	Data Distribution*	GENDER	
		Male	Female
CHARACTERISTICS			
Average weekend worship attendance		368	399
Average church income		$588,940	$688,792
Average # of years employed		6	5
Average # of paid vacation days		17	16
% College graduate or higher		80%	78%
% Who receive auto reimbursement/allowance		45%	58%
% Ordained		82%	73%
% Supervise one or more people		33%	49%
Average % salary increase (for those who had an increase) this year		10.9%	8.8%
HOURLY RATE			
Base Rate	Average	$17	$16
COMPENSATION			
Base Salary	Median	$12,552	$12,000
	Average	$14,768	$14,031
Housing	Median	$11,500	$10,010
	Average	$11,783	$12,004
Parsonage	Median	-	-
	Average	-	-
Total Compensation	**Median**	**$14,584**	**$16,218**
	Average	**$16,836**	**$16,894**
BENEFITS			
Health Insurance	Median	$4,302	-
	Average	$5,234	-
Life Insurance	Median	-	-
	Average	-	-
Disability Insurance	Median	-	-
	Average	-	-
Retirement	Median	$1,550	$2,600
	Average	$2,654	$3,945
Continuing Education	Median	$656	$700
	Average	$811	$1,081
Total Benefits	**Median**	**$2,400**	**$1,435**
	Average	**$4,280**	**$4,582**
TOTAL COMPENSATION PLUS BENEFITS	**Median**	**$14,584**	**$16,614**
	Average	**$17,995**	**$18,776**
Number of Respondents		144	56

- Not enough response to provide meaningful data.

* For detailed description and definitions of Data Distribution (Median and Average), see Chapter 1's "Explanation of Data Distribution."

8

ADULT MINISTRY/ CHRISTIAN EDUCATION PASTORS/DIRECTORS

Employment Profile

For purposes of this book, Adult Ministry and Christian Education Pastors/Directors have been reported together.

Adult Ministry Pastors/Directors include paid pastors and directors of church ministries for adults, married couples, men, singles, seniors, women, young adults, etc.

Christian Education Pastors/Directors include paid pastors and directors of educational ministries based on purpose rather than age gradation, such as Bible studies, cell groups, Christian education, discipleship, equipping, small groups, spiritual formation, etc.

About two-thirds of the full-time Adult Ministry and Christian Education Pastors/Directors who reported are ordained ministers. Almost all are employed by the church, rather than self-employed, and have at least a college degree. Half of those working full-time have a graduate degree.

About 40% of the participants in this survey work on a part-time basis. While more than six in ten part-timers are female, a similar percentage of their full-time counterparts are male.

The following chart provides a demographic profile of this sample:

	Full-Time	Part-Time
Number of respondents	251	165
Ordained	65%	29%
Average years employed	6	5
Male	66%	38%
Female	35%	62%
Self-employed (receives 1099)	6%	9%
Church employee (receives W-2)	94%	91%
High school diploma	9%	12%
Associate Degree	7%	11%
Bachelor's Degree	34%	51%
Master's Degree	46%	19%
Doctoral Degree	4%	7%

Total Compensation plus Benefits Package Analysis

The analyses on the next page are based on the data in the tables that you will find in the remainder of the chapter. The tables show compensation plus benefits data for Adult Ministry and Christian Education Pastors/Directors who serve full time and are presented according to church income, church attendance, church setting, region, education, years employed, denomination, and gender. In this way, Adult Ministry and Christian Education Pastors'/Directors' compensation plus benefits can be analyzed and compared from a variety of useful perspectives. There is also a table showing compensation plus benefit data for those who serve part-time presented according to church income.

The total compensation plus benefits amount includes the base salary, housing and/or parsonage amount, health, life, and disability insurance payments, retirement contribution, and educational funds.

Full-timers in adult and education ministries receive benefits packages comparable to those of other professional and ministerial staff members within the church. About five in ten receive housing and auto allowances, and six in ten receive health insurance and retirement benefits.

Part-timers receive few benefits, with the most common being paid vacation.

Compensation Plus Benefits	Full-Time	Part-Time
Base Salary	99%	95%
Housing	48%	13%
Parsonage	3%	0%
Health Insurance	63%	6%
Life Insurance	34%	5%
Disability Insurance	32%	2%
Retirement	60%	12%
Continuing Education	35%	16%
Received Salary Increase	59%	42%
Received Paid Vacation	96%	48%
Received Auto Reimbursement/ Allowance	52%	27%

KEY POINTS

✱ Almost six in ten full-time Adult Ministry and Christian Education Pastors/Directors reporting serve churches with income higher than $1,000,000 and worship attendance of more than 500.

✱ Slightly more than half of part-time Adult Ministry and Christian Education Pastors/ Directors serve in churches with income of $750,000 or less.

✱ In general, as church attendance and the minister's education level increase, compensation and benefits for full-time adult and education ministers also increase.

Compensation & Benefits: National Averages for Full-Time Adult Ministry/ Christian Education Pastors/Directors*

2000	
2001	
2002	
2003	
2004	
2005	
2006	$67,711
2007	$59,791
2008	$60,312
2009	$58,877**

No historical data available before 2006.

**The above trend is made available for your reference only. In addition to looking at this overall data, please refer to the detailed tables using your church's income, attendance, setting, region, and denomination as well as the person's education, gender, and years employed for guidance in compensating this position.*

Table 8-1: Annual Compensation of Full-Time Adult Ministry/Christian Education Pastors/Directors by Church Income

CHARACTERISTICS	Data Distribution*	CHURCH INCOME				
		$250K & Under	$251-$500K	$501-$750K	$751K-$1M	Over 1 Million
Average weekend worship attendance		212	347	395	547	1,605
Average church income		$152,902	$402,757	$623,147	$910,126	$2,749,271
Average # of years employed		5	6	6	7	7
Average # of paid vacation days		16	16	16	17	18
% College graduate or higher		92%	82%	69%	79%	88%
% Who receive auto reimbursement/allowance		55%	52%	57%	59%	51%
% Ordained		36%	64%	48%	63%	73%
% Supervise one or more people		75%	71%	76%	84%	69%
Average % salary increase (for those who had an increase) this year		3.8%	4.0%	3.1%	4.1%	3.9%
COMPENSATION						
Base Salary	Highest 25%	$28,500	$40,500	$43,376	$46,000	$48,000
	Median	$25,000	$34,500	$34,200	$34,963	$40,000
	Lowest 25%	$24,500	$25,375	$30,333	$22,000	$32,830
	Average	$28,074	$34,041	$36,699	$35,895	$41,021
Housing	Highest 25%	-	$32,400	-	$30,000	$30,746
	Median	-	$20,000	-	$24,500	$25,850
	Lowest 25%	-	$18,000	-	$20,000	$21,030
	Average	-	$25,467	-	$23,471	$27,180
Parsonage	Highest 25%	-	-	-	-	-
	Median	-	-	-	-	-
	Lowest 25%	-	-	-	-	-
	Average	-	-	-	-	-
Total Compensation	**Highest 25%**	**$40,843**	**$45,000**	**$50,114**	**$56,800**	**$65,260**
	Median	**$29,500**	**$37,300**	**$40,000**	**$48,454**	**$56,063**
	Lowest 25%	**$25,433**	**$32,000**	**$33,000**	**$37,500**	**$46,000**
	Average	**$34,546**	**$41,081**	**$40,643**	**$47,546**	**$57,475**
BENEFITS						
Health Insurance	Highest 25%	-	-	-	$10,500	$11,580
	Median	-	-	-	$8,220	$8,000
	Lowest 25%	-	-	-	$4,000	$5,000
	Average	-	-	-	$7,943	$8,284
Life Insurance	Highest 25%	-	-	-	$800	$400
	Median	-	-	-	$307	$200
	Lowest 25%	-	-	-	$188	$113
	Average	-	-	-	$490	$346
Disability Insurance	Highest 25%	-	-	-	$1,000	$638
	Median	-	-	-	$500	$400
	Lowest 25%	-	-	-	$343	$251
	Average	-	-	-	$618	$506
Retirement	Highest 25%	-	$3,000	$5,000	$5,476	$5,957
	Median	-	$2,813	$3,000	$4,000	$2,900
	Lowest 25%	-	$2,000	$1,200	$2,500	$1,746
	Average	-	$3,263	$3,154	$4,366	$3,888
Continuing Education	Highest 25%	-	-	-	-	$1,872
	Median	-	-	-	-	$1,000
	Lowest 25%	-	-	-	-	$500
	Average	-	-	-	-	$1,387
Total Benefits	**Highest 25%**	-	-	-	**$13,470**	**$14,951**
	Median	-	-	-	**$8,785**	**$10,414**
	Lowest 25%	-	-	-	**$5,026**	**$5,195**
	Average	-	-	-	**$9,677**	**$10,425**
TOTAL COMPENSATION PLUS BENEFITS	**Highest 25%**	**$45,369**	**$57,510**	**$52,000**	**$71,000**	**$77,406**
	Median	**$32,800**	**$47,000**	**$42,400**	**$54,349**	**$64,915**
	Lowest 25%	**$26,500**	**$34,000**	**$35,365**	**$39,520**	**$53,663**
	Average	**$37,680**	**$48,628**	**$44,098**	**$55,756**	**$67,460**
Number of Respondents		12	29	29	33	142

- Not enough response to provide meaningful data.

* For detailed description and definitions of Data Distribution (Median and Average), see Chapter 1's "Explanation of Data Distribution."

Table 8-2: Annual Compensation of Full-Time Adult Ministry/Christian Education Pastors/Directors by Worship Attendance

	Data Distribution*	100 or less	101-300	301-500	501-750	751-1,000	Over 1,000
CHARACTERISTICS							
Average weekend worship attendance	-		233	414	625	880	2,335
Average church income	-		$399,346	$841,850	$1,294,050	$1,680,451	$3,616,775
Average # of years employed	-		5	7	6	7	7
Average # of paid vacation days	-		16	18	17	18	18
% College graduate or higher	-		86%	86%	74%	88%	84%
% Who receive auto reimbursement/allowance	-		59%	57%	53%	49%	50%
% Ordained	-		56%	57%	64%	67%	73%
% Supervise one or more people	-		69%	77%	68%	61%	78%
Average % salary increase (for those who had an increase) this year	-		4.0%	3.3%	3.7%	3.1%	4.5%
COMPENSATION							
Base Salary	Median	-	$29,760	$37,882	$37,579	$37,440	$41,000
	Average	-	$32,612	$39,443	$38,201	$37,136	$41,894
Housing	Median	-	$19,000	$26,550	$23,585	$28,420	$26,926
	Average	-	$21,948	$25,776	$23,098	$30,070	$27,670
Parsonage	Median	-	-	-	-	-	-
	Average	-	-	-	-	-	-
Total Compensation	**Median**	-	**$36,343**	**$49,700**	**$51,393**	**$49,827**	**$55,948**
	Average	-	**$38,844**	**$49,757**	**$49,173**	**$52,244**	**$58,597**
BENEFITS							
Health Insurance	Median	-	$6,000	$7,200	$5,300	$6,950	$9,044
	Average	-	$7,976	$8,017	$7,345	$7,596	$8,960
Life Insurance	Median	-	-	$350	$297	$118	$200
	Average	-	-	$713	$377	$276	$351
Disability	Median	-	-	$500	$474	$499	$302
	Average	-	-	$640	$523	$594	$504
Retirement	Median	-	$2,900	$3,567	$5,390	$2,350	$2,902
	Average	-	$3,028	$4,014	$4,503	$3,311	$4,011
Continuing Education	Median	-	$500	$750	$1,200	$1,100	$1,000
	Average	-	$1,146	$1,188	$2,073	$1,260	$1,388
Total Benefits	**Median**	-	**$6,009**	**$6,000**	**$8,110**	**$10,544**	**$11,242**
	Average	-	**$7,877**	**$8,798**	**$9,982**	**$9,622**	**$10,659**
TOTAL COMPENSATION PLUS BENEFITS	**Median**	-	**$41,495**	**$55,000**	**$58,344**	**$58,914**	**$65,650**
	Average	-	**$44,470**	**$56,209**	**$57,408**	**$61,385**	**$68,982**
Number of Respondents		3	42	45	40	40	78

- Not enough response to provide meaningful data.

* For detailed description and definitions of Data Distribution (Median and Average), see Chapter 1's "Explanation of Data Distribution."

Table 8-3: Annual Compensation of Full-Time Adult Ministry/Christian Education Pastors/Directors by Church Setting

	Data Distribution*	CHURCH SETTING			
		Metro-politan city	Suburb of large city	Small town or rural city	Farming area
CHARACTERISTICS					
Average weekend worship attendance		1,479	1,157	722	-
Average church income		$2,693,910	$1,924,218	$1,130,387	-
Average # of years employed		7	7	6	-
Average # of paid vacation days		17	18	17	-
% College graduate or higher		94%	86%	74%	-
% Who receive auto reimbursement/allowance		57%	51%	52%	-
% Ordained		65%	68%	59%	-
% Supervise one or more people		83%	74%	61%	-
Average % salary increase (for those who had an increase) this year		4.1%	3.7%	3.8%	-
COMPENSATION					
Base Salary	Median	$39,663	$38,157	$33,415	-
	Average	$40,813	$38,669	$35,265	-
Housing	Median	$25,000	$26,400	$20,000	-
	Average	$27,141	$28,232	$21,180	-
Parsonage	Median	-	-	-	-
	Average	-	-	-	-
Total Compensation	**Median**	**$53,000**	**$51,000**	**$43,779**	**-**
	Average	**$54,168**	**$52,623**	**$44,870**	**-**
BENEFITS					
Health Insurance	Median	$8,220	$7,200	$8,000	-
	Average	$8,114	$8,108	$8,177	-
Life Insurance	Median	$300	$235	$108	-
	Average	$440	$370	$384	-
Disability Insurance	Median	$368	$500	$492	-
	Average	$408	$575	$701	-
Retirement	Median	$5,000	$2,300	$2,900	-
	Average	$4,856	$3,576	$3,468	-
Continuing Education	Median	$1,000	$600	$1,050	-
	Average	$996	$1,446	$1,504	-
Total Benefits	**Median**	**$10,043**	**$8,484**	**$7,600**	**-**
	Average	**$10,302**	**$9,720**	**$8,887**	**-**
TOTAL COMPENSATION PLUS BENEFITS	**Median**	**$62,594**	**$59,330**	**$52,111**	**-**
	Average	**$63,233**	**$61,195**	**$51,956**	**-**
Number of Respondents		50	127	74	0

- Not enough response to provide meaningful data.

* For detailed description and definitions of Data Distribution (Median and Average), see Chapter 1's "Explanation of Data Distribution."

Table 8-4: Annual Compensation of Full-Time Adult Ministry/Christian Education Pastors/Directors by Region

	Data Distribution*	New England	Middle Atlantic	South Atlantic	E-N Central	E-S Central	W-N Central	W-S Central	Mountain	Pacific
CHARACTERISTICS										
Average weekend worship attendance	-	1,030	1,132	1,073	1,096	954	1,028	957	1,583
Average church income	-	$1,563,286	$1,979,741	$1,706,157	$2,287,043	$1,209,002	$1,999,458	$2,023,737	$2,182,775
Average # of years employed	-	6	6	7	6	7	6	7	7
Average # of paid vacation days	-	17	17	18	17	17	17	17	17
% College graduate or higher	-	88%	82%	80%	88%	92%	93%	53%	85%
% Who receive auto reimbursement/allowance	-	63%	68%	51%	33%	58%	44%	26%	60%
% Ordained	-	50%	64%	64%	78%	40%	68%	59%	88%
% Supervise one or more people	-	81%	73%	78%	60%	60%	69%	53%	81%
Average % salary increase (for those who had an increase) this year	-	3.5%	3.8%	4.1%	3.7%	2.8%	3.9%	5.4%	4.1%
COMPENSATION										
Base Salary	Median	-	$40,000	$37,814	$35,000	$42,221	$37,500	$36,698	$37,440	$34,682
	Average	-	$40,234	$38,747	$36,335	$41,395	$37,291	$40,113	$34,132	$36,825
Housing	Median	-	$26,750	$24,000	$25,000	$26,500	-	$25,350	$26,700	$26,517
	Average	-	$24,375	$24,768	$24,516	$26,411	-	$27,233	$27,358	$26,561
Parsonage	Median	-	-	-	-	-	-	-	-	-
	Average	-	-	-	-	-	-	-	-	-
Total Compensation	**Median**	-	**$48,000**	**$52,000**	**$46,000**	**$57,650**	**$38,729**	**$52,756**	**$52,000**	**$51,832**
	Average	-	**$52,421**	**$50,830**	**$47,916**	**$54,601**	**$42,489**	**$54,892**	**$48,531**	**$53,534**
BENEFITS										
Health Insurance	Median	-	$6,930	$6,816	$7,515	$8,918	$5,656	$9,850	$8,375	$6,000
	Average	-	$7,715	$7,612	$8,380	$7,124	$9,090	$9,281	$7,701	$6,125
Life Insurance	Median	-	-	$397	$157	-	$204	$226	$80	-
	Average	-	-	$567	$347	-	$276	$446	$113	-
Disability Insurance	Median	-	-	$485	$376	-	$650	$363	-	$739
	Average	-	-	$605	$711	-	$670	$454	-	$678
Retirement	Median	-	$4,500	$3,250	$2,405	$1,746	$2,600	$3,800	$3,352	$3,700
	Average	-	$3,998	$4,078	$2,983	$2,701	$3,300	$4,406	$3,862	$4,535
Continuing Education	Median	-	-	$750	$1,050	-	$500	$1,100	-	-
	Average	-	-	$1,623	$1,216	-	$1,113	$1,763	-	-
Total Benefits	**Median**	-	**$6,750**	**$5,840**	**$8,929**	**$7,968**	**$6,156**	**$11,627**	**$10,603**	**$8,110**
	Average	-	**$9,291**	**$8,941**	**$9,220**	**$8,563**	**$8,926**	**$11,487**	**$9,865**	**$8,981**
TOTAL COMPENSATION PLUS BENEFITS	**Median**	-	**$57,750**	**$62,280**	**$55,000**	**$62,661**	**$47,492**	**$66,050**	**$59,330**	**$58,675**
	Average	-	**$60,550**	**$58,986**	**$55,112**	**$60,785**	**$50,385**	**$64,465**	**$57,876**	**$61,479**
Number of Respondents		6	16	57	41	18	26	42	19	26

- Not enough response to provide meaningful data.

* For detailed description and definitions of Data Distribution (Median and Average), see Chapter 1's "Explanation of Data Distribution."

Table 8-5: Annual Compensation of Full-Time Adult Ministry/Christian Education Pastors/Directors by Education

	Data Distribution*	EDUCATION			
		Less than Bachelor	Bachelor	Master	Doctorate
CHARACTERISTICS					
Average weekend worship attendance		825	1,175	1,057	1,912
Average church income		$1,184,286	$1,904,079	$1,801,453	$4,525,300
Average # of years employed		6	6	6	9
Average # of paid vacation days		14	17	19	20
% College graduate or higher		0%	100%	100%	100%
% Who receive auto reimbursement/allowance		45%	43%	61%	70%
% Ordained		48%	54%	77%	80%
% Supervise one or more people		62%	71%	73%	100%
Average % salary increase (for those who had an increase) this year		5.0%	3.6%	3.4%	3.3%
COMPENSATION					
Base Salary	Median	$31,200	$37,850	$38,098	-
	Average	$32,484	$40,235	$38,328	-
Housing	Median	$28,400	$25,000	$25,000	$29,000
	Average	$26,275	$25,513	$25,780	$32,775
Parsonage	Median	-	-	-	-
	Average	-	-	-	-
Total Compensation	**Median**	**$35,000**	**$49,900**	**$54,000**	**$63,850**
	Average	**$37,584**	**$51,374**	**$53,748**	**$61,705**
BENEFITS					
Health Insurance	Median	$4,793	$6,750	$8,110	$8,918
	Average	$6,014	$7,632	$8,916	$9,643
Life Insurance	Median	-	$243	$255	-
	Average	-	$396	$421	-
Disability Insurance	Median	-	$494	$474	-
	Average	-	$547	$595	-
Retirement	Median	$1,955	$2,852	$3,600	$6,691
	Average	$2,267	$3,397	$4,172	$5,326
Continuing Education	Median	$725	$1,160	$500	-
	Average	$1,175	$1,593	$1,136	-
Total Benefits	**Median**	**$4,186**	**$6,600**	**$11,011**	**$12,090**
	Average	**$5,662**	**$8,397**	**$11,317**	**$14,720**
TOTAL COMPENSATION PLUS BENEFITS	**Median**	**$43,106**	**$56,361**	**$62,777**	**$75,940**
	Average	**$41,973**	**$58,872**	**$63,278**	**$76,425**
Number of Respondents		40	84	114	10

- Not enough response to provide meaningful data.

* For detailed description and definitions of Data Distribution (Median and Average), see Chapter 1's "Explanation of Data Distribution."

Table 8-6: Annual Compensation of Full-Time Adult Ministry/Christian Education Pastors/Directors by Years Employed

	Data Distribution*	YEARS EMPLOYED			
		Less than 6 years	6-10 years	11-15 years	Over 15 years
CHARACTERISTICS					
Average weekend worship attendance		1,014	988	1,842	1,049
Average church income		$1,863,619	$1,321,512	$2,465,497	$2,186,293
Average # of years employed		3	8	13	20
Average # of paid vacation days		16	18	21	22
% College graduate or higher		84%	81%	86%	94%
% Who receive auto reimbursement/allowance		53%	56%	45%	50%
% Ordained		67%	54%	76%	76%
% Supervise one or more people		69%	80%	86%	63%
Average % salary increase (for those who had an increase) this year		4.4%	3.4%	2.8%	3.9%
COMPENSATION					
Base Salary	Median	$35,932	$39,157	$30,350	$39,828
	Average	$37,705	$38,239	$33,404	$44,580
Housing	Median	$25,300	$23,405	$26,550	$25,700
	Average	$26,913	$22,737	$27,524	$32,057
Parsonage	Median	-	-	-	-
	Average	-	-	-	-
Total Compensation	**Median**	**$50,000**	**$45,500**	**$50,850**	**$58,602**
	Average	**$50,491**	**$47,115**	**$52,283**	**$60,608**
BENEFITS					
Health Insurance	Median	$7,540	$8,700	$6,664	$6,915
	Average	$8,098	$8,172	$7,459	$7,389
Life Insurance	Median	$218	$225	$300	$323
	Average	$368	$543	$296	$339
Disability Insurance	Median	$400	$739	-	$300
	Average	$518	$791	-	$431
Retirement	Median	$3,000	$2,500	$5,476	$5,676
	Average	$3,549	$3,309	$5,403	$5,513
Continuing Education	Median	$900	$600	-	-
	Average	$1,384	$1,233	-	-
Total Benefits	**Median**	**$7,520**	**$7,945**	**$7,412**	**$13,330**
	Average	**$8,960**	**$9,524**	**$10,324**	**$12,559**
TOTAL COMPENSATION PLUS BENEFITS	**Median**	**$56,363**	**$56,000**	**$54,786**	**$66,625**
	Average	**$58,199**	**$55,832**	**$60,260**	**$71,074**
Number of Respondents		136	59	22	18

- Not enough response to provide meaningful data.

* For detailed description and definitions of Data Distribution (Median and Average), see Chapter 1's "Explanation of Data Distribution."

Table 8-7: Annual Compensation of Full-Time Adult Ministry/Christian Education Pastors/Directors by Denomination

	Data Distribution*	DENOMINATION					
		Assemblies of God	Baptist	Independent/ Nondenom.	Lutheran	Methodist	Presby-terian
CHARACTERISTICS							
Average weekend worship attendance		1,204	1,010	1,267	512	767	916
Average church income		$1,889,500	$2,031,287	$1,891,743	$1,122,764	$1,299,013	$1,687,812
Average # of years employed		4	6	6	7	6	6
Average # of paid vacation days		13	18	16	17	18	19
% College graduate or higher		53%	89%	74%	93%	87%	96%
% Who receive auto reimbursement/allowance		44%	67%	40%	63%	21%	78%
% Ordained		76%	87%	67%	44%	26%	26%
% Supervise one or more people		63%	74%	76%	40%	58%	74%
Average % salary increase (for those who had an increase) this year		5.0%	3.9%	4.7%	2.3%	4.3%	2.8%
COMPENSATION							
Base Salary	Median	$25,000	$36,868	$35,000	$37,829	$36,250	$45,580
	Average	$27,729	$38,655	$38,312	$39,553	$37,592	$43,833
Housing	Median	-	$24,000	$28,400	-	-	-
	Average	-	$24,662	$29,768	-	-	-
Parsonage	Median	-	-	-	-	-	-
	Average	-	-	-	-	-	-
Total Compensation	**Median**	**$42,000**	**$56,910**	**$52,000**	**$42,479**	**$38,500**	**$48,454**
	Average	**$39,063**	**$56,187**	**$54,070**	**$44,678**	**$40,342**	**$49,311**
BENEFITS							
Health Insurance	Median	$5,720	$8,249	$9,000	$6,500	$4,772	$5,578
	Average	$6,097	$8,999	$8,323	$8,403	$5,335	$7,982
Life Insurance	Median	-	$264	$102	-	-	-
	Average	-	$409	$275	-	-	-
Disability Insurance	Median	-	$400	$600	-	-	-
	Average	-	$421	$661	-	-	-
Retirement	Median	-	$3,600	$2,400	$3,374	$2,681	$5,000
	Average	-	$4,058	$2,996	$3,725	$3,061	$5,630
Continuing Education	Median	-	$1,500	$1,000	$500	$660	$625
	Average	-	$2,169	$2,070	$663	$982	$1,071
Total Benefits	**Median**	**$4,950**	**$9,360**	**$10,800**	**$6,629**	**$4,252**	**$6,000**
	Average	**$6,254**	**$10,704**	**$10,125**	**$9,435**	**$6,659**	**$8,830**
TOTAL COMPENSATION PLUS BENEFITS	**Median**	**$47,600**	**$65,837**	**$59,150**	**$53,500**	**$41,165**	**$52,000**
	Average	**$44,213**	**$65,878**	**$62,783**	**$52,934**	**$44,781**	**$56,989**
Number of Respondents		17	74	43	16	24	23

- *Not enough response to provide meaningful data.*

* *For detailed description and definitions of Data Distribution (Median and Average), see Chapter 1's "Explanation of Data Distribution."*

Table 8-8: Annual Compensation of Full-Time Adult Ministry/Christian Education Pastors/Directors by Gender

	Data Distribution*	GENDER	
		Male	Female
CHARACTERISTICS			
Average weekend worship attendance		1,115	1,049
Average church income		$1,989,346	$1,573,192
Average # of years employed		6	7
Average # of paid vacation days		17	17
% College graduate or higher		88%	76%
% Who receive auto reimbursement/allowance		59%	40%
% Ordained		86%	27%
% Supervise one or more people		72%	71%
Average % salary increase (for those who had an increase) this year		4.0%	3.4%
COMPENSATION			
Base Salary	Median	$37,500	$35,000
	Average	$39,098	$36,187
Housing	Median	$25,000	$25,500
	Average	$26,398	$24,691
Parsonage	Median	-	-
	Average	-	-
Total Compensation	**Median**	**$55,907**	**$40,000**
	Average	**$56,024**	**$40,505**
BENEFITS			
Health Insurance	Median	$8,959	$5,000
	Average	$8,961	$5,875
Life Insurance	Median	$254	$169
	Average	$398	$344
Disability Insurance	Median	$450	$485
	Average	$591	$482
Retirement	Median	$3,000	$2,500
	Average	$3,968	$3,407
Continuing Education	Median	$1,000	$600
	Average	$1,644	$993
Total Benefits	**Median**	**$10,884**	**$5,676**
	Average	**$10,923**	**$6,711**
TOTAL COMPENSATION PLUS BENEFITS	**Median**	**$65,200**	**$44,550**
	Average	**$65,882**	**$45,673**
Number of Respondents		164	87

- Not enough response to provide meaningful data.

* For detailed description and definitions of Data Distribution (Median and Average), see Chapter 1's "Explanation of Data Distribution."

Table 8-9: Annual Compensation of Part-Time Adult Ministry/Christian Education Pastors/Directors by Church Income

	Data Distribution*	CHURCH INCOME				
		$250K & Under	$251-$500K	$501-$750K	$751K-$1M	Over 1 Million
CHARACTERISTICS						
Average weekend worship attendance		171	280	478	544	889
Average church income		$165,436	$403,620	$642,311	$907,362	$1,961,443
Average # of years employed		5	3	5	6	6
Average # of paid vacation days		16	12	10	11	12
% College graduate or higher		86%	81%	76%	72%	72%
% Who receive auto reimbursement/allowance		-	-	-	-	28%
% Ordained		32%	28%	31%	25%	25%
% Supervise one or more people		27%	29%	41%	42%	44%
Average % salary increase (for those who had an increase) this year		3.0%	4.5%	6.4%	2.9%	3.9%
HOURLY RATE						
Base Rate	Average	-	$15	-	$15	$17
COMPENSATION						
Base Salary	Median	$7,900	$14,000	-	$13,944	$15,785
	Average	$9,832	$14,499	-	$16,171	$17,535
Housing	Median	-	-	-	-	-
	Average	-	-	-	-	-
Parsonage	Median	-	-	-	-	-
	Average	-	-	-	-	-
Total Compensation	**Median**	**$8,800**	**$15,800**	-	**$17,756**	**$17,296**
	Average	**$10,048**	**$15,732**	-	**$17,718**	**$18,111**
BENEFITS						
Health Insurance	Median	-	-	-	-	-
	Average	-	-	-	-	-
Life Insurance	Median	-	-	-	-	-
	Average	-	-	-	-	-
Disability Insurance	Median	-	-	-	-	-
	Average	-	-	-	-	-
Retirement	Median	-	-	-	-	-
	Average	-	-	-	-	-
Continuing Education	Median	-	-	-	-	-
	Average	-	-	-	-	-
Total Benefits	**Median**	-	-	-	-	**$1,065**
	Average	-	-	-	-	**$3,593**
TOTAL COMPENSATION PLUS BENEFITS	**Median**	**$8,800**	**$15,800**	**$12,700**	**$17,947**	**$17,796**
	Average	**$10,427**	**$15,977**	**$15,624**	**$18,218**	**$19,159**
Number of Respondents		22	32	33	25	48

- Not enough response to provide meaningful data.

* For detailed description and definitions of Data Distribution (Median and Average), see Chapter 1's "Explanation of Data Distribution."

9

YOUTH PASTORS/DIRECTORS

Employment Profile

Youth Pastors/Directors include paid pastors and directors of junior high, senior high, or college students. This category may include such titles as Campus Pastor, College Minister, Junior High Pastor/Director, Senior High Pastor/Director, Youth Center Director, Youth Pastor/Director, etc.

On average, Youth Pastors/Directors have been employed in their current positions for fewer years than other church staff. Nearly all full-time Youth Pastors/Directors are considered church employees, rather than using the "self-employed" designation which the Internal Revenue Service grants many ordained pastors. Among full-timers, almost nine in ten have a college degree and are male.

More than twice as many full-time as part-time Youth Pastors/Directors are ordained. Approximately 30% of the Youth Pastors/Directors in this sample work part time. Of this part-time group, females account for 29%, compared to 9% of full-timers.

The following is a profile of the demographics reported for this position:

	Full-Time	Part-Time
Number of respondents	552	233
Ordained	70%	32%
Average years employed	4	3
Male	91%	71%
Female	9%	29%
Self-employed (receives 1099)	4%	7%
Church employee (receives W-2)	96%	93%
High school diploma	8%	19%
Associate Degree	6%	15%
Bachelor's Degree	60%	53%
Master's Degree	25%	12%
Doctoral Degree	1%	<.5 %

Total Compensation plus Benefits Package Analysis

The analyses on the next page are based on the data in the tables that you will find in the remainder of the chapter. The tables show compensation plus benefits data for full-time and part-time Youth Pastors/Directors and are presented according to church income, church attendance, church setting, region, education, years employed, denomination, and gender. In this way, the compensation plus benefits of Youth Pastors/Directors can be analyzed and compared from a variety of useful perspectives.

The total compensation plus benefits amount includes the base salary, housing and/or parsonage amount, health, life, and disability insurance payments, retirement contribution, and educational funds.

The average compensation for full-time Youth Pastors/Directors is similar to Children's/Preschool Pastors/Directors and about 15% less than that of full-time Adult Ministry/Christian Education Pastors/Directors, but they receive similar benefits packages. A small fraction of part-time Youth Pastors/Directors receive benefits similar to those received by their full-time counterparts.

Compensation Plus Benefits	Full-Time	Part-Time
Base Salary	99%	94%
Housing	60%	16%
Parsonage	5%	5%
Health Insurance	68%	6%
Life Insurance	24%	1%
Disability Insurance	20%	1%
Retirement	54%	5%
Continuing Education	30%	12%
Received Salary Increase	56%	36%
Received Paid Vacation	96%	46%
Received Auto Reimbursement/ Allowance	58%	36%

KEY POINTS

✳ About seven in ten part-time Youth Pastors/Directors serve in smaller churches with 300 or less in attendance or church income of $500,000 or less.

✳ In general, as church income, church attendance, the minister's education level, and years employed increase, compensation and benefits for full-time Youth Pastors/Directors also increase.

✳ The vast majority of full-time Youth Pastors/Directors in this report serve in churches set in a suburb of a large city or a small town/rural city. Youth Pastors/Directors in metropolitan cities and suburbs of large cities have higher compensation packages than their counterparts in small towns/rural cities or farming areas.

✳ Some regional differences emerge across compensation and benefits packages for full-time Youth Pastors/Directors. The lowest package averages are found in the West-North Central, New England, and East-South Central regions, while the highest are found in Pacific region.

Compensation & Benefits: National Averages for Full-Time Solo Pastors*

2000	$42,561
2001	$43,288
2002	$45,043
2003	$47,058
2004	$47,302
2005	$50,371
2006	$51,640
2007	$50,824
2008	$51,484
2009	$50,540*

*The above trend is made available for your reference only. In addition to looking at this overall data, please refer to the detailed tables using your church's income, attendance, setting, region, and denomination as well as the person's education, gender, and years employed for guidance in compensating this position.

Table 9-1: Annual Compensation of Full-Time Youth Pastors/Directors by Church Income

CHARACTERISTICS	Data Distribution*	CHURCH INCOME				
		$250K & Under	$251-$500K	$501-$750K	$751K-$1M	Over 1 Million
Average weekend worship attendance		239	241	367	520	1,291
Average church income		$194,755	$377,008	$630,824	$893,387	$2,172,147
Average # of years employed		3	4	4	4	4
Average # of paid vacation days		15	14	14	16	16
% College graduate or higher		76%	79%	88%	90%	92%
% Who receive auto reimbursement/allowance		63%	63%	52%	56%	57%
% Ordained		65%	65%	75%	77%	72%
% Supervise one or more people		42%	37%	43%	42%	69%
Average % salary increase (for those who had an increase) this year		4.2%	3.7%	4.5%	4.0%	4.2%
COMPENSATION						
Base Salary	Highest 25%	$32,000	$34,000	$37,761	$40,000	$43,761
	Median	$28,000	$27,820	$31,250	$32,000	$35,000
	Lowest 25%	$22,032	$20,060	$25,000	$25,375	$28,249
	Average	$27,312	$27,456	$31,302	$32,542	$36,234
Housing	Highest 25%	$15,122	$21,000	$20,400	$22,416	$26,628
	Median	$11,500	$16,100	$16,800	$18,000	$21,789
	Lowest 25%	$8,000	$12,000	$10,000	$15,000	$16,000
	Average	$11,589	$17,275	$16,336	$19,386	$22,324
Parsonage	Highest 25%	-	-	-	-	-
	Median	-	-	-	-	-
	Lowest 25%	-	-	-	-	-
	Average	-	-	-	-	-
Total Compensation	**Highest 25%**	**$39,500**	**$44,500**	**$48,000**	**$48,959**	**$57,200**
	Median	**$35,592**	**$36,000**	**$40,000**	**$42,120**	**$46,238**
	Lowest 25%	**$30,000**	**$30,000**	**$35,000**	**$37,425**	**$40,000**
	Average	**$36,262**	**$38,136**	**$41,432**	**$43,537**	**$49,359**
BENEFITS						
Health Insurance	Highest 25%	$9,600	$10,000	$10,800	$13,288	$11,137
	Median	$4,800	$5,412	$6,000	$8,412	$8,027
	Lowest 25%	$3,000	$3,106	$3,780	$5,054	$4,612
	Average	$6,481	$7,209	$7,307	$9,321	$8,166
Life Insurance	Highest 25%	-	$397	$360	$344	$276
	Median	-	$190	$145	$200	$146
	Lowest 25%	-	$71	$96	$160	$89
	Average	-	$440	$246	$358	$277
Disability Insurance	Highest 25%	-	$1,000	-	$500	$500
	Median	-	$500	-	$310	$252
	Lowest 25%	-	$350	-	$200	$200
	Average	-	$632	-	$358	$387
Retirement	Highest 25%	$3,154	$2,823	$3,334	$3,887	$4,999
	Median	$1,380	$1,500	$2,000	$2,977	$3,278
	Lowest 25%	$1,050	$1,000	$1,132	$1,525	$2,000
	Average	$2,429	$2,184	$2,290	$3,017	$3,629
Continuing Education	Highest 25%	$1,650	$1,400	$1,500	$1,750	$2,000
	Median	$1,000	$1,000	$1,000	$900	$1,300
	Lowest 25%	$350	$500	$500	$500	$775
	Average	$1,475	$1,155	$1,084	$1,120	$1,558
Total Benefits	**Highest 25%**	**$9,000**	**$10,604**	**$10,500**	**$14,884**	**$13,871**
	Median	**$5,000**	**$5,924**	**$5,258**	**$9,833**	**$9,500**
	Lowest 25%	**$3,000**	**$3,200**	**$2,723**	**$4,574**	**$5,000**
	Average	**$6,278**	**$7,635**	**$7,010**	**$10,175**	**$10,021**
TOTAL COMPENSATION PLUS BENEFITS	**Highest 25%**	**$46,000**	**$50,440**	**$54,650**	**$60,280**	**$67,800**
	Median	**$38,000**	**$42,417**	**$46,900**	**$50,211**	**$54,898**
	Lowest 25%	**$33,600**	**$36,210**	**$39,270**	**$42,437**	**$46,000**
	Average	**$41,003**	**$44,719**	**$47,597**	**$52,056**	**$58,532**
Number of Respondents		49	138	83	86	189

- Not enough response to provide meaningful data.

* For detailed description and definitions of Data Distribution (Median and Average), see Chapter 1's "Explanation of Data Distribution."

111

Table 9-2: Annual Compensation of Full-Time Youth Pastors/Directors by Worship Attendance

	Data Distribution*	WORSHIP ATTENDANCE					
		100 or less	101-300	301-500	501-750	751-1,000	Over 1,000
CHARACTERISTICS							
Average weekend worship attendance		79	221	416	617	903	2,113
Average church income		$221,687	$414,811	$811,602	$1,063,593	$1,660,708	$2,957,999
Average # of years employed		2	4	4	4	4	5
Average # of paid vacation days		18	14	15	16	16	16
% College graduate or higher		75%	80%	89%	90%	89%	93%
% Who receive auto reimbursement/allowance		73%	58%	61%	56%	53%	55%
% Ordained		58%	66%	69%	72%	87%	74%
% Supervise one or more people		33%	37%	53%	44%	69%	78%
Average % salary increase (for those who had an increase) this year		5.8%	4.0%	3.8%	3.5%	4.6%	4.4%
COMPENSATION							
Base Salary	Median	$28,990	$28,000	$31,566	$34,970	$30,250	$38,247
	Average	$27,759	$27,923	$31,629	$33,985	$31,954	$38,752
Housing	Median	-	$16,000	$17,960	$18,000	$22,117	$20,332
	Average	-	$16,612	$18,015	$19,491	$22,111	$21,674
Parsonage	Median	-	$7,000	$9,500	-	-	-
	Average	-	$10,919	$10,900	-	-	-
Total Compensation	**Median**	**$33,050**	**$37,000**	**$40,000**	**$43,000**	**$47,750**	**$48,000**
	Average	**$34,594**	**$38,543**	**$41,542**	**$46,147**	**$48,777**	**$50,935**
BENEFITS							
Health Insurance	Median	-	$5,425	$7,000	$8,322	$8,068	$8,000
	Average	-	$6,581	$9,218	$8,154	$7,797	$8,257
Life Insurance	Median	-	$200	$194	$112	$118	$170
	Average	-	$696	$420	$159	$235	$295
Disability	Median	-	$526	$450	$233	$333	$250
	Average	-	$635	$487	$300	$493	$365
Retirement	Median	-	$1,506	$2,633	$3,000	$3,285	$3,150
	Average	-	$2,100	$3,073	$3,274	$3,281	$3,453
Continuing Education	Median	-	$1,000	$1,000	$1,500	$1,000	$1,200
	Average	-	$1,086	$1,386	$1,495	$1,179	$1,434
Total Benefits	**Median**	-	**$5,400**	**$6,591**	**$8,900**	**$9,450**	**$9,580**
	Average	-	**$6,779**	**$9,431**	**$9,230**	**$9,446**	**$10,194**
TOTAL COMPENSATION PLUS BENEFITS	**Median**	**$35,300**	**$42,000**	**$46,618**	**$50,500**	**$53,700**	**$60,000**
	Average	**$39,721**	**$44,295**	**$49,553**	**$54,236**	**$56,991**	**$60,660**
Number of Respondents		12	198	113	89	46	87

- Not enough response to provide meaningful data.

* For detailed description and definitions of Data Distribution (Median and Average), see Chapter 1's "Explanation of Data Distribution."

Table 9-3: Annual Compensation of Full-Time Youth Pastors/Directors by Church Setting

	Data Distribution*	CHURCH SETTING			
		Metro-politan city	Suburb of large city	Small town or rural city	Farming area
CHARACTERISTICS					
Average weekend worship attendance		881	814	493	519
Average church income		$1,478,098	$1,339,673	$760,466	$588,444
Average # of years employed		4	4	4	5
Average # of paid vacation days		17	16	14	14
% College graduate or higher		86%	86%	86%	88%
% Who receive auto reimbursement/allowance		51%	56%	62%	100%
% Ordained		67%	72%	70%	67%
% Supervise one or more people		57%	55%	43%	33%
Average % salary increase (for those who had an increase) this year		3.6%	4.2%	4.0%	3.3%
COMPENSATION					
Base Salary	Median	$32,000	$32,246	$29,400	$29,700
	Average	$33,991	$32,475	$30,345	$30,270
Housing	Median	$20,000	$20,664	$15,122	-
	Average	$20,358	$21,498	$15,488	-
Parsonage	Median	-	-	$8,500	-
	Average	-	-	$8,489	-
Total Compensation	**Median**	**$42,250**	**$43,500**	**$40,000**	**$39,000**
	Average	**$45,405**	**$45,237**	**$40,251**	**$38,082**
BENEFITS					
Health Insurance	Median	$7,647	$9,000	$5,000	$7,651
	Average	$7,363	$8,642	$7,210	$7,168
Life Insurance	Median	$276	$180	$120	-
	Average	$414	$323	$373	-
Disability Insurance	Median	$358	$300	$230	-
	Average	$543	$386	$415	-
Retirement	Median	$3,445	$2,894	$2,000	-
	Average	$3,603	$3,329	$2,391	-
Continuing Education	Median	$1,160	$1,000	$1,000	-
	Average	$1,369	$1,272	$1,259	-
Total Benefits	**Median**	**$8,475**	**$9,540**	**$5,540**	**$8,541**
	Average	**$9,010**	**$9,748**	**$7,468**	**$8,392**
TOTAL COMPENSATION PLUS BENEFITS	**Median**	**$48,800**	**$50,593**	**$45,371**	**$44,700**
	Average	**$53,156**	**$53,670**	**$46,718**	**$45,541**
Number of Respondents		93	215	231	9

- Not enough response to provide meaningful data.

* For detailed description and definitions of Data Distribution (Median and Average), see Chapter 1's "Explanation of Data Distribution."

Table 9-4: Annual Compensation of Full-Time Youth Pastors/Directors by Region

CHARACTERISTICS	Data Distribution*	New England	Middle Atlantic	South Atlantic	E-N Central	E-S Central	W-N Central	W-S Central	Mountain	Pacific
Average weekend worship attendance		401	514	616	649	820	801	640	753	798
Average church income		$599,360	$797,201	$1,117,302	$964,979	$1,390,625	$1,104,601	$1,214,427	$1,204,575	$1,176,219
Average # of years employed		2	5	4	4	4	4	5	4	4
Average # of paid vacation days		15	16	15	15	13	15	14	18	15
% College graduate or higher		80%	90%	89%	88%	81%	91%	81%	79%	87%
% Who receive auto reimbursement/allowance		50%	63%	61%	62%	58%	61%	59%	45%	49%
% Ordained		50%	69%	68%	67%	84%	58%	76%	60%	80%
% Supervise one or more people		10%	59%	47%	44%	46%	48%	55%	55%	61%
Average % salary increase (for those who had an increase) this year		2.8%	3.8%	3.6%	4.1%	3.5%	3.9%	5.3%	4.5%	3.7%
COMPENSATION										
Base Salary	Median	$31,000	$30,900	$30,975	$29,572	$32,246	$32,000	$30,000	$30,500	$31,250
	Average	$33,367	$30,944	$33,688	$31,435	$33,239	$29,007	$30,693	$31,902	$31,954
Housing	Median	-	$17,437	$16,000	$16,000	$12,600	$18,000	$18,000	$21,600	$20,000
	Average	-	$16,698	$19,268	$17,329	$13,762	$19,458	$18,222	$22,030	$21,703
Parsonage	Median	-	-	-	-	-	-	-	-	-
	Average	-	-	-	-	-	-	-	-	-
Total Compensation	**Median**	**$35,500**	**$40,000**	**$42,800**	**$39,370**	**$40,000**	**$39,000**	**$40,537**	**$45,330**	**$43,911**
	Average	**$38,817**	**$41,384**	**$44,040**	**$42,026**	**$42,431**	**$39,347**	**$42,447**	**$44,571**	**$47,331**
BENEFITS										
Health Insurance	Median	-	$10,600	$6,900	$7,900	$6,000	$6,200	$6,000	$6,980	$8,432
	Average	-	$10,486	$7,442	$9,170	$6,255	$6,426	$7,192	$6,977	$7,538
Life Insurance	Median	-	$480	$162	$158	$85	$120	$150	$113	$216
	Average	-	$668	$329	$284	$212	$172	$542	$192	$296
Disability Insurance	Median	-	$300	$280	$300	$176	$360	$475	$350	$263
	Average	-	$329	$393	$374	$475	$437	$571	$435	$488
Retirement	Median	-	$2,023	$3,263	$2,000	$2,000	$2,528	$2,847	$2,260	$2,765
	Average	-	$2,571	$3,487	$2,372	$2,321	$2,645	$3,104	$2,739	$3,702
Continuing Education	Median	-	$700	$1,100	$1,000	$1,160	$1,000	$900	-	$1,000
	Average	-	$937	$1,457	$1,418	$1,678	$1,068	$1,183	-	$1,129
Total Benefits	**Median**	**$6,450**	**$12,466**	**$7,364**	**$6,900**	**$6,844**	**$6,100**	**$7,126**	**$8,764**	**$7,350**
	Average	**$10,214**	**$11,341**	**$8,520**	**$9,357**	**$6,884**	**$7,388**	**$8,713**	**$8,157**	**$8,150**
TOTAL COMPENSATION PLUS BENEFITS	**Median**	**$40,750**	**$47,400**	**$47,700**	**$46,468**	**$46,000**	**$45,305**	**$47,766**	**$52,227**	**$50,300**
	Average	**$46,989**	**$50,642**	**$51,445**	**$50,213**	**$47,910**	**$45,914**	**$50,192**	**$51,529**	**$54,676**
Number of Respondents		10	49	107	96	49	54	72	34	81

- Not enough response to provide meaningful data.

* For detailed description and definitions of Data Distribution (Median and Average), see Chapter 1's "Explanation of Data Distribution."

Table 9-5: Annual Compensation of Full-Time Youth Pastors/Directors by Education

	Data Distribution*	EDUCATION			
		Less than Bachelor	Bachelor	Master	Doctorate
CHARACTERISTICS					
Average weekend worship attendance		501	658	854	-
Average church income		$807,618	$1,054,041	$1,402,916	-
Average # of years employed		3	4	5	-
Average # of paid vacation days		14	15	16	-
% College graduate or higher		0%	100%	100%	-
% Who receive auto reimbursement/allowance		49%	58%	63%	-
% Ordained		68%	67%	82%	-
% Supervise one or more people		54%	46%	57%	-
Average % salary increase (for those who had an increase) this year		3.8%	3.9%	4.2%	-
COMPENSATION					
Base Salary	Median	$30,338	$30,000	$32,000	-
	Average	$29,628	$31,640	$32,633	-
Housing	Median	$16,000	$17,671	$20,000	-
	Average	$17,832	$18,002	$20,306	-
Parsonage	Median	-	$9,750	-	-
	Average	-	$11,834	-	-
Total Compensation	**Median**	**$40,000**	**$40,000**	**$45,000**	-
	Average	**$39,615**	**$42,186**	**$46,820**	-
BENEFITS					
Health Insurance	Median	$6,996	$6,600	$7,354	-
	Average	$7,420	$7,722	$8,136	-
Life Insurance	Median	-	$146	$185	-
	Average	-	$290	$302	-
Disability Insurance	Median	-	$325	$283	-
	Average	-	$403	$466	-
Retirement	Median	$1,368	$2,374	$3,000	-
	Average	$2,310	$2,724	$3,504	-
Continuing Education	Median	$1,000	$1,000	$1,100	-
	Average	$1,602	$1,163	$1,368	-
Total Benefits	**Median**	**$6,300**	**$6,500**	**$8,604**	-
	Average	**$7,286**	**$8,358**	**$9,683**	-
TOTAL COMPENSATION PLUS BENEFITS	**Median**	**$44,604**	**$46,618**	**$53,000**	-
	Average	**$45,735**	**$49,325**	**$55,571**	-
Number of Respondents		75	329	135	4

- Not enough response to provide meaningful data.

* For detailed description and definitions of Data Distribution (Median and Average), see Chapter 1's "Explanation of Data Distribution."

Table 9-6: Annual Compensation of Full-Time Youth Pastors/Directors by Years Employed

	Data Distribution*	YEARS EMPLOYED			
		Less than 6 years	6-10 years	11-15 years	Over 15 years
CHARACTERISTICS					
Average weekend worship attendance		624	959	917	-
Average church income		$1,063,942	$1,289,005	$1,282,033	-
Average # of years employed		3	7	12	-
Average # of paid vacation days		14	18	20	-
% College graduate or higher		87%	91%	95%	-
% Who receive auto reimbursement/allowance		59%	56%	75%	-
% Ordained		68%	74%	85%	-
% Supervise one or more people		49%	56%	83%	-
Average % salary increase (for those who had an increase) this year		4.2%	4.2%	4.1%	-
COMPENSATION					
Base Salary	Median	$30,000	$32,080	$33,775	-
	Average	$31,380	$32,803	$33,893	-
Housing	Median	$17,773	$20,100	$20,000	-
	Average	$18,105	$20,000	$22,690	-
Parsonage	Median	$10,000	-	-	-
	Average	$11,147	-	-	-
Total Compensation	**Median**	**$40,000**	**$43,706**	**$49,283**	**-**
	Average	**$41,945**	**$45,172**	**$52,311**	**-**
BENEFITS					
Health Insurance	Median	$7,000	$6,995	$7,188	-
	Average	$7,856	$7,552	$8,818	-
Life Insurance	Median	$145	$216	$228	-
	Average	$313	$355	$439	-
Disability Insurance	Median	$300	$231	-	-
	Average	$445	$350	-	-
Retirement	Median	$2,625	$2,300	$3,740	-
	Average	$2,865	$3,058	$4,068	-
Continuing Education	Median	$1,000	$1,000	$1,350	-
	Average	$1,214	$1,282	$1,350	-
Total Benefits	**Median**	**$6,961**	**$8,000**	**$9,128**	**-**
	Average	**$8,632**	**$8,492**	**$11,424**	**-**
TOTAL COMPENSATION PLUS BENEFITS	**Median**	**$46,618**	**$46,900**	**$63,544**	**-**
	Average	**$49,427**	**$52,720**	**$63,164**	**-**
Number of Respondents		375	90	20	4

- Not enough response to provide meaningful data.

* For detailed description and definitions of Data Distribution (Median and Average), see Chapter 1's "Explanation of Data Distribution."

Table 9-7: Annual Compensation of Full-Time Youth Pastors/Directors by Denomination

	Data Distribution*	DENOMINATION					
		Assemblies of God	Baptist	Independent/ Nondenom.	Lutheran	Methodist	Presby-terian
CHARACTERISTICS							
Average weekend worship attendance		591	626	950	526	534	511
Average church income		$998,733	$1,160,719	$1,264,289	$1,003,025	$974,069	$1,115,878
Average # of years employed		3	4	4	4	3	4
Average # of paid vacation days		14	15	16	16	14	17
% College graduate or higher		67%	90%	89%	81%	89%	89%
% Who receive auto reimbursement/allowance		54%	72%	41%	59%	41%	67%
% Ordained		94%	87%	83%	29%	-	23%
% Supervise one or more people		53%	49%	56%	32%	37%	54%
Average % salary increase (for those who had an increase) this year		5.9%	4.1%	4.5%	4.3%	4.7%	3.5%
COMPENSATION							
Base Salary	Median	$25,444	$28,370	$30,000	$33,600	$32,170	$38,300
	Average	$27,687	$29,811	$33,447	$33,331	$34,841	$39,877
Housing	Median	$18,000	$18,000	$19,500	-	-	-
	Average	$18,736	$18,545	$19,367	-	-	-
Parsonage	Median	-	-	-	-	-	-
	Average	-	-	-	-	-	-
Total Compensation	**Median**	**$40,098**	**$43,466**	**$42,937**	**$35,000**	**$33,900**	**$42,250**
	Average	**$41,603**	**$44,250**	**$45,802**	**$35,951**	**$36,486**	**$43,490**
BENEFITS							
Health Insurance	Median	$7,693	$8,340	$6,000	$7,000	$4,140	$8,000
	Average	$8,238	$8,226	$7,287	$7,094	$5,035	$8,075
Life Insurance	Median	$425	$113	$163	-	-	-
	Average	$481	$289	$394	-	-	-
Disability Insurance	Median	-	$241	$231	-	-	-
	Average	-	$398	$374	-	-	-
Retirement	Median	$1,800	$3,389	$1,995	$2,700	$1,703	$3,100
	Average	$2,469	$3,345	$2,167	$2,464	$1,983	$3,358
Continuing Education	Median	-	$1,200	$1,000	$500	$550	$800
	Average	-	$1,605	$1,315	$1,004	$941	$1,182
Total Benefits	**Median**	**$9,600**	**$8,600**	**$5,911**	**$6,800**	**$4,996**	**$4,647**
	Average	**$9,304**	**$9,468**	**$7,725**	**$7,190**	**$5,458**	**$8,581**
TOTAL COMPENSATION PLUS BENEFITS	**Median**	**$46,724**	**$51,000**	**$47,997**	**$42,075**	**$37,930**	**$45,964**
	Average	**$49,098**	**$52,925**	**$52,607**	**$42,814**	**$40,795**	**$50,110**
Number of Respondents		36	179	84	22	38	35

- Not enough response to provide meaningful data.

* For detailed description and definitions of Data Distribution (Median and Average), see Chapter 1's "Explanation of Data Distribution."

Table 9-8: Annual Compensation of Full-Time Youth Pastors/Directors by Gender

	Data Distribution*	GENDER	
		Male	Female
CHARACTERISTICS			
Average weekend worship attendance		677	728
Average church income		$1,110,786	$948,589
Average # of years employed		4	4
Average # of paid vacation days		15	15
% College graduate or higher		86%	83%
% Who receive auto reimbursement/allowance		58%	55%
% Ordained		75%	24%
% Supervise one or more people		51%	37%
Average % salary increase (for those who had an increase) this year		4.1%	3.9%
COMPENSATION			
Base Salary	Median	$30,950	$30,000
	Average	$31,871	$30,992
Housing	Median	$18,000	$16,429
	Average	$18,632	$17,979
Parsonage	Median	$9,750	-
	Average	$10,660	-
Total Compensation	**Median**	**$41,513**	**$32,160**
	Average	**$43,927**	**$34,600**
BENEFITS			
Health Insurance	Median	$7,188	$5,372
	Average	$7,938	$6,151
Life Insurance	Median	$162	-
	Average	$348	-
Disability Insurance	Median	$300	-
	Average	$435	-
Retirement	Median	$2,500	$3,303
	Average	$2,935	$3,097
Continuing Education	Median	$1,000	$500
	Average	$1,348	$846
Total Benefits	**Median**	**$7,367**	**$5,924**
	Average	**$8,835**	**$6,479**
TOTAL COMPENSATION PLUS BENEFITS	**Median**	**$48,784**	**$39,000**
	Average	**$51,616**	**$40,021**
Number of Respondents		501	49

- Not enough response to provide meaningful data.

* For detailed description and definitions of Data Distribution (Median and Average), see Chapter 1's "Explanation of Data Distribution."

Table 9-9: Annual Compensation of Part-Time Youth Pastors/Directors by Church Income

	Data Distribution*	CHURCH INCOME				
		$250K & Under	$251-$500K	$501-$750K	$751K-$1M	Over 1 Million
CHARACTERISTICS						
Average weekend worship attendance		122	216	464	476	889
Average church income		$166,934	$343,827	$634,690	$903,257	$1,764,913
Average # of years employed		2	3	3	3	2
Average # of paid vacation days		11	12	12	10	12
% College graduate or higher		60%	67%	79%	50%	77%
% Who receive auto reimbursement/allowance		28%	45%	48%	10%	41%
% Ordained		26%	35%	36%	30%	32%
% Supervise one or more people		28%	29%	29%	35%	35%
Average % salary increase (for those who had an increase) this year		5.9%	5.4%	2.9%	3.6%	3.4%
HOURLY RATE						
Base Rate	Average	$13	$17	$18	-	$16
COMPENSATION						
Base Salary	Median	$9,000	$15,000	$16,732	$14,400	$13,490
	Average	$9,983	$14,149	$17,166	$18,056	$14,874
Housing	Median	$6,500	$9,000	-	-	-
	Average	$8,072	$8,798	-	-	-
Parsonage	Median	-	-	-	-	-
	Average	-	-	-	-	-
Total Compensation	**Median**	**$9,800**	**$15,000**	**$17,418**	**$17,200**	**$15,936**
	Average	**$11,054**	**$14,999**	**$18,421**	**$18,789**	**$16,523**
BENEFITS						
Health Insurance	Median	-	$4,000	-	-	-
	Average	-	$4,708	-	-	-
Life Insurance	Median	-	-	-	-	-
	Average	-	-	-	-	-
Disability Insurance	Median	-	-	-	-	-
	Average	-	-	-	-	-
Retirement	Median	-	-	-	-	-
	Average	-	-	-	-	-
Continuing Education	Median	-	$500	-	-	-
	Average	-	$606	-	-	-
Total Benefits	**Median**	**$1,200**	**$1,000**	-	-	-
	Average	**$1,957**	**$2,531**	-	-	-
TOTAL COMPENSATION	**Median**	**$9,800**	**$15,000**	**$18,500**	**$17,200**	**$15,936**
PLUS BENEFITS	**Average**	**$11,313**	**$15,664**	**$18,705**	**$19,037**	**$17,132**
Number of Respondents		68	80	34	20	23

- Not enough response to provide meaningful data.

* For detailed description and definitions of Data Distribution (Median and Average), see Chapter 1's "Explanation of Data Distribution."

Table 9-10: Annual Compensation of Part-Time Youth Pastors/Directors by Worship Attendance

	Data Distribution*	WORSHIP ATTENDANCE					
		100 or less	101-300	301-500	501-750	751-1,000	Over 1,000
CHARACTERISTICS							
Average weekend worship attendance		80	189	397	641	-	1,672
Average church income		$156,434	$337,236	$719,555	$1,143,677	-	$2,230,667
Average # of years employed		2	3	3	3	-	2
Average # of paid vacation days		10	11	13	10	-	12
% College graduate or higher		59%	68%	68%	56%	-	67%
% Who receive auto reimbursement/allowance		29%	41%	34%	26%	-	33%
% Ordained		30%	33%	35%	26%	-	33%
% Supervise one or more people		24%	30%	39%	35%	-	44%
Average % salary increase (for those who had an increase) this year		5.6%	5.3%	4.3%	3.6%	-	4.0%
HOURLY RATE							
Base Rate	Average	$15	$16	$16	$22	-	-
COMPENSATION							
Base Salary	Median	$9,000	$12,000	$15,150	$15,468	-	$14,460
	Average	$10,440	$13,251	$15,626	$17,640	-	$14,802
Housing	Median	-	$9,000	-	-	-	-
	Average	-	$9,783	-	-	-	-
Parsonage	Median	-	-	-	-	-	-
	Average	-	-	-	-	-	-
Total Compensation	**Median**	**$8,500**	**$13,800**	**$16,566**	**$17,568**	**-**	**$15,000**
	Average	**$10,869**	**$14,412**	**$16,809**	**$18,705**	**-**	**$15,836**
BENEFITS							
Health Insurance	Median	-	-	-	-	-	-
	Average	-	-	-	-	-	-
Life Insurance	Median	-	-	-	-	-	-
	Average	-	-	-	-	-	-
Disability	Median	-	-	-	-	-	-
	Average	-	-	-	-	-	-
Retirement	Median	-	-	-	-	-	-
	Average	-	-	-	-	-	-
Continuing Education	Median	-	$500	-	-	-	-
	Average	-	$492	-	-	-	-
Total Benefits	**Median**	**-**	**$1,000**	**$1,079**	**-**	**-**	**-**
	Average	**-**	**$1,791**	**$2,652**	**-**	**-**	**-**
TOTAL COMPENSATION PLUS BENEFITS	**Median**	**$8,500**	**$13,800**	**$16,816**	**$17,568**	**-**	**$15,000**
	Average	**$11,251**	**$14,759**	**$17,507**	**$19,011**	**-**	**$16,842**
Number of Respondents		34	129	38	20	3	9

- Not enough response to provide meaningful data.

* For detailed description and definitions of Data Distribution (Median and Average), see Chapter 1's "Explanation of Data Distribution."

Table 9-11: Annual Compensation of Part-Time Youth Pastors/Directors by Church Setting

	Data Distribution*	CHURCH SETTING			
		Metro-politan city	Suburb of large city	Small town or rural city	Farming area
CHARACTERISTICS					
Average weekend worship attendance		385	366	257	210
Average church income		$667,530	$676,485	$385,147	$300,216
Average # of years employed		2	3	3	3
Average # of paid vacation days		11	12	10	13
% College graduate or higher		76%	80%	54%	60%
% Who receive auto reimbursement/allowance		24%	46%	35%	31%
% Ordained		35%	33%	29%	38%
% Supervise one or more people		44%	25%	33%	25%
Average % salary increase (for those who had an increase) this year		3.4%	3.9%	5.6%	6.4%
HOURLY RATE					
Base Rate	Average	$15	$15	$18	$15
COMPENSATION					
Base Salary	Median	$14,100	$10,400	$13,368	$10,000
	Average	$14,484	$13,349	$14,336	$10,756
Housing	Median	-	$9,600	$9,300	-
	Average	-	$10,340	$8,961	-
Parsonage	Median	-	-	-	-
	Average	-	-	-	-
Total Compensation	**Median**	**$14,400**	**$15,000**	**$13,188**	**$10,000**
	Average	**$15,220**	**$15,105**	**$14,910**	**$11,229**
BENEFITS					
Health Insurance	Median	-	-	-	-
	Average	-	-	-	-
Life Insurance	Median	-	-	-	-
	Average	-	-	-	-
Disability Insurance	Median	-	-	-	-
	Average	-	-	-	-
Retirement	Median	-	-	$963	-
	Average	-	-	$1,327	-
Continuing Education	Median	-	$500	$500	-
	Average	-	$594	$525	-
Total Benefits	**Median**	**-**	**$750**	**$1,000**	**-**
	Average	**-**	**$2,259**	**$2,152**	**-**
TOTAL COMPENSATION PLUS BENEFITS	**Median**	**$14,400**	**$15,000**	**$13,466**	**$10,750**
	Average	**$15,552**	**$15,516**	**$15,359**	**$11,822**
Number of Respondents		39	77	96	16

- Not enough response to provide meaningful data.

* For detailed description and definitions of Data Distribution (Median and Average), see Chapter 1's "Explanation of Data Distribution."

121

Table 9-12: Annual Compensation of Part-Time Youth Pastors/Directors by Region

	Data Distribution*	New England	Middle Atlantic	South Atlantic	E-N Central	E-S Central	W-N Central	W-S Central	Mountain	Pacific
CHARACTERISTICS										
Average weekend worship attendance		152	222	264	381	297	269	406	-	371
Average church income		$322,455	$386,494	$502,931	$526,860	$575,914	$429,645	$800,066	-	$518,859
Average # of years employed		2	4	2	3	4	3	3	-	2
Average # of paid vacation days		10	14	10	12	11	13	8	-	13
% College graduate or higher		73%	88%	57%	72%	69%	71%	81%	-	51%
% Who receive auto reimbursement/allowance		45%	71%	32%	36%	44%	46%	30%	-	23%
% Ordained		36%	18%	46%	24%	33%	30%	34%	-	26%
% Supervise one or more people		10%	31%	42%	31%	13%	29%	18%	-	45%
Average % salary increase (for those who had an increase) this year		-	5.9%	3.6%	7.1%	4.6%	3.6%	6.8%	-	3.7%
HOURLY RATE										
Base Rate	Average	$16	$16	$15	$16	-	$17	$21	-	$15
COMPENSATION										
Base Salary	Median	$10,300	$14,400	$13,000	$14,000	$13,564	$17,000	$12,490	-	$9,500
	Average	$10,784	$14,396	$14,483	$14,159	$14,243	$16,764	$14,581	-	$10,793
Housing	Median	-	-	$9,600	-	-	-	-	-	-
	Average	-	-	$9,487	-	-	-	-	-	-
Parsonage	Median	-	-	-	-	-	-	-	-	-
	Average	-	-	-	-	-	-	-	-	-
Total Compensation	**Median**	$12,000	$16,000	$13,368	$14,000	$13,282	$17,750	$15,000	-	$10,000
	Average	$11,929	$16,984	$15,378	$14,486	$14,103	$16,915	$15,899	-	$12,299
BENEFITS										
Health Insurance	Median	-	-	-	-	-	-	-	-	-
	Average	-	-	-	-	-	-	-	-	-
Life Insurance	Median	-	-	-	-	-	-	-	-	-
	Average	-	-	-	-	-	-	-	-	-
Disability Insurance	Median	-	-	-	-	-	-	-	-	-
	Average	-	-	-	-	-	-	-	-	-
Retirement	Median	-	-	-	-	-	-	-	-	-
	Average	152	-	-	-	297	-	406	-	-
Continuing Education	Median	-	-	-	-	-	-	-	-	-
	Average	-	-	-	-	-	-	-	-	-
Total Benefits	**Median**	-	-	-	-	-	$926	-	-	$1,764
	Average	-	-	-	-	-	$1,349	-	-	$2,114
TOTAL COMPENSATION PLUS BENEFITS	**Median**	$12,000	$16,910	$13,368	$15,000	$13,282	$18,150	$15,000	-	$10,500
	Average	$12,535	$17,278	$15,447	$15,576	$15,227	$17,534	$15,978	-	$12,693
Number of Respondents		11	17	55	29	16	24	33	5	43

- Not enough response to provide meaningful data.

* For detailed description and definitions of Data Distribution (Median and Average), see Chapter 1's "Explanation of Data Distribution."

Table 9-13: Annual Compensation of Part-Time Youth Pastors/Directors by Education

	Data Distribution*	EDUCATION			
		Less than Bachelor	Bachelor	Master	Doctorate
CHARACTERISTICS					
Average weekend worship attendance		320	301	324	-
Average church income		$517,963	$519,586	$546,101	-
Average # of years employed		2	3	3	-
Average # of paid vacation days		10	12	13	-
% College graduate or higher		0%	100%	100%	-
% Who receive auto reimbursement/allowance		23%	48%	29%	-
% Ordained		20%	39%	35%	-
% Supervise one or more people		33%	27%	46%	-
Average % salary increase (for those who had an increase) this year		6.1%	4.6%	3.8%	-
HOURLY RATE					
Base Rate	Average	$15	$16	$19	-
COMPENSATION					
Base Salary	Median	$10,400	$15,000	$16,350	-
	Average	$11,933	$14,258	$16,955	-
Housing	Median	-	$9,000	-	-
	Average	-	$9,446	-	-
Parsonage	Median	-	$5,000	-	-
	Average	-	$6,239	-	-
Total Compensation	**Median**	**$11,850**	**$15,936**	**$16,350**	**-**
	Average	**$12,483**	**$15,808**	**$17,133**	**-**
BENEFITS					
Health Insurance	Median	-	$4,900	-	-
	Average	-	$5,389	-	-
Life Insurance	Median	-	-	-	-
	Average	-	-	-	-
Disability Insurance	Median	-	-	-	-
	Average	-	-	-	-
Retirement	Median	-	-	-	-
	Average	-	-	-	-
Continuing Education	Median	$500	$500	-	-
	Average	$609	$630	-	-
Total Benefits	**Median**	**$963**	**$2,000**	**$1,100**	**-**
	Average	**$1,053**	**$2,895**	**$1,540**	**-**
TOTAL COMPENSATION PLUS BENEFITS	**Median**	**$11,850**	**$16,084**	**$16,450**	**-**
	Average	**$12,672**	**$16,406**	**$17,573**	**-**
Number of Respondents		78	121	28	1

- Not enough response to provide meaningful data.

* For detailed description and definitions of Data Distribution (Median and Average), see Chapter 1's "Explanation of Data Distribution."

Table 9-14: Annual Compensation of Part-Time Youth Pastors/Directors by Years Employed

	Data Distribution*	YEARS EMPLOYED			
		Less than 6 years	6-10 years	11-15 years	Over 15 years
CHARACTERISTICS					
Average weekend worship attendance		300	248	-	-
Average church income		$515,888	$407,580	-	-
Average # of years employed		2	7	-	-
Average # of paid vacation days		11	16	-	-
% College graduate or higher		68%	72%	-	-
% Who receive auto reimbursement/allowance		35%	61%	-	-
% Ordained		36%	28%	-	-
% Supervise one or more people		33%	38%	-	-
Average % salary increase (for those who had an increase) this year		5.2%	4.8%	-	-
HOURLY RATE					
Base Rate	Average	$16	$21	-	-
COMPENSATION					
Base Salary	Median	$12,000	$16,132	-	-
	Average	$13,048	$16,811	-	-
Housing	Median	$8,460	-	-	-
	Average	$9,108	-	-	-
Parsonage	Median	$7,200	-	-	-
	Average	$7,306	-	-	-
Total Compensation	**Median**	**$12,801**	**$18,075**	**-**	**-**
	Average	**$14,126**	**$18,972**	**-**	**-**
BENEFITS					
Health Insurance	Median	$4,000	-	-	-
	Average	$4,364	-	-	-
Life Insurance	Median	-	-	-	-
	Average	-	-	-	-
Disability Insurance	Median	-	-	-	-
	Average	-	-	-	-
Retirement	Median	-	-	-	-
	Average	-	-	-	-
Continuing Education	Median	$500	-	-	-
	Average	$587	-	-	-
Total Benefits	**Median**	**$1,000**	**-**	**-**	**-**
	Average	**$1,853**	**-**	**-**	**-**
TOTAL COMPENSATION PLUS BENEFITS	**Median**	**$12,801**	**$19,963**	**-**	**-**
	Average	**$14,510**	**$20,410**	**-**	**-**
Number of Respondents		174	18	3	1

- Not enough response to provide meaningful data.

* For detailed description and definitions of Data Distribution (Median and Average), see Chapter 1's "Explanation of Data Distribution."

Table 9-15: Annual Compensation of Part-Time Youth Pastors/Directors by Denomination

	Data Distribution*	DENOMINATION					
		Assemblies of God	Baptist	Independent/ Nondenom.	Lutheran	Methodist	Presby-terian
CHARACTERISTICS							
Average weekend worship attendance		266	290	357	288	322	245
Average church income		$432,100	$500,247	$557,501	$548,844	$553,933	$566,650
Average # of years employed		2	3	3	3	4	3
Average # of paid vacation days		7	11	11	20	11	14
% College graduate or higher		45%	71%	67%	64%	73%	63%
% Who receive auto reimbursement/allowance		8%	41%	32%	18%	50%	56%
% Ordained		33%	40%	41%	20%	14%	0%
% Supervise one or more people		25%	26%	47%	18%	13%	26%
Average % salary increase (for those who had an increase) this year		-	5.3%	6.8%	3.2%	3.4%	3.9%
HOURLY RATE							
Base Rate	Average	-	$16	$14	$16	$19	$16
COMPENSATION							
Base Salary	Median	$19,094	$13,000	$10,950	$14,400	$16,100	$15,000
	Average	$15,922	$13,377	$11,508	$14,949	$16,246	$14,632
Housing	Median	-	$12,000	$9,000	-	-	-
	Average	-	$12,523	$9,598	-	-	-
Parsonage	Median	-	-	-	-	-	-
	Average	-	-	-	-	-	-
Total Compensation	**Median**	**$14,747**	**$15,000**	**$12,000**	**$14,400**	**$16,100**	**$15,000**
	Average	**$15,745**	**$14,769**	**$13,966**	**$14,949**	**$17,093**	**$14,737**
BENEFITS							
Health Insurance	Median	-	-	-	-	-	-
	Average	-	-	-	-	-	-
Life Insurance	Median	-	-	-	-	-	-
	Average	-	-	-	-	-	-
Disability Insurance	Median	-	-	-	-	-	-
	Average	-	-	-	-	-	-
Retirement	Median	-	-	-	-	-	-
	Average	-	-	-	-	-	-
Continuing Education	Median	-	$600	-	-	-	-
	Average	-	$732	-	-	-	-
Total Benefits	**Median**	-	**$1,000**	-	-	-	-
	Average	-	**$2,198**	-	-	-	-
TOTAL COMPENSATION PLUS BENEFITS	**Median**	**$16,250**	**$15,000**	**$12,000**	**$14,400**	**$16,600**	**$15,000**
	Average	**$16,003**	**$15,172**	**$14,282**	**$15,403**	**$17,214**	**$15,571**
Number of Respondents		12	71	37	11	15	19

- Not enough response to provide meaningful data.

* For detailed description and definitions of Data Distribution (Median and Average), see Chapter 1's "Explanation of Data Distribution."

Table 9-16: Annual Compensation of Part-Time Youth Pastors/Directors by Gender

	Data Distribution*	GENDER	
		Male	Female
CHARACTERISTICS			
Average weekend worship attendance		312	317
Average church income		$535,877	$515,477
Average # of years employed		3	3
Average # of paid vacation days		11	13
% College graduate or higher		69%	61%
% Who receive auto reimbursement/allowance		35%	39%
% Ordained		39%	16%
% Supervise one or more people		38%	18%
Average % salary increase (for those who had an increase) this year		5.9%	3.2%
HOURLY RATE			
Base Rate	Average	$16	$17
COMPENSATION			
Base Salary	Median	$12,000	$15,450
	Average	$13,096	$15,407
Housing	Median	$9,300	-
	Average	$9,845	-
Parsonage	Median	$6,100	-
	Average	$7,415	-
Total Compensation	**Median**	**$13,004**	**$15,500**
	Average	**$14,448**	**$15,588**
BENEFITS			
Health Insurance	Median	$4,000	-
	Average	$4,590	-
Life Insurance	Median	-	-
	Average	-	-
Disability Insurance	Median	-	-
	Average	-	-
Retirement	Median	$963	-
	Average	$1,307	-
Continuing Education	Median	$500	$500
	Average	$635	$492
Total Benefits	**Median**	**$1,200**	**$500**
	Average	**$2,533**	**$1,225**
TOTAL COMPENSATION PLUS BENEFITS	**Median**	**$13,282**	**$15,500**
	Average	**$14,948**	**$15,862**
Number of Respondents		162	67

- Not enough response to provide meaningful data.

* For detailed description and definitions of Data Distribution (Median and Average), see Chapter 1's "Explanation of Data Distribution."

10

CHILDREN'S/ PRESCHOOL PASTORS/DIRECTORS

Employment Profile

Children's/Preschool Pastors/Directors are paid pastors and directors for children's ministries from nursery through elementary school-age. (They are church staff, not school staff.) This category may include such positions as Early Childhood Pastor, Elementary School Pastor, Preschool Pastor/Director, Childcare Director, Daycare Director, etc.

Of the children's ministry leaders who responded to our survey, just over half work full-time. Nearly all are employed by the church rather than self-employed. More than seven in ten full-time children's ministry leaders are female and have at least a Bachelor's degree. Women hold more than 90% of the part-time positions.

The following chart summarizes a demographic profile of this sample:

	Full-Time	Part-Time
Number of respondents	264	224
Ordained	47%	10%
Average years employed	6	4
Male	29%	9%
Female	71%	91%
Self-employed (receives 1099)	3%	4%
Church employee (receives W-2)	97%	96%
High school diploma	15%	22%
Associate Degree	8%	15%
Bachelor's Degree	50%	51%
Master's Degree	24%	11%
Doctoral Degree	2%	1%

Total Compensation plus Benefits Package Analysis

The analyses on the next page are based on the data in the tables that you will find in the remainder of the chapter. The tables show compensation plus benefits data for children's ministry leaders who serve full-time and are presented according to church income, church attendance, church setting, region, education, years employed, denomination, and gender.

There is also a table showing compensation plus benefit data for children's ministry leaders who serve part-time presented by church income. In this way, the compensation plus benefits can be analyzed and compared from a variety of useful perspectives.

The total compensation plus benefits amount includes the base salary, housing and/or parsonage amount, health, life, and disability insurance payments, retirement contribution, and educational funds.

Almost none of the paid children's ministry leaders live in church-provided parsonages, however, about four in ten full-timers receive housing allowances. The percentage of those receiving benefits such as health insurance, retirement, and continuing education is comparable to other pastors, not including Solo or Senior Pastors, for both full-time and part-time positions.

Compensation Plus Benefits	Full-Time	Part-Time
Base Salary	100%	97%
Housing	38%	5%
Parsonage	1%	0%
Health Insurance	57%	5%
Life Insurance	30%	3%
Disability Insurance	24%	5%
Retirement	53%	8%
Continuing Education	23%	11%
Received Salary Increase	58%	40%
Received Paid Vacation	96%	46%
Received Auto Reimbursement/ Allowance	45%	25%

KEY POINTS

✳ **Six out of ten full-time Children's/Preschool Pastors/Directors in this sample serve in larger churches with an income of over $1,000,000.**

✳ **For the most part, as church income, worship attendance, the minister's education level, and years employed increase, average compensation and benefits for children's ministry leaders also increase.**

✳ **About four out of ten full-time Children's/Preschool Pastors/Directors in this sample serve in churches set in a suburb of a large city or in a small town or rural city. The 20% of children's ministry leaders serving in metropolitan cities have the highest compensation and benefits packages compared to those in other settings. Almost no churches in farming areas reported having paid children's ministry leaders.**

✳ **The majority of full-time Children's/Preschool Pastors/Directors in this sample are female. However, the 76 reported full-time males in these positions receive higher compensation and benefits packages than the females (about 28% higher).**

**Compensation & Benefits: National Averages for
Full-Time Children's Preschool Pastors/Directors***

2000	
2001	
2002	
2003	
2004	
2005	
2006	$46,361
2007	$52,434
2008	$53,033
2009	$50,782**

No historical data available before 2006.

**The above trend is made available for your reference only. In addition to looking at this overall data, please refer to the detailed tables using your church's income, attendance, setting, region, and denomination as well as the person's education, gender, and years employed for guidance in compensating this position.*

Table 10-1: Annual Compensation of Full-Time Children's/Preschool Pastors/Directors by Church Income

CHARACTERISTICS	Data Distribution*	$250K & Under	$251-$500K	$501-$750K	$751K-$1M	Over 1 Million
Average weekend worship attendance	-		286	402	565	1,393
Average church income	-		$428,924	$637,698	$905,888	$2,451,542
Average # of years employed	-		5	6	5	6
Average # of paid vacation days	-		16	15	16	16
% College graduate or higher	-		68%	82%	66%	80%
% Who receive auto reimbursement/allowance	-		64%	44%	43%	47%
% Ordained	-		50%	33%	61%	47%
% Supervise one or more people	-		55%	63%	63%	83%
Average % salary increase (for those who had an increase) this year	-		6%	4%	4%	5%
COMPENSATION						
Base Salary	Highest 25%	-	$32,500	$39,500	$36,000	$48,100
	Median	-	$29,610	$31,938	$31,200	$37,500
	Lowest 25%	-	$21,620	$28,620	$24,172	$29,400
	Average	-	$28,721	$32,698	$30,611	$38,873
Housing	Highest 25%	-	$20,200	$23,000	$28,500	$27,000
	Median	-	$16,000	$16,139	$18,000	$24,000
	Lowest 25%	-	$12,060	$11,810	$15,350	$18,000
	Average	-	$16,907	$18,032	$22,148	$22,877
Parsonage	Highest 25%	-	-	-	-	-
	Median	-	-	-	-	-
	Lowest 25%	-	-	-	-	-
	Average	-	-	-	-	-
Total Compensation	**Highest 25%**	-	**$38,500**	**$44,114**	**$48,000**	**$53,416**
	Median	-	**$34,300**	**$36,740**	**$37,822**	**$46,000**
	Lowest 25%	-	**$30,329**	**$31,871**	**$34,086**	**$38,000**
	Average	-	**$35,638**	**$37,850**	**$41,390**	**$47,846**
BENEFITS						
Health Insurance	Highest 25%	-	$8,822	$6,534	$10,000	$10,638
	Median	-	$6,114	$4,800	$5,500	$7,093
	Lowest 25%	-	$3,900	$3,251	$3,000	$4,537
	Average	-	$6,613	$6,073	$6,408	$8,078
Life Insurance	Highest 25%	-	-	-	-	$500
	Median	-	-	-	-	$159
	Lowest 25%	-	-	-	-	$113
	Average	-	-	-	-	$352
Disability Insurance	Highest 25%	-	-	-	-	$575
	Median	-	-	-	-	$360
	Lowest 25%	-	-	-	-	$210
	Average	-	-	-	-	$640
Retirement	Highest 25%	-	-	$2,550	$2,998	$4,694
	Median	-	-	$2,000	$2,077	$3,070
	Lowest 25%	-	-	$1,500	$1,200	$1,743
	Average	-	-	$2,324	$2,647	$3,385
Continuing Education	Highest 25%	-	-	-	-	$2,000
	Median	-	-	-	-	$1,500
	Lowest 25%	-	-	-	-	$1,000
	Average	-	-	-	-	$1,526
Total Benefits	**Highest 25%**	-	**$9,010**	**$8,502**	**$9,950**	**$13,625**
	Median	-	**$6,000**	**$6,810**	**$5,625**	**$8,000**
	Lowest 25%	-	**$3,645**	**$3,500**	**$2,955**	**$3,900**
	Average	-	**$6,468**	**$6,861**	**$6,816**	**$9,098**
TOTAL COMPENSATION PLUS BENEFITS	**Highest 25%**	-	**$43,425**	**$50,026**	**$53,794**	**$65,290**
	Median	-	**$38,100**	**$43,180**	**$43,175**	**$54,251**
	Lowest 25%	-	**$35,250**	**$32,700**	**$36,450**	**$42,109**
	Average	-	**$40,342**	**$42,505**	**$47,276**	**$55,448**
Number of Respondents		9	22	28	44	152

- Not enough response to provide meaningful data.

* For detailed description and definitions of Data Distribution (Median and Average), see Chapter 1's "Explanation of Data Distribution."

131

Table 10-2: Annual Compensation of Full-Time Children's/Preschool Pastors/Directors by Worship Attendance

	Data Distribution*	WORSHIP ATTENDANCE					
		100 or less	101-300	301-500	501-750	751-1,000	Over 1,000
CHARACTERISTICS							
Average weekend worship attendance	-		243	423	618	886	2,312
Average church income	-		$514,791	$889,167	$1,126,396	$1,610,508	$3,490,042
Average # of years employed	-		6	6	4	6	6
Average # of paid vacation days	-		14	17	15	16	16
% College graduate or higher	-		73%	82%	69%	78%	78%
% Who receive auto reimbursement/allowance	-		50%	54%	40%	54%	36%
% Ordained	-		52%	38%	54%	41%	51%
% Supervise one or more people	-		47%	65%	75%	82%	89%
Average % salary increase (for those who had an increase) this year	-		5.3%	4.3%	3.5%	5.2%	5.2%
COMPENSATION							
Base Salary	Median	-	$30,000	$35,000	$33,460	$33,000	$43,000
	Average	-	$27,803	$34,181	$33,768	$34,665	$42,312
Housing	Median	-	$12,860	$25,000	$18,000	$20,000	$25,000
	Average	-	$16,224	$24,848	$22,406	$20,111	$23,193
Parsonage	Median	-	-	-	-	-	-
	Average	-	-	-	-	-	-
Total Compensation	**Median**	-	**$35,000**	**$40,000**	**$43,424**	**$43,000**	**$50,500**
	Average	-	**$34,686**	**$41,946**	**$44,611**	**$42,583**	**$51,153**
BENEFITS							
Health Insurance	Median	-	$6,000	$5,220	$4,719	$6,986	$8,400
	Average	-	$6,747	$6,814	$5,777	$7,760	$8,665
Life Insurance	Median	-	-	$193	$150	$120	$183
	Average	-	-	$364	$271	$393	$372
Disability	Median	-	-	-	$391	$509	$336
	Average	-	-	-	$386	$664	$714
Retirement	Median	-	$2,157	$3,000	$2,436	$2,700	$3,000
	Average	-	$2,180	$3,250	$2,756	$3,440	$3,258
Continuing Education	Median	-	-	$1,000	$1,350	$1,350	$1,500
	Average	-	-	$1,173	$1,470	$1,729	$1,575
Total Benefits	**Median**	-	**$6,000**	**$6,500**	**$4,256**	**$8,834**	**$8,900**
	Average	-	**$6,594**	**$7,579**	**$5,987**	**$9,068**	**$9,817**
TOTAL COMPENSATION PLUS BENEFITS	**Median**	-	**$37,000**	**$44,164**	**$46,164**	**$51,500**	**$58,968**
	Average	-	**$38,882**	**$47,554**	**$49,743**	**$49,873**	**$59,792**
Number of Respondents		5	33	50	49	51	75

- Not enough response to provide meaningful data.

* For detailed description and definitions of Data Distribution (Median and Average), see Chapter 1's "Explanation of Data Distribution."

Table 10-3: Annual Compensation of Full-Time Children's/Preschool Pastors/Directors by Church Setting

	Data Distribution*	CHURCH SETTING			
		Metro-politan city	Suburb of large city	Small town or rural city	Farming area
CHARACTERISTICS					
Average weekend worship attendance		1,115	1,343	724	-
Average church income		$2,115,893	$2,073,152	$1,193,674	-
Average # of years employed		5	6	5	-
Average # of paid vacation days		17	16	15	-
% College graduate or higher		83%	78%	71%	-
% Who receive auto reimbursement/allowance		29%	41%	57%	-
% Ordained		55%	49%	43%	-
% Supervise one or more people		78%	77%	70%	-
Average % salary increase (for those who had an increase) this year		4.2%	5.6%	4.1%	-
COMPENSATION					
Base Salary	Median	$37,342	$35,000	$30,330	-
	Average	$40,667	$36,540	$32,707	-
Housing	Median	$18,549	$23,911	$18,000	-
	Average	$19,626	$24,262	$19,872	-
Parsonage	Median	-	-	-	-
	Average	-	-	-	-
Total Compensation	**Median**	**$45,000**	**$44,000**	**$40,159**	**-**
	Average	**$48,246**	**$45,857**	**$40,818**	**-**
BENEFITS					
Health Insurance	Median	$8,400	$6,066	$6,000	-
	Average	$8,124	$7,683	$6,661	-
Life Insurance	Median	$167	$183	$150	-
	Average	$391	$351	$339	-
Disability Insurance	Median	$321	$418	$427	-
	Average	$357	$661	$1,208	-
Retirement	Median	$3,000	$2,500	$2,475	-
	Average	$3,193	$3,133	$3,023	-
Continuing Education	Median	$1,250	$1,150	$1,500	-
	Average	$1,243	$1,270	$1,681	-
Total Benefits	**Median**	**$5,935**	**$7,778**	**$6,500**	**-**
	Average	**$8,447**	**$8,402**	**$7,445**	**-**
TOTAL COMPENSATION PLUS BENEFITS	**Median**	**$52,290**	**$48,700**	**$44,671**	**-**
	Average	**$55,556**	**$52,518**	**$46,668**	**-**
Number of Respondents		52	111	98	2

- Not enough response to provide meaningful data.

* For detailed description and definitions of Data Distribution (Median and Average), see Chapter 1's "Explanation of Data Distribution."

Table 10-4: Annual Compensation of Full-Time Children's/Preschool Pastors/Directors by Region

	Data Distribution*	REGION								
		New England	Middle Atlantic	South Atlantic	E-N Central	E-S Central	W-N Central	W-S Central	Mountain	Pacific
CHARACTERISTICS										
Average weekend worship attendance	-	889	916	1,285	951	1,155	1,143	1,007	1,027
Average church income	-	$1,438,743	$1,575,236	$2,042,353	$1,828,523	$1,481,621	$2,318,729	$1,315,209	$1,384,479
Average # of years employed	-	6	6	6	4	4	5	5	6
Average # of paid vacation days	-	16	15	17	14	16	15	15	19
% College graduate or higher	-	69%	78%	79%	81%	77%	78%	75%	68%
% Who receive auto reimbursement/allowance	-	54%	48%	60%	55%	32%	44%	30%	30%
% Ordained	-	69%	36%	69%	38%	44%	51%	40%	42%
% Supervise one or more people	-	77%	70%	79%	60%	65%	84%	80%	72%
Average % salary increase (for those who had an increase) this year	-	5.0%	3.2%	4.3%	3.9%	5.6%	4.6%	5.7%	6.9%
COMPENSATION										
Base Salary	Median	-	$27,270	$36,382	$30,250	$36,121	$31,603	$35,000	$33,500	$35,000
	Average	-	$31,243	$35,872	$33,556	$37,305	$34,725	$37,823	$34,909	$37,109
Housing	Median	-	-	$20,000	$20,100	-	$23,860	$17,600	$17,370	$25,842
	Average	-	-	$21,555	$21,536	-	$22,233	$19,713	$20,187	$27,916
Parsonage	Median	-	-	-	-	-	-	-	-	-
	Average	-	-	-	-	-	-	-	-	-
Total Compensation	**Median**	-	**$45,000**	**$40,475**	**$44,983**	**$40,000**	**$38,500**	**$45,100**	**$43,000**	**$43,977**
	Average	-	**$43,255**	**$42,480**	**$44,837**	**$41,557**	**$44,131**	**$46,584**	**$42,984**	**$45,966**
BENEFITS										
Health Insurance	Median	-	$8,066	$5,452	$9,665	$7,300	$5,352	$6,000	$6,118	$6,000
	Average	-	$8,314	$6,031	$8,713	$7,732	$7,001	$8,137	$6,894	$6,556
Life Insurance	Median	-	-	$123	$158	-	$98	$183	$138	-
	Average	-	-	$315	$275	-	$116	$417	$280	-
Disability Insurance	Median	-	-	$366	$500	-	-	$409	-	-
	Average	-	-	$437	$1,380	-	-	$431	-	-
Retirement	Median	-	-	$3,253	$2,570	$1,736	$2,600	$3,500	$1,725	$2,500
	Average	-	-	$3,548	$2,741	$2,173	$3,325	$3,827	$2,278	$2,958
Continuing Education	Median	-	-	$1,000	$1,000	-	$1,700	$1,500	-	-
	Average	-	-	$1,175	$1,287	-	$1,863	$1,370	-	-
Total Benefits	**Median**	-	**$9,532**	**$5,400**	**$9,167**	**$7,486**	**$5,199**	**$8,513**	**$3,200**	**$4,650**
	Average	-	**$10,299**	**$6,711**	**$9,084**	**$8,014**	**$7,518**	**$10,530**	**$6,297**	**$6,479**
TOTAL COMPENSATION PLUS BENEFITS	**Median**	-	**$53,300**	**$44,321**	**$53,291**	**$42,243**	**$44,100**	**$52,415**	**$45,714**	**$46,628**
	Average	-	**$50,385**	**$47,727**	**$53,056**	**$47,021**	**$50,493**	**$54,540**	**$48,021**	**$51,423**
Number of Respondents		3	13	55	42	22	26	45	20	38

- Not enough response to provide meaningful data.

* For detailed description and definitions of Data Distribution (Median and Average), see Chapter 1's "Explanation of Data Distribution."

Table 10-5: Annual Compensation of Full-Time Children's/Preschool Pastors/Directors by Education

	Data Distribution*	EDUCATION			
		Less than Bachelor	Bachelor	Master	Doctorate
CHARACTERISTICS					
Average weekend worship attendance		1,130	977	1,149	-
Average church income		$1,430,297	$1,871,944	$1,736,017	-
Average # of years employed		6	5	6	-
Average # of paid vacation days		15	16	16	-
% College graduate or higher		0%	100%	100%	-
% Who receive auto reimbursement/allowance		38%	44%	52%	-
% Ordained		41%	47%	49%	-
% Supervise one or more people		75%	70%	83%	-
Average % salary increase (for those who had an increase) this year		4.4%	5.5%	3.5%	-
COMPENSATION					
Base Salary	Median	$31,631	$33,680	$38,625	-
	Average	$31,768	$36,076	$38,684	-
Housing	Median	$21,600	$20,000	$18,000	-
	Average	$21,959	$21,063	$21,279	-
Parsonage	Median	-	-	-	-
	Average	-	-	-	-
Total Compensation	**Median**	**$35,403**	**$43,000**	**$48,000**	**-**
	Average	**$38,523**	**$43,801**	**$48,756**	**-**
BENEFITS					
Health Insurance	Median	$5,000	$6,743	$6,066	-
	Average	$6,027	$7,896	$7,082	-
Life Insurance	Median	$150	$159	$221	-
	Average	$291	$308	$527	-
Disability Insurance	Median	$405	$383	$500	-
	Average	$706	$531	$1,298	-
Retirement	Median	$1,912	$2,760	$3,000	-
	Average	$2,172	$3,096	$3,324	-
Continuing Education	Median	$1,000	$1,100	$1,200	-
	Average	$1,383	$1,336	$1,488	-
Total Benefits	**Median**	**$4,764**	**$6,686**	**$8,000**	**-**
	Average	**$5,935**	**$8,273**	**$8,907**	**-**
TOTAL COMPENSATION PLUS BENEFITS	**Median**	**$39,924**	**$47,016**	**$56,000**	**-**
	Average	**$42,927**	**$50,684**	**$55,684**	**-**
Number of Respondents		62	131	63	5

- Not enough response to provide meaningful data.

* For detailed description and definitions of Data Distribution (Median and Average), see Chapter 1's "Explanation of Data Distribution."

Table 10-6: Annual Compensation of Full-Time Children's/Preschool Pastors/Directors by Years Employed

	Data Distribution*	YEARS EMPLOYED			
		Less than 6 years	6-10 years	11-15 years	Over 15 years
CHARACTERISTICS					
Average weekend worship attendance		906	1,319	1,512	-
Average church income		$1,535,599	$2,080,779	$1,946,381	-
Average # of years employed		3	8	13	-
Average # of paid vacation days		14	18	20	-
% College graduate or higher		78%	77%	64%	-
% Who receive auto reimbursement/allowance		43%	52%	38%	-
% Ordained		47%	48%	56%	-
% Supervise one or more people		72%	75%	92%	-
Average % salary increase (for those who had an increase) this year		5.0%	4.6%	4.1%	-
COMPENSATION					
Base Salary	Median	$32,495	$35,748	$35,000	-
	Average	$35,117	$37,586	$35,457	-
Housing	Median	$20,000	$23,000	$30,000	-
	Average	$20,775	$21,748	$28,665	-
Parsonage	Median	-	-	-	-
	Average	-	-	-	-
Total Compensation	**Median**	**$40,660**	**$43,911**	**$50,000**	**-**
	Average	**$42,805**	**$45,909**	**$50,469**	**-**
BENEFITS					
Health Insurance	Median	$6,000	$5,500	$8,916	-
	Average	$6,906	$7,360	$9,618	-
Life Insurance	Median	$148	$153	$541	-
	Average	$319	$239	$629	-
Disability Insurance	Median	$371	$406	$1,250	-
	Average	$400	$833	$2,287	-
Retirement	Median	$2,500	$2,475	$3,000	-
	Average	$2,829	$3,082	$3,667	-
Continuing Education	Median	$1,075	$1,200	-	-
	Average	$1,318	$1,265	-	-
Total Benefits	**Median**	**$5,643**	**$7,183**	**$9,404**	**-**
	Average	**$7,353**	**$8,166**	**$10,678**	**-**
TOTAL COMPENSATION PLUS BENEFITS	**Median**	**$45,646**	**$50,052**	**$56,900**	**-**
	Average	**$48,816**	**$52,603**	**$59,012**	**-**
Number of Respondents		148	61	25	8

- Not enough response to provide meaningful data.

* For detailed description and definitions of Data Distribution (Median and Average), see Chapter 1's "Explanation of Data Distribution."

Table 10-7: Annual Compensation of Full-Time Children's/Preschool Pastors/Directors by Denomination

CHARACTERISTICS	Data Distribution*	Assemblies of God	Baptist	Independent/ Nondenom.	Lutheran	Methodist	Presby-terian
Average weekend worship attendance		957	1,151	1,219	-	810	684
Average church income		$1,576,620	$1,911,843	$1,763,931	-	$1,452,397	$1,614,940
Average # of years employed		6	5	5	-	4	6
Average # of paid vacation days		16	15	17	-	11	15
% College graduate or higher		71%	81%	64%	-	84%	86%
% Who receive auto reimbursement/allowance		56%	53%	38%	-	28%	23%
% Ordained		76%	37%	58%	-	17%	7%
% Supervise one or more people		63%	75%	78%	-	74%	93%
Average % salary increase (for those who had an increase) this year		4.9%	4.5%	6.0%	-	3.2%	3.0%
COMPENSATION							
Base Salary	Median	$20,000	$37,000	$32,600	-	$33,902	$36,644
	Average	$22,279	$38,513	$37,215	-	$33,977	$40,159
Housing	Median	$25,500	$20,000	$20,800	-	-	-
	Average	$27,391	$21,402	$20,438	-	-	-
Parsonage	Median	-	-	-	-	-	-
	Average	-	-	-	-	-	-
Total Compensation	**Median**	**$42,500**	**$45,100**	**$43,652**	-	**$35,000**	**$36,644**
	Average	**$40,303**	**$45,965**	**$46,404**	-	**$35,924**	**$40,159**
BENEFITS							
Health Insurance	Median	$10,697	$5,551	$6,000	-	-	-
	Average	$10,218	$6,297	$7,769	-	-	-
Life Insurance	Median	-	$145	$138	-	-	-
	Average	-	$443	$279	-	-	-
Disability Insurance	Median	-	$354	$384	-	-	-
	Average	-	$1,019	$486	-	-	-
Retirement	Median	-	$3,850	$1,584	-	$1,926	$2,690
	Average	-	$3,682	$1,878	-	$2,123	$2,793
Continuing Education	Median	-	$1,625	$1,600	-	-	-
	Average	-	$1,463	$1,844	-	-	-
Total Benefits	**Median**	**$11,131**	**$7,213**	**$6,000**	-	**$4,364**	**$5,000**
	Average	**$10,927**	**$8,171**	**$7,466**	-	**$4,624**	**$7,495**
TOTAL COMPENSATION PLUS BENEFITS	**Median**	**$55,500**	**$51,218**	**$47,917**	-	**$36,750**	**$42,860**
	Average	**$49,302**	**$52,542**	**$52,326**	-	**$38,845**	**$46,048**
Number of Respondents		17	82	58	4	19	14

- Not enough response to provide meaningful data.

* For detailed description and definitions of Data Distribution (Median and Average), see Chapter 1's "Explanation of Data Distribution."

Table 10-8: Annual Compensation of Full-Time Children's/Preschool Pastors/Directors by Gender

	Data Distribution*	GENDER	
		Male	Female
CHARACTERISTICS			
Average weekend worship attendance		1,100	1,041
Average church income		$1,709,690	$1,740,467
Average # of years employed		5	6
Average # of paid vacation days		16	16
% College graduate or higher		87%	72%
% Who receive auto reimbursement/allowance		55%	41%
% Ordained		86%	32%
% Supervise one or more people		73%	75%
Average % salary increase (for those who had an increase) this year		4.0%	5.0%
COMPENSATION			
Base Salary	Median	$30,922	$35,000
	Average	$33,710	$36,805
Housing	Median	$21,450	$20,000
	Average	$21,293	$22,010
Parsonage	Median	-	-
	Average	-	-
Total Compensation	**Median**	**$48,818**	**$38,845**
	Average	**$50,680**	**$41,769**
BENEFITS			
Health Insurance	Median	$9,687	$5,000
	Average	$9,284	$6,139
Life Insurance	Median	$192	$156
	Average	$390	$331
Disability Insurance	Median	$383	$405
	Average	$824	$740
Retirement	Median	$3,366	$2,500
	Average	$3,256	$3,030
Continuing Education	Median	$1,300	$1,100
	Average	$1,475	$1,400
Total Benefits	**Median**	**$10,594**	**$5,400**
	Average	**$10,800**	**$6,748**
TOTAL COMPENSATION PLUS BENEFITS	**Median**	**$57,146**	**$43,650**
	Average	**$60,201**	**$46,974**
Number of Respondents		76	188

- Not enough response to provide meaningful data.

* For detailed description and definitions of Data Distribution (Median and Average), see Chapter 1's "Explanation of Data Distribution."

Table 10-9: Annual Compensation of Part-Time Children's/Preschool Pastors/Directors by Church Income

	Data Distribution*	CHURCH INCOME				
		$250K & Under	$251-$500K	$501-$750K	$751K-$1M	Over 1 Million
CHARACTERISTICS						
Average weekend worship attendance		151	226	360	556	1,041
Average church income		$183,115	$387,515	$620,970	$896,615	$2,209,773
Average # of years employed		4	3	4	5	4
Average # of paid vacation days		15	11	12	11	12
% College graduate or higher		62%	69%	63%	55%	63%
% Who receive auto reimbursement/allowance		-	25%	21%	42%	29%
% Ordained		15%	11%	14%	3%	8%
% Supervise one or more people		64%	47%	49%	48%	43%
Average % salary increase (for those who had an increase) this year		-	4.6%	6.2%	4.1%	4.0%
HOURLY RATE						
Base Rate	Average	$13	$15	$16	$16	$17
COMPENSATION						
Base Salary	Median	$9,100	$11,370	$14,400	$17,500	$18,200
	Average	$10,030	$11,361	$15,364	$16,935	$17,484
Housing	Median	-	-	-	-	-
	Average	-	-	-	-	-
Parsonage	Median	-	-	-	-	-
	Average	-	-	-	-	-
Total Compensation	**Median**	**$8,750**	**$11,685**	**$14,316**	**$17,500**	**$18,200**
	Average	**$10,687**	**$12,009**	**$15,563**	**$16,935**	**$17,876**
BENEFITS						
Health Insurance	Median	-	-	-	-	-
	Average	-	-	-	-	-
Life Insurance	Median	-	-	-	-	-
	Average	-	-	-	-	-
Disability Insurance	Median	-	-	-	-	-
	Average	-	-	-	-	-
Retirement	Median	-	-	-	-	-
	Average	-	-	-	-	-
Continuing Education	Median	-	-	$750	-	-
	Average	-	-	$1,794	-	-
Total Benefits	**Median**	-	**$419**	**$1,487**	-	**$4,994**
	Average	-	**$1,978**	**$2,677**	-	**$4,615**
TOTAL COMPENSATION PLUS BENEFITS	**Median**	**$9,550**	**$11,725**	**$14,604**	**$17,640**	**$19,231**
	Average	**$10,971**	**$12,362**	**$16,203**	**$17,290**	**$18,967**
Number of Respondents		28	56	46	32	55

- Not enough response to provide meaningful data.

* For detailed description and definitions of Data Distribution (Median and Average), see Chapter 1's "Explanation of Data Distribution."

11

MUSIC/CHOIR/
WORSHIP
PASTORS/DIRECTORS

Employment Profile

Music/Choir/Worship Pastors/Directors include paid pastors and directors of church music programs, including band, bell/chimes choir, music ministry, orchestra, praise and worship team, vocal choir, etc. This category may include such positions as Music Pastor, Worship Pastor, Worship Leader, Choir Director, Choir Master, Director of Music Ministries, etc.

Of the reported music ministry leaders, nearly six in ten work part-time. While men occupy most of the full-time positions, part-time positions are almost evenly split between males and females. About nine in ten full-time music ministry leaders hold at least a Bachelor's degree. Two-thirds of full-time music ministry leaders are ordained. The following chart provides a demographic profile of this sample:

	Full-Time	Part-Time
Number of respondents	314	448
Ordained	68%	17%
Average years employed	7	7
Male	88%	55%
Female	12%	45%
Self-employed (receives 1099)	4%	11%
Church employee (receives W-2)	96%	89%
High school diploma	6%	14%
Associate Degree	7%	8%
Bachelor's Degree	48%	47%
Master's Degree	34%	28%
Doctoral Degree	5%	4%

Total Compensation plus Benefits Package Analysis

The analyses on the next page are based on the data in the tables that you will find in the remainder of the chapter. The tables show compensation plus benefits data for full-time and part-time Music/Choir/Worship Pastors/Directors and are presented according to church income, church attendance, church setting, region, education, years employed, denomination, and gender. In this way, the music ministry leaders' compensation plus benefits can be analyzed and compared from a variety of useful perspectives.

The total compensation plus benefits amount includes the base salary, housing and/or parsonage amount, health, life, and disability insurance payments, retirement contribution, and educational funds.

Most benefits reported by music ministry leaders are comparable to those of Youth Pastors/Directors, Adult Ministry/Christian Education, and Children's/Preschool Pastors/Directors. Few of the music ministry leaders live in church-provided parsonages, but nearly six in ten of those who work full time receive housing allowances.

Compensation Plus Benefits	Full-Time	Part-Time
Base Salary	99%	96%
Housing	58%	6%
Parsonage	2%	1%
Health Insurance	63%	3%
Life Insurance	25%	1%
Disability Insurance	19%	2%
Retirement	Reti60%	5%
Continuing Education	29%	10%
Received Salary Increase	58%	45%
Received Paid Vacation	95%	46%
Received Auto Reimbursement/ Allowance	49%	9%

KEY POINTS

✳ About two-thirds of full-time Music/Choir/Worship Pastors/Directors serve in larger congregations (those with more than $750,000 in church income) while an almost similar percentage of part-time staff serve in smaller churches (income $500,000 or less).

✳ Full-time male Music/Choir/Worship Pastors/Directors earn 28% more than females.

✳ The vast majority of the Music/Choir/Worship Pastors/Directors, both full-time and part-time, serve in churches set in a suburb of a large city or in a small town or rural city.

✳ Full-time music ministry leaders who work in a metropolitan city are paid almost as much as those in the suburbs. Part-time music ministry leaders are paid almost equally whether they live in a suburb of a large city, a metropolitan city, or a small town or rural city.

Compensation & Benefits: National Averages for Full-Time Music/Choir/Worship Pastor/Director

2000	$50,911
2001	$53,200
2002	$55,046
2003	$56,875
2004	$57,279
2005	$60,316
2006	$64,075
2007	$65,133
2008	$61,373
2009	$61,754*

The above trend is made available for your reference only. In addition to looking at this overall data, please refer to the detailed tables using your church's income, attendance, setting, region, and denomination as well as the person's education, gender, and years employed for guidance in compensating this position.

Table 11-1: Annual Compensation of Full-Time Music/Choir/Worship Pastors/Directors by Church Income

CHARACTERISTICS	Data Distribution*	CHURCH INCOME				
		$250K & Under	$251-$500K	$501-$750K	$751K-$1M	Over 1 Million
Average weekend worship attendance		259	305	368	607	1,363
Average church income		$177,786	$399,814	$623,118	$895,067	$2,273,904
Average # of years employed		8	7	8	7	8
Average # of paid vacation days		13	15	17	16	18
% College graduate or higher		50%	80%	84%	84%	92%
% Who receive auto reimbursement/allowance		8%	39%	41%	56%	55%
% Ordained		64%	65%	62%	72%	71%
% Supervise one or more people		57%	50%	54%	60%	82%
Average % salary increase (for those who had an increase) this year		8.4%	5.1%	3.9%	3.7%	3.8%
COMPENSATION						
Base Salary	Highest 25%	$34,000	$36,000	$46,865	$40,000	$59,500
	Median	$26,627	$30,002	$40,000	$32,736	$45,000
	Lowest 25%	$18,600	$18,917	$29,500	$26,337	$33,313
	Average	$27,283	$29,539	$38,329	$35,294	$46,630
Housing	Highest 25%	-	$24,500	$27,000	$27,083	$33,500
	Median	-	$19,990	$14,610	$22,500	$24,981
	Lowest 25%	-	$15,300	$7,199	$19,000	$20,000
	Average	-	$21,189	$16,657	$23,608	$27,078
Parsonage	Highest 25%	-	-	-	-	-
	Median	-	-	-	-	-
	Lowest 25%	-	-	-	-	-
	Average	-	-	-	-	-
Total Compensation	**Highest 25%**	**$45,170**	**$46,625**	**$51,870**	**$59,448**	**$71,910**
	Median	**$39,687**	**$38,449**	**$44,883**	**$49,325**	**$61,000**
	Lowest 25%	**$26,760**	**$32,000**	**$38,360**	**$40,541**	**$50,347**
	Average	**$38,597**	**$39,883**	**$46,965**	**$50,912**	**$62,609**
BENEFITS						
Health Insurance	Highest 25%	-	$12,000	$11,449	$12,432	$12,000
	Median	-	$6,500	$6,780	$10,000	$8,650
	Lowest 25%	-	$3,900	$3,720	$6,064	$5,000
	Average	-	$7,727	$7,562	$9,735	$9,559
Life Insurance	Highest 25%	-	$320	-	$701	$500
	Median	-	$208	-	$260	$186
	Lowest 25%	-	$183	-	$78	$113
	Average	-	$263	-	$339	$396
Disability Insurance	Highest 25%	-	-	-	$1,000	$603
	Median	-	-	-	$500	$376
	Lowest 25%	-	-	-	$230	$251
	Average	-	-	-	$833	$459
Retirement	Highest 25%	-	$3,600	$3,215	$5,407	$6,500
	Median	-	$2,400	$1,782	$4,010	$4,251
	Lowest 25%	-	$1,000	$1,181	$2,500	$2,094
	Average	-	$2,657	$2,281	$4,014	$4,439
Continuing Education	Highest 25%	-	$1,150	$1,200	$1,100	$2,000
	Median	-	$1,000	$1,000	$1,000	$1,200
	Lowest 25%	-	$500	$500	$700	$750
	Average	-	$1,194	$1,081	$1,050	$1,649
Total Benefits	**Highest 25%**	**$8,325**	**$12,000**	**$12,782**	**$15,504**	**$16,102**
	Median	**$5,970**	**$5,800**	**$7,699**	**$9,500**	**$10,150**
	Lowest 25%	**$1,370**	**$3,510**	**$3,915**	**$6,127**	**$5,100**
	Average	**$6,158**	**$7,200**	**$8,531**	**$10,802**	**$11,430**
TOTAL COMPENSATION PLUS BENEFITS	**Highest 25%**	**$49,300**	**$52,429**	**$59,914**	**$71,000**	**$83,946**
	Median	**$43,227**	**$44,164**	**$50,950**	**$58,828**	**$71,378**
	Lowest 25%	**$26,760**	**$35,600**	**$43,279**	**$52,206**	**$57,950**
	Average	**$42,995**	**$45,412**	**$53,790**	**$59,719**	**$73,283**
Number of Respondents		14	56	50	65	151

- Not enough response to provide meaningful data.

* For detailed description and definitions of Data Distribution (Median and Average), see Chapter 1's "Explanation of Data Distribution."

Table 11-2: Annual Compensation of Full-Time Music/Choir/Worship Pastors/Directors by Worship Attendance

	Data Distribution*	WORSHIP ATTENDANCE					
		100 or less	101-300	301-500	501-750	751-1,000	Over 1,000
CHARACTERISTICS							
Average weekend worship attendance		-	223	417	609	905	2,262
Average church income		-	$442,765	$845,706	$1,084,498	$1,671,983	$3,190,720
Average # of years employed		-	8	6	7	6	7
Average # of paid vacation days		-	16	17	16	16	18
% College graduate or higher		-	81%	89%	83%	84%	94%
% Who receive auto reimbursement/allowance		-	33%	55%	57%	54%	49%
% Ordained		-	63%	74%	63%	76%	72%
% Supervise one or more people		-	51%	58%	69%	83%	85%
Average % salary increase (for those who had an increase) this year		-	4.3%	4.3%	3.8%	3.8%	4.1%
COMPENSATION							
Base Salary	Median	-	$31,200	$33,016	$38,000	$41,944	$48,075
	Average	-	$32,199	$36,384	$38,579	$43,272	$51,563
Housing	Median	-	$19,980	$22,000	$24,000	$25,000	$24,000
	Average	-	$20,640	$22,183	$24,447	$28,155	$25,966
Parsonage	Median	-	-	-	-	-	-
	Average	-	-	-	-	-	-
Total Compensation	**Median**	-	**$40,750**	**$49,000**	**$52,000**	**$61,000**	**$66,147**
	Average	-	**$42,867**	**$50,380**	**$51,859**	**$61,054**	**$67,789**
BENEFITS							
Health Insurance	Median	-	$6,000	$8,743	$8,400	$9,050	$9,942
	Average	-	$6,624	$8,718	$9,987	$9,735	$9,483
Life Insurance	Median	-	$260	$540	$158	$186	$184
	Average	-	$654	$584	$197	$420	$360
Disability	Median	-	-	$413	$296	$628	$350
	Average	-	-	$718	$449	$623	$465
Retirement	Median	-	$2,200	$3,200	$3,569	$3,000	$4,408
	Average	-	$2,895	$3,700	$3,625	$3,615	$4,797
Continuing Education	Median	-	$1,000	$1,150	$1,000	$900	$1,300
	Average	-	$1,002	$1,333	$1,193	$1,075	$2,123
Total Benefits	**Median**	-	**$6,000**	**$8,298**	**$8,082**	**$10,561**	**$12,351**
	Average	-	**$6,903**	**$9,751**	**$10,361**	**$10,774**	**$12,188**
TOTAL COMPENSATION PLUS BENEFITS	**Median**	-	**$45,656**	**$55,919**	**$58,500**	**$71,408**	**$79,300**
	Average	-	**$48,476**	**$57,963**	**$60,430**	**$70,694**	**$79,623**
Number of Respondents		2	80	72	81	38	69

- Not enough response to provide meaningful data.

* For detailed description and definitions of Data Distribution (Median and Average), see Chapter 1's "Explanation of Data Distribution."

Table 11-3: Annual Compensation of Full-Time Music/Choir/Worship Pastors/Directors by Church Setting

	Data Distribution*	Metro-politan city	Suburb of large city	Small town or rural city	Farming area
CHARACTERISTICS					
Average weekend worship attendance		1,050	931	651	-
Average church income		$1,859,756	$1,538,317	$950,178	-
Average # of years employed		8	7	7	-
Average # of paid vacation days		17	17	16	-
% College graduate or higher		89%	90%	80%	-
% Who receive auto reimbursement/allowance		40%	48%	54%	-
% Ordained		65%	68%	70%	-
% Supervise one or more people		72%	70%	60%	-
Average % salary increase (for those who had an increase) this year		4.5%	3.9%	4.1%	-
COMPENSATION					
Base Salary	Median	$41,000	$36,245	$38,000	-
	Average	$42,199	$38,983	$39,505	-
Housing	Median	$20,800	$24,000	$21,500	-
	Average	$23,374	$25,876	$21,708	-
Parsonage	Median	-	-	-	-
	Average	-	-	-	-
Total Compensation	**Median**	**$53,000**	**$50,000**	**$50,170**	**-**
	Average	**$54,289**	**$54,445**	**$51,814**	**-**
BENEFITS					
Health Insurance	Median	$6,850	$8,833	$8,986	-
	Average	$7,059	$9,859	$8,544	-
Life Insurance	Median	$276	$207	$146	-
	Average	$456	$428	$387	-
Disability Insurance	Median	$534	$360	$340	-
	Average	$708	$509	$400	-
Retirement	Median	$3,100	$3,500	$3,311	-
	Average	$4,246	$3,977	$3,381	-
Continuing Education	Median	$1,000	$1,050	$1,000	-
	Average	$1,278	$1,588	$1,001	-
Total Benefits	**Median**	**$8,082**	**$11,538**	**$7,863**	**-**
	Average	**$9,057**	**$11,362**	**$9,037**	**-**
TOTAL COMPENSATION PLUS BENEFITS	**Median**	**$60,122**	**$59,350**	**$57,254**	**-**
	Average	**$62,253**	**$64,048**	**$59,357**	**-**
Number of Respondents		58	155	127	4

- Not enough response to provide meaningful data.

* For detailed description and definitions of Data Distribution (Median and Average), see Chapter 1's "Explanation of Data Distribution."

Table 11-4: Annual Compensation of Full-Time Music/Choir/Worship Pastors/Directors by Region

	Data Distribution*	New England	Middle Atlantic	South Atlantic	E-N Central	E-S Central	W-N Central	W-S Central	Mountain	Pacific
CHARACTERISTICS										
Average weekend worship attendance	-	987	708	884	715	900	868	939	1,056
Average church income	-	$1,526,897	$1,258,475	$1,245,966	$1,054,983	$1,406,727	$1,566,132	$1,669,308	$1,429,317
Average # of years employed	-	5	7	6	8	6	8	7	8
Average # of paid vacation days	-	16	17	17	15	17	16	17	18
% College graduate or higher	-	82%	85%	93%	83%	87%	83%	96%	82%
% Who receive auto reimbursement/allowance	-	55%	53%	53%	48%	42%	57%	26%	38%
% Ordained	-	64%	66%	58%	77%	66%	82%	64%	68%
% Supervise one or more people	-	73%	68%	74%	61%	61%	74%	71%	51%
Average % salary increase (for those who had an increase) this year	-	6.7%	4.1%	4.1%	2.8%	3.9%	3.9%	3.4%	4.7%
COMPENSATION										
Base Salary	Median	-	$35,000	$44,650	$32,392	$41,000	$39,375	$34,479	$33,016	$35,500
	Average	-	$38,392	$43,419	$35,275	$40,060	$39,014	$38,778	$37,531	$37,562
Housing	Median	-	-	$24,000	$19,500	$19,865	$19,980	$20,820	$23,124	$29,240
	Average	-	-	$25,043	$19,099	$20,629	$20,465	$23,257	$26,895	$29,200
Parsonage	Median	-	-	-	-	-	-	-	-	-
	Average	-	-	-	-	-	-	-	-	-
Total Compensation	**Median**	-	**$55,000**	**$54,939**	**$47,690**	**$53,000**	**$42,420**	**$49,250**	**$49,570**	**$49,450**
	Average	-	**$53,512**	**$57,168**	**$45,259**	**$52,897**	**$48,170**	**$56,435**	**$54,340**	**$52,683**
BENEFITS										
Health Insurance	Median	-	$12,532	$8,280	$10,850	$8,037	$6,430	$7,993	$6,000	$6,900
	Average	-	$12,015	$9,101	$10,720	$7,730	$7,460	$8,359	$6,842	$10,376
Life Insurance	Median	-	-	$199	$155	-	$178	$400	$132	-
	Average	-	-	$430	$203	-	$265	$758	$253	-
Disability Insurance	Median	-	$450	$500	$319	$534	$264	$441	$597	$180
	Average	-	$450	$558	$366	$632	$475	$700	$539	$324
Retirement	Median	-	-	$3,732	$2,318	$3,200	$2,400	$4,500	$3,600	$4,780
	Average	-	-	$3,905	$2,406	$3,098	$3,073	$4,518	$4,542	$5,083
Continuing Education	Median	-	-	$1,000	$1,000	-	$1,000	$1,200	-	-
	Average	-	-	$1,121	$1,031	-	$1,450	$1,442	-	-
Total Benefits	**Median**	-	**$14,300**	**$8,082**	**$6,139**	**$6,180**	**$7,591**	**$9,500**	**$8,076**	**$8,760**
	Average	-	**$14,184**	**$10,184**	**$8,660**	**$6,890**	**$9,215**	**$11,160**	**$9,837**	**$11,347**
TOTAL COMPENSATION PLUS BENEFITS	**Median**	-	**$74,200**	**$62,375**	**$53,880**	**$55,715**	**$51,853**	**$60,597**	**$57,822**	**$55,503**
	Average	-	**$67,696**	**$65,824**	**$52,541**	**$58,898**	**$56,899**	**$65,403**	**$62,128**	**$61,761**
Number of Respondents		2	11	100	44	31	38	56	24	40

- Not enough response to provide meaningful data.

* For detailed description and definitions of Data Distribution (Median and Average), see Chapter 1's "Explanation of Data Distribution."

Table 11-5: Annual Compensation of Full-Time Music/Choir/Worship Pastors/Directors by Education

	Data Distribution*	EDUCATION			
		Less than Bachelor	Bachelor	Master	Doctorate
CHARACTERISTICS					
Average weekend worship attendance		626	899	786	1,321
Average church income		$903,475	$1,339,873	$1,542,428	$1,774,119
Average # of years employed		6	7	8	6
Average # of paid vacation days		14	17	18	18
% College graduate or higher		0%	100%	100%	100%
% Who receive auto reimbursement/allowance		38%	44%	59%	47%
% Ordained		60%	70%	72%	53%
% Supervise one or more people		70%	67%	65%	74%
Average % salary increase (for those who had an increase) this year		5.4%	4.2%	3.6%	3.3%
COMPENSATION					
Base Salary	Median	$35,000	$36,245	$41,200	$46,475
	Average	$35,242	$38,367	$41,650	$48,001
Housing	Median	$20,000	$21,800	$24,000	-
	Average	$19,639	$23,782	$24,905	-
Parsonage	Median	-	-	-	-
	Average	-	-	-	-
Total Compensation	**Median**	**$45,000**	**$49,325**	**$55,000**	**$48,606**
	Average	**$43,353**	**$52,672**	**$57,459**	**$56,133**
BENEFITS					
Health Insurance	Median	$8,162	$8,550	$8,000	$10,045
	Average	$10,095	$8,693	$8,506	$10,902
Life Insurance	Median	$180	$184	$326	-
	Average	$618	$260	$478	-
Disability Insurance	Median	-	$310	$492	-
	Average	-	$509	$495	-
Retirement	Median	$2,468	$2,650	$3,672	$4,551
	Average	$3,371	$3,302	$4,240	$5,175
Continuing Education	Median	$1,000	$1,000	$1,100	$710
	Average	$1,040	$1,652	$1,274	$690
Total Benefits	**Median**	**$6,497**	**$8,601**	**$8,520**	**$13,459**
	Average	**$10,611**	**$9,730**	**$9,875**	**$11,434**
TOTAL COMPENSATION PLUS BENEFITS	**Median**	**$50,000**	**$58,045**	**$64,200**	**$60,000**
	Average	**$51,481**	**$60,750**	**$66,476**	**$65,160**
Number of Respondents		47	159	115	19

- Not enough response to provide meaningful data.

* For detailed description and definitions of Data Distribution (Median and Average), see Chapter 1's "Explanation of Data Distribution."

Table 11-6: Annual Compensation of Full-Time Music/Choir/Worship Pastors/Directors by Years Employed

	Data Distribution*	YEARS EMPLOYED			
		Less than 6 years	6-10 years	11-15 years	Over 15 years
CHARACTERISTICS					
Average weekend worship attendance		747	1,058	1,072	720
Average church income		$1,192,624	$1,658,934	$1,691,636	$1,261,108
Average # of years employed		3	8	13	24
Average # of paid vacation days		15	17	21	22
% College graduate or higher		85%	86%	92%	90%
% Who receive auto reimbursement/allowance		47%	51%	56%	55%
% Ordained		71%	72%	64%	66%
% Supervise one or more people		61%	75%	83%	67%
Average % salary increase (for those who had an increase) this year		4.5%	3.9%	3.4%	3.4%
COMPENSATION					
Base Salary	Median	$32,892	$38,120	$44,136	$42,000
	Average	$35,697	$41,478	$48,188	$43,566
Housing	Median	$22,750	$22,398	$20,733	$19,000
	Average	$23,779	$24,992	$22,837	$20,209
Parsonage	Median	-	-	-	-
	Average	-	-	-	-
Total Compensation	**Median**	**$48,747**	**$51,657**	**$57,265**	**$57,640**
	Average	**$50,620**	**$54,566**	**$60,533**	**$55,688**
BENEFITS					
Health Insurance	Median	$8,986	$6,900	$7,200	$7,200
	Average	$9,343	$8,889	$7,245	$7,328
Life Insurance	Median	$184	$186	$132	$276
	Average	$357	$323	$341	$489
Disability Insurance	Median	$300	$549	$394	$376
	Average	$390	$746	$491	$446
Retirement	Median	$3,000	$3,500	$3,200	$4,500
	Average	$3,503	$3,877	$3,813	$4,545
Continuing Education	Median	$1,050	$800	$1,200	-
	Average	$1,356	$1,593	$1,357	-
Total Benefits	**Median**	**$8,000**	**$8,400**	**$8,057**	**$8,000**
	Average	**$10,117**	**$9,963**	**$8,975**	**$9,425**
TOTAL COMPENSATION PLUS BENEFITS	**Median**	**$55,327**	**$59,746**	**$68,000**	**$64,000**
	Average	**$59,051**	**$63,349**	**$68,780**	**$64,505**
Number of Respondents		174	76	37	31

- Not enough response to provide meaningful data.

* For detailed description and definitions of Data Distribution (Median and Average), see Chapter 1's "Explanation of Data Distribution."

149

Table 11-7: Annual Compensation of Full-Time Music/Choir/Worship Pastors/Directors by Denomination

	Data Distribution*	DENOMINATION					
		Assemblies of God	Baptist	Independent/ Nondenom.	Lutheran	Methodist	Presby-terian
CHARACTERISTICS							
Average weekend worship attendance		679	696	1,170	614	715	841
Average church income		$1,159,000	$1,226,009	$1,683,342	$1,123,628	$1,278,308	$1,552,407
Average # of years employed		5	7	6	6	10	7
Average # of paid vacation days		17	16	16	14	17	17
% College graduate or higher		71%	84%	87%	93%	88%	95%
% Who receive auto reimbursement/allowance		57%	63%	41%	33%	28%	42%
% Ordained		77%	86%	88%	33%	23%	15%
% Supervise one or more people		57%	67%	69%	67%	87%	45%
Average % salary increase (for those who had an increase) this year		4.8%	3.8%	4.3%	3.2%	3.4%	4.1%
COMPENSATION							
Base Salary	Median	$31,500	$36,023	$34,510	$37,000	$48,564	$48,075
	Average	$33,335	$37,307	$39,086	$38,034	$49,187	$48,471
Housing	Median	$19,500	$22,500	$21,000	-	-	-
	Average	$22,979	$24,241	$24,712	-	-	-
Parsonage	Median	-	-	-	-	-	-
	Average	-	-	-	-	-	-
Total Compensation	**Median**	**$46,700**	**$52,180**	**$54,000**	**$40,000**	**$49,808**	**$49,000**
	Average	**$48,921**	**$54,716**	**$58,570**	**$42,634**	**$51,648**	**$50,328**
BENEFITS							
Health Insurance	Median	$11,000	$8,717	$8,100	$6,000	$5,931	$8,512
	Average	$8,985	$9,709	$8,313	$7,774	$7,227	$8,825
Life Insurance	Median	-	$250	$250	-	-	-
	Average	-	$455	$692	-	-	-
Disability Insurance	Median	-	$476	$319	-	-	-
	Average	-	$603	$438	-	-	-
Retirement	Median	-	$4,500	$2,080	$3,975	$2,305	$5,015
	Average	-	$4,377	$2,837	$3,902	$2,448	$5,210
Continuing Education	Median	-	$1,050	$1,300	$600	$1,000	$800
	Average	-	$1,279	$1,787	$889	$1,078	$867
Total Benefits	**Median**	**$11,538**	**$9,450**	**$8,238**	**$7,224**	**$6,231**	**$11,906**
	Average	**$10,590**	**$10,887**	**$9,643**	**$9,992**	**$7,142**	**$9,856**
TOTAL COMPENSATION PLUS BENEFITS	**Median**	**$53,912**	**$60,365**	**$62,572**	**$56,837**	**$57,925**	**$56,595**
	Average	**$57,242**	**$64,152**	**$67,101**	**$51,960**	**$57,451**	**$58,306**
Number of Respondents		14	135	52	15	32	21

- Not enough response to provide meaningful data.

* For detailed description and definitions of Data Distribution (Median and Average), see Chapter 1's "Explanation of Data Distribution."

Table 11-8: Annual Compensation of Full-Time Music/Choir/Worship Pastors/Directors by Gender

CHARACTERISTICS	Data Distribution*	Male	Female
Average weekend worship attendance		879	601
Average church income		$1,393,903	$1,148,279
Average # of years employed		7	10
Average # of paid vacation days		16	18
% College graduate or higher		86%	86%
% Who receive auto reimbursement/allowance		52%	31%
% Ordained		74%	31%
% Supervise one or more people		66%	76%
Average % salary increase (for those who had an increase) this year		4.2%	3.0%
COMPENSATION			
Base Salary	Median	$37,000	$39,875
	Average	$39,561	$40,669
Housing	Median	$22,500	$12,000
	Average	$24,301	$13,442
Parsonage	Median	-	-
	Average	-	-
Total Compensation	**Median**	**$52,000**	**$39,875**
	Average	**$54,861**	**$43,549**
BENEFITS			
Health Insurance	Median	$8,550	$6,141
	Average	$9,098	$7,136
Life Insurance	Median	$208	$185
	Average	$435	$272
Disability Insurance	Median	$376	-
	Average	$520	-
Retirement	Median	$3,325	$2,600
	Average	$3,859	$3,307
Continuing Education	Median	$1,000	$875
	Average	$1,483	$961
Total Benefits	**Median**	**$9,000**	**$6,493**
	Average	**$10,387**	**$7,226**
TOTAL COMPENSATION PLUS BENEFITS	**Median**	**$60,047**	**$46,760**
	Average	**$63,690**	**$49,915**
Number of Respondents		300	42

- Not enough response to provide meaningful data.

* For detailed description and definitions of Data Distribution (Median and Average), see Chapter 1's "Explanation of Data Distribution."

151

Table 11-9: Annual Compensation of Part-Time Music/Choir/Worship Pastors/Directors by Church Income

	Data Distribution*	CHURCH INCOME				
		$250K & Under	$251-$500K	$501-$750K	$751K-$1M	Over 1 Million
CHARACTERISTICS						
Average weekend worship attendance		123	223	380	480	854
Average church income		$180,759	$366,717	$640,488	$900,539	$1,645,956
Average # of years employed		7	7	7	7	7
Average # of paid vacation days		11	11	12	16	12
% College graduate or higher		79%	77%	78%	77%	88%
% Who receive auto reimbursement/allowance		6%	8%	16%	-	-
% Ordained		18%	19%	12%	15%	14%
% Supervise one or more people		35%	44%	44%	62%	41%
Average % salary increase (for those who had an increase) this year		9.7%	4.5%	5.7%	3.3%	3.3%
HOURLY RATE						
Base Rate	Average	$20	$20	$22	$20	$19
COMPENSATION						
Base Salary	Median	$7,800	$11,400	$14,445	$16,115	$14,181
	Average	$8,953	$12,875	$15,480	$18,071	$17,742
Housing	Median	$12,000	$14,000	-	-	-
	Average	$11,751	$13,622	-	-	-
Parsonage	Median	-	-	-	-	-
	Average	-	-	-	-	-
Total Compensation	**Median**	**$7,974**	**$11,896**	**$14,752**	**$16,115**	**$14,181**
	Average	**$9,360**	**$13,179**	**$16,552**	**$18,071**	**$19,097**
BENEFITS						
Health Insurance	Median	-	-	-	-	-
	Average	-	-	-	-	-
Life Insurance	Median	-	-	-	-	-
	Average	-	-	-	-	-
Disability Insurance	Median	-	-	-	-	-
	Average	-	-	-	-	-
Retirement	Median	-	-	-	-	-
	Average	-	-	-	-	-
Continuing Education	Median	$500	$400	$500	-	-
	Average	$599	$456	$590	-	-
Total Benefits	**Median**	**$600**	**$500**	**$500**	**$1,188**	**$1,498**
	Average	**$1,646**	**$1,081**	**$1,433**	**$3,631**	**$2,247**
TOTAL COMPENSATION PLUS BENEFITS	**Median**	**$7,974**	**$12,000**	**$14,850**	**$16,115**	**$14,181**
	Average	**$9,548**	**$13,353**	**$16,868**	**$18,925**	**$19,704**
Number of Respondents		149	149	68	34	37

- Not enough response to provide meaningful data.

* For detailed description and definitions of Data Distribution (Median and Average), see Chapter 1's "Explanation of Data Distribution."

Table 11-10: Annual Compensation of Part-Time Music/Choir/Worship Pastors/Directors by Worship Attendance

	Data Distribution*	WORSHIP ATTENDANCE					
		100 or less	101-300	301-500	501-750	751-1,000	Over 1,000
CHARACTERISTICS							
Average weekend worship attendance		71	184	387	621	-	-
Average church income		$166,119	$338,868	$676,107	$1,074,900	-	-
Average # of years employed		6	7	9	6	-	-
Average # of paid vacation days		9	11	14	10	-	-
% College graduate or higher		77%	81%	75%	81%	-	-
% Who receive auto reimbursement/allowance		-	10%	-	-	-	-
% Ordained		19%	17%	13%	25%	-	-
% Supervise one or more people		36%	41%	49%	54%	-	-
Average % salary increase (for those who had an increase) this year		11.4%	6.0%	4.8%	3.5%	-	-
HOURLY RATE							
Base Rate	Average	$24	$20	$20	$22	-	-
COMPENSATION							
Base Salary	Median	$8,215	$10,400	$14,000	$20,600	-	-
	Average	$9,540	$11,996	$14,427	$20,193	-	-
Housing	Median	-	$13,265	-	-	-	-
	Average	-	$13,572	-	-	-	-
Parsonage	Median	-	-	-	-	-	-
	Average	-	-	-	-	-	-
Total Compensation	**Median**	**$8,293**	**$11,000**	**$14,286**	**$15,600**	**-**	**-**
	Average	**$9,973**	**$12,606**	**$14,664**	**$20,360**	**-**	**-**
BENEFITS							
Health Insurance	Median	-	-	-	-	-	-
	Average	-	-	-	-	-	-
Life Insurance	Median	-	-	-	-	-	-
	Average	-	-	-	-	-	-
Disability	Median	-	-	-	-	-	-
	Average	-	-	-	-	-	-
Retirement	Median	-	$1,600	-	-	-	-
	Average	-	$2,301	-	-	-	-
Continuing Education	Median	-	$500	$750	-	-	-
	Average	-	$416	$694	-	-	-
Total Benefits	**Median**	**$660**	**$500**	**$1,000**	**$1,201**	**-**	**-**
	Average	**$1,770**	**$1,208**	**$2,898**	**$2,082**	**-**	**-**
TOTAL COMPENSATION PLUS BENEFITS	**Median**	**$8,293**	**$11,000**	**$14,286**	**$15,600**	**-**	**-**
	Average	**$10,207**	**$12,781**	**$15,207**	**$20,979**	**-**	**-**
Number of Respondents		68	241	80	37	8	10

- Not enough response to provide meaningful data.

* For detailed description and definitions of Data Distribution (Median and Average), see Chapter 1's "Explanation of Data Distribution."

Table 11-11: Annual Compensation of Part-Time Music/Choir/Worship/Directors by Church Setting

	Data Distribution*	CHURCH SETTING			
		Metro-politan city	Suburb of large city	Small town or rural city	Farming area
CHARACTERISTICS					
Average weekend worship attendance		288	317	266	209
Average church income		$536,841	$570,958	$411,671	$325,636
Average # of years employed		8	6	7	3
Average # of paid vacation days		12	12	11	12
% College graduate or higher		72%	81%	79%	64%
% Who receive auto reimbursement/allowance		6%	8%	12%	12%
% Ordained		15%	13%	21%	18%
% Supervise one or more people		47%	46%	37%	41%
Average % salary increase (for those who had an increase) this year		4.5%	6.2%	5.2%	9.0%
HOURLY RATE					
Base Rate	Average	$20	$20	$21	$23
COMPENSATION					
Base Salary	Median	$12,100	$12,000	$10,450	$5,500
	Average	$12,856	$13,338	$12,968	$7,313
Housing	Median	-	$12,950	$13,390	-
	Average	-	$13,278	$13,127	-
Parsonage	Median	-	-	-	-
	Average	-	-	-	-
Total Compensation	**Median**	**$12,500**	**$12,000**	**$10,960**	**$7,000**
	Average	**$13,590**	**$13,731**	**$13,373**	**$8,214**
BENEFITS					
Health Insurance	Median	-	-	-	-
	Average	-	-	-	-
Life Insurance	Median	-	-	-	-
	Average	-	-	-	-
Disability Insurance	Median	-	-	-	-
	Average	-	-	-	-
Retirement	Median	-	$1,367	$1,200	-
	Average	-	$1,596	$1,755	-
Continuing Education	Median	-	$500	$500	-
	Average	-	$388	$524	-
Total Benefits	**Median**	**$450**	**$845**	**$700**	**-**
	Average	**$687**	**$2,725**	**$1,287**	**-**
TOTAL COMPENSATION PLUS BENEFITS	**Median**	**$12,500**	**$12,000**	**$11,200**	**$7,000**
	Average	**$13,683**	**$14,146**	**$13,652**	**$8,270**
Number of Respondents		81	177	166	17

- Not enough response to provide meaningful data.

* For detailed description and definitions of Data Distribution (Median and Average), see Chapter 1's "Explanation of Data Distribution."

Table 11-12: Annual Compensation of Part-Time Music/Choir/Worship Pastors/Directors by Region

	Data Distribution*	REGION								
		New England	Middle Atlantic	South Atlantic	E-N Central	E-S Central	W-N Central	W-S Central	Mountain	Pacific
CHARACTERISTICS										
Average weekend worship attendance		187	196	249	334	237	280	412	376	286
Average church income		$334,029	$363,253	$451,746	$553,959	$400,661	$471,251	$727,505	$476,202	$531,312
Average # of years employed		8	8	6	6	5	8	7	5	7
Average # of paid vacation days		10	14	10	13	8	15	9	10	9
% College graduate or higher		67%	88%	76%	80%	88%	81%	77%	68%	74%
% Who receive auto reimbursement/allowance		-	-	10%	-	-	-	-	-	-
% Ordained		9%	8%	23%	9%	21%	11%	27%	21%	21%
% Supervise one or more people		36%	43%	41%	45%	42%	31%	35%	50%	58%
Average % salary increase (for those who had an increase) this year		7.8%	4.2%	3.2%	5.2%	3.9%	3.4%	-	-	5.7%
HOURLY RATE										
Base Rate	Average	$23	$24	$22	$20	$17	$17	$20	$17	$20
COMPENSATION										
Base Salary	Median	$13,000	$10,708	$11,544	$11,300	$16,794	$7,800	$9,100	$8,775	$12,002
	Average	$13,854	$12,761	$13,454	$12,933	$15,447	$10,573	$12,239	$10,974	$13,229
Housing	Median	-	-	$12,950	-	-	-	-	-	-
	Average	-	-	$14,010	-	-	-	-	-	-
Parsonage	Median	-	-	-	-	-	-	-	-	-
	Average	-	-	-	-	-	-	-	-	-
Total Compensation	**Median**	**$13,000**	**$10,865**	**$12,000**	**$11,150**	**$16,794**	**$7,800**	**$10,100**	**$8,775**	**$12,447**
	Average	**$13,854**	**$12,803**	**$14,411**	**$12,902**	**$15,605**	**$10,543**	**$13,731**	**$10,974**	**$14,129**
BENEFITS										
Health Insurance	Median	-	-	-	-	-	-	-	-	-
	Average	-	-	-	-	-	-	-	-	-
Life Insurance	Median	-	-	-	-	-	-	-	-	-
	Average	-	-	-	-	-	-	-	-	-
Disability Insurance	Median	-	-	-	-	-	-	-	-	-
	Average	-	-	-	-	-	-	-	-	-
Retirement	Median	-	-	-	-	-	-	-	-	-
	Average	-	-	-	-	-	-	-	-	-
Continuing Education	Median	-	$500	$570	-	-	-	-	-	-
	Average	-	$558	$668	-	-	-	-	-	-
Total Benefits	**Median**	-	**$500**	**$1,000**	**$429**	-	**$405**	**$1,125**	-	**$845**
	Average	-	**$776**	**$1,704**	**$1,768**	-	**$1,960**	**$1,758**	-	**$2,728**
TOTAL COMPENSATION PLUS BENEFITS	**Median**	**$13,000**	**$11,000**	**$12,040**	**$11,150**	**$16,794**	**$7,800**	**$10,186**	**$8,775**	**$12,880**
	Average	**$14,105**	**$12,993**	**$14,679**	**$13,143**	**$15,752**	**$10,960**	**$14,013**	**$10,974**	**$14,706**
Number of Respondents		23	53	89	88	26	47	50	20	52

- Not enough response to provide meaningful data.

* For detailed description and definitions of Data Distribution (Median and Average), see Chapter 1's "Explanation of Data Distribution."

Table 11-13: Annual Compensation of Part-Time Music/Choir/Worship Pastors/Directors by Education

	Data Distribution*	EDUCATION			
		Less than Bachelor	Bachelor	Master	Doctorate
CHARACTERISTICS					
Average weekend worship attendance		306	314	219	268
Average church income		$459,223	$522,768	$451,370	$477,200
Average # of years employed		6	6	8	9
Average # of paid vacation days		11	11	12	14
% College graduate or higher		0%	100%	100%	100%
% Who receive auto reimbursement/allowance		-	12%	9%	-
% Ordained		17%	14%	20%	13%
% Supervise one or more people		42%	40%	46%	50%
Average % salary increase (for those who had an increase) this year		6.4%	7.0%	5.8%	3.1%
HOURLY RATE					
Base Rate	Average	$20	$20	$21	$24
COMPENSATION					
Base Salary	Median	$9,100	$11,150	$12,000	$13,091
	Average	$12,444	$12,467	$13,252	$17,434
Housing	Median	-	$11,100	$13,750	-
	Average	-	$12,347	$13,830	-
Parsonage	Median	-	-	-	-
	Average	-	-	-	-
Total Compensation	**Median**	**$10,000**	**$11,500**	**$12,650**	**$13,091**
	Average	**$12,592**	**$13,021**	**$13,741**	**$17,434**
BENEFITS					
Health Insurance	Median	-	-	-	-
	Average	-	-	-	-
Life Insurance	Median	-	-	-	-
	Average	-	-	-	-
Disability Insurance	Median	-	-	-	-
	Average	-	-	-	-
Retirement	Median	-	$743	$2,169	-
	Average	-	$1,286	$2,449	-
Continuing Education	Median	-	$500	$500	-
	Average	-	$471	$518	-
Total Benefits	**Median**	**$909**	**$530**	**$600**	**-**
	Average	**$1,899**	**$1,624**	**$1,735**	**-**
TOTAL COMPENSATION PLUS BENEFITS	**Median**	**$10,000**	**$11,576**	**$12,650**	**$13,091**
	Average	**$12,902**	**$13,263**	**$14,079**	**$17,677**
Number of Respondents		92	201	118	16

- Not enough response to provide meaningful data.

* For detailed description and definitions of Data Distribution (Median and Average), see Chapter 1's "Explanation of Data Distribution."

Table 11-14: Annual Compensation of Part-Time Music/Choir/Worship Pastors/Directors by Years Employed

		YEARS EMPLOYED			
	Data Distribution*	Less than 6 years	6-10 years	11-15 years	Over 15 years
CHARACTERISTICS					
Average weekend worship attendance		294	267	242	282
Average church income		$489,223	$470,256	$418,689	$479,694
Average # of years employed		3	8	13	24
Average # of paid vacation days		10	11	16	12
% College graduate or higher		77%	81%	75%	86%
% Who receive auto reimbursement/allowance		9%	-	-	-
% Ordained		19%	15%	18%	9%
% Supervise one or more people		41%	45%	55%	42%
Average % salary increase (for those who had an increase) this year		7.6%	5.9%	3.9%	3.5%
HOURLY RATE					
Base Rate	Average	$20	$22	$19	$21
COMPENSATION					
Base Salary	Median	$10,000	$12,722	$13,500	$9,081
	Average	$12,474	$13,677	$12,718	$11,761
Housing	Median	$13,265	-	-	-
	Average	$12,808	-	-	-
Parsonage	Median	-	-	-	-
	Average	-	-	-	-
Total Compensation	**Median**	**$11,150**	**$12,800**	**$14,000**	**$9,081**
	Average	**$13,087**	**$13,964**	**$12,843**	**$11,761**
BENEFITS					
Health Insurance	Median	-	-	-	-
	Average	-	-	-	-
Life Insurance	Median	-	-	-	-
	Average	-	-	-	-
Disability Insurance	Median	-	-	-	-
	Average	-	-	-	-
Retirement	Median	$2,169	-	-	-
	Average	$2,101	-	-	-
Continuing Education	Median	$500	$500	-	-
	Average	$536	$559	-	-
Total Benefits	**Median**	**$750**	**$529**	**$1,200**	**$475**
	Average	**$1,932**	**$1,081**	**$2,090**	**$1,938**
TOTAL COMPENSATION PLUS BENEFITS	**Median**	**$11,150**	**$13,200**	**$14,250**	**$9,184**
	Average	**$13,353**	**$14,218**	**$13,314**	**$12,180**
Number of Respondents		240	85	40	37

- Not enough response to provide meaningful data.

* For detailed description and definitions of Data Distribution (Median and Average), see Chapter 1's "Explanation of Data Distribution."

Table 11-15: Annual Compensation of Part-Time Music/Choir/Worship Pastors/Directors by Denomination

	Data Distribution*	DENOMINATION					
		Assemblies of God	Baptist	Independent/ Nondenom.	Lutheran	Methodist	Presby-terian
CHARACTERISTICS							
Average weekend worship attendance		330	277	415	282	242	202
Average church income		$619,958	$432,483	$588,735	$549,723	$414,715	$414,060
Average # of years employed		7	6	6	9	8	6
Average # of paid vacation days		9	10	11	17	10	14
% College graduate or higher		45%	76%	63%	88%	80%	93%
% Who receive auto reimbursement/allowance		-	16%	-	-	-	-
% Ordained		9%	31%	20%	0%	9%	0%
% Supervise one or more people		33%	39%	47%	41%	46%	46%
Average % salary increase (for those who had an increase) this year		8.0%	4.4%	8.5%	4.8%	6.5%	3.8%
HOURLY RATE							
Base Rate	Average	$22	$18	$19	$18	$21	$21
COMPENSATION							
Base Salary	Median	$9,550	$11,500	$11,400	$7,749	$10,000	$11,000
	Average	$13,154	$12,823	$13,221	$12,359	$10,366	$13,250
Housing	Median	-	-	-	-	-	-
	Average	-	-	-	-	-	-
Parsonage	Median	-	-	-	-	-	-
	Average	-	-	-	-	-	-
Total Compensation	**Median**	**$9,550**	**$13,000**	**$11,400**	**$7,749**	**$10,000**	**$11,000**
	Average	**$13,154**	**$13,872**	**$13,741**	**$12,359**	**$10,366**	**$13,250**
BENEFITS							
Health Insurance	Median	-	-	-	-	-	-
	Average	-	-	-	-	-	-
Life Insurance	Median	-	-	-	-	-	-
	Average	-	-	-	-	-	-
Disability Insurance	Median	-	-	-	-	-	-
	Average	-	-	-	-	-	-
Retirement	Median	-	-	-	$1,697	-	-
	Average	-	-	-	$2,268	-	-
Continuing Education	Median	-	-	-	$200	-	$500
	Average	-	-	-	$256	-	$531
Total Benefits	**Median**	-	**$750**	-	**$529**	-	**$500**
	Average	-	**$880**	-	**$1,540**	-	**$542**
TOTAL COMPENSATION PLUS BENEFITS	**Median**	**$9,550**	**$13,228**	**$11,675**	**$7,849**	**$10,091**	**$11,353**
	Average	**$13,695**	**$13,974**	**$14,043**	**$12,927**	**$10,482**	**$13,388**
Number of Respondents		12	120	49	38	56	59

- Not enough response to provide meaningful data.

* For detailed description and definitions of Data Distribution (Median and Average), see Chapter 1's "Explanation of Data Distribution."

Table 11-16: Annual Compensation of Part-Time Music/Choir/Worship Pastors/Directors by Gender

	Data Distribution*	GENDER	
		Male	Female
CHARACTERISTICS			
Average weekend worship attendance		315	255
Average church income		$527,724	$454,806
Average # of years employed		6	8
Average # of paid vacation days		11	12
% College graduate or higher		75%	83%
% Who receive auto reimbursement/allowance		10%	8%
% Ordained		24%	8%
% Supervise one or more people		43%	42%
Average % salary increase (for those who had an increase) this year		5.9%	6.7%
HOURLY RATE			
Base Rate	Average	$21	$20
COMPENSATION			
Base Salary	Median	$11,747	$10,558
	Average	$13,512	$12,051
Housing	Median	$13,445	-
	Average	$13,792	-
Parsonage	Median	-	-
	Average	-	-
Total Compensation	**Median**	**$12,051**	**$10,555**
	Average	**$14,217**	**$12,207**
BENEFITS			
Health Insurance	Median	-	-
	Average	-	-
Life Insurance	Median	-	-
	Average	-	-
Disability Insurance	Median	-	-
	Average	-	-
Retirement	Median	$1,200	$1,106
	Average	$1,603	$1,634
Continuing Education	Median	$500	$500
	Average	$552	$542
Total Benefits	**Median**	**$750**	**$520**
	Average	**$2,096**	**$1,378**
TOTAL COMPENSATION PLUS BENEFITS	**Median**	**$12,056**	**$10,653**
	Average	**$14,501**	**$12,500**
Number of Respondents		244	202

- Not enough response to provide meaningful data.

* For detailed description and definitions of Data Distribution (Median and Average), see Chapter 1's "Explanation of Data Distribution."

12

ADMINISTRATORS

Employment Profile

Administrators include paid, but not usually ordained, staff who supervise the business aspects of church operations, such as financial management, business operations, and some staff oversight. This may include such positions as Business Administrator, Business Manager, Chief Financial Officer, Chief Operating Officer, etc.

Three-quarters of Administrators who reported serve in a full-time capacity. In this study, 21% of those working full time are ordained ministers. The majority of Administrators (both full-time and part-time) are female and have a minimum of a Bachelor's degree. Nearly all are employed by the church, rather than self-employed.

This group of administrators provided the following employment profile:

	Full-Time	Part-Time
Number of respondents	257	84
Ordained	21%	10%
Average years employed	8	7
Male	48%	33%
Female	52%	67%
Self-employed (receives 1099)	2%	5%
Church employee (receives W-2)	98%	95%
High school diploma	22%	29%
Associate Degree	18%	10%
Bachelor's Degree	35%	43%
Master's Degree	21%	18%
Doctoral Degree	4%	1%

Total Compensation plus Benefits Package Analysis

The analyses on the next page are based on the data in the tables that you will find in the remainder of the chapter. The tables show compensation plus benefits data for Administrators who serve full time and are presented according to church income, church attendance, church setting, region, education, years employed, denomination, and gender.

There is also a table showing compensation plus benefit data for Administrators who serve part time presented by church income. In this way, the Administrator's compensation plus benefits can be analyzed and compared from a variety of useful perspectives.

The total compensation plus benefits amount includes the base salary, housing allowance and/or parsonage, health, life, and disability insurance payments, retirement contribution, and educational funds.

About six in ten full-time Administrators receive health insurance and retirement benefits. Most church administrators do not receive housing or parsonage allowances.

Compensation Plus Benefits	Full-Time	Part-Time
Base Salary	100%	99%
Housing	13%	3%
Parsonage	1%	0%
Health Insurance	60%	8%
Life Insurance	31%	5%
Disability Insurance	24%	3%
Retirement	56%	14%
Continuing Education	23%	7%
Received Salary Increase	57%	51%
Received Paid Vacation	97%	71%
Received Auto Reimbursement/ Allowance	39%	19%

KEY POINTS

✳ More than half of the full-time Administrators reported serve in larger churches with an income over $1,000,000.

✳ In general, as church income, worship attendance, and the minister's education level increase, compensation and benefits for full-time Administrators also increase.

✳ Almost half of the full-time Administrators in this survey serve in churches set in a suburb of a large city. Compensation varies based on setting, with those serving in metropolitan churches receiving the highest compensation.

✳ Full-time male Administrators receive higher compensation and benefits packages than females (45% higher). A contributing factor to this discrepancy is that, on average, male Administrators work in churches that are twice the size and collect almost twice the income of churches that employed female Administrators.

Compensation & Benefits: National Averages for Full-Time Administrators

2000	$44,768
2001	$48,064
2002	$47,305
2003	$50,615
2004	$49,907
2005	$53,153
2006	$52,036
2007	$57,639
2008	$54,237
2009	$56,637*

*The above trend is made available for your reference only. In addition to looking at this overall data, please refer to the detailed tables using your church's income, attendance, setting, region, and denomination as well as the person's education, gender, and years employed for guidance in compensating this position.

Table 12-1: Annual Compensation of Full-Time Administrators by Church Income

CHARACTERISTICS	Data Distribution*	CHURCH INCOME				
		$250K & Under	$251-$500K	$501-$750K	$751K-$1M	Over 1 Million
Average weekend worship attendance		170	257	409	524	1,541
Average church income		$161,738	$382,125	$649,672	$904,706	$2,513,951
Average # of years employed		8	9	7	9	8
Average # of paid vacation days		15	15	17	17	18
% College graduate or higher		27%	41%	47%	57%	74%
% Who receive auto reimbursement/allowance		47%	33%	22%	36%	45%
% Ordained		21%	18%	15%	20%	24%
% Supervise one or more people		80%	85%	85%	96%	95%
Average % salary increase (for those who had an increase) this year		4.7%	4.1%	5.3%	4.1%	4.5%
COMPENSATION						
Base Salary	Highest 25%	$42,000	$41,900	$39,728	$50,000	$64,394
	Median	$24,600	$34,500	$35,158	$45,000	$51,798
	Lowest 25%	$20,800	$30,672	$32,211	$37,346	$40,854
	Average	$34,002	$36,950	$35,757	$44,957	$53,134
Housing	Highest 25%	-	-	-	-	$38,520
	Median	-	-	-	-	$29,736
	Lowest 25%	-	-	-	-	$22,200
	Average	-	-	-	-	$30,249
Parsonage	Highest 25%	-	-	-	-	-
	Median	-	-	-	-	-
	Lowest 25%	-	-	-	-	-
	Average	-	-	-	-	-
Total Compensation	**Highest 25%**	**$42,000**	**$43,850**	**$43,500**	**$51,184**	**$68,000**
	Median	**$27,200**	**$34,500**	**$36,228**	**$46,275**	**$59,007**
	Lowest 25%	**$20,800**	**$30,672**	**$33,075**	**$38,198**	**$45,000**
	Average	**$34,602**	**$37,480**	**$39,454**	**$47,411**	**$57,757**
BENEFITS						
Health Insurance	Highest 25%	-	$7,500	$9,310	$11,227	$10,274
	Median	-	$5,568	$7,320	$5,000	$6,600
	Lowest 25%	-	$2,400	$4,100	$2,031	$4,703
	Average	-	$5,939	$6,938	$6,501	$7,899
Life Insurance	Highest 25%	-	-	-	-	$340
	Median	-	-	-	-	$159
	Lowest 25%	-	-	-	-	$100
	Average	-	-	-	-	$296
Disability Insurance	Highest 25%	-	-	-	-	$586
	Median	-	-	-	-	$300
	Lowest 25%	-	-	-	-	$200
	Average	-	-	-	-	$513
Retirement	Highest 25%	-	$3,698	$3,720	$3,750	$6,000
	Median	-	$2,450	$3,095	$3,078	$3,119
	Lowest 25%	-	$1,260	$1,978	$1,884	$2,220
	Average	-	$2,467	$3,375	$3,218	$4,155
Continuing Education	Highest 25%	-	-	-	-	$1,500
	Median	-	-	-	-	$1,000
	Lowest 25%	-	-	-	-	$600
	Average	-	-	-	-	$1,363
Total Benefits	**Highest 25%**	**$11,605**	**$8,750**	**$10,904**	**$10,850**	**$13,926**
	Median	**$7,195**	**$4,845**	**$4,300**	**$6,693**	**$9,575**
	Lowest 25%	**$863**	**$2,075**	**$2,530**	**$1,890**	**$4,800**
	Average	**$8,162**	**$6,003**	**$6,654**	**$7,872**	**$10,084**
TOTAL COMPENSATION PLUS BENEFITS	**Highest 25%**	**$50,000**	**$47,491**	**$50,928**	**$64,174**	**$79,154**
	Median	**$39,000**	**$40,000**	**$41,418**	**$51,070**	**$65,357**
	Lowest 25%	**$24,192**	**$31,800**	**$37,225**	**$41,227**	**$52,800**
	Average	**$40,043**	**$41,364**	**$44,028**	**$53,914**	**$66,681**
Number of Respondents		15	34	32	46	139

- Not enough response to provide meaningful data.

* For detailed description and definitions of Data Distribution (Median and Average), see Chapter 1's "Explanation of Data Distribution."

Table 12-2: Annual Compensation of Full-Time Administrators by Worship Attendance

	Data Distribution*	WORSHIP ATTENDANCE					
		100 or less	101-300	301-500	501-750	751-1,000	Over 1,000
CHARACTERISTICS							
Average weekend worship attendance		-	213	422	613	877	2,331
Average church income		-	$442,000	$913,842	$1,254,096	$1,688,219	$3,320,360
Average # of years employed		-	9	9	7	8	7
Average # of paid vacation days		-	16	18	17	17	18
% College graduate or higher		-	33%	58%	72%	63%	78%
% Who receive auto reimbursement/allowance		-	30%	39%	36%	50%	40%
% Ordained		-	20%	14%	27%	16%	27%
% Supervise one or more people		-	84%	96%	89%	91%	99%
Average % salary increase (for those who had an increase) this year		-	4.5%	3.8%	4.7%	5.7%	4.4%
COMPENSATION							
Base Salary	Median	-	$33,690	$40,707	$48,000	$45,000	$54,000
	Average	-	$35,252	$43,976	$47,172	$49,849	$55,191
Housing	Median	-	-	-	-	-	$35,000
	Average	-	-	-	-	-	$32,853
Parsonage	Median	-	-	-	-	-	-
	Average	-	-	-	-	-	-
Total Compensation	**Median**	-	**$33,800**	**$41,037**	**$50,000**	**$54,000**	**$62,000**
	Average	-	**$37,379**	**$45,537**	**$49,737**	**$53,915**	**$61,491**
BENEFITS							
Health Insurance	Median	-	$5,900	$4,332	$6,700	$8,016	$6,500
	Average	-	$6,989	$5,250	$7,757	$8,276	$8,039
Life Insurance	Median	-	-	$127	$340	$168	$154
	Average	-	-	$249	$681	$370	$263
Disability	Median	-	-	-	-	$281	$280
	Average	-	-	-	-	$413	$503
Retirement	Median	-	$2,550	$3,175	$3,000	$4,680	$3,100
	Average	-	$2,714	$3,696	$3,408	$4,710	$4,110
Continuing Education	Median	-	-	$500	$1,000	-	$1,200
	Average	-	-	$558	$938	-	$1,828
Total Benefits	**Median**	-	**$4,459**	**$4,542**	**$8,400**	**$9,238**	**$10,490**
	Average	-	**$6,457**	**$6,084**	**$9,317**	**$9,872**	**$11,048**
TOTAL COMPENSATION PLUS BENEFITS	**Median**	-	**$39,000**	**$46,028**	**$61,483**	**$57,403**	**$70,230**
	Average	-	**$41,371**	**$50,535**	**$57,398**	**$62,553**	**$71,329**
Number of Respondents		8	55	56	45	32	73

- Not enough response to provide meaningful data.

* For detailed description and definitions of Data Distribution (Median and Average), see Chapter 1's "Explanation of Data Distribution."

Table 12-3: Annual Compensation of Full-Time Administrators by Church Setting

	Data Distribution*	CHURCH SETTING			
		Metro-politan city	Suburb of large city	Small town or rural city	Farming area
CHARACTERISTICS					
Average weekend worship attendance		1,197	1,104	678	-
Average church income		$1,970,894	$1,823,617	$1,121,540	-
Average # of years employed		9	8	8	-
Average # of paid vacation days		18	17	17	-
% College graduate or higher		67%	62%	57%	-
% Who receive auto reimbursement/allowance		44%	42%	31%	-
% Ordained		26%	19%	22%	-
% Supervise one or more people		93%	89%	93%	-
Average % salary increase (for those who had an increase) this year		3.9%	4.7%	4.7%	-
COMPENSATION					
Base Salary	Median	$48,000	$45,000	$39,000	-
	Average	$49,640	$47,813	$41,587	-
Housing	Median	$28,000	$27,000	$27,700	-
	Average	$26,904	$27,969	$26,691	-
Parsonage	Median	-	-	-	-
	Average	-	-	-	-
Total Compensation	**Median**	**$50,000**	**$45,457**	**$43,359**	**-**
	Average	**$54,588**	**$49,471**	**$46,419**	**-**
BENEFITS					
Health Insurance	Median	$6,000	$6,014	$8,008	-
	Average	$6,937	$7,128	$8,374	-
Life Insurance	Median	$168	$190	$250	-
	Average	$427	$284	$534	-
Disability Insurance	Median	$250	$410	$568	-
	Average	$283	$559	$676	-
Retirement	Median	$3,307	$3,000	$3,176	-
	Average	$4,670	$3,309	$3,752	-
Continuing Education	Median	$800	$950	$900	-
	Average	$901	$1,280	$1,000	-
Total Benefits	**Median**	**$8,339**	**$7,800**	**$7,929**	**-**
	Average	**$9,227**	**$8,241**	**$9,572**	**-**
TOTAL COMPENSATION PLUS BENEFITS	**Median**	**$60,620**	**$54,430**	**$51,000**	**-**
	Average	**$62,473**	**$56,238**	**$53,625**	**-**
Number of Respondents		55	123	89	3

- Not enough response to provide meaningful data.

* For detailed description and definitions of Data Distribution (Median and Average), see Chapter 1's "Explanation of Data Distribution."

Table 12-4: Annual Compensation of Full-Time Administrators by Region

	Data Distribution*	New England	Middle Atlantic	South Atlantic	E-N Central	E-S Central	W-N Central	W-S Central	Mountain	Pacific
CHARACTERISTICS										
Average weekend worship attendance	-		713	834	984	1,058	853	865	846	1,505
Average church income	-		$1,394,442	$1,441,551	$1,660,346	$2,019,347	$1,322,945	$1,751,803	$1,245,092	$1,957,651
Average # of years employed	-		6	8	6	9	7	10	9	9
Average # of paid vacation days	-		18	17	17	16	18	18	18	17
% College graduate or higher	-		52%	63%	72%	67%	59%	63%	67%	46%
% Who receive auto reimbursement/allowance	-		24%	43%	40%	47%	38%	45%	40%	33%
% Ordained	-		28%	24%	14%	27%	24%	24%	19%	18%
% Supervise one or more people	-		92%	93%	98%	93%	95%	84%	100%	82%
Average % salary increase (for those who had an increase) this year	-		6.3%	3.3%	4.7%	3.7%	4.2%	5.5%	5.5%	4.2%
COMPENSATION										
Base Salary	Median	-	$37,250	$41,490	$43,285	$52,522	$46,157	$48,200	$45,000	$46,182
	Average	-	$42,748	$41,747	$47,128	$50,254	$51,132	$45,786	$46,271	$50,489
Housing	Median	-	-	$28,000	-	-	-	-	-	-
	Average	-	-	$26,960	-	-	-	-	-	-
Parsonage	Median	-	-	-	-	-	-	-	-	-
	Average	-	-	-	-	-	-	-	-	-
Total Compensation	**Median**	-	**$40,000**	**$45,000**	**$43,500**	**$60,312**	**$48,000**	**$52,298**	**$48,800**	**$48,988**
	Average	-	**$45,388**	**$45,661**	**$47,686**	**$55,342**	**$53,923**	**$51,849**	**$51,138**	**$52,772**
BENEFITS										
Health Insurance	Median	-	$9,600	$6,800	$6,582	$4,800	$5,202	$5,760	$5,784	$6,000
	Average	-	$8,913	$8,221	$7,636	$6,461	$7,086	$6,941	$6,859	$6,648
Life Insurance	Median	-	-	$240	$163	-	-	$120	$130	-
	Average	-	-	$505	$281	-	-	$288	$314	-
Disability Insurance	Median	-	-	$391	$456	-	-	$284	$401	-
	Average	-	-	$402	$570	-	-	$332	$487	-
Retirement	Median	-	$2,400	$3,088	$2,588	$3,100	$2,800	$2,525	$3,539	$3,454
	Average	-	$3,472	$3,872	$3,166	$3,665	$3,369	$3,684	$3,772	$4,458
Continuing Education	Median	-	$900	$1,250	$600	-	-	$800	-	-
	Average		$1,256	$1,357	$944			$1,063		-
Total Benefits	**Median**	-	**$9,665**	**$8,209**	**$7,303**	**$9,203**	**$9,138**	**$7,402**	**$8,307**	**$7,695**
	Average	-	**$9,788**	**$9,958**	**$7,221**	**$9,863**	**$9,266**	**$7,570**	**$8,930**	**$8,934**
TOTAL COMPENSATION PLUS BENEFITS	**Median**	-	**$47,100**	**$53,468**	**$45,825**	**$67,952**	**$60,282**	**$57,351**	**$54,172**	**$55,812**
	Average	-	**$53,219**	**$53,370**	**$53,396**	**$63,232**	**$61,504**	**$58,025**	**$58,367**	**$60,082**
Number of Respondents		1	25	62	43	15	22	38	21	44

- Not enough response to provide meaningful data.

* For detailed description and definitions of Data Distribution (Median and Average), see Chapter 1's "Explanation of Data Distribution."

Table 12-5: Annual Compensation of Full-Time Administrators by Education

	Data Distribution*	EDUCATION			
		Less than Bachelor	Bachelor	Master	Doctorate
CHARACTERISTICS					
Average weekend worship attendance		627	1,046	1,527	-
Average church income		$1,086,074	$1,672,878	$2,442,653	-
Average # of years employed		10	7	7	-
Average # of paid vacation days		17	17	18	-
% College graduate or higher		0%	100%	100%	-
% Who receive auto reimbursement/allowance		30%	38%	54%	-
% Ordained		10%	26%	28%	-
% Supervise one or more people		88%	92%	98%	-
Average % salary increase (for those who had an increase) this year		4.3%	4.5%	5.1%	-
COMPENSATION					
Base Salary	Median	$40,000	$46,000	$52,000	-
	Average	$42,387	$45,813	$55,528	-
Housing	Median	-	$27,000	$26,000	-
	Average	-	$28,709	$24,140	-
Parsonage	Median	-	-	-	-
	Average	-	-	-	-
Total Compensation	**Median**	**$40,000**	**$48,750**	**$60,000**	**-**
	Average	**$43,034**	**$50,420**	**$60,765**	**-**
BENEFITS					
Health Insurance	Median	$6,654	$6,000	$6,000	-
	Average	$7,286	$7,298	$7,800	-
Life Insurance	Median	$250	$142	$276	-
	Average	$510	$217	$455	-
Disability Insurance	Median	$450	$300	$300	-
	Average	$765	$487	$397	-
Retirement	Median	$2,504	$3,000	$4,736	-
	Average	$2,817	$3,569	$4,897	-
Continuing Education	Median	$500	$1,000	$1,000	-
	Average	$546	$1,597	$1,200	-
Total Benefits	**Median**	**$5,658**	**$7,890**	**$9,820**	**-**
	Average	**$7,231**	**$8,887**	**$10,636**	**-**
TOTAL COMPENSATION PLUS BENEFITS	**Median**	**$44,100**	**$55,820**	**$67,952**	**-**
	Average	**$48,337**	**$57,733**	**$70,095**	**-**
Number of Respondents		105	96	57	10

- Not enough response to provide meaningful data.

* For detailed description and definitions of Data Distribution (Median and Average), see Chapter 1's "Explanation of Data Distribution."

Table 12-6: Annual Compensation of Full-Time Administrators by Years Employed

	Data Distribution*	YEARS EMPLOYED			
		Less than 6 years	6-10 years	11-15 years	Over 15 years
CHARACTERISTICS					
Average weekend worship attendance		1,074	861	906	1,117
Average church income		$1,712,239	$1,412,622	$1,869,829	$1,531,590
Average # of years employed		3	8	13	22
Average # of paid vacation days		15	18	19	20
% College graduate or higher		68%	64%	53%	31%
% Who receive auto reimbursement/allowance		40%	34%	38%	39%
% Ordained		19%	22%	24%	21%
% Supervise one or more people		91%	92%	97%	86%
Average % salary increase (for those who had an increase) this year		5.1%	4.4%	3.4%	4.2%
COMPENSATION					
Base Salary	Median	$46,350	$46,000	$40,500	$42,569
	Average	$48,281	$45,931	$44,590	$43,130
Housing	Median	$28,868	$29,700	-	-
	Average	$28,539	$28,252	-	-
Parsonage	Median	-	-	-	-
	Average	-	-	-	-
Total Compensation	**Median**	**$48,000**	**$49,500**	**$42,500**	**$44,100**
	Average	**$50,290**	**$50,373**	**$49,866**	**$47,061**
BENEFITS					
Health Insurance	Median	$7,023	$6,000	$9,508	$6,000
	Average	$7,824	$6,588	$9,449	$6,974
Life Insurance	Median	$200	$165	$370	$108
	Average	$451	$262	$470	$187
Disability Insurance	Median	$450	$351	$500	-
	Average	$520	$431	$729	-
Retirement	Median	$2,960	$3,575	$3,257	$3,039
	Average	$3,468	$3,948	$4,338	$3,734
Continuing Education	Median	$975	$1,000	$1,000	-
	Average	$1,158	$1,106	$1,256	-
Total Benefits	**Median**	**$7,800**	**$7,486**	**$10,253**	**$7,992**
	Average	**$8,750**	**$8,051**	**$10,821**	**$9,456**
TOTAL COMPENSATION PLUS BENEFITS	**Median**	**$55,132**	**$55,302**	**$47,121**	**$54,534**
	Average	**$56,890**	**$57,378**	**$58,409**	**$54,235**
Number of Respondents		118	77	38	29

- Not enough response to provide meaningful data.

* For detailed description and definitions of Data Distribution (Median and Average), see Chapter 1's "Explanation of Data Distribution."

Table 12-7: Annual Compensation of Full-Time Administrators by Denomination

	Data Distribution*	DENOMINATION					
		Assemblies of God	Baptist	Independent/ Nondenom.	Lutheran	Methodist	Presby-terian
CHARACTERISTICS							
Average weekend worship attendance		685	856	1,197	605	716	503
Average church income		$1,101,601	$1,497,478	$1,818,812	$1,249,422	$1,535,817	$1,162,989
Average # of years employed		9	9	6	7	7	7
Average # of paid vacation days		17	17	17	18	16	17
% College graduate or higher		27%	59%	59%	74%	67%	68%
% Who receive auto reimbursement/allowance		27%	54%	28%	38%	40%	43%
% Ordained		33%	27%	30%	8%	7%	9%
% Supervise one or more people		93%	89%	90%	100%	90%	91%
Average % salary increase (for those who had an increase) this year		5.2%	5.2%	4.9%	3.1%	4.1%	3.9%
COMPENSATION							
Base Salary	Median	$40,000	$44,251	$43,000	$48,870	$46,804	$40,891
	Average	$39,719	$44,586	$44,387	$51,166	$46,006	$48,529
Housing	Median	-	$20,000	$31,000	-	-	-
	Average	-	$25,333	$29,063	-	-	-
Parsonage	Median	-	-	-	-	-	-
	Average	-	-	-	-	-	-
Total Compensation	**Median**	**$43,500**	**$49,500**	**$46,875**	**$48,870**	**$47,500**	**$40,891**
	Average	**$47,013**	**$49,946**	**$48,262**	**$51,166**	**$46,997**	**$48,529**
BENEFITS							
Health Insurance	Median	-	$8,952	$5,760	$6,365	$4,900	$6,267
	Average	-	$8,947	$7,028	$7,274	$5,280	$7,844
Life Insurance	Median	-	$450	$120	-	-	-
	Average	-	$595	$196	-	-	-
Disability Insurance	Median	-	$260	$262	$1,200	-	-
	Average	-	$316	$349	$1,158	-	-
Retirement	Median	-	$3,250	$2,310	$3,709	$2,737	$4,778
	Average	-	$4,018	$2,707	$4,172	$2,952	$5,885
Continuing Education	Median	-	-	$1,000	$500	$1,125	$600
	Average	-	-	$2,128	$845	$996	$683
Total Benefits	**Median**	**$8,741**	**$9,840**	**$5,666**	**$8,900**	**$6,902**	**$10,320**
	Average	**$7,691**	**$10,827**	**$7,655**	**$9,526**	**$6,451**	**$10,980**
TOTAL COMPENSATION PLUS BENEFITS	**Median**	**$48,400**	**$57,490**	**$48,570**	**$62,138**	**$56,039**	**$50,799**
	Average	**$51,115**	**$58,852**	**$54,003**	**$60,296**	**$52,158**	**$57,014**
Number of Respondents		15	62	60	24	30	22

- Not enough response to provide meaningful data.

. * For detailed description and definitions of Data Distribution (Median and Average), see Chapter 1's "Explanation of Data Distribution."

Table 12-8: Annual Compensation of Full-Time Administrators by Gender

	Data Distribution*	GENDER	
		Male	Female
CHARACTERISTICS			
Average weekend worship attendance		1,304	659
Average church income		$2,077,188	$1,144,501
Average # of years employed		7	9
Average # of paid vacation days		17	17
% College graduate or higher		78%	45%
% Who receive auto reimbursement/allowance		52%	26%
% Ordained		36%	7%
% Supervise one or more people		96%	87%
Average % salary increase (for those who had an increase) this year		4.6%	4.4%
COMPENSATION			
Base Salary	Median	$50,000	$39,000
	Average	$52,254	$40,529
Housing	Median	$27,000	-
	Average	$26,780	-
Parsonage	Median	-	-
	Average	-	-
Total Compensation	**Median**	**$58,820**	**$40,000**
	Average	**$57,992**	**$41,567**
BENEFITS			
Health Insurance	Median	$8,062	$5,525
	Average	$8,572	$6,002
Life Insurance	Median	$200	$159
	Average	$443	$276
Disability Insurance	Median	$420	$300
	Average	$566	$439
Retirement	Median	$3,799	$2,737
	Average	$4,383	$2,947
Continuing Education	Median	$1,000	$500
	Average	$1,308	$882
Total Benefits	**Median**	**$9,600**	**$5,973**
	Average	**$10,699**	**$6,719**
TOTAL COMPENSATION PLUS BENEFITS	**Median**	**$66,150**	**$43,800**
	Average	**$67,313**	**$46,498**
Number of Respondents		132	139

- Not enough response to provide meaningful data.

* For detailed description and definitions of Data Distribution (Median and Average), see Chapter 1's "Explanation of Data Distribution."

Table 12-9: Annual Compensation of Part-Time Administrators by Church Income

	Data Distribution*	CHURCH INCOME				
		$250K & Under	$251-$500K	$501-$750K	$751K-$1M	Over 1 Million
CHARACTERISTICS						
Average weekend worship attendance		138	252	358	479	933
Average church income		$171,852	$350,870	$631,253	$889,777	$1,946,070
Average # of years employed		10	7	5	6	5
Average # of paid vacation days		13	15	11	14	15
% College graduate or higher		39%	47%	74%	73%	100%
% Who receive auto reimbursement/allowance		17%	18%	22%	10%	25%
% Ordained		14%	0%	9%	9%	25%
% Supervise one or more people		45%	47%	74%	82%	91%
Average % salary increase (for those who had an increase) this year		-	-	5.1%	4.1%	-
HOURLY RATE						
Base Rate	Average	$18	$20	$17	$18	$22
COMPENSATION						
Base Salary	Median	$15,013	$17,950	$25,750	$21,120	$27,620
	Average	$15,970	$19,616	$24,202	$22,326	$26,954
Housing	Median	-	-	-	-	-
	Average	-	-	-	-	-
Parsonage	Median	-	-	-	-	-
	Average	-	-	-	-	-
Total Compensation	**Median**	**$15,576**	**$17,950**	**$25,750**	-	**$27,620**
	Average	**$15,971**	**$19,616**	**$24,202**	-	**$29,466**
BENEFITS						
Health Insurance	Median	-	-	-	-	-
	Average	-	-	-	-	-
Life Insurance	Median	-	-	-	-	-
	Average	-	-	-	-	-
Disability Insurance	Median	-	-	-	-	-
	Average	-	-	-	-	-
Retirement	Median	-	-	-	-	-
	Average	-	-	-	-	-
Continuing Education	Median	-	-	-	-	-
	Average	-	-	-	-	-
Total Benefits	**Median**	-	-	-	-	-
	Average	-	-	-	-	-
TOTAL COMPENSATION PLUS BENEFITS	**Median**	**$15,576**	**$18,000**	**$25,750**	-	**$27,800**
	Average	**$16,661**	**$19,665**	**$25,617**	-	**$29,910**
Number of Respondents		23	17	23	11	12

- Not enough response to provide meaningful data.

* For detailed description and definitions of Data Distribution (Median and Average), see Chapter 1's "Explanation of Data Distribution."

13

BOOKKEEPERS/ ACCOUNTANTS

Employment Profile

Bookkeepers/Accountants include paid personnel who assist with day-to-day financial matters in the church. This category may include such positions as Accountant, Controller, Financial Administrative Assistant, Financial Secretary, Payroll Secretary, Treasurer, etc.

Almost six out of ten Bookkeeper/Accountant positions reported are part time. In general, most Bookkeepers/Accountants are female and employed by the church, rather than self-employed. The majority of part-time Bookkeepers/Accountants have a minimum of a Bachelor's degree.

The statistical profile of Bookkeepers/Accountants is as follows:

	Full-Time	Part-Time
Number of respondents	170	232
Ordained	3%	3%
Average years employed	10	7
Male	6%	17%
Female	94%	83%
Self-employed (receives 1099)	0%	5%
Church employee (receives W-2)	100%	95%
High school diploma	39%	30%
Associate Degree	24%	17%
Bachelor's Degree	29%	46%
Master's Degree	7%	7%
Doctoral Degree	1%	<.5%

Total Compensation plus Benefits Package Analysis

The analyses on the next page are based on the data in the tables that you will find in the remainder of the chapter. The tables show compensation plus benefits data for full-time and part-time Bookkeepers/Accountants and are presented according to church income, church attendance, church setting, region, education, years employed, denomination, and gender. In this way, the Bookkeepers/Accountants' compensation plus benefits can be analyzed and compared from a variety of useful perspectives.

The total compensation plus benefits amount includes the base salary, housing and/or parsonage amount, health, life, and disability insurance payments, retirement contribution, and educational funds.

Nearly all full-time Bookkeepers/Accountants receive paid vacation. More than half receive health insurance and retirement benefits. Few part-time Bookkeepers/Accountants reported fringe benefits other than paid vacation, which is received by four out of ten.

Compensation Plus Benefits	Full-Time	Part-Time
Base Salary	100%	100%
Housing	2%	0%
Parsonage	0%	0%
Health Insurance	54%	4%
Life Insurance	26%	2%
Disability Insurance	21%	2%
Retirement	56%	9%
Continuing Education	12%	2%
Received Salary Increase	58%	53%
Received Paid Vacation	97%	39%
Received Auto Reimbursement/ Allowance	24%	11%

KEY POINTS

✳ Larger churches are more likely to employ full-time financial assistants, while small churches account for more than half of the part-timers. More than half of the full-time Bookkeepers/Accountants serve in churches with income more than $1,000,000, contrasted with about six in ten part-time Bookkeepers/Accountants serve in churches with income $500,000 or less.

✳ In general, as church income, church attendance, and the staff member's education level increase, compensation and benefits for full-time Bookkeepers/Accountants also increase.

✳ Full-time and part-time Bookkeepers/Accountants serving in churches in a suburb of a large city or in a metropolitan city have higher compensation and benefits packages compared to those serving in small towns and rural cities or farming areas.

Compensation & Benefits: National Averages for Full-Time Bookkeepers/Accountants

2000	$27,992
2001	$29,220
2002	$29,398
2003	$30,457
2004	$32,765
2005	$33,336
2006	$36,122
2007	$38,185
2008	$37,631
2009	$38,809*

The above trend is made available for your reference only. In addition to looking at this overall data, please refer to the detailed tables using your church's income, attendance, setting, region, and denomination as well as the person's education, gender, and years employed for guidance in compensating this position.

Table 13-1: Annual Compensation of Full-Time Bookkeepers/Accountants by Church Income

CHARACTERISTICS	Data Distribution*	CHURCH INCOME				
		$250K & Under	$251-$500K	$501-$750K	$751K-$1M	Over 1 Million
Average weekend worship attendance	-	245	333	488	1,238	
Average church income	-	$421,522	$630,475	$896,350	$2,244,683	
Average # of years employed	-	12	11	9	9	
Average # of paid vacation days	-	16	17	18	16	
% College graduate or higher	-	33%	26%	19%	47%	
% Who receive auto reimbursement/allowance	-	36%	26%	-	29%	
% Ordained	-	0%	4%	0%	5%	
% Supervise one or more people	-	17%	50%	40%	31%	
Average % salary increase (for those who had an increase) this year	-	3.2%	6.5%	5.8%	6.0%	
COMPENSATION						
Base Salary	Highest 25%	-	$34,000	$34,631	$34,142	$43,242
	Median	-	$26,464	$30,000	$31,346	$35,100
	Lowest 25%	-	$21,536	$24,637	$26,801	$30,000
	Average	-	$27,316	$29,709	$30,901	$37,484
Housing	Highest 25%	-	-	-	-	-
	Median	-	-	-	-	-
	Lowest 25%	-	-	-	-	-
	Average	-	-	-	-	-
Parsonage	Highest 25%	-	-	-	-	-
	Median	-	-	-	-	-
	Lowest 25%	-	-	-	-	-
	Average	-	-	-	-	-
Total Compensation	**Highest 25%**	-	**$34,000**	**$34,631**	**$34,142**	**$43,242**
	Median	-	**$26,464**	**$30,000**	**$31,346**	**$35,100**
	Lowest 25%	-	**$21,536**	**$24,637**	**$26,801**	**$30,000**
	Average	-	**$27,316**	**$29,871**	**$30,901**	**$37,722**
BENEFITS						
Health Insurance	Highest 25%	-	-	$6,719	$8,733	$7,623
	Median	-	-	$5,498	$7,889	$5,010
	Lowest 25%	-	-	$4,086	$4,656	$3,550
	Average	-	-	$6,331	$8,057	$5,523
Life Insurance	Highest 25%	-	-	-	$431	$175
	Median	-	-	-	$260	$120
	Lowest 25%	-	-	-	$107	$72
	Average	-	-	-	$270	$298
Disability Insurance	Highest 25%	-	-	-	-	$390
	Median	-	-	-	-	$210
	Lowest 25%	-	-	-	-	$153
	Average	-	-	-	-	$340
Retirement	Highest 25%	-	-	$1,940	$2,541	$2,980
	Median	-	-	$1,500	$2,064	$2,100
	Lowest 25%	-	-	$1,347	$1,048	$1,300
	Average	-	-	$1,737	$1,901	$2,523
Continuing Education	Highest 25%	-	-	-	-	$1,100
	Median	-	-	-	-	$750
	Lowest 25%	-	-	-	-	$425
	Average	-	-	-	-	$830
Total Benefits	**Highest 25%**	-	**$5,126**	**$7,686**	**$8,206**	**$8,384**
	Median	-	**$3,451**	**$6,020**	**$4,352**	**$5,987**
	Lowest 25%	-	**$991**	**$2,867**	**$1,823**	**$2,282**
	Average	-	**$3,794**	**$6,545**	**$6,024**	**$6,190**
TOTAL COMPENSATION PLUS BENEFITS	**Highest 25%**	-	**$39,650**	**$39,000**	**$40,062**	**$49,640**
	Median	-	**$30,951**	**$31,849**	**$34,438**	**$40,524**
	Lowest 25%	-	**$21,669**	**$27,689**	**$30,673**	**$35,000**
	Average	-	**$30,478**	**$33,689**	**$35,252**	**$43,028**
Number of Respondents		6	12	24	36	91

- Not enough response to provide meaningful data.

* For detailed description and definitions of Data Distribution (Median and Average), see Chapter 1's "Explanation of Data Distribution."

Table 13-2: Annual Compensation of Full-Time Bookkeepers/Accountants by Worship Attendance

	Data Distribution*	WORSHIP ATTENDANCE					
		100 or less	101-300	301-500	501-750	751-1,000	Over 1,000
CHARACTERISTICS							
Average weekend worship attendance	-		229	426	616	916	2,219
Average church income	-		$524,125	$946,864	$1,216,392	$1,836,465	$3,447,821
Average # of years employed	-		12	10	10	9	8
Average # of paid vacation days	-		16	19	16	15	15
% College graduate or higher	-		22%	37%	29%	30%	61%
% Who receive auto reimbursement/allowance	-		25%	23%	18%	30%	28%
% Ordained	-		3%	0%	6%	0%	6%
% Supervise one or more people	-		41%	28%	37%	35%	35%
Average % salary increase (for those who had an increase) this year	-		3.3%	4.6%	6.1%	11.7%	4.4%
COMPENSATION							
Base Salary	Median	-	$29,178	$31,200	$31,405	$37,000	$39,000
	Average	-	$28,039	$31,066	$33,063	$36,132	$42,352
Housing	Median	-	-	-	-	-	-
	Average	-	-	-	-	-	-
Parsonage	Median	-	-	-	-	-	-
	Average	-	-	-	-	-	-
Total Compensation	**Median**	-	**$29,178**	**$31,200**	**$31,405**	**$37,000**	**$39,000**
	Average	-	**$28,157**	**$31,066**	**$33,663**	**$36,132**	**$42,352**
BENEFITS							
Health Insurance	Median	-	$5,000	$6,000	$4,998	$5,616	$5,451
	Average	-	$5,882	$6,566	$5,505	$6,043	$6,356
Life Insurance	Median	-	-	-	$107	-	$124
	Average	-	-	-	$463	-	$265
Disability	Median	-	-	-	-	-	$210
	Average	-	-	-	-	-	$399
Retirement	Median	-	$1,560	$2,087	$1,600	$2,150	$2,163
	Average	-	$1,941	$2,006	$2,215	$2,171	$2,856
Continuing Education	Median	-	-	-	-	-	$750
	Average	-	-	-	-	-	$837
Total Benefits	**Median**	-	**$4,947**	**$4,452**	**$5,683**	**$4,800**	**$7,517**
	Average	-	**$5,412**	**$5,710**	**$5,466**	**$4,746**	**$8,035**
TOTAL COMPENSATION PLUS BENEFITS	**Median**	-	**$31,801**	**$35,300**	**$35,697**	**$40,124**	**$45,018**
	Average	-	**$31,601**	**$35,383**	**$38,067**	**$40,052**	**$49,634**
Number of Respondents		1	33	41	36	23	32

- Not enough response to provide meaningful data.

* For detailed description and definitions of Data Distribution (Median and Average), see Chapter 1's "Explanation of Data Distribution."

Table 13-3: Annual Compensation of Full-Time Bookkeepers/Accountants by Church Setting

	Data Distribution*	CHURCH SETTING			
		Metro-politan city	Suburb of large city	Small town or rural city	Farming area
CHARACTERISTICS					
Average weekend worship attendance		1,033	1,053	576	-
Average church income		$1,699,781	$1,990,465	$1,007,489	-
Average # of years employed		12	9	9	-
Average # of paid vacation days		16	17	16	-
% College graduate or higher		36%	46%	25%	-
% Who receive auto reimbursement/allowance		35%	19%	24%	-
% Ordained		4%	3%	3%	-
% Supervise one or more people		29%	39%	31%	-
Average % salary increase (for those who had an increase) this year		3.9%	6.5%	5.8%	-
COMPENSATION					
Base Salary	Median	$33,974	$35,000	$30,340	-
	Average	$35,930	$36,842	$29,673	-
Housing	Median	-	-	-	-
	Average	-	-	-	-
Parsonage	Median	-	-	-	-
	Average	-	-	-	-
Total Compensation	**Median**	**$33,974**	**$35,000**	**$30,600**	**-**
	Average	**$36,230**	**$37,037**	**$30,105**	**-**
BENEFITS					
Health Insurance	Median	$5,665	$5,318	$4,896	-
	Average	$5,951	$5,957	$6,006	-
Life Insurance	Median	$135	$119	$120	-
	Average	$133	$326	$221	-
Disability Insurance	Median	-	$219	-	-
	Average	-	$342	-	-
Retirement	Median	$2,400	$1,993	$1,787	-
	Average	$2,928	$2,344	$1,889	-
Continuing Education	Median	-	$725	-	-
	Average	-	$849	-	-
Total Benefits	**Median**	**$7,272**	**$5,683**	**$4,554**	**-**
	Average	**$7,260**	**$6,106**	**$5,215**	**-**
TOTAL COMPENSATION PLUS BENEFITS	**Median**	**$37,771**	**$40,062**	**$34,093**	**-**
	Average	**$42,280**	**$42,070**	**$33,884**	**-**
Number of Respondents		24	74	69	1

- Not enough response to provide meaningful data.

* For detailed description and definitions of Data Distribution (Median and Average), see Chapter 1's "Explanation of Data Distribution."

Table 13-4: Annual Compensation of Full-Time Bookkeepers/Accountants by Region

	Data Distribution*	New England	Middle Atlantic	South Atlantic	E-N Central	E-S Central	W-N Central	W-S Central	Mountain	Pacific
CHARACTERISTICS										
Average weekend worship attendance		-	-	720	690	719	1,372	994	730	1,189
Average church income		-	-	$1,404,252	$1,373,916	$1,171,558	$2,980,221	$1,771,342	$1,349,263	$1,591,367
Average # of years employed		-	-	9	14	12	5	10	11	6
Average # of paid vacation days		-	-	17	20	16	14	16	15	14
% College graduate or higher		-	-	37%	32%	47%	70%	27%	27%	47%
% Who receive auto reimbursement/allowance		-	-	31%	28%	25%	0%	24%	36%	13%
% Ordained		-	-	4%	0%	0%	0%	3%	9%	6%
% Supervise one or more people		-	-	27%	42%	32%	60%	39%	27%	38%
Average % salary increase (for those who had an increase) this year		-	-	3.5%	3.2%	4.3%	6.0%	6.0%	6.6%	20.3%
COMPENSATION										
Base Salary	Median	-	-	$31,000	$33,674	$30,655	$40,145	$33,000	$32,130	$35,578
	Average	-	-	$32,019	$33,548	$30,560	$41,504	$33,539	$36,107	$39,132
Housing	Median	-	-	-	-	-	-	-	-	-
	Average	-	-	-	-	-	-	-	-	-
Parsonage	Median	-	-	-	-	-	-	-	-	-
	Average	-	-	-	-	-	-	-	-	-
Total Compensation	**Median**	-	-	**$31,000**	**$33,950**	**$30,655**	**$40,145**	**$33,000**	**$32,130**	**$35,578**
	Average	-	-	**$32,099**	**$34,843**	**$30,560**	**$41,504**	**$33,928**	**$36,107**	**$39,582**
BENEFITS										
Health Insurance	Median	-	-	$4,947	$4,311	$4,800	$6,853	$5,451	-	$5,088
	Average	-	-	$5,311	$5,367	$6,144	$7,522	$5,866	-	$6,173
Life Insurance	Median	-	-	$115	$106	-	-	$142	-	-
	Average	-	-	$231	$460	-	-	$159	-	-
Disability Insurance	Median	-	-	$257	-	-	-	-	-	-
	Average	-	-	$237	-	-	-	-	-	-
Retirement	Median	-	-	$1,735	$1,755	$1,440	-	$1,885	-	-
	Average	-	-	$2,199	$1,879	$1,628	-	$2,000	-	-
Continuing Education	Median	-	-	$750	-	-	-	-	-	-
	Average	-	-	$828	-	-	-	-	-	-
Total Benefits	**Median**	-	-	**$6,028**	**$2,839**	**$2,500**	**$10,153**	**$5,405**	-	**$5,290**
	Average	-	-	**$5,943**	**$4,626**	**$4,557**	**$9,849**	**$5,624**	-	**$7,220**
TOTAL COMPENSATION PLUS BENEFITS	**Median**	-	-	**$37,219**	**$36,417**	**$33,409**	**$51,237**	**$36,588**	**$41,330**	**$39,091**
	Average	-	-	**$36,222**	**$39,007**	**$34,433**	**$50,368**	**$38,336**	**$41,179**	**$46,351**
Number of Respondents		1	6	49	20	20	10	37	11	16

- Not enough response to provide meaningful data.

* For detailed description and definitions of Data Distribution (Median and Average), see Chapter 1's "Explanation of Data Distribution."

Table 13-5: Annual Compensation of Full-Time Bookkeepers/Accountants by Education

CHARACTERISTICS	Data Distribution*	EDUCATION			
		Less than Bachelor	Bachelor	Master	Doctorate
Average weekend worship attendance		687	1,129	1,142	-
Average church income		$1,327,294	$1,727,250	$2,540,716	-
Average # of years employed		10	9	5	-
Average # of paid vacation days		17	16	14	-
% College graduate or higher		0%	100%	100%	-
% Who receive auto reimbursement/allowance		20%	33%	25%	-
% Ordained		2%	2%	17%	-
% Supervise one or more people		35%	30%	50%	-
Average % salary increase (for those who had an increase) this year		5.1%	8.5%	4.0%	-
COMPENSATION					
Base Salary	Median	$31,200	$34,825	$44,081	-
	Average	$31,399	$36,287	$43,838	-
Housing	Median	-	-	-	-
	Average	-	-	-	-
Parsonage	Median	-	-	-	-
	Average	-	-	-	-
Total Compensation	**Median**	**$31,200**	**$34,825**	**$44,081**	**-**
	Average	**$31,535**	**$36,368**	**$44,438**	**-**
BENEFITS					
Health Insurance	Median	$5,665	$4,845	-	-
	Average	$6,447	$5,266	-	-
Life Insurance	Median	$118	$135	-	-
	Average	$286	$284	-	-
Disability Insurance	Median	$200	$270	-	-
	Average	$271	$500	-	-
Retirement	Median	$1,560	$2,250	$2,275	-
	Average	$1,876	$2,274	$3,161	-
Continuing Education	Median	-	$625	-	-
	Average	-	$853	-	-
Total Benefits	**Median**	**$4,947**	**$5,842**	**$6,131**	**-**
	Average	**$5,648**	**$5,979**	**$7,267**	**-**
TOTAL COMPENSATION PLUS BENEFITS	**Median**	**$35,227**	**$38,895**	**$50,504**	**-**
	Average	**$35,744**	**$41,351**	**$51,100**	**-**
Number of Respondents		106	48	12	1

- Not enough response to provide meaningful data.

** For detailed description and definitions of Data Distribution (Median and Average), see Chapter 1's "Explanation of Data Distribution."*

Table 13-6: Annual Compensation of Full-Time Bookkeepers/Accountants by Years Employed

	Data Distribution*	YEARS EMPLOYED			
		Less than 6 years	6-10 years	11-15 years	Over 15 years
CHARACTERISTICS					
Average weekend worship attendance		958	794	987	694
Average church income		$1,725,450	$1,470,418	$1,706,742	$1,238,357
Average # of years employed		3	8	12	22
Average # of paid vacation days		13	16	21	20
% College graduate or higher		51%	36%	26%	23%
% Who receive auto reimbursement/allowance		17%	24%	35%	32%
% Ordained		4%	6%	0%	0%
% Supervise one or more people		25%	35%	47%	47%
Average % salary increase (for those who had an increase) this year		6.9%	7.0%	5.5%	3.1%
COMPENSATION					
Base Salary	Median	$32,599	$32,850	$31,200	$33,000
	Average	$33,927	$34,947	$33,617	$32,440
Housing	Median	-	-	-	-
	Average	-	-	-	-
Parsonage	Median	-	-	-	-
	Average	-	-	-	-
Total Compensation	**Median**	**$32,599**	**$32,850**	**$31,410**	**$33,000**
	Average	**$34,066**	**$35,274**	**$34,980**	**$32,440**
BENEFITS					
Health Insurance	Median	$5,829	$6,350	$4,000	$5,451
	Average	$6,085	$7,053	$3,833	$6,237
Life Insurance	Median	$124	$107	-	$184
	Average	$168	$176	-	$216
Disability Insurance	Median	$166	$237	-	-
	Average	$269	$363	-	-
Retirement	Median	$1,993	$2,041	$1,297	$1,976
	Average	$2,648	$2,447	$1,675	$1,969
Continuing Education	Median	-	-	-	-
	Average	-	-	-	-
Total Benefits	**Median**	**$6,000**	**$7,255**	**$4,048**	**$5,052**
	Average	**$6,253**	**$6,586**	**$4,186**	**$6,083**
TOTAL COMPENSATION PLUS BENEFITS	**Median**	**$37,704**	**$39,589**	**$36,000**	**$36,894**
	Average	**$38,755**	**$40,448**	**$38,726**	**$37,738**
Number of Respondents		52	56	19	31

- Not enough response to provide meaningful data.

* For detailed description and definitions of Data Distribution (Median and Average), see Chapter 1's "Explanation of Data Distribution."

Table 13-7: Annual Compensation of Full-Time Bookkeepers/Accountants by Denomination

	Data Distribution*	DENOMINATION					
		Assemblies of God	Baptist	Independent/ Nondenom.	Lutheran	Methodist	Presby- terian
CHARACTERISTICS							
Average weekend worship attendance		655	705	1,150	-	700	-
Average church income		$1,574,911	$1,294,829	$1,791,072	-	$1,352,400	-
Average # of years employed		7	10	11	-	8	-
Average # of paid vacation days		14	17	15	-	16	-
% College graduate or higher		27%	32%	33%	-	47%	-
% Who receive auto reimbursement/allowance		13%	31%	14%	-	12%	-
% Ordained		0%	3%	10%	-	0%	-
% Supervise one or more people		33%	28%	53%	-	47%	-
Average % salary increase (for those who had an increase) this year		10.4%	3.8%	10.2%	-	4.3%	-
COMPENSATION							
Base Salary	Median	$30,340	$30,569	$36,653	-	$32,700	-
	Average	$30,158	$31,124	$37,821	-	$32,581	-
Housing	Median	-	-	-	-	-	-
	Average	-	-	-	-	-	-
Parsonage	Median	-	-	-	-	-	-
	Average	-	-	-	-	-	-
Total Compensation	**Median**	**$30,340**	**$30,569**	**$36,653**	**-**	**$32,700**	**-**
	Average	**$30,158**	**$31,219**	**$38,411**	**-**	**$32,581**	**-**
BENEFITS							
Health Insurance	Median	-	$5,195	$4,947	-	$4,572	-
	Average	-	$6,256	$5,920	-	$4,444	-
Life Insurance	Median	-	$113	$128	-	-	-
	Average	-	$147	$182	-	-	-
Disability Insurance	Median	-	$153	-	-	-	-
	Average	-	$165	-	-	-	-
Retirement	Median	-	$2,100	$1,350	-	$1,200	-
	Average	-	$2,123	$1,886	-	$1,504	-
Continuing Education	Median	-	-	-	-	$625	-
	Average	-	-	-	-	$831	-
Total Benefits	**Median**	**$7,574**	**$5,714**	**$5,224**	**-**	**$4,800**	**-**
	Average	**$8,268**	**$6,147**	**$5,934**	**-**	**$4,587**	**-**
TOTAL COMPENSATION PLUS BENEFITS	**Median**	**$31,345**	**$36,512**	**$40,900**	**-**	**$38,131**	**-**
	Average	**$34,568**	**$36,152**	**$42,622**	**-**	**$36,628**	**-**
Number of Respondents		15	76	31	4	17	3

- Not enough response to provide meaningful data.

* For detailed description and definitions of Data Distribution (Median and Average), see Chapter 1's "Explanation of Data Distribution."

Table 13-8: Annual Compensation of Full-Time Bookkeepers/Accountants by Gender

	Data Distribution*	GENDER	
		Male	Female
CHARACTERISTICS			
Average weekend worship attendance		986	828
Average church income		$1,813,738	$1,498,950
Average # of years employed		6	10
Average # of paid vacation days		14	16
% College graduate or higher		80%	34%
% Who receive auto reimbursement/allowance		30%	24%
% Ordained		22%	2%
% Supervise one or more people		40%	35%
Average % salary increase (for those who had an increase) this year		5.6%	5.8%
COMPENSATION			
Base Salary	Median	$32,580	$32,130
	Average	$35,444	$33,648
Housing	Median	-	-
	Average	-	-
Parsonage	Median	-	-
	Average	-	-
Total Compensation	**Median**	**$35,280**	**$32,130**
	Average	**$39,144**	**$33,739**
BENEFITS			
Health Insurance	Median	-	$5,154
	Average	-	$5,943
Life Insurance	Median	-	$118
	Average	-	$239
Disability Insurance	Median	-	$205
	Average	-	$314
Retirement	Median	-	$1,885
	Average	-	$2,184
Continuing Education	Median	-	$725
	Average	-	$787
Total Benefits	**Median**	**-**	**$5,245**
	Average	**-**	**$5,789**
TOTAL COMPENSATION PLUS BENEFITS	**Median**	**$41,654**	**$37,219**
	Average	**$45,268**	**$38,327**
Number of Respondents		10	159

- Not enough response to provide meaningful data.

* For detailed description and definitions of Data Distribution (Median and Average), see Chapter 1's "Explanation of Data Distribution."

Table 13-9: Annual Compensation of Part-Time Bookkeepers/Accountants by Church Income

	Data Distribution*	CHURCH INCOME				
		$250K & Under	$251-$500K	$501-$750K	$751K-$1M	Over 1 Million
CHARACTERISTICS						
Average weekend worship attendance		119	234	447	503	1,066
Average church income		$180,591	$378,097	$636,450	$883,772	$1,850,281
Average # of years employed		7	7	9	7	7
Average # of paid vacation days		10	12	13	11	12
% College graduate or higher		53%	46%	48%	63%	66%
% Who receive auto reimbursement/allowance		5%	10%	17%	14%	14%
% Ordained		5%	1%	0%	4%	3%
% Supervise one or more people		5%	10%	7%	14%	25%
Average % salary increase (for those who had an increase) this year		5.4%	4.5%	3.3%	7.3%	4.4%
HOURLY RATE						
Base Rate	Average	$13	$14	$20	$18	$18
COMPENSATION						
Base Salary	Median	$5,160	$8,360	$11,801	$16,273	$20,800
	Average	$6,540	$9,871	$13,942	$16,975	$20,954
Housing	Median	-	-	-	-	-
	Average	-	-	-	-	-
Parsonage	Median	-	-	-	-	-
	Average	-	-	-	-	-
Total Compensation	**Median**	**$5,160**	**$8,320**	**$11,801**	**$16,273**	**$20,800**
	Average	**$6,540**	**$9,819**	**$13,942**	**$16,975**	**$20,954**
BENEFITS						
Health Insurance	Median	-	-	-	-	-
	Average	-	-	-	-	-
Life Insurance	Median	-	-	-	-	-
	Average	-	-	-	-	-
Disability Insurance	Median	-	-	-	-	-
	Average	-	-	-	-	-
Retirement	Median	-	-	-	-	$1,360
	Average	-	-	-	-	$1,304
Continuing Education	Median	-	-	-	-	-
	Average	-	-	-	-	-
Total Benefits	**Median**	**-**	**-**	**-**	**-**	**$1,500**
	Average	**-**	**-**	**-**	**-**	**$2,808**
TOTAL COMPENSATION PLUS BENEFITS	**Median**	**$5,160**	**$8,320**	**$11,801**	**$16,273**	**$20,800**
	Average	**$6,608**	**$10,062**	**$14,201**	**$17,437**	**$22,093**
Number of Respondents		63	71	30	28	37

- Not enough response to provide meaningful data.

* For detailed description and definitions of Data Distribution (Median and Average), see Chapter 1's "Explanation of Data Distribution."

185

Table 13-10: Annual Compensation of Part-Time Bookkeepers/Accountants by Worship Attendance

	Data Distribution*	WORSHIP ATTENDANCE					
		100 or less	101-300	301-500	501-750	751-1,000	Over 1,000
CHARACTERISTICS							
Average weekend worship attendance		82	201	398	609	850	2,575
Average church income		$164,578	$382,815	$722,265	$1,164,918	$1,371,776	$3,014,511
Average # of years employed		7	8	8	7	7	5
Average # of paid vacation days		9	13	12	11	9	12
% College graduate or higher		37%	55%	57%	58%	45%	70%
% Who receive auto reimbursement/allowance		6%	7%	18%	14%	10%	30%
% Ordained		6%	2%	2%	5%	0%	0%
% Supervise one or more people		6%	8%	7%	29%	27%	30%
Average % salary increase (for those who had an increase) this year		7.7%	4.3%	4.1%	3.5%	-	3.8%
HOURLY RATE							
Base Rate	Average	$14	$15	$17	$16	$18	$18
COMPENSATION							
Base Salary	Median	$5,240	-	$12,350	$16,266	$17,700	$21,143
	Average	$6,863	-	$14,210	$16,954	$20,089	$22,416
Housing	Median	-	-	-	-	-	-
	Average	-	-	-	-	-	-
Parsonage	Median	-	-	-	-	-	-
	Average	-	-	-	-	-	-
Total Compensation	**Median**	**$5,240**	**$7,650**	**$12,350**	**$16,266**	**$17,700**	**$21,143**
	Average	**$6,863**	**$10,118**	**$14,210**	**$16,954**	**$20,089**	**$22,416**
BENEFITS							
Health Insurance	Median	-	-	-	-	-	-
	Average	-	-	-	-	-	-
Life Insurance	Median	-	-	-	-	-	-
	Average	-	-	-	-	-	-
Disability	Median	-	-	-	-	-	-
	Average	-	-	-	-	-	-
Retirement	Median	-	-	$1,085	-	-	-
	Average	-	-	$1,546	-	-	-
Continuing Education	Median	-	-	-	-	-	-
	Average	-	-	-	-	-	-
Total Benefits	**Median**	-	**$1,988**	**$3,335**	-	-	-
	Average	-	**$2,616**	**$3,576**	-	-	-
TOTAL COMPENSATION PLUS BENEFITS	**Median**	**$5,240**	**$7,650**	**$12,350**	**$16,266**	**$17,700**	**$21,466**
	Average	**$6,874**	**$10,365**	**$15,023**	**$17,283**	**$20,257**	**$23,705**
Number of Respondents		36	106	44	22	11	10

- Not enough response to provide meaningful data.

* For detailed description and definitions of Data Distribution (Median and Average), see Chapter 1's "Explanation of Data Distribution."

Table 13-11: Annual Compensation of Part-Time Bookkeepers/Accountants by Church Setting

	Data Distribution*	CHURCH SETTING			
		Metro-politan city	Suburb of large city	Small town or rural city	Farming area
CHARACTERISTICS					
Average weekend worship attendance		558	444	314	174
Average church income		$1,007,237	$746,374	$480,697	$252,132
Average # of years employed		6	8	7	10
Average # of paid vacation days		8	14	10	10
% College graduate or higher		56%	56%	52%	43%
% Who receive auto reimbursement/allowance		6%	11%	14%	0%
% Ordained		9%	0%	2%	14%
% Supervise one or more people		6%	17%	9%	0%
Average % salary increase (for those who had an increase) this year		4.3%	4.7%	5.3%	3.0%
HOURLY RATE					
Base Rate	Average	$17	$17	$14	-
COMPENSATION					
Base Salary	Median	$9,750	$11,900	$9,600	$7,372
	Average	$12,605	$13,870	$10,614	$7,035
Housing	Median	-	-	-	-
	Average	-	-	-	-
Parsonage	Median	-	-	-	-
	Average	-	-	-	-
Total Compensation	**Median**	**$9,750**	**$11,900**	**$9,488**	**$7,372**
	Average	**$12,605**	**$13,870**	**$10,567**	**$7,035**
BENEFITS					
Health Insurance	Median	-	-	-	-
	Average	-	-	-	-
Life Insurance	Median	-	-	-	-
	Average	-	-	-	-
Disability Insurance	Median	-	-	-	-
	Average	-	-	-	-
Retirement	Median	-	$1,360	$598	-
	Average	-	$1,703	$924	-
Continuing Education	Median	-	-	-	-
	Average	-	-	-	-
Total Benefits	**Median**	**-**	**$1,500**	**$645**	**-**
	Average	**-**	**$3,285**	**$2,098**	**-**
TOTAL COMPENSATION PLUS BENEFITS	**Median**	**$9,750**	**$11,900**	**$9,488**	**$7,372**
	Average	**$12,819**	**$14,406**	**$10,857**	**$7,095**
Number of Respondents		34	92	94	8

- Not enough response to provide meaningful data.

* For detailed description and definitions of Data Distribution (Median and Average), see Chapter 1's "Explanation of Data Distribution."

Table 13-12: Annual Compensation of Part-Time Bookkeepers/Accountants by Region

	Data Distribution*	New England	Middle Atlantic	South Atlantic	E-N Central	E-S Central	W-N Central	W-S Central	Mountain	Pacific
CHARACTERISTICS										
Average weekend worship attendance		163	259	324	484	378	421	663	292	453
Average church income		$399,360	$450,368	$654,449	$761,759	$583,040	$602,704	$1,029,190	$573,878	$644,883
Average # of years employed		6	6	7	7	8	7	8	8	8
Average # of paid vacation days		18	8	13	12	11	22	9	12	12
% College graduate or higher		70%	44%	55%	55%	44%	75%	42%	36%	60%
% Who receive auto reimbursement/allowance		0%	12%	10%	8%	11%	33%	10%	7%	12%
% Ordained		0%	0%	6%	2%	0%	0%	11%	0%	0%
% Supervise one or more people		0%	3%	13%	14%	11%	0%	15%	29%	9%
Average % salary increase (for those who had an increase) this year		5.5%	4.7%	4.0%	6.9%	-	3.3%	3.8%	6.2%	4.4%
HOURLY RATE										
Base Rate	Average	$17	$12	$18	$15	-	$15	$14	$17	$16
COMPENSATION										
Base Salary	Median	$7,200	$6,760	$14,080	$8,320	$10,225	$9,892	$11,250	$8,680	$11,900
	Average	$11,615	$8,777	$14,833	$11,254	$11,182	$11,056	$11,580	$11,341	$14,037
Housing	Median	-	-	-	-	-	-	-	-	-
	Average	-	-	-	-	-	-	-	-	-
Parsonage	Median	-	-	-	-	-	-	-	-	-
	Average	-	-	-	-	-	-	-	-	-
Total Compensation	**Median**	**$7,200**	**$6,466**	**$14,080**	**$8,320**	**$10,225**	**$9,892**	**$11,250**	**$8,680**	**$11,900**
	Average	**$11,615**	**$8,701**	**$14,833**	**$11,254**	**$11,182**	**$11,056**	**$11,580**	**$11,341**	**$14,037**
BENEFITS										
Health Insurance	Median	-	-	-	-	-	-	-	-	-
	Average	-	-	-	-	-	-	-	-	-
Life Insurance	Median	-	-	-	-	-	-	-	-	-
	Average	-	-	-	-	-	-	-	-	-
Disability Insurance	Median	-	-	-	-	-	-	-	-	-
	Average	-	-	-	-	-	-	-	-	-
Retirement	Median	-	-	-	-	-	-	-	-	-
	Average	-	-	-	-	-	-	-	-	-
Continuing Education	Median	-	-	-	-	-	-	-	-	-
	Average	-	-	-	-	-	-	-	-	-
Total Benefits	**Median**	-	-	**$3,335**	-	-	-	-	-	-
	Average	-	-	**$3,635**	-	-	-	-	-	-
TOTAL COMPENSATION PLUS BENEFITS	**Median**	**$7,200**	**$6,466**	**$14,080**	**$8,320**	**$10,705**	**$10,046**	**$11,250**	**$8,680**	**$11,900**
	Average	**$11,982**	**$8,716**	**$15,414**	**$11,344**	**$11,235**	**$11,400**	**$11,941**	**$11,652**	**$14,933**
Number of Respondents		10	34	50	49	9	12	20	14	34

- Not enough response to provide meaningful data.

* For detailed description and definitions of Data Distribution (Median and Average), see Chapter 1's "Explanation of Data Distribution."

Table 13-13: Annual Compensation of Part-Time Bookkeepers/Accountants by Education

	Data Distribution*	EDUCATION			
		Less than Bachelor	Bachelor	Master	Doctorate
CHARACTERISTICS					
Average weekend worship attendance		324	478	348	-
Average church income		$536,720	$772,676	$702,268	-
Average # of years employed		8	7	7	-
Average # of paid vacation days		12	13	9	-
% College graduate or higher		0%	100%	100%	-
% Who receive auto reimbursement/allowance		10%	13%	7%	-
% Ordained		4%	1%	0%	-
% Supervise one or more people		13%	9%	6%	-
Average % salary increase (for those who had an increase) this year		4.6%	4.9%	-	-
HOURLY RATE					
Base Rate	Average	$15	$15	$18	-
COMPENSATION					
Base Salary	Median	$10,800	$9,404	$11,643	-
	Average	$11,813	$12,402	$13,919	-
Housing	Median	-	-	-	-
	Average	-	-	-	-
Parsonage	Median	-	-	-	-
	Average	-	-	-	-
Total Compensation	**Median**	**$10,800**	**$9,390**	**$11,643**	**-**
	Average	**$11,813**	**$12,341**	**$13,919**	**-**
BENEFITS					
Health Insurance	Median	-	-	-	-
	Average	-	-	-	-
Life Insurance	Median	-	-	-	-
	Average	-	-	-	-
Disability Insurance	Median	-	-	-	-
	Average	-	-	-	-
Retirement	Median	$690	$1,500	-	-
	Average	$888	$1,867	-	-
Continuing Education	Median	-	-	-	-
	Average	-	-	-	-
Total Benefits	**Median**	**$2,632**	**$1,500**	**-**	**-**
	Average	**$3,414**	**$2,277**	**-**	**-**
TOTAL COMPENSATION PLUS BENEFITS	**Median**	**$10,800**	**$9,390**	**$11,643**	**-**
	Average	**$12,268**	**$12,676**	**$14,067**	**-**
Number of Respondents		105	102	16	1

- Not enough response to provide meaningful data.

* For detailed description and definitions of Data Distribution (Median and Average), see Chapter 1's "Explanation of Data Distribution."

Table 13-14: Annual Compensation of Part-Time Bookkeepers/Accountants by Years Employed

	Data Distribution*	YEARS EMPLOYED			
		Less than 6 years	6-10 years	11-15 years	Over 15 years
CHARACTERISTICS					
Average weekend worship attendance		390	310	322	453
Average church income		$672,088	$570,018	$551,930	$640,652
Average # of years employed		3	8	13	22
Average # of paid vacation days		9	13	15	17
% College graduate or higher		59%	49%	67%	45%
% Who receive auto reimbursement/allowance		13%	7%	10%	15%
% Ordained		4%	2%	0%	5%
% Supervise one or more people		8%	14%	16%	20%
Average % salary increase (for those who had an increase) this year		6.0%	4.2%	3.8%	3.1%
HOURLY RATE					
Base Rate	Average	$16	$15	$15	$17
COMPENSATION					
Base Salary	Median	$10,000	$10,000	$11,193	$14,642
	Average	$12,095	$11,381	$12,822	$16,208
Housing	Median	-	-	-	-
	Average	-	-	-	-
Parsonage	Median	-	-	-	-
	Average	-	-	-	-
Total Compensation	**Median**	**$10,000**	**$10,000**	**$10,800**	**$14,642**
	Average	**$12,095**	**$11,381**	**$12,607**	**$16,208**
BENEFITS					
Health Insurance	Median	-	-	-	-
	Average	-	-	-	-
Life Insurance	Median	-	-	-	-
	Average	-	-	-	-
Disability Insurance	Median	-	-	-	-
	Average	-	-	-	-
Retirement	Median	$737	-	-	-
	Average	$753	-	-	-
Continuing Education	Median	-	-	-	-
	Average	-	-	-	-
Total Benefits	**Median**	**$900**	**-**	**-**	**-**
	Average	**$2,535**	**-**	**-**	**-**
TOTAL COMPENSATION PLUS BENEFITS	**Median**	**$10,000**	**$10,000**	**$10,800**	**$14,642**
	Average	**$12,395**	**$11,759**	**$12,929**	**$16,813**
Number of Respondents		110	43	31	20

- Not enough response to provide meaningful data.

* For detailed description and definitions of Data Distribution (Median and Average), see Chapter 1's "Explanation of Data Distribution."

Table 13-15: Annual Compensation of Part-Time Bookkeepers/Accountants by Denomination

	Data Distribution*	DENOMINATION					
		Assemblies of God	Baptist	Independent/ Nondenom.	Lutheran	Methodist	Presby-terian
CHARACTERISTICS							
Average weekend worship attendance		374	264	665	383	353	278
Average church income		$632,225	$522,111	$980,572	$911,610	$526,933	$591,279
Average # of years employed		5	7	6	8	6	9
Average # of paid vacation days		6	12	11	10	10	13
% College graduate or higher		40%	35%	59%	50%	77%	61%
% Who receive auto reimbursement/allowance		0%	5%	21%	0%	9%	16%
% Ordained		9%	5%	0%	0%	0%	3%
% Supervise one or more people		0%	12%	17%	13%	0%	9%
Average % salary increase (for those who had an increase) this year		5.3%	3.6%	6.4%	3.8%	6.2%	3.4%
HOURLY RATE							
Base Rate	Average	$14	$15	$17	-	$15	$18
COMPENSATION							
Base Salary	Median	$5,772	$9,075	$11,750	$4,005	$6,143	$12,692
	Average	$9,667	$11,253	$14,488	$6,997	$8,836	$14,855
Housing	Median	-	-	-	-	-	-
	Average	-	-	-	-	-	-
Parsonage	Median	-	-	-	-	-	-
	Average	-	-	-	-	-	-
Total Compensation	**Median**	**$5,772**	**$9,075**	**$11,750**	**$4,005**	**$6,143**	**$12,692**
	Average	**$9,667**	**$11,253**	**$14,488**	**$6,997**	**$8,836**	**$14,855**
BENEFITS							
Health Insurance	Median	-	-	-	-	-	-
	Average	-	-	-	-	-	-
Life Insurance	Median	-	-	-	-	-	-
	Average	-	-	-	-	-	-
Disability Insurance	Median	-	-	-	-	-	-
	Average	-	-	-	-	-	-
Retirement	Median	-	-	-	-	-	-
	Average	-	-	-	-	-	-
Continuing Education	Median	-	-	-	-	-	-
	Average	-	-	-	-	-	-
Total Benefits	**Median**	-	-	-	-	-	-
	Average	-	-	-	-	-	-
TOTAL COMPENSATION PLUS BENEFITS	**Median**	**$5,772**	**$9,075**	**$11,750**	**$4,005**	**$6,143**	**$12,692**
	Average	**$10,053**	**$11,590**	**$14,685**	**$7,066**	**$8,869**	**$15,950**
Number of Respondents		11	58	42	8	23	32

- Not enough response to provide meaningful data.

* For detailed description and definitions of Data Distribution (Median and Average), see Chapter 1's "Explanation of Data Distribution."

Table 13-16: Annual Compensation of Part-Time Bookkeepers/Accountants by Gender

	Data Distribution*	GENDER	
		Male	Female
CHARACTERISTICS			
Average weekend worship attendance		338	406
Average church income		$607,064	$667,611
Average # of years employed		6	7
Average # of paid vacation days		10	12
% College graduate or higher		72%	49%
% Who receive auto reimbursement/allowance		13%	11%
% Ordained		3%	3%
% Supervise one or more people		15%	10%
Average % salary increase (for those who had an increase) this year		3.5%	5.1%
HOURLY RATE			
Base Rate	Average	$16	$16
COMPENSATION			
Base Salary	Median	$8,320	$10,787
	Average	$10,374	$12,475
Housing	Median	-	-
	Average	-	-
Parsonage	Median	-	-
	Average	-	-
Total Compensation	**Median**	**$8,320**	**$10,773**
	Average	**$10,374**	**$12,443**
BENEFITS			
Health Insurance	Median	-	$6,159
	Average	-	$5,901
Life Insurance	Median	-	-
	Average	-	-
Disability Insurance	Median	-	-
	Average	-	-
Retirement	Median	-	$829
	Average	-	$1,161
Continuing Education	Median	-	-
	Average	-	-
Total Benefits	**Median**	-	**$1,058**
	Average	-	**$2,444**
TOTAL COMPENSATION PLUS BENEFITS	**Median**	**$8,320**	**$10,773**
	Average	**$10,719**	**$12,810**
Number of Respondents		39	193

- Not enough response to provide meaningful data.

* For detailed description and definitions of Data Distribution (Median and Average), see Chapter 1's "Explanation of Data Distribution."

14
SECRETARIES/ ADMINISTRATIVE ASSISTANTS

Employment Profile

Secretaries/Administrative Assistants include paid personnel who provide clerical or administrative support. This category may include such positions as Administrative Assistant, Clerical Assistant, Executive Secretary, Lead Secretary, Office Assistant, Office Clerk, Office Manager, Publications Coordinator, Receptionist, Church Secretary, Secretary to any pastor or ministry, Secretary's Assistant, etc.

Nearly six in ten of the reported Secretaries/Administrative Assistants are employed on a part-time basis. Almost all, regardless of employment status, are females employed by the church, rather than self-employed. More than half of the Secretaries/Administrative Assistants have more than a high school diploma.

This sample of Secretaries/Administrative Assistants provided the following employment profile:

	Full-Time	Part-Time
Number of respondents	552	744
Ordained	3%	2%
Average years employed	8	6
Male	3%	2%
Female	97%	98%
Self-employed (receives 1099)	1%	4%
Church employee (receives W-2)	99%	96%
High school diploma	48%	49%
Associate Degree	20%	18%
Bachelor's Degree	28%	28%
Master's Degree	4%	4%
Doctoral Degree	<.5%	<.5%

Total Compensation plus Benefits Package Analysis

The analyses on the next page are based on the data in the tables that you will find in the remainder of the chapter. The tables show compensation plus benefits data for full-time and part-time Secretaries/Administrative Assistants and are presented according to church income, church attendance, church setting, region, education, years employed, denomination, and gender. In this way, the Secretaries/Administrative Assistants' compensation plus benefits can be analyzed and compared from a variety of useful perspectives.

The total compensation plus benefits amount includes the base salary, housing and/or parsonage amount, health, life, and disability insurance payments, retirement contribution, and educational funds.

Secretaries/Administrative Assistants receive fewer benefits for full-time work than pastoral staff members receive. Less than half of them receive health insurance and retirement benefits. While nearly all full-time Secretaries/Administrative Assistants receive paid vacation, nearly all receive no housing or continuing education allowances. Three-quarters or more do not receive life or disability insurances or auto allowances. Few benefits are provided for part-time Secretaries/Administrative Assistants apart from paid vacation.

Compensation Plus Benefits	Full-Time	Part-Time
Base Salary	100%	100%
Housing	1%	0%
Parsonage	0%	0%
Health Insurance	41%	4%
Life Insurance	16%	1%
Disability Insurance	14%	2%
Retirement	40%	8%
Continuing Education	8%	4%
Received Salary Increase	59%	50%
Received Paid Vacation	95%	57%
Received Auto Reimbursement/ Allowance	18%	11%

KEY POINTS

✳ Almost half of full-time Secretaries/Administrative Assistants who reported serve in larger churches with income over $750,000, or churches with attendance of more than 500.

✳ For the most part, as church income increases, compensation and benefits for full-time Secretaries/Administrative Assistants also increase. For those holding part-time positions, the number of years employed has more impact on increased compensation than does church income.

✳ Eight out of ten full-time and part-time Secretaries/Administrative Assistants who reported serve in churches located in a suburb of large city or in a small town or rural city. In both cases, those working in the suburbs are compensated at a higher rate than those in small-town churches.

✳ Although few full-time Secretaries/Administrative Assistants were male (14 of 552 respondents), the males reported earning about 40% more than females. However, the part-time Secretaries/Administrative Assistants who were male (13 of 744 respondents) reported earning 15% less than their female counterparts.

Compensation & Benefits: National Averages for Full-Time Secretaries/Administrative Assistants

2000	$21,965
2001	$23,316
2002	$24,132
2003	$24,875
2004	$25,007
2005	$26,624
2006	$29,551
2007	$30,840
2008	$30,835
2009	$30,727*

*The above trend is made available for your reference only. In addition to looking at this overall data, please refer to the detailed tables using your church's income, attendance, setting, region, and denomination as well as the person's education, gender, and years employed for guidance in compensating this position.

Table 14-1: Annual Compensation of Full-Time Secretaries/Administrative Assistants by Church Income

CHARACTERISTICS	Data Distribution*	CHURCH INCOME				
		$250K & Under	$251-$500K	$501-$750K	$751K-$1M	Over 1 Million
Average weekend worship attendance		288	251	407	532	1,148
Average church income		$188,639	$382,241	$638,576	$893,415	$2,105,883
Average # of years employed		10	8	9	8	8
Average # of paid vacation days		12	14	16	15	15
% College graduate or higher		23%	27%	23%	29%	42%
% Who receive auto reimbursement/allowance		11%	17%	16%	10%	26%
% Ordained		6%	2%	0%	1%	3%
% Supervise one or more people		27%	25%	29%	27%	22%
Average % salary increase (for those who had an increase) this year		4.0%	4.8%	3.9%	3.5%	4.3%
COMPENSATION						
Base Salary	Highest 25%	$25,000	$29,120	$31,278	$33,000	$34,530
	Median	$20,800	$24,445	$28,000	$26,520	$29,174
	Lowest 25%	$16,380	$21,216	$23,462	$22,000	$24,000
	Average	$19,935	$25,455	$27,835	$28,037	$30,152
Housing	Highest 25%	-	-	-	-	-
	Median	-	-	-	-	-
	Lowest 25%	-	-	-	-	-
	Average	-	-	-	-	-
Parsonage	Highest 25%	-	-	-	-	-
	Median	-	-	-	-	-
	Lowest 25%	-	-	-	-	-
	Average	-	-	-	-	-
Total Compensation	**Highest 25%**	**$25,000**	**$29,120**	**$31,200**	**$33,000**	**$34,900**
	Median	**$20,800**	**$24,445**	**$28,000**	**$26,520**	**$29,422**
	Lowest 25%	**$16,380**	**$21,216**	**$23,004**	**$22,000**	**$24,185**
	Average	**$20,076**	**$25,455**	**$27,522**	**$28,037**	**$30,633**
BENEFITS						
Health Insurance	Highest 25%	$6,084	$6,200	$8,000	$6,315	$8,627
	Median	$3,000	$4,920	$5,170	$4,416	$5,256
	Lowest 25%	$2,045	$3,500	$3,400	$3,425	$4,117
	Average	$5,509	$5,026	$5,881	$5,474	$6,105
Life Insurance	Highest 25%	-	-	-	$236	$215
	Median	-	-	-	$174	$158
	Lowest 25%	-	-	-	$71	$100
	Average	-	-	-	$196	$459
Disability Insurance	Highest 25%	-	$422	-	-	$360
	Median	-	$363	-	-	$200
	Lowest 25%	-	$150	-	-	$154
	Average	-	$438	-	-	$279
Retirement	Highest 25%	$2,400	$2,470	$2,500	$2,506	$2,874
	Median	$1,743	$1,200	$1,260	$1,733	$1,982
	Lowest 25%	$944	$876	$1,000	$1,026	$1,230
	Average	$2,059	$1,956	$1,942	$1,897	$2,339
Continuing Education	Highest 25%	-	$900	-	-	$500
	Median	-	$500	-	-	$450
	Lowest 25%	-	$250	-	-	$250
	Average	-	$730	-	-	$515
Total Benefits	**Highest 25%**	**$7,250**	**$7,050**	**$7,477**	**$6,192**	**$8,887**
	Median	**$3,200**	**$3,700**	**$3,419**	**$3,288**	**$5,671**
	Lowest 25%	**$1,320**	**$2,000**	**$1,395**	**$1,660**	**$2,300**
	Average	**$5,629**	**$4,687**	**$4,609**	**$4,795**	**$6,158**
TOTAL COMPENSATION PLUS BENEFITS	**Highest 25%**	**$27,308**	**$31,000**	**$35,090**	**$35,983**	**$41,015**
	Median	**$21,632**	**$26,275**	**$29,413**	**$30,000**	**$34,753**
	Lowest 25%	**$16,973**	**$22,880**	**$26,328**	**$23,866**	**$27,343**
	Average	**$22,614**	**$27,816**	**$30,526**	**$31,056**	**$35,486**
Number of Respondents		51	133	89	81	184

- *Not enough response to provide meaningful data.*

* *For detailed description and definitions of Data Distribution (Median and Average), see Chapter 1's "Explanation of Data Distribution."*

Table 14-2: Annual Compensation of Full-Time Secretaries/Administrative Assistants by Worship Attendance

	Data Distribution*	WORSHIP ATTENDANCE					
		100 or less	101- 300	301- 500	501- 750	751- 1,000	Over 1,000
CHARACTERISTICS							
Average weekend worship attendance		81	211	411	604	878	2,229
Average church income		$201,371	$412,348	$804,277	$1,135,220	$1,733,814	$3,030,311
Average # of years employed		8	9	9	7	8	6
Average # of paid vacation days		11	14	16	14	15	15
% College graduate or higher		18%	28%	31%	32%	39%	38%
% Who receive auto reimbursement/allowance		18%	16%	20%	16%	30%	16%
% Ordained		12%	3%	2%	0%	0%	7%
% Supervise one or more people		24%	27%	25%	28%	27%	19%
Average % salary increase (for those who had an increase) this year		5.7%	4.3%	3.8%	3.3%	5.1%	4.6%
COMPENSATION							
Base Salary	Median	$19,200	$24,648	$26,780	$27,024	$29,422	$30,095
	Average	$18,214	$24,755	$27,871	$28,578	$30,596	$30,362
Housing	Median	-	-	-	-	-	-
	Average	-	-	-	-	-	-
Parsonage	Median	-	-	-	-	-	-
	Average	-	-	-	-	-	-
Total Compensation	**Median**	**$19,200**	**$24,624**	**$26,780**	**$27,024**	**$29,422**	**$30,329**
	Average	**$18,638**	**$24,627**	**$27,871**	**$28,578**	**$30,596**	**$31,508**
BENEFITS							
Health Insurance	Median	-	$4,567	$4,411	$5,695	$5,737	$5,256
	Average	-	$5,121	$5,206	$6,220	$6,914	$5,238
Life Insurance	Median	-	$162	$165	$126	$118	$177
	Average	-	$325	$224	$829	$218	$241
Disability	Median	-	$320	$316	$184	$294	$225
	Average	-	$395	$401	$260	$344	$610
Retirement	Median	-	$1,300	$1,624	$1,714	$2,286	$1,687
	Average	-	$1,942	$1,873	$2,247	$2,385	$2,389
Continuing Education	Median	-	$400	$270	-	-	-
	Average	-	$612	$456	-	-	-
Total Benefits	**Median**	-	**$3,788**	**$3,400**	**$5,600**	**$6,457**	**$5,451**
	Average	-	**$4,651**	**$4,141**	**$5,968**	**$7,498**	**$5,351**
TOTAL COMPENSATION PLUS BENEFITS	**Median**	**$23,000**	**$26,637**	**$29,447**	**$30,957**	**$35,090**	**$35,500**
	Average	**$21,086**	**$26,952**	**$30,679**	**$32,665**	**$35,952**	**$35,877**
Number of Respondents		17	194	115	92	63	60

- Not enough response to provide meaningful data.

* For detailed description and definitions of Data Distribution (Median and Average), see Chapter 1's "Explanation of Data Distribution."

Table 14-3: Annual Compensation of Full-Time Secretaries/Administrative Assistants by Church Setting

	Data Distribution*	CHURCH SETTING			
		Metro-politan city	Suburb of large city	Small town or rural city	Farming area
CHARACTERISTICS					
Average weekend worship attendance		668	793	464	459
Average church income		$1,174,529	$1,408,124	$773,378	$425,030
Average # of years employed		7	8	9	9
Average # of paid vacation days		15	15	14	11
% College graduate or higher		41%	34%	27%	17%
% Who receive auto reimbursement/allowance		18%	18%	19%	25%
% Ordained		6%	3%	1%	0%
% Supervise one or more people		29%	27%	25%	17%
Average % salary increase (for those who had an increase) this year		4.4%	4.1%	4.1%	4.9%
COMPENSATION					
Base Salary	Median	$28,500	$28,500	$25,000	$23,557
	Average	$29,218	$29,203	$25,069	$20,537
Housing	Median	-	-	-	-
	Average	-	-	-	-
Parsonage	Median	-	-	-	-
	Average	-	-	-	-
Total Compensation	**Median**	**$28,500**	**$28,765**	**$25,000**	**$23,557**
	Average	**$29,715**	**$29,305**	**$25,069**	**$20,537**
BENEFITS					
Health Insurance	Median	$4,441	$5,510	$4,411	-
	Average	$5,308	$6,230	$5,229	-
Life Insurance	Median	$137	$177	$118	-
	Average	$257	$508	$250	-
Disability Insurance	Median	$266	$224	$310	-
	Average	$294	$457	$419	-
Retirement	Median	$1,523	$2,250	$1,464	-
	Average	$1,987	$2,442	$1,933	-
Continuing Education	Median	$333	$450	$625	-
	Average	$414	$567	$922	-
Total Benefits	**Median**	**$3,600**	**$5,670**	**$3,864**	**-**
	Average	**$4,997**	**$5,889**	**$4,835**	**-**
TOTAL COMPENSATION PLUS BENEFITS	**Median**	**$30,750**	**$31,754**	**$27,083**	**$25,576**
	Average	**$33,102**	**$33,250**	**$27,903**	**$25,116**
Number of Respondents		90	212	232	12

- Not enough response to provide meaningful data.

* For detailed description and definitions of Data Distribution (Median and Average), see Chapter 1's "Explanation of Data Distribution."

Table 14-4: Annual Compensation of Full-Time Secretaries/Administrative Assistants by Region

	Data Distribution*	REGION								
		New England	Middle Atlantic	South Atlantic	E-N Central	E-S Central	W-N Central	W-S Central	Mountain	Pacific
CHARACTERISTICS										
Average weekend worship attendance		244	355	579	714	661	482	735	569	768
Average church income		$441,250	$604,996	$1,097,071	$1,221,232	$991,867	$756,997	$1,460,905	$874,989	$1,115,567
Average # of years employed		13	10	7	8	9	8	9	7	9
Average # of paid vacation days		14	15	14	15	14	15	15	15	16
% College graduate or higher		50%	26%	33%	32%	43%	38%	25%	25%	30%
% Who receive auto reimbursement/allowance		13%	6%	26%	12%	28%	16%	18%	16%	15%
% Ordained		11%	0%	3%	6%	0%	2%	1%	0%	4%
% Supervise one or more people		33%	24%	24%	31%	27%	29%	19%	26%	27%
Average % salary increase (for those who had an increase) this year		5.7%	4.5%	3.5%	4.7%	4.3%	4.3%	4.8%	4.0%	3.7%
COMPENSATION										
Base Salary	Median	$30,000	$28,000	$27,500	$26,000	$24,801	$24,000	$25,000	$25,000	$29,016
	Average	$29,231	$28,396	$28,247	$26,791	$25,372	$25,527	$26,720	$26,285	$28,953
Housing	Median	-	-	-	-	-	-	-	-	-
	Average	-	-	-	-	-	-	-	-	-
Parsonage	Median	-	-	-	-	-	-	-	-	-
	Average	-	-	-	-	-	-	-	-	-
Total Compensation	**Median**	**$30,000**	**$28,000**	**$27,500**	**$27,039**	**$24,801**	**$24,000**	**$25,000**	**$25,000**	**$29,016**
	Average	**$29,231**	**$28,396**	**$28,395**	**$26,989**	**$25,372**	**$25,527**	**$26,720**	**$26,285**	**$29,500**
BENEFITS										
Health Insurance	Median	-	$5,782	$4,860	$5,510	$4,368	$4,500	$5,256	$5,250	$6,000
	Average	-	$6,313	$5,903	$6,207	$4,321	$4,848	$5,754	$5,072	$6,672
Life Insurance	Median	-	-	$175	$158	-	$118	$183	-	-
	Average	-	-	$302	$1,171	-	$113	$333	-	-
Disability Insurance	Median	-	-	$368	$230	-	$200	$203	-	$258
	Average	-	-	$762	$275	-	$290	$370	-	$330
Retirement	Median	-	$1,510	$2,211	$1,955	$1,500	$1,468	$1,289	$1,300	$1,622
	Average	-	$1,753	$2,246	$2,530	$1,841	$1,894	$2,011	$1,320	$2,155
Continuing Education	Median	-	-	$400	-	-	$500	-	-	-
	Average	-	-	$669	-	-	$422	-	-	-
Total Benefits	**Median**	-	**$4,100**	**$4,700**	**$3,469**	**$2,500**	**$3,689**	**$4,950**	**$3,700**	**$6,658**
	Average	-	**$5,404**	**$5,884**	**$5,267**	**$3,913**	**$4,600**	**$4,933**	**$4,636**	**$6,969**
TOTAL COMPENSATION PLUS BENEFITS	**Median**	**$30,000**	**$32,745**	**$30,993**	**$28,930**	**$27,700**	**$26,690**	**$27,300**	**$27,500**	**$34,200**
	Average	**$31,050**	**$31,834**	**$32,359**	**$30,173**	**$27,620**	**$28,524**	**$29,704**	**$28,748**	**$34,513**
Number of Respondents		9	33	141	86	47	66	81	32	57

- Not enough response to provide meaningful data.

* For detailed description and definitions of Data Distribution (Median and Average), see Chapter 1's "Explanation of Data Distribution."

Table 14-5: Annual Compensation of Full-Time Secretaries/Administrative Assistants by Education

	Data Distribution*	EDUCATION			
		Less than Bachelor	Bachelor	Master	Doctorate
CHARACTERISTICS					
Average weekend worship attendance		596	690	412	-
Average church income		$986,802	$1,262,168	$1,041,911	-
Average # of years employed		9	6	5	-
Average # of paid vacation days		15	14	13	-
% College graduate or higher		0%	100%	100%	-
% Who receive auto reimbursement/allowance		19%	17%	24%	-
% Ordained		1%	5%	15%	-
% Supervise one or more people		25%	26%	50%	-
Average % salary increase (for those who had an increase) this year		4.1%	4.2%	5.9%	-
COMPENSATION					
Base Salary	Median	$25,273	$28,000	$25,625	-
	Average	$26,286	$29,385	$26,948	-
Housing	Median	-	-	-	-
	Average	-	-	-	-
Parsonage	Median	-	-	-	-
	Average	-	-	-	-
Total Compensation	**Median**	**$25,274**	**$28,028**	**$28,000**	**-**
	Average	**$26,233**	**$29,856**	**$27,890**	**-**
BENEFITS					
Health Insurance	Median	$5,000	$5,510	$3,595	-
	Average	$5,749	$5,812	$4,251	-
Life Insurance	Median	$170	$149	-	-
	Average	$270	$644	-	-
Disability Insurance	Median	$279	$200	-	-
	Average	$499	$268	-	-
Retirement	Median	$1,560	$2,350	-	-
	Average	$2,059	$2,387	-	-
Continuing Education	Median	$450	$375	-	-
	Average	$638	$504	-	-
Total Benefits	**Median**	**$3,990**	**$4,886**	**$3,595**	**-**
	Average	**$5,299**	**$5,483**	**$4,990**	**-**
TOTAL COMPENSATION PLUS BENEFITS	**Median**	**$28,534**	**$30,304**	**$28,000**	**-**
	Average	**$29,569**	**$33,311**	**$30,979**	**-**
Number of Respondents		359	146	21	2

- Not enough response to provide meaningful data.

* For detailed description and definitions of Data Distribution (Median and Average), see Chapter 1's "Explanation of Data Distribution."

Table 14-6: Annual Compensation of Full-Time Secretaries/Administrative Assistants by Years Employed

	Data Distribution*	YEARS EMPLOYED			
		Less than 6 years	6-10 years	11-15 years	Over 15 years
CHARACTERISTICS					
Average weekend worship attendance		662	686	614	404
Average church income		$1,110,628	$1,201,641	$1,117,868	$763,217
Average # of years employed		3	8	13	23
Average # of paid vacation days		12	15	18	20
% College graduate or higher		42%	28%	23%	17%
% Who receive auto reimbursement/allowance		18%	20%	15%	18%
% Ordained		2%	5%	2%	2%
% Supervise one or more people		23%	26%	36%	37%
Average % salary increase (for those who had an increase) this year		4.5%	4.2%	3.7%	3.8%
COMPENSATION					
Base Salary	Median	$25,000	$28,000	$27,876	$27,436
	Average	$26,155	$28,229	$28,091	$28,574
Housing	Median	-	-	-	-
	Average	-	-	-	-
Parsonage	Median	-	-	-	-
	Average	-	-	-	-
Total Compensation	**Median**	**$25,016**	**$28,000**	**$27,876**	**$27,682**
	Average	**$26,240**	**$28,593**	**$28,091**	**$28,680**
BENEFITS					
Health Insurance	Median	$4,703	$5,628	$6,500	$4,724
	Average	$5,321	$6,356	$7,175	$5,193
Life Insurance	Median	$134	$183	$139	-
	Average	$153	$317	$279	-
Disability Insurance	Median	$210	$500	$293	$186
	Average	$487	$462	$367	$237
Retirement	Median	$1,607	$1,505	$1,631	$1,856
	Average	$2,010	$1,990	$2,138	$2,607
Continuing Education	Median	$500	$500	-	-
	Average	$767	$455	-	-
Total Benefits	**Median**	**$3,710**	**$5,677**	**$5,344**	**$4,567**
	Average	**$4,973**	**$5,940**	**$6,281**	**$4,973**
TOTAL COMPENSATION PLUS BENEFITS	**Median**	**$27,950**	**$31,097**	**$30,410**	**$30,195**
	Average	**$29,190**	**$32,733**	**$32,906**	**$32,117**
Number of Respondents		231	132	60	68

- Not enough response to provide meaningful data.

* For detailed description and definitions of Data Distribution (Median and Average), see Chapter 1's "Explanation of Data Distribution."

Table 14-7: Annual Compensation of Full-Time Secretaries/Administrative Assistants by Denomination

	Data Distribution*	Assemblies of God	Baptist	Independent/ Nondenom.	Lutheran	Methodist	Presby- terian
CHARACTERISTICS							
Average weekend worship attendance		397	575	962	492	531	396
Average church income		$758,874	$1,082,829	$1,341,704	$915,403	$1,014,200	$902,256
Average # of years employed		10	9	7	9	7	9
Average # of paid vacation days		15	15	14	16	14	15
% College graduate or higher		20%	28%	29%	30%	41%	42%
% Who receive auto reimbursement/allowance		13%	24%	12%	19%	12%	13%
% Ordained		16%	3%	4%	0%	0%	0%
% Supervise one or more people		29%	20%	29%	27%	27%	39%
Average % salary increase (for those who had an increase) this year		8.5%	3.9%	3.9%	3.5%	5.4%	3.3%
COMPENSATION							
Base Salary	Median	$23,920	$25,000	$26,000	$28,252	$26,000	$31,200
	Average	$25,820	$26,285	$27,126	$29,409	$26,571	$31,924
Housing	Median	-	-	-	-	-	-
	Average	-	-	-	-	-	-
Parsonage	Median	-	-	-	-	-	-
	Average	-	-	-	-	-	-
Total Compensation	**Median**	**$24,000**	**$25,000**	**$26,000**	**$28,252**	**$26,000**	**$31,200**
	Average	**$26,053**	**$26,386**	**$27,678**	**$29,409**	**$26,571**	**$31,105**
BENEFITS							
Health Insurance	Median	$3,454	$4,877	$4,703	$5,676	$4,099	$5,641
	Average	$4,938	$5,854	$5,982	$6,423	$4,398	$5,250
Life Insurance	Median	-	$132	$118	-	-	-
	Average	-	$414	$207	-	-	-
Disability Insurance	Median	-	$200	$219	$593	-	-
	Average	-	$266	$828	$583	-	-
Retirement	Median	-	$1,837	$1,300	$2,350	$1,500	$2,617
	Average	-	$2,132	$1,875	$2,347	$1,754	$2,945
Continuing Education	Median	-	$300	-	-	$625	-
	Average	-	$379	-	-	$752	-
Total Benefits	**Median**	**$3,115**	**$4,000**	**$4,821**	**$3,636**	**$3,300**	**$5,772**
	Average	**$4,425**	**$5,399**	**$5,884**	**$6,266**	**$3,785**	**$6,354**
TOTAL COMPENSATION PLUS BENEFITS	**Median**	**$24,090**	**$28,000**	**$30,000**	**$31,356**	**$28,000**	**$34,882**
	Average	**$27,908**	**$30,069**	**$30,947**	**$34,282**	**$28,723**	**$35,993**
Number of Respondents		31	195	81	27	51	39

- Not enough response to provide meaningful data.

* For detailed description and definitions of Data Distribution (Median and Average), see Chapter 1's "Explanation of Data Distribution."

Table 14-8: Annual Compensation of Full-Time Secretaries/Administrative Assistants by Gender

CHARACTERISTICS	Data Distribution*	Male	Female
Average weekend worship attendance		669	618
Average church income		$1,345,042	$1,069,658
Average # of years employed		6	8
Average # of paid vacation days		14	15
% College graduate or higher		57%	31%
% Who receive auto reimbursement/allowance		29%	18%
% Ordained		15%	2%
% Supervise one or more people		43%	25%
Average % salary increase (for those who had an increase) this year		3.0%	4.2%
COMPENSATION			
Base Salary	Median	$33,200	$26,000
	Average	$34,780	$27,056
Housing	Median	-	-
	Average	-	-
Parsonage	Median	-	-
	Average	-	-
Total Compensation	**Median**	**$33,200**	**$26,000**
	Average	**$36,193**	**$27,147**
BENEFITS			
Health Insurance	Median	$6,193	$4,993
	Average	$6,888	$5,673
Life Insurance	Median	-	$139
	Average	-	$325
Disability Insurance	Median	-	$250
	Average	-	$434
Retirement	Median	-	$1,631
	Average	-	$2,083
Continuing Education	Median	-	$450
	Average	-	$593
Total Benefits	**Median**	**$7,878**	**$4,130**
	Average	**$9,433**	**$5,233**
TOTAL COMPENSATION PLUS BENEFITS	**Median**	**$41,150**	**$29,000**
	Average	**$43,605**	**$30,447**
Number of Respondents		14	536

- Not enough response to provide meaningful data.

* For detailed description and definitions of Data Distribution (Median and Average), see Chapter 1's "Explanation of Data Distribution."

Table 14-9: Annual Compensation of Part-Time Secretaries/Administrative Assistants by Church Income

	Data Distribution*	CHURCH INCOME				
		$250K & Under	$251-$500K	$501-$750K	$751K-$1M	Over 1 Million
CHARACTERISTICS						
Average weekend worship attendance		113	232	407	514	1,038
Average church income		$168,244	$356,592	$637,585	$890,001	$1,639,274
Average # of years employed		7	7	5	6	5
Average # of paid vacation days		11	12	12	12	12
% College graduate or higher		30%	36%	30%	36%	38%
% Who receive auto reimbursement/allowance		9%	8%	10%	10%	23%
% Ordained		2%	2%	4%	3%	0%
% Supervise one or more people		8%	10%	10%	10%	9%
Average % salary increase (for those who had an increase) this year		5.9%	4.1%	4.3%	3.5%	3.2%
HOURLY RATE						
Base Rate	Average	$11	$12	$13	$13	$13
COMPENSATION						
Base Salary	Median	-	-	-	-	-
	Average	-	-	-	-	-
Housing	Median	-	-	-	-	-
	Average	-	-	-	-	-
Parsonage	Median	-	-	-	-	-
	Average	-	-	-	-	-
Total Compensation	**Median**	**$9,800**	**$14,566**	**$13,830**	**$14,780**	**$15,425**
	Average	**$10,351**	**$14,446**	**$14,721**	**$15,972**	**$15,891**
BENEFITS						
Health Insurance	Median	-	$1,500	-	-	-
	Average	-	$3,473	-	-	-
Life Insurance	Median	-	-	-	-	-
	Average	-	-	-	-	-
Disability Insurance	Median	-	-	-	-	-
	Average	-	-	-	-	-
Retirement	Median	-	$1,200	$1,018	-	$1,080
	Average	-	$1,866	$2,011	-	$1,345
Continuing Education	Median	$250	-	$213	-	-
	Average	$409	-	$188	-	-
Total Benefits	**Median**	**$555**	**$1,153**	**$568**	**-**	**$1,800**
	Average	**$1,167**	**$2,125**	**$1,324**	**-**	**$2,521**
TOTAL COMPENSATION PLUS BENEFITS	**Median**	**$9,800**	**$14,693**	**$13,975**	**$14,780**	**$15,425**
	Average	**$10,446**	**$14,798**	**$14,952**	**$16,293**	**$16,544**
Number of Respondents		295	175	103	62	85

- Not enough response to provide meaningful data.

* For detailed description and definitions of Data Distribution (Median and Average), see Chapter 1's "Explanation of Data Distribution."

Table 14-10: Annual Compensation of Part-Time Secretaries/Administrative Assistants by Worship Attendance

	Data Distribution*	WORSHIP ATTENDANCE					
		100 or less	101-300	301-500	501-750	751-1,000	Over 1,000
CHARACTERISTICS							
Average weekend worship attendance		74	187	406	626	852	1,645
Average church income		$154,047	$308,660	$744,683	$970,034	$1,264,514	$2,065,571
Average # of years employed		7	7	6	5	6	5
Average # of paid vacation days		11	12	11	11	11	10
% College graduate or higher		29%	31%	37%	33%	38%	42%
% Who receive auto reimbursement/allowance		9%	8%	11%	20%	22%	18%
% Ordained		2%	3%	2%	0%	0%	3%
% Supervise one or more people		6%	9%	13%	9%	13%	8%
Average % salary increase (for those who had an increase) this year		6.8%	4.5%	3.8%	3.6%	4.5%	3.1%
HOURLY RATE							
Base Rate	Average	$11	$12	$13	$12	$12	$11
COMPENSATION							
Base Salary	Median	$8,580	$12,650	$14,586	$15,656	$14,269	$12,532
	Average	$9,358	$13,278	$15,688	$15,241	$15,413	$13,314
Housing	Median	-	-	-	-	-	-
	Average	-	-	-	-	-	-
Parsonage	Median	-	-	-	-	-	-
	Average	-	-	-	-	-	-
Total Compensation	**Median**	**$8,580**	**$12,650**	**$14,586**	**$15,656**	**$14,269**	**$12,532**
	Average	**$9,358**	**$13,278**	**$15,688**	**$15,241**	**$15,413**	**$13,314**
BENEFITS							
Health Insurance	Median	-	$2,000	-	-	-	-
	Average	-	$3,285	-	-	-	-
Life Insurance	Median	-	-	-	-	-	-
	Average	-	-	-	-	-	-
Disability	Median	-	-	-	-	-	-
	Average	-	-	-	-	-	-
Retirement	Median	-	$1,209	$2,080	-	-	-
	Average	-	$2,217	$1,679	-	-	-
Continuing Education	Median	-	$200	-	-	-	-
	Average	-	$244	-	-	-	-
Total Benefits	**Median**	**$450**	**$1,137**	**$975**	-	-	-
	Average	**$930**	**$2,136**	**$1,693**	-	-	-
TOTAL COMPENSATION PLUS BENEFITS	**Median**	**$8,600**	**$13,000**	**$15,000**	**$15,656**	**$14,269**	**$12,792**
	Average	**$9,461**	**$13,558**	**$15,988**	**$15,710**	**$15,903**	**$13,554**
Number of Respondents		163	344	113	61	24	36

- Not enough response to provide meaningful data.

* For detailed description and definitions of Data Distribution (Median and Average), see Chapter 1's "Explanation of Data Distribution."

Table 14-11: Annual Compensation of Part-Time Secretaries/Administrative Assistants by Church Setting

	Data Distribution*	CHURCH SETTING			
		Metro-politan city	Suburb of large city	Small town or rural city	Farming area
CHARACTERISTICS					
Average weekend worship attendance		270	455	270	159
Average church income		$525,121	$736,476	$398,129	$235,369
Average # of years employed		5	6	7	7
Average # of paid vacation days		10	12	12	9
% College graduate or higher		52%	33%	28%	26%
% Who receive auto reimbursement/allowance		11%	12%	9%	10%
% Ordained		5%	4%	1%	0%
% Supervise one or more people		13%	8%	8%	4%
Average % salary increase (for those who had an increase) this year		3.5%	4.0%	4.3%	12.5%
HOURLY RATE					
Base Rate	Average	$13	$13	$11	$10
COMPENSATION					
Base Salary	Median	$13,263	$13,000	$12,355	$7,800
	Average	$13,764	$13,889	$12,906	$8,549
Housing	Median	-	-	-	-
	Average	-	-	-	-
Parsonage	Median	-	-	-	-
	Average	-	-	-	-
Total Compensation	**Median**	**$13,263**	**$13,000**	**$12,355**	**$7,800**
	Average	**$13,764**	**$13,889**	**$12,906**	**$8,549**
BENEFITS					
Health Insurance	Median	-	$1,200	$4,303	-
	Average	-	$2,608	$3,442	-
Life Insurance	Median	-	-	-	-
	Average	-	-	-	-
Disability Insurance	Median	-	-	-	-
	Average	-	-	-	-
Retirement	Median	-	$1,142	$1,177	-
	Average	-	$1,632	$1,606	-
Continuing Education	Median	-	$200	$250	-
	Average	-	$259	$286	-
Total Benefits	**Median**	**$1,500**	**$1,050**	**$1,074**	**-**
	Average	**$2,875**	**$1,816**	**$1,757**	**-**
TOTAL COMPENSATION PLUS BENEFITS	**Median**	**$13,263**	**$13,172**	**$12,480**	**$7,800**
	Average	**$14,116**	**$14,177**	**$13,165**	**$8,584**
Number of Respondents		90	252	346	49

- Not enough response to provide meaningful data.

* For detailed description and definitions of Data Distribution (Median and Average), see Chapter 1's "Explanation of Data Distribution."

Table 14-12: Annual Compensation of Part-Time Secretaries/Administrative Assistants by Region

	Data Distribution*	New England	Middle Atlantic	South Atlantic	E-N Central	E-S Central	W-N Central	W-S Central	Mountain	Pacific
CHARACTERISTICS										
Average weekend worship attendance		129	251	338	408	361	315	282	279	307
Average church income		$273,740	$394,842	$504,848	$634,248	$494,361	$449,473	$597,005	$432,722	$537,428
Average # of years employed		9	8	7	6	6	7	6	5	6
Average # of paid vacation days		13	13	11	11	11	12	9	14	12
% College graduate or higher		32%	26%	34%	34%	31%	29%	35%	31%	35%
% Who receive auto reimbursement/allowance		0%	4%	9%	7%	21%	18%	25%	9%	11%
% Ordained		4%	5%	4%	1%	0%	0%	2%	0%	2%
% Supervise one or more people		8%	4%	6%	9%	6%	6%	9%	18%	14%
Average % salary increase (for those who had an increase) this year		3.5%	4.2%	5.6%	4.2%	3.8%	5.6%	4.6%	4.6%	4.3%
HOURLY RATE										
Base Rate	Average	$15	$12	$12	$12	$10	$12	$11	$12	$13
COMPENSATION										
Base Salary	Median	$12,115	$12,584	$12,800	$11,880	$12,037	$12,240	$11,882	$12,285	$14,000
	Average	$14,632	$12,967	$13,104	$12,467	$12,212	$12,610	$11,846	$13,002	$14,658
Housing	Median	-	-	-	-	-	-	-	-	-
	Average	-	-	-	-	-	-	-	-	-
Parsonage	Median	-	-	-	-	-	-	-	-	-
	Average	-	-	-	-	-	-	-	-	-
Total Compensation	**Median**	**$12,115**	**$12,584**	**$12,800**	**$11,880**	**$12,037**	**$12,240**	**$11,882**	**$12,285**	**$14,000**
	Average	**$14,632**	**$12,967**	**$13,104**	**$12,467**	**$12,212**	**$12,610**	**$11,846**	**$13,002**	**$14,658**
BENEFITS										
Health Insurance	Median	-	-	-	-	-	-	-	-	$4,206
	Average	-	-	-	-	-	-	-	-	$4,293
Life Insurance	Median	-	-	-	-	-	-	-	-	-
	Average	-	-	-	-	-	-	-	-	-
Disability Insurance	Median	-	-	-	-	-	-	-	-	-
	Average	-	-	-	-	-	-	-	-	-
Retirement	Median	-	-	$1,567	$873	-	-	$600	-	$2,102
	Average	-	-	$1,859	$993	-	-	$788	-	$2,755
Continuing Education	Median	-	-	$238	-	-	-	-	-	-
	Average	-	-	$338	-	-	-	-	-	-
Total Benefits	**Median**	**$1,473**	**$360**	**$1,000**	**$873**	**-**	**$448**	**$878**	**-**	**$2,770**
	Average	**$1,609**	**$1,028**	**$2,056**	**$1,216**	**-**	**$509**	**$1,893**	**-**	**$3,441**
TOTAL COMPENSATION PLUS BENEFITS	**Median**	**$12,115**	**$12,584**	**$13,000**	**$11,997**	**$12,447**	**$12,240**	**$11,882**	**$12,285**	**$14,625**
	Average	**$15,127**	**$13,110**	**$13,416**	**$12,601**	**$12,355**	**$12,660**	**$12,190**	**$13,027**	**$15,335**
Number of Respondents		26	79	125	181	34	81	55	46	117

- Not enough response to provide meaningful data.

* For detailed description and definitions of Data Distribution (Median and Average), see Chapter 1's "Explanation of Data Distribution."

Table 14-13: Annual Compensation of Part-Time Secretaries/Administrative Assistants by Education

	Data Distribution*	EDUCATION			
		Less than Bachelor	Bachelor	Master	Doctorate
CHARACTERISTICS					
Average weekend worship attendance		316	355	292	-
Average church income		$496,891	$575,353	$465,868	-
Average # of years employed		7	5	5	-
Average # of paid vacation days		12	11	8	-
% College graduate or higher		0%	100%	100%	-
% Who receive auto reimbursement/allowance		9%	12%	14%	-
% Ordained		2%	2%	10%	-
% Supervise one or more people		8%	8%	21%	-
Average % salary increase (for those who had an increase) this year		4.6%	4.6%	4.9%	-
HOURLY RATE					
Base Rate	Average	$12	$12	$12	-
COMPENSATION					
Base Salary	Median	$12,480	$12,000	$12,500	-
	Average	$12,970	$13,199	$13,340	-
Housing	Median	-	-	-	-
	Average	-	-	-	-
Parsonage	Median	-	-	-	-
	Average	-	-	-	-
Total Compensation	**Median**	**$12,480**	**$12,000**	**$12,500**	-
	Average	**$12,970**	**$13,199**	**$13,340**	-
BENEFITS					
Health Insurance	Median	$4,400	-	-	-
	Average	$3,965	-	-	-
Life Insurance	Median	-	-	-	-
	Average	-	-	-	-
Disability Insurance	Median	$100	-	-	-
	Average	$266	-	-	-
Retirement	Median	$1,200	$1,153	-	-
	Average	$1,886	$1,121	-	-
Continuing Education	Median	$225	-	-	-
	Average	$248	-	-	-
Total Benefits	**Median**	**$850**	**$1,149**	-	-
	Average	**$1,898**	**$1,452**	-	-
TOTAL COMPENSATION PLUS BENEFITS	**Median**	**$12,592**	**$12,000**	**$13,200**	-
	Average	**$13,243**	**$13,399**	**$13,382**	-
Number of Respondents		486	203	29	1

- Not enough response to provide meaningful data.

* For detailed description and definitions of Data Distribution (Median and Average), see Chapter 1's "Explanation of Data Distribution."

Table 14-14: Annual Compensation of Part-Time Secretaries/Administrative Assistants by Years Employed

	Data Distribution*	YEARS EMPLOYED			
		Less than 6 years	6-10 years	11-15 years	Over 15 years
CHARACTERISTICS					
Average weekend worship attendance		361	288	316	236
Average church income		$561,449	$475,450	$503,461	$378,771
Average # of years employed		3	8	13	21
Average # of paid vacation days		10	13	14	16
% College graduate or higher		37%	27%	24%	23%
% Who receive auto reimbursement/allowance		11%	12%	9%	10%
% Ordained		1%	2%	5%	4%
% Supervise one or more people		5%	16%	19%	13%
Average % salary increase (for those who had an increase) this year		4.8%	3.8%	5.4%	4.6%
HOURLY RATE					
Base Rate	Average	$11	$12	$13	$14
COMPENSATION					
Base Salary	Median	$11,725	$13,500	$14,230	$16,000
	Average	$12,017	$13,760	$15,089	$16,689
Housing	Median	-	-	-	-
	Average	-	-	-	-
Parsonage	Median	-	-	-	-
	Average	-	-	-	-
Total Compensation	**Median**	**$11,725**	**$13,500**	**$14,230**	**$16,000**
	Average	**$12,017**	**$13,760**	**$15,089**	**$16,689**
BENEFITS					
Health Insurance	Median	$3,050	-	-	-
	Average	$2,746	-	-	-
Life Insurance	Median	-	-	-	-
	Average	-	-	-	-
Disability Insurance	Median	-	-	-	-
	Average	-	-	-	-
Retirement	Median	$800	$1,200	$1,384	-
	Average	$1,395	$1,729	$1,826	-
Continuing Education	Median	$250	-	-	-
	Average	$338	-	-	-
Total Benefits	**Median**	**$575**	**$1,200**	**$1,200**	**$1,621**
	Average	**$1,496**	**$2,165**	**$1,811**	**$2,886**
TOTAL COMPENSATION PLUS BENEFITS	**Median**	**$11,798**	**$13,500**	**$15,287**	**$17,100**
	Average	**$12,174**	**$14,128**	**$15,507**	**$17,396**
Number of Respondents		382	147	78	49

- Not enough response to provide meaningful data.

* For detailed description and definitions of Data Distribution (Median and Average), see Chapter 1's "Explanation of Data Distribution."

Table 14-15: Annual Compensation of Part-Time Secretaries/Administrative Assistants by Denomination

	Data Distribution*	DENOMINATION					
		Assemblies of God	Baptist	Independent/ Nondenom.	Lutheran	Methodist	Presby- terian
CHARACTERISTICS							
Average weekend worship attendance		281	319	502	230	232	251
Average church income		$451,200	$475,917	$741,918	$467,701	$385,415	$453,545
Average # of years employed		5	7	6	5	5	7
Average # of paid vacation days		11	11	11	13	12	12
% College graduate or higher		17%	29%	36%	42%	31%	33%
% Who receive auto reimbursement/allowance		6%	12%	6%	9%	21%	14%
% Ordained		3%	0%	3%	4%	0%	5%
% Supervise one or more people		14%	8%	9%	5%	13%	9%
Average % salary increase (for those who had an increase) this year		4.6%	5.1%	4.1%	3.8%	4.0%	3.5%
HOURLY RATE							
Base Rate	Average	$11	$12	$13	$12	$12	$12
COMPENSATION							
Base Salary	Median	$11,940	$12,837	$13,000	$12,500	$12,384	$13,650
	Average	$11,400	$13,280	$14,074	$12,676	$12,137	$14,389
Housing	Median	-	-	-	-	-	-
	Average	-	-	-	-	-	-
Parsonage	Median	-	-	-	-	-	-
	Average	-	-	-	-	-	-
Total Compensation	**Median**	**$11,940**	**$12,837**	**$13,000**	**$12,500**	**$12,384**	**$13,650**
	Average	**$11,400**	**$13,280**	**$14,074**	**$12,676**	**$12,137**	**$14,389**
BENEFITS							
Health Insurance	Median	-	$4,638	$2,500	-	-	-
	Average	-	$4,367	$3,683	-	-	-
Life Insurance	Median	-	-	-	-	-	-
	Average	-	-	-	-	-	-
Disability Insurance	Median	-	-	-	-	-	-
	Average	-	-	-	-	-	-
Retirement	Median	-	$1,708	$1,111	-	-	-
	Average	-	$1,794	$1,036	-	-	-
Continuing Education	Median	-	$275	-	-	$225	-
	Average	-	$294	-	-	$267	-
Total Benefits	**Median**	-	**$1,248**	**$1,145**	**$1,037**	**$375**	-
	Average	-	**$2,375**	**$2,018**	**$1,330**	**$479**	-
TOTAL COMPENSATION PLUS BENEFITS	**Median**	**$12,360**	**$12,925**	**$13,406**	**$12,695**	**$12,384**	**$13,650**
	Average	**$11,611**	**$13,574**	**$14,489**	**$12,907**	**$12,245**	**$14,745**
Number of Respondents		36	210	112	46	53	65

- Not enough response to provide meaningful data.

* For detailed description and definitions of Data Distribution (Median and Average), see Chapter 1's "Explanation of Data Distribution."

Table 14-16: Annual Compensation of Part-Time Secretaries/Administrative Assistants by Gender

	Data Distribution*	GENDER	
		Male	Female
CHARACTERISTICS			
Average weekend worship attendance		213	327
Average church income		$398,590	$520,981
Average # of years employed		7	6
Average # of paid vacation days		11	11
% College graduate or higher		46%	32%
% Who receive auto reimbursement/allowance		15%	11%
% Ordained		8%	2%
% Supervise one or more people		8%	9%
Average % salary increase (for those who had an increase) this year		4.0%	4.6%
HOURLY RATE			
Base Rate	Average	$12	$12
COMPENSATION			
Base Salary	Median	$11,882	$12,432
	Average	$11,587	$13,054
Housing	Median	-	-
	Average	-	-
Parsonage	Median	-	-
	Average	-	-
Total Compensation	**Median**	**$11,882**	**$12,432**
	Average	**$11,587**	**$13,054**
BENEFITS			
Health Insurance	Median	-	$4,097
	Average	-	$3,583
Life Insurance	Median	-	-
	Average	-	-
Disability Insurance	Median	-	$100
	Average	-	$238
Retirement	Median	-	$1,200
	Average	-	$1,606
Continuing Education	Median	-	$238
	Average	-	$284
Total Benefits	**Median**	**-**	**$1,090**
	Average	**-**	**$1,871**
TOTAL COMPENSATION PLUS BENEFITS	**Median**	**$11,882**	**$12,482**
	Average	**$11,587**	**$13,322**
Number of Respondents		13	726

- Not enough response to provide meaningful data.

* For detailed description and definitions of Data Distribution (Median and Average), see Chapter 1's "Explanation of Data Distribution."

15

CUSTODIANS

Employment Profile

Custodians include paid personnel who provide care and maintenance of facilities, buildings, grounds, and security. This category may include such positions as Building and Grounds Manager, Building Supervisor, Custodian, Facilities Manager, Grounds Keeper, Housekeeper, Lawn Maintenance Assistant, Maid, Maintenance Assistant, Plant Manager, Property Manager, Security Manager or Assistant, Sexton, Traffic Coordinator, etc.

Two-thirds of Custodians in this survey serve part-time. Most full-time Custodians are men while part-time Custodians are split about evenly between males and females. The highest level of education for about three-quarters of full-time and part-time Custodians is a high school diploma.

The following chart summarizes a demographic profile of this sample:

	Full-Time	Part-Time
Number of respondents	251	526
Ordained	2%	2%
Average years employed	9	6
Male	83%	56%
Female	17%	44%
Self-employed (receives 1099)	1%	9%
Church employee (receives W-2)	99%	91%
High school diploma	77%	79%
Associate Degree	10%	7%
Bachelor's Degree	13%	12%
Master's Degree	1%	1%
Doctoral Degree	0%	0%

Total Compensation plus Benefits Package Analysis

The analyses on the next page are based on the data in the tables that you will find in the remainder of the chapter. The tables show compensation plus benefits data for full-time and part-time Custodians and are presented according to church income, church attendance, church setting, region, education, years employed, denomination, and gender. In this way, Custodians' compensation plus benefits can be analyzed and compared from a variety of useful perspectives.

The total compensation plus benefits amount includes the base salary, housing allowance and/or parsonage amount, health, life, and disability insurance payments, retirement contribution, and educational funds.

Custodians receive fewer benefits than pastoral positions but they are aligned with other non-pastoral positions. More than half of full-time Custodians receive health insurance and slightly less than half receive retirement benefits. Paid vacation is part of nearly all full-time Custodians' compensation plus benefit packages. Churches provide part-time Custodians with very few benefits compared to full-time employees.

Compensation Plus Benefits	Full-Time	Part-Time
Base Salary	100%	100%
Housing	1%	1%
Parsonage	2%	0%
Health Insurance	55%	2%
Life Insurance	26%	1%
Disability Insurance	20%	2%
Retirement	45%	2%
Continuing Education	4%	0%
Received Salary Increase	60%	41%
Received Paid Vacation	98%	27%
Received Auto Reimbursement/ Allowance	18%	6%

KEY POINTS

* Nearly half of full-time Custodians reported in this sample serve in larger churches with income of over $1,000,000, while four in ten part-time workers serve in smaller churches with income of $250,000 or less.

* About four in ten full-time Custodians are serving in churches set in a small town or rural city. Full-time Custodians serving in churches located in a suburb of a large city receive the highest compensation and benefits packages.

* Regional differences emerge in Custodians' compensation and benefits packages. Both full-time and part-time Custodians from the Pacific have the highest compensation packages.

Compensation & Benefits: National Averages for Full-Time Custodians

2000	$26,161
2001	$26,725
2002	$27,913
2003	$29,047
2004	$30,052
2005	$31,026
2006	$32,884
2007	$33,893
2008	$36,462
2009	$35,425*

The above trend is made available for your reference only. In addition to looking at this overall data, please refer to the detailed tables using your church's income, attendance, setting, region, and denomination as well as the person's education, gender, and years employed for guidance in compensating this position.

Table 15-1: Annual Compensation of Full-Time Custodians by Church Income

CHARACTERISTICS	Data Distribution*	CHURCH INCOME				
		$250K & Under	$251-$500K	$501-$750K	$751K-$1M	Over 1 Million
Average weekend worship attendance	-		249	424	480	1,136
Average church income	-		$404,073	$634,607	$892,188	$2,062,286
Average # of years employed	-		9	8	11	8
Average # of paid vacation days	-		15	15	16	15
% College graduate or higher	-		7%	5%	14%	18%
% Who receive auto reimbursement/allowance	-		11%	16%	12%	24%
% Ordained	-		0%	2%	4%	3%
% Supervise one or more people	-		11%	37%	46%	53%
Average % salary increase (for those who had an increase) this year	-		3.1%	4.7%	3.4%	3.8%
COMPENSATION						
Base Salary	Highest 25%	-	$25,000	$32,000	$33,315	$40,721
	Median	-	$20,000	$27,666	$27,022	$31,824
	Lowest 25%	-	$17,232	$22,000	$23,762	$26,111
	Average	-	$21,813	$27,825	$28,785	$33,134
Housing	Highest 25%	-	-	-	-	-
	Median	-	-	-	-	-
	Lowest 25%	-	-	-	-	-
	Average	-	-	-	-	-
Parsonage	Highest 25%	-	-	-	-	-
	Median	-	-	-	-	-
	Lowest 25%	-	-	-	-	-
	Average	-	-	-	-	-
Total Compensation	**Highest 25%**	-	**$25,000**	**$33,666**	**$33,587**	**$40,721**
	Median	-	**$20,000**	**$28,805**	**$27,357**	**$32,000**
	Lowest 25%	-	**$17,425**	**$22,000**	**$23,762**	**$26,187**
	Average	-	**$22,169**	**$29,241**	**$28,939**	**$33,231**
BENEFITS						
Health Insurance	Highest 25%	-	$9,546	$9,468	$8,866	$10,200
	Median	-	$6,559	$6,679	$6,438	$5,805
	Lowest 25%	-	$4,220	$4,075	$3,764	$3,353
	Average	-	$7,738	$6,965	$7,075	$6,869
Life Insurance	Highest 25%	-	-	-	-	$222
	Median	-	-	-	-	$120
	Lowest 25%	-	-	-	-	$58
	Average	-	-	-	-	$209
Disability Insurance	Highest 25%	-	-	-	-	$462
	Median	-	-	-	-	$210
	Lowest 25%	-	-	-	-	$166
	Average	-	-	-	-	$335
Retirement	Highest 25%	-	-	$2,516	$2,556	$2,961
	Median	-	-	$1,995	$2,048	$1,979
	Lowest 25%	-	-	$1,136	$1,446	$1,268
	Average	-	-	$1,854	$2,108	$2,283
Continuing Education	Highest 25%	-	-	-	-	-
	Median	-	-	-	-	-
	Lowest 25%	-	-	-	-	-
	Average	-	-	-	-	-
Total Benefits	**Highest 25%**	-	**$7,525**	**$10,261**	**$9,343**	**$10,536**
	Median	-	**$5,750**	**$6,000**	**$5,785**	**$6,181**
	Lowest 25%	-	**$1,836**	**$2,090**	**$2,554**	**$2,417**
	Average	-	**$7,052**	**$6,706**	**$6,584**	**$7,217**
TOTAL COMPENSATION PLUS BENEFITS	**Highest 25%**	-	**$29,150**	**$39,400**	**$39,983**	**$48,000**
	Median	-	**$22,800**	**$33,666**	**$32,253**	**$38,300**
	Lowest 25%	-	**$18,720**	**$23,100**	**$24,784**	**$29,640**
	Average	-	**$24,781**	**$33,452**	**$32,991**	**$39,451**
Number of Respondents	5	27	43	52	123	

- Not enough response to provide meaningful data.

* For detailed description and definitions of Data Distribution (Median and Average), see Chapter 1's "Explanation of Data Distribution."

Table 15-2: Annual Compensation of Full-Time Custodians by Worship Attendance

	Data Distribution*	\#WORSHIP ATTENDANCE 100 or less	101-300	301-500	501-750	751-1,000	Over 1,000
CHARACTERISTICS							
Average weekend worship attendance		-	243	410	613	876	1,931
Average church income		-	$605,783	$848,306	$1,181,131	$1,679,918	$2,749,261
Average # of years employed		-	10	9	8	9	8
Average # of paid vacation days		-	15	17	15	15	14
% College graduate or higher		-	7%	11%	17%	13%	20%
% Who receive auto reimbursement/allowance		-	17%	13%	13%	30%	25%
% Ordained		-	2%	3%	2%	0%	4%
% Supervise one or more people		-	28%	39%	42%	63%	59%
Average % salary increase (for those who had an increase) this year		-	3.8%	3.9%	3.4%	4.1%	4.4%
COMPENSATION							
Base Salary	Median	-	$26,790	$26,994	$27,857	$31,632	$35,000
	Average	-	$25,675	$28,181	$30,563	$31,938	$35,468
Housing	Median	-	-	-	-	-	-
	Average	-	-	-	-	-	-
Parsonage	Median	-	-	-	-	-	-
	Average	-	-	-	-	-	-
Total Compensation	**Median**	-	**$26,790**	**$27,000**	**$27,857**	**$31,632**	**$35,000**
	Average	-	**$27,067**	**$28,411**	**$30,563**	**$31,938**	**$35,713**
BENEFITS							
Health Insurance	Median	-	$6,600	$5,500	$4,638	$8,400	$7,762
	Average	-	$6,843	$6,899	$6,204	$7,379	$8,029
Life Insurance	Median	-	-	-	$38	$118	$184
	Average	-	-	-	$111	$174	$294
Disability	Median	-	-	-	$220	-	$201
	Average	-	-	-	$244	-	$514
Retirement	Median	-	$2,189	$1,992	$1,955	$1,342	$1,979
	Average	-	$2,085	$1,994	$2,165	$2,167	$2,391
Continuing Education	Median	-	-	-	-	-	-
	Average	-	-	-	-	-	-
Total Benefits	**Median**	-	**$8,019**	**$4,488**	**$5,446**	**$7,776**	**$7,682**
	Average	-	**$7,341**	**$5,639**	**$6,773**	**$7,326**	**$8,531**
TOTAL COMPENSATION PLUS BENEFITS	**Median**	-	**$29,075**	**$27,664**	**$33,141**	**$39,334**	**$42,100**
	Average	-	**$30,577**	**$32,081**	**$34,997**	**$38,776**	**$43,547**
Number of Respondents		3	46	63	55	30	49

- Not enough response to provide meaningful data.

* For detailed description and definitions of Data Distribution (Median and Average), see Chapter 1's "Explanation of Data Distribution."

Table 15-3: Annual Compensation of Full-Time Custodians by Church Setting

	Data Distribution*	CHURCH SETTING			
		Metro-politan city	Suburb of large city	Small town or rural city	Farming area
CHARACTERISTICS					
Average weekend worship attendance		846	951	620	-
Average church income		$1,531,612	$1,666,044	$1,025,697	-
Average # of years employed		8	9	9	-
Average # of paid vacation days		15	15	15	-
% College graduate or higher		15%	20%	7%	-
% Who receive auto reimbursement/allowance		21%	15%	19%	-
% Ordained		4%	4%	1%	-
% Supervise one or more people		45%	46%	42%	-
Average % salary increase (for those who had an increase) this year		3.2%	4.2%	3.9%	-
COMPENSATION					
Base Salary	Median	$28,669	$30,300	$26,780	-
	Average	$30,630	$31,897	$28,304	-
Housing	Median	-	-	-	-
	Average	-	-	-	-
Parsonage	Median	-	-	-	-
	Average	-	-	-	-
Total Compensation	**Median**	**$28,990**	**$30,663**	**$26,780**	**-**
	Average	**$31,037**	**$32,035**	**$28,837**	**-**
BENEFITS					
Health Insurance	Median	$6,480	$6,242	$6,000	-
	Average	$6,460	$7,040	$7,397	-
Life Insurance	Median	$117	$167	$118	-
	Average	$174	$235	$251	-
Disability Insurance	Median	$277	$201	$308	-
	Average	$301	$479	$429	-
Retirement	Median	$2,000	$2,400	$1,706	-
	Average	$2,074	$2,459	$1,966	-
Continuing Education	Median	-	-	-	-
	Average	-	-	-	-
Total Benefits	**Median**	**$5,609**	**$7,957**	**$5,000**	**-**
	Average	**$6,576**	**$7,915**	**$6,645**	**-**
TOTAL COMPENSATION PLUS BENEFITS	**Median**	**$33,404**	**$37,482**	**$30,721**	**-**
	Average	**$36,138**	**$38,130**	**$33,030**	**-**
Number of Respondents		58	87	103	3

- Not enough response to provide meaningful data.

* For detailed description and definitions of Data Distribution (Median and Average), see Chapter 1's "Explanation of Data Distribution."

Table 15-4: Annual Compensation of Full-Time Custodians by Region

	Data Distribution*	REGION								
		New England	Middle Atlantic	South Atlantic	E-N Central	E-S Central	W-N Central	W-S Central	Mountain	Pacific
CHARACTERISTICS										
Average weekend worship attendance	-	508	673	989	718	687	764	842	905
Average church income	-	$768,522	$1,300,422	$1,613,782	$952,802	$1,160,961	$1,521,067	$1,364,095	$1,572,459
Average # of years employed	-	9	8	7	10	9	10	7	10
Average # of paid vacation days	-	15	16	14	14	16	15	13	17
% College graduate or higher	-	7%	18%	14%	0%	13%	13%	13%	19%
% Who receive auto reimbursement/allowance	-	0%	35%	18%	10%	21%	14%	13%	10%
% Ordained	-	0%	2%	2%	0%	0%	5%	0%	7%
% Supervise one or more people	-	27%	46%	39%	37%	58%	40%	39%	55%
Average % salary increase (for those who had an increase) this year	-	3.8%	3.4%	4.3%	3.2%	4.4%	3.7%	4.6%	3.5%
COMPENSATION										
Base Salary	Median	-	$29,417	$29,169	$30,150	$25,240	$32,380	$26,994	$25,500	$30,284
	Average	-	$27,578	$30,721	$30,944	$27,841	$32,243	$27,591	$28,115	$32,990
Housing	Median	-	-	-	-	-	-	-	-	-
	Average	-	-	-	-	-	-	-	-	-
Parsonage	Median	-	-	-	-	-	-	-	-	-
	Average	-	-	-	-	-	-	-	-	-
Total Compensation	**Median**	-	**$29,500**	**$29,460**	**$30,150**	**$25,240**	**$32,380**	**$26,994**	**$25,500**	**$31,600**
	Average	-	**$30,618**	**$30,837**	**$30,944**	**$27,841**	**$32,243**	**$27,686**	**$28,115**	**$34,153**
BENEFITS										
Health Insurance	Median	-	$6,500	$6,263	$9,930	$6,438	$4,854	$5,260	$3,610	$6,730
	Average	-	$7,109	$5,960	$8,712	$6,831	$6,057	$6,216	$3,573	$8,416
Life Insurance	Median	-	-	$114	$150	-	$109	$174	-	-
	Average	-	-	$174	$297	-	$124	$214	-	-
Disability Insurance	Median	-	-	$340	$172	-	-	$206	-	-
	Average	-	-	$813	$345	-	-	$232	-	-
Retirement	Median	-	-	$2,189	$1,960	$1,650	$1,526	$2,245	-	$2,448
	Average	-	-	$2,417	$2,222	$2,014	$1,879	$2,095	-	$2,412
Continuing Education	Median	-	-	-	-	-	-	-	-	-
	Average	-	-	-	-	-	-	-	-	-
Total Benefits	**Median**	-	**$6,000**	**$5,746**	**$7,860**	**$7,328**	**$4,994**	**$6,623**	**$5,390**	**$7,700**
	Average	-	**$6,874**	**$6,349**	**$8,002**	**$7,594**	**$5,842**	**$6,871**	**$4,571**	**$8,528**
TOTAL COMPENSATION PLUS BENEFITS	**Median**	-	**$38,885**	**$36,896**	**$36,000**	**$30,623**	**$34,569**	**$28,340**	**$26,200**	**$39,336**
	Average	-	**$35,659**	**$35,965**	**$36,946**	**$32,777**	**$36,381**	**$31,613**	**$30,102**	**$41,829**
Number of Respondents		1	15	52	44	20	24	42	23	30

- Not enough response to provide meaningful data.

* For detailed description and definitions of Data Distribution (Median and Average), see Chapter 1's "Explanation of Data Distribution."

Table 15-5: Annual Compensation of Full-Time Custodians by Education

CHARACTERISTICS	Data Distribution*	Less than Bachelor	Bachelor	Master	Doctorate
Average weekend worship attendance		748	1,029	-	-
Average church income		$1,279,597	$1,843,773	-	-
Average # of years employed		9	7	-	-
Average # of paid vacation days		15	17	-	-
% College graduate or higher		0%	100%	-	-
% Who receive auto reimbursement/allowance		19%	13%	-	-
% Ordained		1%	10%	-	-
% Supervise one or more people		38%	73%	-	-
Average % salary increase (for those who had an increase) this year		4.0%	3.1%	-	-
COMPENSATION					
Base Salary	Median	$27,675	$36,635	-	-
	Average	$28,875	$36,810	-	-
Housing	Median	-	-	-	-
	Average	-	-	-	-
Parsonage	Median	-	-	-	-
	Average	-	-	-	-
Total Compensation	**Median**	**$27,695**	**$36,635**	**-**	**-**
	Average	**$29,316**	**$36,810**	**-**	**-**
BENEFITS					
Health Insurance	Median	$6,438	$6,475	-	-
	Average	$7,058	$7,358	-	-
Life Insurance	Median	$150	$100	-	-
	Average	$227	$197	-	-
Disability Insurance	Median	$271	-	-	-
	Average	$418	-	-	-
Retirement	Median	$1,910	$2,616	-	-
	Average	$2,063	$2,968	-	-
Continuing Education	Median	-	-	-	-
	Average	-	-	-	-
Total Benefits	**Median**	**$6,141**	**$6,803**	**-**	**-**
	Average	**$7,065**	**$7,737**	**-**	**-**
TOTAL COMPENSATION PLUS BENEFITS	**Median**	**$33,141**	**$42,489**	**-**	**-**
	Average	**$34,210**	**$42,484**	**-**	**-**
Number of Respondents		205	30	2	0

- Not enough response to provide meaningful data.

* For detailed description and definitions of Data Distribution (Median and Average), see Chapter 1's "Explanation of Data Distribution."

Table 15-6: Annual Compensation of Full-Time Custodians by Years Employed

	Data Distribution*	YEARS EMPLOYED			
		Less than 6 years	6-10 years	11-15 years	Over 15 years
CHARACTERISTICS					
Average weekend worship attendance		963	679	820	650
Average church income		$1,513,871	$1,321,101	$1,364,279	$1,234,048
Average # of years employed		3	8	13	23
Average # of paid vacation days		12	16	17	20
% College graduate or higher		15%	16%	17%	3%
% Who receive auto reimbursement/allowance		19%	18%	10%	26%
% Ordained		2%	5%	0%	3%
% Supervise one or more people		41%	43%	43%	61%
Average % salary increase (for those who had an increase) this year		4.6%	3.6%	3.6%	3.0%
COMPENSATION					
Base Salary	Median	$26,705	$29,818	$28,300	$29,726
	Average	$28,576	$31,282	$31,280	$31,376
Housing	Median	-	-	-	-
	Average	-	-	-	-
Parsonage	Median	-	-	-	-
	Average	-	-	-	-
Total Compensation	**Median**	**$26,705**	**$30,965**	**$29,500**	**$29,870**
	Average	**$28,717**	**$31,684**	**$31,474**	**$32,034**
BENEFITS					
Health Insurance	Median	$5,125	$7,271	$6,881	$6,438
	Average	$6,029	$7,535	$7,700	$7,384
Life Insurance	Median	$123	$67	$154	$233
	Average	$197	$207	$127	$310
Disability Insurance	Median	$175	$531	-	$251
	Average	$212	$519	-	$329
Retirement	Median	$1,500	$2,008	$2,500	$2,516
	Average	$1,751	$2,075	$2,494	$2,521
Continuing Education	Median	-	-	-	-
	Average	-	-	-	-
Total Benefits	**Median**	**$4,764**	**$6,180**	**$8,472**	**$7,682**
	Average	**$5,500**	**$7,704**	**$8,984**	**$7,669**
TOTAL COMPENSATION PLUS BENEFITS	**Median**	**$28,969**	**$36,255**	**$38,203**	**$37,482**
	Average	**$32,384**	**$37,170**	**$38,429**	**$38,713**
Number of Respondents		96	66	31	31

- Not enough response to provide meaningful data.

* For detailed description and definitions of Data Distribution (Median and Average), see Chapter 1's "Explanation of Data Distribution."

Table 15-7: Annual Compensation of Full-Time Custodians by Denomination

	Data Distribution*	DENOMINATION					
		Assemblies of God	Baptist	Independent/ Nondenom.	Lutheran	Methodist	Presby-terian
CHARACTERISTICS							
Average weekend worship attendance		674	598	1,272	717	616	494
Average church income		$1,147,580	$1,165,352	$1,814,535	$1,407,231	$1,155,417	$1,060,674
Average # of years employed		10	9	7	13	9	7
Average # of paid vacation days		15	15	14	18	16	14
% College graduate or higher		0%	10%	19%	33%	15%	24%
% Who receive auto reimbursement/allowance		9%	18%	9%	22%	15%	18%
% Ordained		0%	2%	2%	0%	0%	0%
% Supervise one or more people		18%	45%	51%	44%	44%	31%
Average % salary increase (for those who had an increase) this year		6.0%	3.8%	3.9%	2.9%	4.0%	3.5%
COMPENSATION							
Base Salary	Median	$29,417	$26,497	$31,000	$35,000	$28,830	$30,000
	Average	$28,960	$27,205	$32,552	$37,229	$29,028	$31,229
Housing	Median	-	-	-	-	-	-
	Average	-	-	-	-	-	-
Parsonage	Median	-	-	-	-	-	-
	Average	-	-	-	-	-	-
Total Compensation	**Median**	**$29,417**	**$26,629**	**$31,000**	**$35,000**	**$29,150**	**$30,000**
	Average	**$28,960**	**$27,381**	**$32,552**	**$37,229**	**$29,250**	**$31,229**
BENEFITS							
Health Insurance	Median	-	$5,500	$5,900	-	$3,720	$6,045
	Average	-	$5,775	$7,986	-	$4,223	$5,376
Life Insurance	Median	-	$125	$120	-	-	-
	Average	-	$197	$205	-	-	-
Disability Insurance	Median	-	$155	$275	-	-	-
	Average	-	$172	$505	-	-	-
Retirement	Median	-	$2,135	$1,719	$2,990	$1,311	-
	Average	-	$2,224	$2,345	$3,074	$1,523	-
Continuing Education	Median	-	-	-	-	-	-
	Average	-	-	-	-	-	-
Total Benefits	**Median**	-	**$5,473**	**$6,321**	**$8,677**	**$4,560**	**$4,917**
	Average	-	**$6,085**	**$8,213**	**$8,668**	**$4,257**	**$5,649**
TOTAL COMPENSATION PLUS BENEFITS	**Median**	**$30,930**	**$28,880**	**$36,360**	**$49,509**	**$33,666**	**$34,938**
	Average	**$35,162**	**$31,259**	**$38,941**	**$44,934**	**$32,246**	**$35,548**
Number of Respondents		11	91	45	9	27	17

- Not enough response to provide meaningful data.

* For detailed description and definitions of Data Distribution (Median and Average), see Chapter 1's "Explanation of Data Distribution."

Table 15-8: Annual Compensation of Full-Time Custodians by Gender

	Data Distribution*	GENDER	
		Male	Female
CHARACTERISTICS			
Average weekend worship attendance		819	606
Average church income		$1,403,206	$1,115,129
Average # of years employed		9	9
Average # of paid vacation days		15	15
% College graduate or higher		16%	2%
% Who receive auto reimbursement/allowance		19%	14%
% Ordained		3%	0%
% Supervise one or more people		48%	28%
Average % salary increase (for those who had an increase) this year		3.9%	3.9%
COMPENSATION			
Base Salary	Median	$29,726	$23,712
	Average	$31,330	$24,019
Housing	Median	-	-
	Average	-	-
Parsonage	Median	-	-
	Average	-	-
Total Compensation	**Median**	**$30,236**	**$23,712**
	Average	**$31,772**	**$24,019**
BENEFITS			
Health Insurance	Median	$6,445	$5,625
	Average	$7,257	$6,138
Life Insurance	Median	$150	$114
	Average	$227	$231
Disability Insurance	Median	$265	-
	Average	$420	-
Retirement	Median	$2,090	$1,408
	Average	$2,302	$1,605
Continuing Education	Median	-	-
	Average	-	-
Total Benefits	**Median**	**$6,476**	**$5,170**
	Average	**$7,335**	**$5,949**
TOTAL COMPENSATION PLUS BENEFITS	**Median**	**$36,750**	**$25,544**
	Average	**$37,068**	**$27,754**
Number of Respondents		205	43

- Not enough response to provide meaningful data.

* For detailed description and definitions of Data Distribution (Median and Average), see Chapter 1's "Explanation of Data Distribution."

Table 15-9: Annual Compensation of Part-Time Custodians by Church Income

	Data Distribution*	CHURCH INCOME				
		$250K & Under	$251-$500K	$501-$750K	$751K-$1M	Over 1 Million
CHARACTERISTICS						
Average weekend worship attendance		109	230	362	491	902
Average church income		$164,322	$364,257	$627,958	$867,604	$1,637,842
Average # of years employed		7	6	6	6	6
Average # of paid vacation days		10	12	13	11	9
% College graduate or higher		10%	13%	18%	24%	17%
% Who receive auto reimbursement/allowance		3%	3%	5%	7%	25%
% Ordained		3%	1%	3%	3%	0%
% Supervise one or more people		2%	4%	7%	9%	8%
Average % salary increase (for those who had an increase) this year		5.4%	3.9%	3.6%	3.6%	3.1%
HOURLY RATE						
Base Rate	Average	$12	$13	$13	$13	$11
COMPENSATION						
Base Salary	Median	$5,200	$9,767	$11,892	$12,000	$11,142
	Average	$5,870	$10,697	$12,836	$13,271	$12,114
Housing	Median	-	-	-	-	-
	Average	-	-	-	-	-
Parsonage	Median	-	-	-	-	-
	Average	-	-	-	-	-
Total Compensation	**Median**	**$5,200**	**$9,828**	**$11,783**	**$12,000**	**$11,142**
	Average	**$5,997**	**$10,839**	**$12,685**	**$13,271**	**$12,114**
BENEFITS						
Health Insurance	Median	-	-	-	-	-
	Average	-	-	-	-	-
Life Insurance	Median	-	-	-	-	-
	Average	-	-	-	-	-
Disability Insurance	Median	-	-	-	-	-
	Average	-	-	-	-	-
Retirement	Median	-	-	-	-	-
	Average	-	-	-	-	-
Continuing Education	Median	-	-	-	-	-
	Average	-	-	-	-	-
Total Benefits	**Median**	**$203**	-	-	-	**$627**
	Average	**$1,824**	-	-	-	**$1,353**
TOTAL COMPENSATION PLUS BENEFITS	**Median**	**$5,200**	**$9,828**	**$11,783**	**$12,000**	**$11,376**
	Average	**$6,068**	**$10,894**	**$12,880**	**$13,496**	**$12,304**
Number of Respondents		205	147	61	44	64

- Not enough response to provide meaningful data.

* For detailed description and definitions of Data Distribution (Median and Average), see Chapter 1's "Explanation of Data Distribution."

Table 15-10: Annual Compensation of Part-Time Custodians by Worship Attendance

	Data Distribution*	WORSHIP ATTENDANCE					
		100 or less	101-300	301-500	501-750	751-1,000	Over 1,000
CHARACTERISTICS							
Average weekend worship attendance		75	190	396	607	858	1,398
Average church income		$148,199	$329,901	$713,415	$1,086,073	$1,487,559	$1,905,905
Average # of years employed		7	6	6	6	5	7
Average # of paid vacation days		10	11	13	11	12	12
% College graduate or higher		9%	13%	16%	31%	0%	10%
% Who receive auto reimbursement/allowance		1%	4%	10%	5%	18%	48%
% Ordained		5%	1%	3%	0%	0%	0%
% Supervise one or more people		3%	3%	5%	16%	6%	5%
Average % salary increase (for those who had an increase) this year		6.4%	3.6%	3.6%	5.7%	4.3%	2.9%
HOURLY RATE							
Base Rate	Average	$12	$13	$13	$12	$12	$11
COMPENSATION							
Base Salary	Median	$4,500	$8,086	$12,000	$11,825	$10,456	$11,000
	Average	$5,144	$9,005	$13,946	$12,683	$11,350	$13,236
Housing	Median	-	-	-	-	-	-
	Average	-	-	-	-	-	-
Parsonage	Median	-	-	-	-	-	-
	Average	-	-	-	-	-	-
Total Compensation	**Median**	**$4,680**	**$8,111**	**$12,000**	**$11,534**	**$10,456**	**$11,000**
	Average	**$5,238**	**$9,152**	**$13,946**	**$12,490**	**$11,350**	**$13,236**
BENEFITS							
Health Insurance	Median	-	-	-	-	-	-
	Average	-	-	-	-	-	-
Life Insurance	Median	-	-	-	-	-	-
	Average	-	-	-	-	-	-
Disability	Median	-	-	-	-	-	-
	Average	-	-	-	-	-	-
Retirement	Median	-	-	-	-	-	-
	Average	-	-	-	-	-	-
Continuing Education	Median	-	-	-	-	-	-
	Average	-	-	-	-	-	-
Total Benefits	**Median**	-	-	-	$472	-	-
	Average	-	-	-	$1,404	-	-
TOTAL COMPENSATION PLUS BENEFITS	**Median**	**$4,680**	**$8,111**	**$12,000**	**$11,534**	**$10,456**	**$11,550**
	Average	**$5,305**	**$9,249**	**$14,114**	**$12,729**	**$11,397**	**$13,292**
Number of Respondents		117	255	65	47	17	21

- Not enough response to provide meaningful data.

* For detailed description and definitions of Data Distribution (Median and Average), see Chapter 1's "Explanation of Data Distribution."

Table 15-11: Annual Compensation of Part-Time Custodians by Church Setting

	Data Distribution*	CHURCH SETTING			
		Metro-politan city	Suburb of large city	Small town or rural city	Farming area
CHARACTERISTICS					
Average weekend worship attendance		306	421	246	145
Average church income		$596,800	$742,147	$398,760	$195,462
Average # of years employed		7	6	6	10
Average # of paid vacation days		11	12	11	11
% College graduate or higher		13%	19%	10%	15%
% Who receive auto reimbursement/allowance		1%	14%	3%	5%
% Ordained		0%	2%	3%	0%
% Supervise one or more people		9%	5%	4%	0%
Average % salary increase (for those who had an increase) this year		3.1%	3.3%	4.4%	8.3%
HOURLY RATE					
Base Rate	Average	$13	$14	$12	$14
COMPENSATION					
Base Salary	Median	$9,100	$10,140	$7,248	$4,992
	Average	$10,178	$11,540	$8,292	$6,163
Housing	Median	-	-	-	-
	Average	-	-	-	-
Parsonage	Median	-	-	-	-
	Average	-	-	-	-
Total Compensation	**Median**	**$9,100**	**$10,232**	**$7,235**	**$4,992**
	Average	**$10,396**	**$11,739**	**$8,273**	**$6,163**
BENEFITS					
Health Insurance	Median	-	-	-	-
	Average	-	-	-	-
Life Insurance	Median	-	-	-	-
	Average	-	-	-	-
Disability Insurance	Median	-	-	-	-
	Average	-	-	-	-
Retirement	Median	-	-	-	-
	Average	-	-	-	-
Continuing Education	Median	-	-	-	-
	Average	-	-	-	-
Total Benefits	**Median**	**$1,000**	**-**	**$980**	**-**
	Average	**$3,333**	**-**	**$1,191**	**-**
TOTAL COMPENSATION PLUS BENEFITS	**Median**	**$9,100**	**$10,232**	**$7,235**	**$4,992**
	Average	**$10,830**	**$11,811**	**$8,334**	**$6,163**
Number of Respondents		69	156	255	39

- Not enough response to provide meaningful data.

* For detailed description and definitions of Data Distribution (Median and Average), see Chapter 1's "Explanation of Data Distribution."

Table 15-12: Annual Compensation of Part-Time Custodians by Region

	Data Distribution*	REGION								
		New England	Middle Atlantic	South Atlantic	E-N Central	E-S Central	W-N Central	W-S Central	Mountain	Pacific
CHARACTERISTICS										
Average weekend worship attendance		133	180	260	367	350	308	415	269	300
Average church income		$303,204	$331,554	$512,698	$578,780	$542,735	$470,094	$798,824	$387,369	$554,335
Average # of years employed		5	6	8	8	6	7	5	6	4
Average # of paid vacation days		9	13	9	13	12	14	9	9	10
% College graduate or higher		27%	20%	9%	14%	12%	12%	13%	10%	11%
% Who receive auto reimbursement/allowance		0%	4%	6%	11%	7%	5%	8%	0%	3%
% Ordained		9%	0%	3%	2%	3%	2%	3%	3%	0%
% Supervise one or more people		0%	6%	1%	5%	3%	3%	6%	7%	10%
Average % salary increase (for those who had an increase) this year		4.5%	3.2%	4.6%	3.3%	2.7%	5.3%	5.6%	7.9%	4.1%
HOURLY RATE										
Base Rate	Average	$11	$12	$13	$12	$13	$12	$11	$15	$13
COMPENSATION										
Base Salary	Median	$7,240	$8,056	$7,310	$7,488	$10,000	$8,230	$10,000	$6,120	$9,600
	Average	$7,892	$8,621	$8,529	$9,478	$10,943	$9,985	$10,474	$7,663	$10,643
Housing	Median	-	-	-	-	-	-	-	-	-
	Average	-	-	-	-	-	-	-	-	-
Parsonage	Median	-	-	-	-	-	-	-	-	-
	Average	-	-	-	-	-	-	-	-	-
Total Compensation	**Median**	**$7,280**	**$8,056**	**$7,430**	**$7,488**	**$10,000**	**$8,060**	**$10,000**	**$6,120**	**$9,600**
	Average	**$8,919**	**$8,621**	**$8,633**	**$9,478**	**$10,943**	**$9,881**	**$10,474**	**$7,663**	**$10,874**
BENEFITS										
Health Insurance	Median	-	-	-	-	-	-	-	-	-
	Average	-	-	-	-	-	-	-	-	-
Life Insurance	Median	-	-	-	-	-	-	-	-	-
	Average	-	-	-	-	-	-	-	-	-
Disability Insurance	Median	-	-	-	-	-	-	-	-	-
	Average	-	-	-	-	-	-	-	-	-
Retirement	Median	-	-	-	-	-	-	-	-	-
	Average	-	-	-	-	-	-	-	-	-
Continuing Education	Median	-	-	-	-	-	-	-	-	-
	Average	-	-	-	-	-	-	-	-	-
Total Benefits	**Median**	-	-	-	-	-	-	-	-	-
	Average	-	-	-	-	-	-	-	-	-
TOTAL COMPENSATION PLUS BENEFITS	**Median**	**$7,280**	**$8,056**	**$7,430**	**$7,488**	**$10,000**	**$8,060**	**$10,000**	**$6,120**	**$9,600**
	Average	**$8,919**	**$8,750**	**$8,847**	**$9,554**	**$10,943**	**$9,976**	**$10,680**	**$7,663**	**$10,941**
Number of Respondents		23	54	106	121	29	61	37	30	65

- Not enough response to provide meaningful data.

* For detailed description and definitions of Data Distribution (Median and Average), see Chapter 1's "Explanation of Data Distribution."

Table 15-13: Annual Compensation of Part-Time Custodians by Education

	Data Distribution*	EDUCATION			
		Less than Bachelor	Bachelor	Master	Doctorate
CHARACTERISTICS					
Average weekend worship attendance		294	306	-	-
Average church income		$482,806	$588,004	-	-
Average # of years employed		7	6	-	-
Average # of paid vacation days		11	13	-	-
% College graduate or higher		0%	100%	-	-
% Who receive auto reimbursement/allowance		7%	5%	-	-
% Ordained		2%	0%	-	-
% Supervise one or more people		4%	7%	-	-
Average % salary increase (for those who had an increase) this year		4.3%	3.9%	-	-
HOURLY RATE					
Base Rate	Average	$12	$14	-	-
COMPENSATION					
Base Salary	Median	$7,800	$7,500	-	-
	Average	$9,073	$11,119	-	-
Housing	Median	-	-	-	-
	Average	-	-	-	-
Parsonage	Median	-	-	-	-
	Average	-	-	-	-
Total Compensation	**Median**	**$7,800**	**$7,500**	**-**	**-**
	Average	**$9,134**	**$11,337**	**-**	**-**
BENEFITS					
Health Insurance	Median	$4,943	-	-	-
	Average	$4,631	-	-	-
Life Insurance	Median	-	-	-	-
	Average	-	-	-	-
Disability Insurance	Median	-	-	-	-
	Average	-	-	-	-
Retirement	Median	$885	-	-	-
	Average	$758	-	-	-
Continuing Education	Median	-	-	-	-
	Average	-	-	-	-
Total Benefits	**Median**	**$990**	**-**	**-**	**-**
	Average	**$2,113**	**-**	**-**	**-**
TOTAL COMPENSATION PLUS BENEFITS	**Median**	**$7,840**	**$7,500**	**-**	**-**
	Average	**$9,244**	**$11,347**	**-**	**-**
Number of Respondents		425	59	7	0

- Not enough response to provide meaningful data.

* For detailed description and definitions of Data Distribution (Median and Average), see Chapter 1's "Explanation of Data Distribution."

Table 15-14: Annual Compensation of Part-Time Custodians by Years Employed

	Data Distribution*	Less than 6 years	6-10 years	11-15 years	Over 15 years
CHARACTERISTICS					
Average weekend worship attendance		332	294	287	275
Average church income		$577,174	$493,660	$476,785	$508,940
Average # of years employed		2	8	13	24
Average # of paid vacation days		10	11	13	14
% College graduate or higher		14%	17%	9%	13%
% Who receive auto reimbursement/allowance		8%	6%	6%	9%
% Ordained		3%	1%	3%	3%
% Supervise one or more people		4%	5%	6%	10%
Average % salary increase (for those who had an increase) this year		4.4%	4.1%	4.9%	3.5%
HOURLY RATE					
Base Rate	Average	$12	$14	$13	$13
COMPENSATION					
Base Salary	Median	$7,900	$8,400	$7,000	$10,205
	Average	$9,036	$10,284	$10,152	$11,978
Housing	Median	-	-	-	-
	Average	-	-	-	-
Parsonage	Median	-	-	-	-
	Average	-	-	-	-
Total Compensation	**Median**	$7,800	$8,400	$8,200	$10,205
	Average	$9,015	$10,430	$10,467	$11,978
BENEFITS					
Health Insurance	Median	-	-	-	-
	Average	-	-	-	-
Life Insurance	Median	-	-	-	-
	Average	-	-	-	-
Disability Insurance	Median	$83	-	-	-
	Average	$216	-	-	-
Retirement	Median	-	-	-	-
	Average	-	-	-	-
Continuing Education	Median	-	-	-	-
	Average	-	-	-	-
Total Benefits	**Median**	$469	-	-	-
	Average	$774	-	-	-
TOTAL COMPENSATION PLUS BENEFITS	**Median**	$7,850	$8,400	$8,200	$10,205
	Average	$9,054	$10,495	$10,638	$12,386
Number of Respondents		257	103	35	33

- Not enough response to provide meaningful data.

* For detailed description and definitions of Data Distribution (Median and Average), see Chapter 1's "Explanation of Data Distribution."

Table 15-15: Annual Compensation of Part-Time Custodians by Denomination

	Data Distribution*	DENOMINATION					
		Assemblies of God	Baptist	Independent/ Nondenom.	Lutheran	Methodist	Presby- terian
CHARACTERISTICS							
Average weekend worship attendance		256	315	327	232	192	191
Average church income		$525,264	$589,483	$510,451	$405,680	$307,090	$368,495
Average # of years employed		5	6	7	7	10	6
Average # of paid vacation days		8	10	12	13	15	13
% College graduate or higher		0%	8%	14%	4%	18%	19%
% Who receive auto reimbursement/allowance		0%	7%	7%	8%	3%	6%
% Ordained		4%	5%	3%	0%	0%	0%
% Supervise one or more people		4%	4%	5%	4%	0%	7%
Average % salary increase (for those who had an increase) this year		3.4%	3.9%	5.7%	3.9%	6.0%	4.4%
HOURLY RATE							
Base Rate	Average	$11	$13	$12	$12	$12	$14
COMPENSATION							
Base Salary	Median	$7,400	$9,600	$5,200	$9,592	$5,600	$8,200
	Average	$8,803	$10,209	$6,397	$9,756	$8,776	$10,153
Housing	Median	-	-	-	-	-	-
	Average	-	-	-	-	-	-
Parsonage	Median	-	-	-	-	-	-
	Average	-	-	-	-	-	-
Total Compensation	**Median**	**$7,400**	**$9,600**	**$5,200**	**$9,880**	**$5,600**	**$8,350**
	Average	**$8,803**	**$10,296**	**$6,351**	**$10,149**	**$8,776**	**$10,548**
BENEFITS							
Health Insurance	Median	-	-	-	-	-	-
	Average	-	-	-	-	-	-
Life Insurance	Median	-	-	-	-	-	-
	Average	-	-	-	-	-	-
Disability Insurance	Median	-	-	-	-	-	-
	Average	-	-	-	-	-	-
Retirement	Median	-	-	-	-	-	-
	Average	-	-	-	-	-	-
Continuing Education	Median	-	-	-	-	-	-
	Average	-	-	-	-	-	-
Total Benefits	**Median**	-	-	-	-	-	-
	Average	-	-	-	-	-	-
TOTAL COMPENSATION PLUS BENEFITS	**Median**	**$7,400**	**$9,600**	**$5,200**	**$9,880**	**$5,600**	**$8,350**
	Average	**$8,803**	**$10,420**	**$6,571**	**$10,186**	**$8,839**	**$10,644**
Number of Respondents		28	172	61	28	35	54

- Not enough response to provide meaningful data.

* For detailed description and definitions of Data Distribution (Median and Average), see Chapter 1's "Explanation of Data Distribution."

Table 15-16: Annual Compensation of Part-Time Custodians by Gender

CHARACTERISTICS	Data Distribution*	Male	Female
Average weekend worship attendance		337	242
Average church income		$576,807	$426,542
Average # of years employed		6	7
Average # of paid vacation days		12	11
% College graduate or higher		16%	10%
% Who receive auto reimbursement/allowance		8%	4%
% Ordained		3%	1%
% Supervise one or more people		7%	2%
Average % salary increase (for those who had an increase) this year		4.1%	4.3%
HOURLY RATE			
Base Rate	Average	$12	$13
COMPENSATION			
Base Salary	Median	$9,293	$6,630
	Average	$10,293	$8,257
Housing	Median	-	-
	Average	-	-
Parsonage	Median	-	-
	Average	-	-
Total Compensation	**Median**	**$9,293**	**$6,900**
	Average	**$10,394**	**$8,305**
BENEFITS			
Health Insurance	Median	-	-
	Average	-	-
Life Insurance	Median	-	-
	Average	-	-
Disability Insurance	Median	-	-
	Average	-	-
Retirement	Median	$589	-
	Average	$628	-
Continuing Education	Median	-	-
	Average	-	-
Total Benefits	**Median**	**$474**	**$1,200**
	Average	**$1,376**	**$3,379**
TOTAL COMPENSATION PLUS BENEFITS	**Median**	**$9,293**	**$6,900**
	Average	**$10,483**	**$8,438**
Number of Respondents		292	229

- Not enough response to provide meaningful data.

* For detailed description and definitions of Data Distribution (Median and Average), see Chapter 1's "Explanation of Data Distribution."

16

PART-TIME MUSICIANS/ ACCOMPANISTS/ VOCALISTS

Employment Profile

Musician/Accompanist/Vocalist includes paid personnel who provide vocal or instrumental music or accompaniment. Titles under this category include such positions as Accompanist, Instrumentalist (of any kind), Organist, Pianist, Soloist, Vocalist, Worship Team member, Praise Band Member, etc.

Three-quarters of these part-time musicians are female. They report long tenures, averaging twelve years.

The following chart provides a demographic profile of this sample:

	Full-Time	Part-Time
Number of respondents	4	273
Ordained	-	3%
Average years employed	-	12
Male	-	23%
Female	-	77%
Self-employed (receives 1099)	-	8%
Church employee (receives W-2)	-	92%
High school diploma	-	20%
Associate Degree	-	10%
Bachelor's Degree	-	45%
Master's Degree	-	20%
Doctoral Degree	-	5%

Total Compensation plus Benefits Package Analysis

The analyses on the next page are based on the data in the tables that you will find in the remainder of the chapter. The tables show compensation plus benefits data for Musicians/Accompanists/Vocalists who serve part-time and are presented according to church income, church attendance, church setting, region, education, years employed, denomination, and gender. In this way, the musicians' compensation plus benefits can be analyzed and compared from a variety of useful perspectives.

The total compensation plus benefits amount includes the base salary, housing and/or parsonage amount, health, life, and disability insurance payments, retirement contribution, and educational funds.

Very few part-time church musicians receive fringe benefits such as retirement, health insurance, auto allowance, and funds for continuing education. However, one-third receive paid vacation.

Compensation Plus Benefits	Full-Time	Part-Time
Base Salary	-	99%
Housing	-	1%
Parsonage	-	0%
Health Insurance	-	1%
Life Insurance	-	0%
Disability Insurance	-	1%
Retirement	-	2%
Continuing Education	-	4%
Received Salary Increase	-	38%
Received Paid Vacation	-	33%
Received Auto Reimbursement/Allowance	-	3%

KEY POINTS

✳ Almost seven in ten part-time Musicians/Accompanists/Vocalists serve in smaller churches with attendance of 300 or less. Six in ten serve in churches whose income is $500,000 or less.

✳ The hourly rate paid to Musicians/Accompanist/Vocalists fluctuates across church income, worship attendance, education, and years employed. This means that it is not necessarily true, with this sample, that part-time church musicians earn more on an hourly rate basis if they work in a larger church, have a higher education, or have more years in their position.

✳ Note: There were not enough respondents to provide meaningful data to determine the average compensation and benefits packages for full-time musicians/vocalists.

Table 16-1: Annual Compensation of Part-Time Musicians/Accompanists/Vocalists by Church Income

	Data Distribution*	CHURCH INCOME				
		$250K & Under	$251-$500K	$501-$750K	$751K-$1M	Over 1 Million
CHARACTERISTICS						
Average weekend worship attendance		107	202	325	404	865
Average church income		$160,234	$367,265	$660,899	$880,613	$1,787,639
Average # of years employed		12	14	8	16	10
Average # of paid vacation days		10	8	9	11	6
% College graduate or higher		71%	61%	69%	85%	82%
% Who receive auto reimbursement/allowance		1%	3%	2%	0%	13%
% Ordained		1%	4%	2%	0%	3%
% Supervise one or more people		7%	7%	6%	0%	7%
Average % salary increase (for those who had an increase) this year		4.3%	4.5%	3.4%	3.0%	2.8%
HOURLY RATE						
Base Rate	Average	$22	$23	$27	$22	$22
COMPENSATION						
Base Salary	Median	$4,925	$6,368	$8,275	$9,000	$9,250
	Average	$5,771	$7,592	$8,168	$10,905	$11,139
Housing	Median	-	-	-	-	-
	Average	-	-	-	-	-
Parsonage	Median	-	-	-	-	-
	Average	-	-	-	-	-
Total Compensation	**Median**	**$4,925**	**$6,498**	**$8,275**	**$9,000**	**$10,000**
	Average	**$5,771**	**$7,703**	**$8,168**	**$10,905**	**$11,553**
BENEFITS						
Health Insurance	Median	-	-	-	-	-
	Average	-	-	-	-	-
Life Insurance	Median	-	-	-	-	-
	Average	-	-	-	-	-
Disability Insurance	Median	-	-	-	-	-
	Average	-	-	-	-	-
Retirement	Median	-	-	-	-	-
	Average	-	-	-	-	-
Continuing Education	Median	-	-	-	-	-
	Average	-	-	-	-	-
Total Benefits	**Median**	-	-	-	-	-
	Average	-	-	-	-	-
TOTAL COMPENSATION PLUS BENEFITS	**Median**	**$4,925**	**$6,498**	**$8,275**	**$9,000**	**$10,000**
	Average	**$5,814**	**$7,924**	**$8,202**	**$11,039**	**$11,553**
Number of Respondents		92	72	52	20	31

- Not enough response to provide meaningful data.

* For detailed description and definitions of Data Distribution (Median and Average), see Chapter 1's "Explanation of Data Distribution."

Table 16-2: Annual Compensation of Part-Time Musicians/Accompanists/Vocalists by Worship Attendance

	Data Distribution*	WORSHIP ATTENDANCE					
		100 or less	101-300	301-500	501-750	751-1,000	Over 1,000
CHARACTERISTICS							
Average weekend worship attendance		71	192	376	603	-	1,730
Average church income		$141,564	$376,296	$815,738	$1,117,551	-	$2,566,889
Average # of years employed		11	14	10	11	-	12
Average # of paid vacation days		10	8	11	4	-	10
% College graduate or higher		63%	71%	77%	80%	-	56%
% Who receive auto reimbursement/allowance		2%	2%	7%	0%	-	0%
% Ordained		3%	2%	2%	0%	-	0%
% Supervise one or more people		5%	9%	5%	0%	-	0%
Average % salary increase (for those who had an increase) this year		4.8%	4.0%	3.2%	-	-	2.5%
HOURLY RATE							
Base Rate	Average	$21	$22	$26	$22	-	-
COMPENSATION							
Base Salary	Median	$5,300	$6,000	$7,500	$7,793	-	$7,020
	Average	$6,163	$7,225	$8,780	$9,892	-	$11,421
Housing	Median	-	-	-	-	-	-
	Average	-	-	-	-	-	-
Parsonage	Median	-	-	-	-	-	-
	Average	-	-	-	-	-	-
Total Compensation	**Median**	**$5,400**	**$6,000**	**$7,500**	**$7,793**	**-**	**$7,020**
	Average	**$6,233**	**$7,269**	**$9,052**	**$9,892**	**-**	**$11,421**
BENEFITS							
Health Insurance	Median	-	-	-	-	-	-
	Average	-	-	-	-	-	-
Life Insurance	Median	-	-	-	-	-	-
	Average	-	-	-	-	-	-
Disability	Median	-	-	-	-	-	-
	Average	-	-	-	-	-	-
Retirement	Median	-	-	-	-	-	-
	Average	-	-	-	-	-	-
Continuing Education	Median	-	$300	-	-	-	-
	Average	-	$325	-	-	-	-
Total Benefits	**Median**	**-**	**$494**	**-**	**-**	**-**	**-**
	Average	**-**	**$1,512**	**-**	**-**	**-**	**-**
TOTAL COMPENSATION PLUS BENEFITS	**Median**	**$5,400**	**$6,120**	**$7,500**	**$7,793**	**-**	**$7,020**
	Average	**$6,289**	**$7,410**	**$9,102**	**$9,892**	**-**	**$11,421**
Number of Respondents		60	128	56	14	5	10

- Not enough response to provide meaningful data.

* For detailed description and definitions of Data Distribution (Median and Average), see Chapter 1's "Explanation of Data Distribution."

237

Table 16-3: Annual Compensation of Part-Time Musicians/Accompanists/Vocalists by Church Setting

	Data Distribution*	CHURCH SETTING			
		Metro-politan city	Suburb of large city	Small town or rural city	Farming area
CHARACTERISTICS					
Average weekend worship attendance		309	363	225	-
Average church income		$541,097	$764,160	$380,117	-
Average # of years employed		11	11	13	-
Average # of paid vacation days		7	9	10	-
% College graduate or higher		71%	73%	66%	-
% Who receive auto reimbursement/allowance		0%	4%	4%	-
% Ordained		4%	1%	4%	-
% Supervise one or more people		6%	7%	7%	-
Average % salary increase (for those who had an increase) this year		4.3%	4.5%	3.4%	-
HOURLY RATE					
Base Rate	Average	$25	$22	$22	-
COMPENSATION					
Base Salary	Median	$7,377	$7,215	$6,000	-
	Average	$8,493	$8,574	$6,773	-
Housing	Median	-	-	-	-
	Average	-	-	-	-
Parsonage	Median	-	-	-	-
	Average	-	-	-	-
Total Compensation	**Median**	**$7,377**	**$7,230**	**$6,000**	**-**
	Average	**$8,493**	**$8,617**	**$6,960**	**-**
BENEFITS					
Health Insurance	Median	-	-	-	-
	Average	-	-	-	-
Life Insurance	Median	-	-	-	-
	Average	-	-	-	-
Disability Insurance	Median	-	-	-	-
	Average	-	-	-	-
Retirement	Median	-	-	-	-
	Average	-	-	-	-
Continuing Education	Median	-	-	-	-
	Average	-	-	-	-
Total Benefits	**Median**	**-**	**-**	**$300**	**-**
	Average	**-**	**-**	**$844**	**-**
TOTAL COMPENSATION PLUS BENEFITS	**Median**	**$7,377**	**$7,230**	**$6,000**	**-**
	Average	**$8,545**	**$8,740**	**$7,044**	**-**
Number of Respondents		53	99	111	7

- Not enough response to provide meaningful data.

* For detailed description and definitions of Data Distribution (Median and Average), see Chapter 1's "Explanation of Data Distribution."

Table 16-4: Annual Compensation of Part-Time Musicians/Accompanists/Vocalists by Region

	Data Distribution*	New England	Middle Atlantic	South Atlantic	E-N Central	E-S Central	W-N Central	W-S Central	Mountain	Pacific
CHARACTERISTICS										
Average weekend worship attendance		119	162	336	251	425	225	436	-	198
Average church income		$316,850	$333,139	$579,599	$504,380	$668,959	$378,924	$935,511	-	$394,949
Average # of years employed		8	10	14	13	12	14	10	-	9
Average # of paid vacation days		10	15	7	10	7	9	5	-	12
% College graduate or higher		57%	75%	67%	62%	68%	78%	79%	-	74%
% Who receive auto reimbursement/allowance		0%	0%	6%	2%	4%	4%	3%	-	0%
% Ordained		0%	0%	3%	2%	5%	0%	8%	-	0%
% Supervise one or more people		0%	4%	8%	8%	5%	0%	8%	-	16%
Average % salary increase (for those who had an increase) this year		-	3.1%	4.9%	3.6%	3.4%	3.5%	3.8%	-	3.6%
HOURLY RATE										
Base Rate	Average	-	$24	$24	$24	$24	$20	$20	-	$22
COMPENSATION										
Base Salary	Median	$8,400	$9,000	$6,722	$3,900	$6,400	$4,561	$8,275	-	$7,377
	Average	$8,437	$8,825	$8,746	$6,125	$6,741	$6,778	$8,212	-	$8,383
Housing	Median	-	-	-	-	-	-	-	-	-
	Average	-	-	-	-	-	-	-	-	-
Parsonage	Median	-	-	-	-	-	-	-	-	-
	Average	-	-	-	-	-	-	-	-	-
Total Compensation	**Median**	$8,400	$9,000	$6,722	$3,900	$6,400	$4,561	$8,408	-	$7,377
	Average	$8,437	$8,825	$8,746	$6,125	$7,491	$6,778	$8,391	-	$8,383
BENEFITS										
Health Insurance	Median	-	-	-	-	-	-	-	-	-
	Average	-	-	-	-	-	-	-	-	-
Life Insurance	Median	-	-	-	-	-	-	-	-	-
	Average	-	-	-	-	-	-	-	-	-
Disability Insurance	Median	-	-	-	-	-	-	-	-	-
	Average	-	-	-	-	-	-	-	-	-
Retirement	Median	-	-	-	-	-	-	-	-	-
	Average	-	-	-	-	-	-	-	-	-
Continuing Education	Median	-	-	-	-	-	-	-	-	-
	Average	-	-	-	-	-	-	-	-	-
Total Benefits	**Median**	-	-	-	-	-	-	-	-	-
	Average	-	-	-	-	-	-	-	-	-
TOTAL COMPENSATION PLUS BENEFITS	**Median**	$8,400	$9,000	$6,722	$3,900	$6,400	$4,561	$8,438	-	$7,377
	Average	$8,437	$8,861	$8,910	$6,229	$7,491	$6,909	$8,449	-	$8,410
Number of Respondents		10	25	68	54	23	29	38	7	19

- Not enough response to provide meaningful data.

* For detailed description and definitions of Data Distribution (Median and Average), see Chapter 1's "Explanation of Data Distribution."

Table 16-5: Annual Compensation of Part-Time Musicians/Accompanists/Vocalists by Education

	Data Distribution*	EDUCATION			
		Less than Bachelor	Bachelor	Master	Doctorate
CHARACTERISTICS					
Average weekend worship attendance		334	294	272	210
Average church income		$508,057	$579,423	$608,776	$443,186
Average # of years employed		13	12	12	15
Average # of paid vacation days		9	8	10	7
% College graduate or higher		0%	100%	100%	100%
% Who receive auto reimbursement/allowance		3%	5%	2%	0%
% Ordained		3%	2%	4%	0%
% Supervise one or more people		6%	7%	13%	0%
Average % salary increase (for those who had an increase) this year		5.1%	3.1%	3.5%	6.1%
HOURLY RATE					
Base Rate	Average	$25	$22	$23	-
COMPENSATION					
Base Salary	Median	$6,000	$6,898	$9,000	$6,518
	Average	$6,328	$8,469	$9,440	$7,945
Housing	Median	-	-	-	-
	Average	-	-	-	-
Parsonage	Median	-	-	-	-
	Average	-	-	-	-
Total Compensation	**Median**	**$6,000**	**$6,953**	**$9,413**	**$6,518**
	Average	**$6,421**	**$8,487**	**$9,743**	**$7,945**
BENEFITS					
Health Insurance	Median	-	-	-	-
	Average	-	-	-	-
Life Insurance	Median	-	-	-	-
	Average	-	-	-	-
Disability Insurance	Median	-	-	-	-
	Average	-	-	-	-
Retirement	Median	-	-	-	-
	Average	-	-	-	-
Continuing Education	Median	-	-	-	-
	Average	-	-	-	-
Total Benefits	**Median**	-	-	**$424**	-
	Average	-	-	**$824**	-
TOTAL COMPENSATION PLUS BENEFITS	**Median**	**$6,000**	**$6,953**	**$9,413**	**$6,518**
	Average	**$6,425**	**$8,558**	**$9,881**	**$7,991**
Number of Respondents		70	105	48	11

- Not enough response to provide meaningful data.

* For detailed description and definitions of Data Distribution (Median and Average), see Chapter 1's "Explanation of Data Distribution."

Table 16-6: Annual Compensation of Part-Time Musicians/Accompanists/Vocalists by Years Employed

	Data Distribution*	YEARS EMPLOYED			
		Less than 6 years	6-10 years	11-15 years	Over 15 years
CHARACTERISTICS					
Average weekend worship attendance		292	340	269	327
Average church income		$625,307	$580,049	$551,641	$549,087
Average # of years employed		3	8	13	29
Average # of paid vacation days		6	9	9	8
% College graduate or higher		66%	74%	71%	69%
% Who receive auto reimbursement/allowance		7%	1%	0%	2%
% Ordained		1%	6%	0%	0%
% Supervise one or more people		3%	10%	5%	5%
Average % salary increase (for those who had an increase) this year		4.3%	3.9%	2.8%	4.3%
HOURLY RATE					
Base Rate	Average	$23	$25	$22	$22
COMPENSATION					
Base Salary	Median	$6,700	$6,974	$6,185	$5,250
	Average	$8,156	$8,523	$6,938	$7,044
Housing	Median	-	-	-	-
	Average	-	-	-	-
Parsonage	Median	-	-	-	-
	Average	-	-	-	-
Total Compensation	**Median**	$6,965	$7,104	$6,185	$5,250
	Average	$8,186	$8,582	$6,938	$7,044
BENEFITS					
Health Insurance	Median	-	-	-	-
	Average	-	-	-	-
Life Insurance	Median	-	-	-	-
	Average	-	-	-	-
Disability Insurance	Median	-	-	-	-
	Average	-	-	-	-
Retirement	Median	-	-	-	-
	Average	-	-	-	-
Continuing Education	Median	-	-	-	-
	Average	-	-	-	-
Total Benefits	**Median**	-	-	-	-
	Average	-	-	-	-
TOTAL COMPENSATION PLUS BENEFITS	**Median**	$6,965	$7,104	$6,185	$5,770
	Average	$8,270	$8,762	$6,942	$7,124
Number of Respondents		76	73	24	56

- Not enough response to provide meaningful data.

* For detailed description and definitions of Data Distribution (Median and Average), see Chapter 1's "Explanation of Data Distribution."

Table 16-7: Annual Compensation of Part-Time Musicians/Accompanists/Vocalists by Denomination

	Data Distribution*	Assemblies of God	Baptist	Independent/ Nondenom.	Lutheran	Methodist	Presby- terian
CHARACTERISTICS							
Average weekend worship attendance	-		329	281	238	385	182
Average church income	-		$636,121	$636,670	$501,475	$541,205	$423,813
Average # of years employed	-		13	6	15	14	7
Average # of paid vacation days	-		6	6	12	9	11
% College graduate or higher	-		63%	40%	79%	70%	83%
% Who receive auto reimbursement/allowance	-		5%	11%	0%	0%	3%
% Ordained	-		5%	11%	0%	0%	0%
% Supervise one or more people	-		5%	10%	8%	0%	14%
Average % salary increase (for those who had an increase) this year	-		5.0%	4.0%	3.7%	2.9%	3.8%
HOURLY RATE							
Base Rate	Average	-	$22	-	$24	$23	$24
COMPENSATION							
Base Salary	Median	-	$6,400	$8,034	$6,000	$4,800	$6,495
	Average	-	$7,330	$9,709	$7,647	$8,122	$7,844
Housing	Median	-	-	-	-	-	-
	Average	-	-	-	-	-	-
Parsonage	Median	-	-	-	-	-	-
	Average	-	-	-	-	-	-
Total Compensation	**Median**	-	**$6,400**	**$9,217**	**$6,000**	**$4,800**	**$6,495**
	Average	-	**$7,550**	**$9,778**	**$7,647**	**$8,122**	**$7,844**
BENEFITS							
Health Insurance	Median	-	-	-	-	-	-
	Average	-	-	-	-	-	-
Life Insurance	Median	-	-	-	-	-	-
	Average	-	-	-	-	-	-
Disability Insurance	Median	-	-	-	-	-	-
	Average	-	-	-	-	-	-
Retirement	Median	-	-	-	-	-	-
	Average	-	-	-	-	-	-
Continuing Education	Median	-	-	-	-	-	-
	Average	-	-	-	-	-	-
Total Benefits	**Median**	-	-	-	-	-	-
	Average	-	-	-	-	-	-
TOTAL COMPENSATION PLUS BENEFITS	**Median**	-	**$6,400**	**$9,217**	**$6,000**	**$5,278**	**$6,495**
	Average	-	**$7,579**	**$9,778**	**$7,756**	**$8,178**	**$7,920**
Number of Respondents		3	101	10	41	41	37

- Not enough response to provide meaningful data.

* For detailed description and definitions of Data Distribution (Median and Average), see Chapter 1's "Explanation of Data Distribution."

Table 16-8: Annual Compensation of Part-Time Musicians/Accompanists/Vocalists by Gender

	Data Distribution*	GENDER	
		Male	Female
CHARACTERISTICS			
Average weekend worship attendance		268	298
Average church income		$534,453	$562,143
Average # of years employed		8	13
Average # of paid vacation days		9	9
% College graduate or higher		75%	68%
% Who receive auto reimbursement/allowance		5%	2%
% Ordained		10%	0%
% Supervise one or more people		13%	5%
Average % salary increase (for those who had an increase) this year		4.8%	3.7%
HOURLY RATE			
Base Rate	Average	$26	$22
COMPENSATION			
Base Salary	Median	$7,397	$6,240
	Average	$8,803	$7,449
Housing	Median	-	-
	Average	-	-
Parsonage	Median	-	-
	Average	-	-
Total Compensation	**Median**	**$7,500**	**$6,240**
	Average	**$9,133**	**$7,449**
BENEFITS			
Health Insurance	Median	-	-
	Average	-	-
Life Insurance	Median	-	-
	Average	-	-
Disability Insurance	Median	-	-
	Average	-	-
Retirement	Median	-	-
	Average	-	-
Continuing Education	Median	-	$300
	Average	-	$375
Total Benefits	**Median**	-	**$494**
	Average	-	**$838**
TOTAL COMPENSATION PLUS BENEFITS	**Median**	**$7,500**	**$6,240**
	Average	**$9,332**	**$7,506**
Number of Respondents		63	206

- Not enough response to provide meaningful data.

* For detailed description and definitions of Data Distribution (Median and Average), see Chapter 1's "Explanation of Data Distribution."

17

STATISTICAL ABSTRACT OF CHURCHES REPRESENTED IN DATA

In addition to the individual compensation surveys, respondents were also asked to complete a congregational profile. That information, as well as some detailed information about full-time

Senior/Solo Pastors is summarized here. The data is presented according to worship attendance, and six size categories are portrayed. Second, worship size and region are presented according to both church attendance and finances.

Key Findings

Church Profile

On average, 44% of the churches' income/budget is devoted to salaries.

On average, churches have two full-time ordained staff and two full-time non-ordained staff.

On average, churches have one part-time ordained staff and three part-time non-ordained staff.

Senior/Solo Pastor Profile

More than one-third (36%) of churches provide additional salary to their Senior or Solo Pastor to assist them with their Social Security payments. Of those churches that do help, 72% pay one-half of the social security tax, while 28% pay all of it.

Seven in ten (70%) churches reimburse the Senior or Solo Pastor's professional expenses. Those churches generally reimburse the pastor about 79% of his or her professional expenses per year.

One in ten churches counts reimbursements as income for the Senior or Solo Pastor's W-2 or 1099 form. Most (85%) Senior or Solo Pastors are treated as employees of the church, meaning they receive a W-2 rather than a 1099 form reporting their income at year's end.

About two-thirds (68%) of the churches help their Senior or Solo Pastor with auto expense.

Some four in ten (40%) churches experienced an increase in attendance over the past year.

About one quarter (27%) reported that their income exceeded expenses in the past year.

Table 17-1: Church and Full-time Senior/Solo Pastor Profiles by Worship Attendance

	All Churches Represented	WORSHIP ATTENDANCE					
		100 or less	101-300	301-500	501-750	751-1,000	Over 1,000
CHURCH PROFILE							
Average worship attendance	355	64	189	406	624	892	2,096
Average total church budget/income	$566,610	$112,090	$313,251	$740,157	$1,060,358	$1,564,808	$2,913,095
Average percentage compensation is of total church budget/income	44%	43%	45%	46%	47%	44%	44%
Average number of ordained staff							
Full-time	2	1	1	3	4	5	8
Part-time	1	0	0	1	1	1	1
Average number of non-ordained staff							
Full-time	2	0	1	2	4	7	13
Part-time	3	1	3	4	5	7	13
Number of Respondents	4998	1611	1952	596	318	190	331
FULL-TIME SENIOR/ SOLO PASTOR PROFILE	All Full-Time Senior/Solo Pastors Represented	100 or less	101-300	301-500	501-750	751-1,000	Over 1,000
Percentage that contribute to social security payments of pastors	36%	31%	37%	38%	42%	29%	41%
Breakdown of church's contribution to pastor's social security payments							
Exempt	21%	18%	21%	23%	27%	29%	24%
Pays 0%	43%	51%	42%	39%	31%	42%	35%
Pays 50%	26%	22%	28%	30%	31%	18%	23%
Pays 100%	10%	10%	9%	8%	11%	11%	18%
Percentage of churches that reimburse the pastor for professional expenses	70%	64%	71%	72%	73%	73%	74%
Average percentage among those who get reimbursed	79%	73%	80%	82%	84%	84%	81%
Percentage of pastors receiving tax form							
1099	15%	20%	14%	9%	7%	8%	7%
W2	85%	80%	86%	91%	93%	92%	93%
Percentage of churches that reimburse pastors' expense	90%	85%	89%	91%	95%	96%	93%
Percentage of churches that count reimbursements as income	10%	10%	10%	9%	10%	12%	10%
Percentage of churches that do not count reimbursements as income	80%	75%	80%	82%	85%	84%	82%
Percentage of churches that help the pastor with auto expense	68%	63%	70%	74%	69%	68%	62%
Number of Respondents	3224	1051	1406	344	180	101	127

Table 17-2: Church and Full-time Senior/Solo Pastor Profiles by Worship Attendance

Worship Size	Church Attendance Over the Past Year		
	Decline	Stable	Increase
All Churches Represented (4,998)	16%	44%	40%
100 or less (1,611)	19%	48%	33%
101-300 (1,952)	17%	43%	40%
301-500 (596)	15%	43%	42%
501-750 (318)	11%	39%	50%
751-1,000 (190)	13%	39%	48%
Over 1,000 (331)	10%	37%	52%

Worship Size	Church Finances Over the Past Year		
	Below expenses	Meets expenses	Exceeds expenses
All Churches Represented (4,998)	31%	42%	27%
100 or less (1,611)	35%	42%	23%
101-300 (1,952)	29%	44%	27%
301-500 (596)	31%	40%	29%
501-750 (318)	30%	37%	33%
751-1,000 (190)	29%	42%	28%
Over 1,000 (331)	25%	40%	35%

Table 17-3: Region by Church Attendance and Finances

Region	Church Attendance Over the Past Year		
	Decline	Stable	Increase
All Churches Represented (4,998)	16%	44%	40%
New England (181)	17%	49%	34%
Middle Atlantic (502)	18%	48%	34%
South Atlantic (1,007)	15%	42%	42%
East-North Central (975)	18%	44%	37%
East-South Central (317)	12%	45%	43%
West-North Central (527)	15%	48%	36%
West-South Central (573)	15%	43%	42%
Mountain (257)	14%	41%	45%
Pacific (659)	18%	40%	42%

Region	Church Finances Over the Past Year		
	Below expenses	Meets expenses	Exceeds expenses
All Churches Represented (4,998)	31%	42%	27%
New England (181)	43%	36%	22%
Middle Atlantic (502)	35%	39%	26%
South Atlantic (1,007)	30%	42%	27%
East-North Central (975)	33%	41%	26%
East-South Central (317)	24%	50%	27%
West-North Central (527)	29%	45%	26%
West-South Central (573)	22%	43%	35%
Mountain (257)	31%	39%	30%
Pacific (659)	34%	42%	24%

For breakdowns of regions by state, refer to the Appendix.

COMPENSATION SURVEY FOR 2009
MINISTRY PAID STAFF POSITION DESCRIPTIONS
PASTORAL/MINISTRY STAFF

Solo Pastor/Minister
This is the only ministry staff position. No other paid pastors or ministers in church.

Senior Pastor/Minister
Lead pastor in a church where there are multiple paid ministry positions.

Executive/Administrative Pastor/Minister
Pastor who handles ministry staff supervision, management, and development.

Associate Pastor/Minister
Any paid pastor who assists the Senior Pastor in general or specific ministries other than those specifically listed in the survey. This may include such positions as Assimilation Pastor, Care Pastor, Church Life Pastor, Congregational Care Pastor, Connecting Pastor, Counseling Pastor, Disabilities Ministry Pastor (any), Ethnic Ministries Pastor (any), Evangelism Pastor, Family Life Pastor, Lay Pastor, Membership Pastor, Missions Pastor, Outreach Pastor, Pastoral Care Pastor, Pastoral Counselor, Prayer Pastor, Teaching/Preaching Pastor, Visitation Pastor, and so on.

Youth Pastor/Minister/Director
This includes paid pastors and directors to junior high, senior high, or college students. It may include such positions as Campus Pastor, College Minister, Junior High Pastor/Director, Senior High Pastor/Director, Youth Center Director, Youth Pastor/Minister/Director, and so on.

Adult Ministry Pastor/Minister/Director
Includes paid pastors and directors for adults, married couples, men, singles, seniors, women, young adults, and so on.

Children's/Preschool Pastor/Minister/Director
Church staff (not school staff) that includes paid pastors and directors for children from nursery through elementary school. This may include such positions as Early Childhood Pastor, Elementary School Pastor, Preschool Pastor/Director, Childcare Director, Daycare Director, and so on.

Christian Education Pastor/Minister/Director
Includes paid pastors and directors of broad educational ministries such as Bible studies, cell groups, Christian education, discipleship, equipping, small groups, spiritual formation, and so on.

Music/Choir/Worship Pastor/Minister/Director
This includes paid pastors and directors of band, bell/chimes choir, music ministry, orchestra, praise & worship team, vocal choir, and so on. It may include such positions as Music Pastor/Director, Worship Pastor/Director/Leader, and so on.

Media/Production/Arts Pastor/Minister/Director*
Includes paid pastors and directors who oversee drama, technical ministries, video, sound production, and so on. This may include positions such as Technical Director, Media Director, Drama Director, Production Director, Video Producer, Minister of Arts, and so on.

Not reported due to low response.

MINISTRY PAID STAFF POSITION DESCRIPTIONS
SUPPORT/ADMINISTRATIVE STAFF

Administrator
Includes paid staff (usually not ordained) who supervise the business aspect of running the church, such as business or financial management. This may include such positions as Business Administrator, Business Manager, Chief Financial Officer, Chief Operating Officer, and so on.

Bookkeeper/Accountant
Includes paid personnel who assist with day-to-day financial matters in the church. This may include such positions as Accountant, Controller, Financial Administrative Assistant, Financial Secretary, Payroll Secretary, Treasurer, and so on.

Child Care
Includes paid personnel who provide regular or occasional childcare and are on the church's payroll (not school staff). This may include such positions as Babysitters, Child Care Assistant, Child Care Providers, Daycare Staff, Nursery Attendant, Nursery Director, Nursery Helper, Nursery Worker, and so on.

Custodian/Maintenance
Includes paid personnel who provide care and maintenance of physical facilities, buildings, grounds, and security. This may include such positions as Building and Grounds Manager, Building Supervisor, Custodian, Facilities Manager, Grounds Keeper, Housekeeper, Lawn Maintenance Assistant, Maid, Maintenance Assistant, Plant Manager, Property Manager, Security Manager/Assistant, Sexton, Traffic Coordinator, and so on.

Musician/Accompanist/Vocalist
Includes paid personnel who provide vocal or instrumental music or accompaniment. This may include such positions as Accompanist, Instrumentalist of any kind, Organist, Pianist, Soloist, Vocalist, and so on.

Secretary/Administrative Assistant
Includes paid personnel who provide clerical or administrative support. This may include such positions as Administrative Assistant, Clerical Assistant, Executive Secretary, Lead Secretary, Office Assistant, Office Clerk, Office Manager, Publications Secretary/Coordinator, Receptionist, Secretary to any pastor or ministry, Secretary's Assistant, and so on.

Communications/Design Publications*
Includes paid personnel who provide design services, create publications, or otherwise oversee church communications. This may include such positions as Designer, Communications Coordinator, Publicist, Writer, Editor, and so on.

* Not reported due to low response.

TAX LAW & COMPENSATION PLANNING

Welcome to the Special Section on Essentials in Tax Law and Compensation Planning. Compensation planning for clergy and other church staff presents several unique tax issues that are not well understood by many church leaders and their advisers. This special section eliminates confusion and presents the key considerations to review when structuring compensation plans.

In adopting 2010 and 2011 compensation packages for your ministers and lay staff members, review these possible components of the compensation package.

1. SALARY The most basic component of church staff compensation is salary. There are two important considerations to keep in mind with respect to staff salaries—the amount of the salary, and the use of "salary reduction agreements." These two issues will be discussed separately.

a. Amount. Staff salaries ordinarily are set by the church board. Churches generally may pay any amount they wish, with one important exception—if a church pays unreasonably high compensation to a pastor or other employee there are two possible consequences:

(1) Loss of tax-exempt status. In order for a church or any other charity to maintain its tax-exempt status it must meet a number of conditions. One condition is that it cannot pay unreasonably high compensation to any person. There are two considerations to note. First, very few charities have lost their exempt status for paying unreasonable compensation. The IRS has been very reluctant to impose this remedy. Second, the law does not define what amount of compensation is unreasonable, and neither the IRS nor the courts have provided much clarification.

> **Example.** *A federal appeals court concluded that combined annual income of $115,680 paid by a religious organization to its founder and his wife was not excessive.*

> **Example.** *A court ruled that maximum reasonable compensation for a prominent televangelist was $133,100 in 1984, $146,410 in 1985, $161,051 in 1986, and $177,156 in 1987. The court based its conclusions on a comparison of the salaries of other nonprofit officers in the state.*

(2) Intermediate sanctions. The IRS can assess substantial excise taxes called "intermediate sanctions" against "disqualified persons" that are paid an "excess benefit" by a church or other charity. A disqualified person is any officer or director, or a relative of such a person. An excess benefit is compensation and fringe benefits in excess of what the IRS deems "reasonable." Note that the IRS still can revoke the exempt status of any charity that pays excessive compensation to an employee. However, it is more likely that excessive compensation will result in intermediate sanctions rather than loss of exempt status. To illustrate, why should a major university lose its tax-exempt status because it pays excessive compensation to its head football coach?

The intermediate sanctions the IRS can impose include the following:

- **Tax on disqualified persons.** A disqualified person who benefits from an excess benefit transaction is subject to an excise tax equal to 25 percent of the amount of the "excess benefit" (the amount by which actual compensation exceeds the fair market value of services rendered). This tax is assessed against the disqualified person directly, not his or her employer.

- **Additional tax on disqualified persons.** If a disqualified person fails to "correct" the excess benefit by the time the IRS assesses the 25 percent tax, then the IRS can assess an additional tax of up to 200 percent of the excess benefit. The law specifies that a disqualified person can "correct" the excess benefit transaction by "undoing the excess benefit to the extent possible, and taking any additional measures necessary to place the organization in a financial position not worse than that in which it would be if the disqualified person were dealing under the highest fiduciary standards."

■ **Tax on organization managers.** If the IRS assesses the 25 percent tax against a disqualified person, it is permitted to impose an additional 20 percent tax (up to a maximum of $20,000) on any "organization manager" who participates in an excess benefit transaction knowing it is such a transaction, unless the manager's participation "is not willful and is due to reasonable cause." A "manager" is an officer, director, or trustee. IRS regulations clarify that the managers collectively cannot be liable for more than $20,000 for any one transaction.

>**Key point**< The intermediate sanctions law imposes an excise tax on members of a church's governing board who vote for a compensation package that the IRS determines to be excessive. This makes it essential for board members to carefully review the reasonableness of compensation packages.

Charities, disqualified persons, and governing boards may rely on a "presumption of reasonableness" with respect to a compensation arrangement if it was approved by a board of directors (or committee of the board) that: (1) was composed entirely of individuals unrelated to and not subject to the control of the disqualified person involved in the arrangement; (2) obtained and relied upon objective "comparability" information, such as (a) compensation paid by similar organizations, both taxable and tax-exempt, for comparable positions, (b) independent compensation surveys by nationally recognized independent firms, or (c) actual written offers from similar institutions competing for the services of the disqualified person; and (3) adequately documented the basis for its decision.

>**Key point**< The law creates a presumption that a minister's compensation package is reasonable if approved by a church board that relied upon objective "comparability" information, including independent compensation surveys by nationally recognized independent firms. One of the more comprehensive compensation surveys for church workers is this text. This means that most ministers will be able to use this text to establish the presumption of reasonableness. But it also suggests that the IRS may rely on the data in this text in any attempt to impose intermediate sanctions against ministers.

IRS regulations clarify that "revenue based pay" arrangements in which an employee's compensation is based on a percentage of the employer's total revenues do not automatically result in an excess benefit transaction triggering intermediate sanctions. Rather, "all relevant facts and circumstances" must be considered.

Caution. In a series of rulings published in 2004 the IRS assessed intermediate sanctions against a pastor as a result of excess benefits paid to him and members of his family by his church. The IRS concluded that taxable compensation and benefits a church pays to a disqualified person (any church officer, and members of his or her family), that are not reported as taxable income to the recipient, constitute "automatic excess benefits" that trigger intermediate sanctions regardless of the amount involved. The IRS concluded that the following transactions resulted in excess benefits to the pastor because they were not reported as taxable income: (1) personal use of church property (vehicles, cell phones, credit cards, computers, etc.) by the pastor and members of his family; (2) reimbursements of personal expenses; and (3) nonaccountable reimbursements of business expenses (i.e., reimbursements of expenses that were not supported by adequate documentation of the business purpose of each expense). Since these taxable benefits were not reported as taxable income, they amounted to "automatic" excess benefits resulting in intermediate sanctions. This is a stunning interpretation of the tax code and regulations that directly affects the compensation practices of every church, and exposes some church staff members to intermediate sanctions.

Recommendation. *Churches that pay a minister (or any staff member) significantly more than the highest 25 percent for comparable positions should obtain a legal opinion from an experienced tax attorney confirming that the amount paid is not "unreasonable" and will not expose the employee or the board to intermediate sanctions*

Tax savings tip. *Ministers and other church staff members should carefully review their W-2 or 1099 to be sure that it does not report more income than was actually received. If an error was made, the church should issue a corrected tax form (Form W-2c for an employee, or a "corrected" Form 1099 for a self-employed worker).*

b. Salary reduction agreements. Many churches have established "salary reduction agreements" to handle certain staff expenses. The objective is to reduce a worker's taxable income since only the income remaining after the various "reductions" is reported on the worker's W-2 or 1099 form at the end of the year. It is important for churches to understand that they cannot reduce a worker's taxable income through salary reductions unless specifically allowed by law.

Here are three ways that taxable income can be reduced through salary reduction agreements:

(1) Tax-sheltered annuity contributions. Salary reduction agreements can be used to contribute to a tax-sheltered annuity (sometimes called a "403(b) annuity") if the salary reductions meet certain conditions.

(2) "Cafeteria plans." Salary reduction agreements also can be used to fund "cafeteria plans" (including "flexible spending arrangements") if several conditions are met. A cafeteria plan is a written plan established by an employer that allows employees to choose between cash and a "menu" of nontaxable benefits specified by law (including employer-provided medical insurance premiums, group-term life insurance, and dependent care).

(3) Housing allowances. A church can designate a portion of a minister's salary as a housing allowance, and the amount so designated is not subject to income tax if certain conditions are met. Housing allowances are addressed in detail just below.

Observation. In some cases "salary reductions" will not accomplish the goal of reducing a minister's taxable income. The income tax regulations prohibit the widespread practice of funding "accountable" reimbursement arrangements through salary reductions. This topic is addressed later in this chapter.

▢ Recommended Resources.

For more detailed information on salaries for church staff members,
see chapter 4 in the *Church & Clergy Tax Guide.*

2. HOUSING ALLOWANCES. The most important tax benefit available to ministers who own or rent their homes is the housing allowance. Ministers who own their home do not pay federal income taxes on the amount of their compensation that their employing church designates in advance as a housing allowance, to the extent that the allowance represents compensation for ministerial services, is used to pay housing expenses, and does not exceed the annual fair rental value of the home (furnished, plus utilities). Housing-related expenses include mortgage payments, utilities, repairs, furnishings, insurance, property taxes, additions, and maintenance.

Ministers who rent a home or apartment do not pay federal income taxes on the amount of their compensation that their employing church designates in advance as a housing allowance to the extent that the allowance represents compensation for "ministerial services" and is used to pay rental expenses such as rent, furnishings, utilities, and insurance.

Unfortunately, many churches fail to designate a portion of a minister's compensation as a housing allowance. This deprives their minister of an important tax benefit.

Ministers who live in a church-owned parsonage that is provided "rent-free" as compensation for ministerial services do not include the annual fair rental value of the parsonage as income in computing their federal income taxes. The annual fair rental value is not "deducted" from the minister's income. Rather, it is not reported as additional income anywhere on Form 1040 (as it generally would be by non-clergy workers). Ministers who live in a church-provided parsonage do not pay federal income taxes on the amount of their compensation that their employing church designates in advance as a parsonage allowance, to the extent that the allowance represents compensation for ministerial services and is used to pay parsonage-related expenses such as utilities, repairs, and furnishings.

Tax savings tip. *Ministers who live in church parsonages, and who incur any out-of-pocket expenses in maintaining the parsonage (such as utilities, property taxes, insurance, furnishings, or lawn care) should ask their employing church to designate a portion of their annual compensation in advance as a "parsonage allowance." Such an allowance is not included on the minister's W-2 or 1099 at the end of the year and is nontaxable in computing federal income taxes to the extent the minister incurs housing expenses of at least that amount. This is a very important tax benefit for ministers living in church-provided parsonages. Many ministers and church boards are not aware of this benefit, or are not taking advantage of it.*

Note that these exclusions are for federal income tax purposes only. Ministers cannot exclude the fair rental value of a parsonage or a housing allowance when computing their self-employment (Social Security) taxes.

Recommendation. *Be sure that the designation of a housing or parsonage allowance for year 2010 and 2011 is on the agenda of the church board for one of its final meetings in 2009 and 2010. The designation should be an official action of the board or congregation, and it should be duly recorded in the minutes of the meeting. The IRS also recognizes designations included in employment contracts and budget line items—assuming in each case that the designation was duly adopted by the church board (or the congregation in a business meeting). Also, if the minister is a new hire, be sure the church designates a housing allowance prior to the date he or she begins working.*

How much should a church board or congregation designate as a housing allowance? Many churches base the allowance on their minister's estimate of actual housing expenses for the new year. The church provides the minister with a form on which anticipated housing expenses for the new year are reported. For ministers who own their homes, the form asks for projected expenses in the following categories: down payment, mortgage payments, property taxes, property insurance, utilities, furnishings and appliances, repairs and improvements, maintenance, and miscellaneous. Many churches designate an allowance in excess of the anticipated expenses itemized by the minister. Basing the allowance solely on a minister's actual expenses will penalize the minister if housing expenses in fact turn out to be higher than expected. In other words, the allowance should take into account unexpected housing costs or inaccurate projections of expenses.

Recommendation. *Plan a mid-year review of the housing allowance to make sure that the designated amount is sufficient to cover actual expenses. If a pastor's expenses will exceed the allowance, then the church may amend the allowance. But any amendment will only operate prospectively.*

Observation. *The compensation survey summarized in previous chapters reveals that housing allowances are claimed by several associate ministers, administrators, music directors, secretaries, and custodians. However, it is important to note that the housing allowance is available only if two conditions are met: (1) the recipient is a minister, and (2) the allowance is provided as compensation for services performed in the exercise of ministry. In many cases, these conditions will not be satisfied by administrators, music directors, secretaries, or custodians. See chapter 3 of Richard Hammar's annual* Church & Clergy Tax Guide *(available from* YOUR CHURCH RESOURCES*) for more information.*

⬚ Recommended Resources.

For more detailed information about tax law and housing allowances, see chapter 6 in the *Church & Clergy Tax Guide*.

3. EQUITY ALLOWANCES. Ministers who live in church-owned parsonages are denied one very important benefit of home ownership—the opportunity to accumulate "equity" in a home over the course of many years. Many ministers who have lived in parsonages during much of their active ministry often face retirement without housing. Their fellow ministers who purchased a home early in their ministry often can look forward to retirement with a home that is

THE 2010-2011 COMPENSATION HANDBOOK FOR CHURCH STAFF

either substantially or completely debt-free. To avoid the potential hardship often suffered by a minister who lives in a parsonage, some churches increase their minister's compensation by an amount that is sometimes referred to as an "equity allowance." The idea is to provide the minister with the equivalent of equity in a home. This is an excellent idea that should be considered by any church having one or more ministers living in church-provided housing. Of course, for the concept to work properly, the equity allowance should not be accessible by the minister until retirement. Therefore, some churches choose to place the allowance directly in a minister's tax-sheltered retirement account.

Recommendation. *Equity allowances should also be considered by a church whose minister rents a home.*

⬚ Recommended Resources.
For more detailed information about tax law and equity allowances,
see chapter 6, section A.7, in the *Church & Clergy Tax Guide.*

4. ACCOUNTABLE BUSINESS EXPENSE REIMBURSEMENT POLICY. One of the most important components of church staff compensation packages is an "accountable" business expense reimbursement arrangement. This benefit is available to both ministers and lay staff members alike. Under such an arrangement a church (1) reimburses only those business expenses that are properly substantiated within a reasonable time as to date, amount, place, and business purpose, and (2) requires any excess reimbursements (in excess of substantiated expenses) to be returned to the church. Churches should seriously consider adopting an accountable reimbursement policy for reimbursing staff business expenses. Such a policy has the following advantages:

- Church staff report their business expenses to the church rather than to the IRS.

- Church staff who report their income taxes as employees, or who report as self-employed and who are reclassified as employees by the IRS in an audit, avoid the limitations on the deductibility of employee business expenses. These limitations include (1) the elimination of any deduction if the worker cannot itemize deductions on Schedule A (most taxpayers cannot), and (2) the deductibility of business expenses on Schedule A as an itemized expense only to the extent that these expenses exceed two percent of the worker's adjusted gross income.

- The so-called *Deason* allocation rule is avoided. Under this rule, ministers must reduce their business expense deduction by the percentage of their total compensation that consists of a tax-exempt housing allowance.

- The "50 percent limitation" that applies to the deductibility of business meals and entertainment expenses is avoided. Unless these expenses are reimbursed by an employer under an accountable plan, only 50 percent of them are deductible by either employees or self-employed workers.

- Church staff who report their income taxes as self-employed avoid the risk of being reclassified as an employee by the IRS in an audit and assessed additional taxes.

Observation. *The compensation data summarized in this text reveal that many churches provide automobile allowances to their ministers and lay staff. In many cases, a church will simply provide a fixed dollar amount every month to a worker (for example, $300), and require no substantiation of business miles or a return of any "excess reimbursements" (in excess of substantiated business miles). This is referred to as a "nonaccountable" reimbursement arrangement. What are the tax consequences of such an arrangement? The allowances must be added to the worker's W-2 or 1099 at the end of the year, and the worker can claim a business deduction on Schedule A (if an employee) or on Schedule C (if self-employed). If a worker is an employee with insufficient itemized deductions to use Schedule*

256

For Recommended Resources, order at www.YourChurchResources.com

A, there is no deduction available for business expenses even though the full amount of the monthly allowances are added to taxable income. This is a very unfortunate tax result that can be avoided completely through an accountable reimbursement arrangement. For a sample board resolution adopting an accountable business expense reimbursement arrangement, see chapter 7 of Richard Hammar's annual Church & Clergy Tax Guide.

Example. *A church pays its senior pastor an annual salary of $45,000 this year. In addition, it provides the pastor with a monthly car allowance of $400. This is an example of a nonaccountable reimbursement arrangement. Assume that the church treasurer reports none of these reimbursements as taxable income on the pastor's Form W-2 since she assumes that the pastor had "at least" $4,800 in expenses associated with the business use of his car and so there was no need to report the nonaccountable reimbursements as taxable income. This assumption not only is incorrect, but it also converts the nonaccountable reimbursements into an "automatic" excess benefit exposing the pastor to intermediate sanctions, as noted previously in this chapter. This assumes that the senior pastor is an officer or director (or relative of an officer or director).*

The income tax regulations prohibit the funding of accountable reimbursement arrangements through salary reductions.

Example. *Assume that a church pays Pastor Gary $500 each week, and also agrees to reimburse his substantiated business expenses for each month out of the first weekly payroll check for the following month. Assume further that Pastor Gary substantiated $300 of business expenses for January. The church issued Pastor Gary his customary check of $500 for the first week of February, but only $200 of this check represents taxable salary while the remaining $300 represents a nontaxable reimbursement under an accountable plan. Only the $200 salary component of this check is included on Pastor Gary's W-2 (or 1099) form at the end of the year. This arrangement was once common, and still is practiced by some churches. The income tax regulations do not prohibit the funding of business expense reimbursements out of salary reductions. Rather, a church's reimbursements under such arrangements cannot be "accountable." This means that a church cannot reduce W-2 income by reducing an employee's salary to pay for business expense reimbursements. In our example, the full $500 paycheck must be accumulated to Pastor Gary's W-2. If it is not, the arrangement may constitute an automatic excess benefit transaction exposing Pastor Gary to intermediate sanctions, as explained previously in this chapter.*

>**Key point**< Many churches set aside a certain amount each year to cover an employee's total compensation. For ministers, this amount often includes salary, housing allowance, fringe benefits, and an amount for the reimbursement of business expenses. To illustrate, a church board determines in December of 2009 that Pastor Ted's compensation package for 2010 will consist of salary ($30,000), housing allowance ($10,000), fringe benefits ($5,000), and business expense reimbursements ($3,000). This is what is sometimes called a salary "restructuring" arrangement. Are such arrangements treated as salary reductions, meaning that the entire $3,000 must be accumulated to Pastor Teds W-2 income? Not necessarily. A possible basis exists for not reporting the $3,000 as taxable income to Pastor Ted if all of the following conditions are met: (1) the $3,000 is used to reimburse Pastor Ted for business expenses only if the substantiation requirements of an accountable arrangement are met; (2) the salary "restructuring" occurs prior to the start of the year; (3) any undistributed portion of the $3,000 is not given to Pastor Ted at the end of the year; and (4) the church adopts two resolutions—a "compensation" resolution consisting of salary, housing, and fringe benefits, and a "business expense" resolution consisting of the $3,000 reimbursement amount. If the IRS audits Pastor Ted and asks to see the church resolution specifying his compensation, the church would produce the first resolution. This is an aggressive position that may be rejected by the IRS in an audit. No court has addressed the issue. It should not be adopted without first consulting with a tax attorney.

⬥ Recommended Resources.

For more detailed information about tax law and business expense reimbursement policies,
see chapter 7, section E, in the *Church & Clergy Tax Guide.*

5. TRAVEL EXPENSES OF A SPOUSE. A church should decide if it will be paying for any of the travel expenses of a spouse accompanying a minister or other staff member on a business trip. Reimbursing these expenses represents a significant benefit. Unfortunately, there is much confusion regarding the correct reporting of such reimbursements for tax purposes. If the spouse's presence on the trip serves a legitimate business purpose, and the spouse's travel expenses are reimbursed by the church under an accountable arrangement (described above) then the reimbursements represent a nontaxable fringe benefit. If these two requirements are not met, the reimbursements represent taxable income to the minister or staff member.

Caution. If either of these conditions is not met, then a church's reimbursement of a nonemployee spouse's travel expenses will represent taxable income to the minister or other staff member. The same applies to children who accompany a minister or staff member on a business trip. Further, the IRS may assert that the church's failure to report the reimbursement of the spouse's expenses as taxable income to the minister makes the reimbursement an "automatic" excess benefit triggering intermediate sanctions, as noted previously in this chapter.

> **Tax savings tip.** *If a church does not reimburse the travel expenses of a pastor's spouse who accompanies the pastor on a business trip, then the spouse may be able to deduct travel expenses as a charitable contribution (assuming that the spouse's presence on the trip serves a legitimate "business" purpose).*

▯ Recommended Resources.

For more detailed information about tax law and the travel expense of a spouse,
see chapter 7, section C.2, in the *Church & Clergy Tax Guide*.

6. CHURCH-OWNED VEHICLES. Churches should consider the advantages of acquiring an automobile for staff members' church-related travel. Here's why. If a church purchases a car, and the church board adopts a resolution restricting use of the car to church-related activities, then the worker reports no income or deductions, and better yet, there are no accountings, reimbursements, allowances, or recordkeeping requirements. This assumes that the car is in fact used exclusively for church-related purposes, and the strict conditions specified in the income tax regulations are satisfied.

Commuting is always considered to be personal use of a car, and so this procedure would not be available if a church allowed a worker to commute to work in a church-owned vehicle. Fortunately, the income tax regulations permit certain church employees who use a church-owned vehicle exclusively for business purposes except for commuting to receive all of the benefits associated with business use of a church-owned vehicle, if certain additional conditions are met.

Unfortunately, most churches that provide a staff member with a car do not consider either of these alternatives. Rather, they simply transfer the car to the individual and impose no limitations on personal use. This arrangement results in taxable income to the staff member, whether the staff member is a minister or a lay employee.

▯ Recommended Resources.

For more detailed information about tax law and church owned vehicles,
see chapter 4, section B.8, in the *Church & Clergy Tax Guide*.

7. SELF-EMPLOYMENT TAX. There is one provision in the tax code that has caused more confusion for ministers and church treasurers than any other, and it is this: Ministers are always treated as self-employed for Social Security with regard to services they perform in the exercise of their ministry. This is true even if they are employees for federal income tax reporting purposes. This is sometimes referred to as the "dual tax status" of ministers.

Social Security benefits are financed through two tax systems. Employers and employees each pay "Social Security" and "Medicare" (sometimes collectively referred to as "FICA") taxes which for 2010 amount to 7.65 percent of an employee's taxable wages (a total tax of 15.3 percent) up to a specified amount. Self-employed persons pay the "self-employment tax," which for 2010 is 15.3 percent of net self-employment earnings up to a specified amount. Note that self-employed workers are responsible for paying their entire Social Security tax liability, while employees pay only half (their employer pays the other half). (Watch for updates on the 2011 FICA and self-employment tax amounts in Richard Hammar's *2011 Church & Clergy Tax Guide*.)

>**Key point**< Ministers always are treated as self-employed for Social Security with respect to services performed in the exercise of their ministry, and so they do not pay "Social Security" and "Medicare" taxes. Rather, they pay the "self-employment tax" with respect to church compensation, unless they have filed a timely application for exemption from Social Security taxes (and received back a copy of their exemption application from the IRS marked "approved"). As a result, ministers must be familiar with the self-employment tax rules. So must lay church employees who work for a church that filed a timely exemption from Social Security coverage (Form 8274), since they are considered self-employed for Social Security.

>**Key point**< Many churches pay some or all of their pastor's self-employment taxes. This is perfectly appropriate. After all, churches pay half of a non-minister employee's Social Security and Medicare taxes, so why shouldn't it do the same for its pastor? Research conducted by *Your Church* reveals that in 2009 more than one-third (36 percent) of churches paid some or all of their senior pastor's self-employment taxes. Of those churches that did, 26 percent paid one-half of the self-employment tax, while 10 percent paid all of it. Any portion paid by the church is a taxable fringe benefit that must be reported as additional wages on the pastor's W-2 or 1099 form, and Form 1040. It also should be reported as additional income by the pastor in computing self-employment taxes.

>**Key point**< Housing allowances and the fair rental value of parsonages are includable in self-employment earnings for Social Security purposes.

Caution. Many churches withhold the employees' share of Social Security and Medicare taxes from ministers' compensation, and then pay the employer's share. In other words, they treat their minister as an employee for Social Security. This is understandable, especially when the church treats the minister as an employee for purposes of federal income taxation. But, it is always incorrect for a church to treat a minister as an employee for Social Security with respect to services performed in the exercise of ministry.

Ministers may exempt themselves from self-employment taxes with respect to services performed in the exercise of ministry if several requirements are met. Among other things, the exemption must be filed by the due date of a minister's federal tax return (Form 1040) for the second year in which he or she had net self-employment earnings of $400 or more, any part of which derived from the performance of ministerial duties. In most cases, this means the form is due by April 15 of the third year of ministry. Also, the minister must be opposed on the basis of religious convictions to accepting Social Security benefits.

As a self-employed person for Social Security, a minister computes self-employment taxes on Schedule SE of Form 1040.

⬚ Recommended Resources.

For more detailed information about tax law and self-employment tax,
see chapter 9 in the *Church & Clergy Tax Guide*.

8. INSURANCE. Churches often provide ministers with life, health, or disability insurance coverage and pay all of the premiums for such coverage. In some cases, churches make the same benefits available to lay staff members. The income tax regulations specify that the gross income of an *employee* does not include

■ contributions which his employer makes to an accident or health plan for compensation (through insurance or otherwise) to the employee for personal injuries or sickness incurred by him, his spouse, or his dependents .... The employer may contribute to an accident or health plan by paying the premium (or a portion of the premium) on a policy of accident or health insurance covering one or more of his employees, or by contributing to a separate trust or fund...

The exclusion of employer-paid health insurance premiums from the taxable income of employees is one of the main reasons why ministers and other staff members often are better off reporting their income taxes as employees. This important benefit is not available to workers who report their income taxes as self-employed. A church wishing to make this benefit available to its ministers (or other employees) should adopt a plan in an appropriate board resolution. Plans that benefit only ministers are exempted from the "nondiscrimination" rules that apply to most of these kinds of plans.

Observation. *The compensation survey data summarized in this text reveal that many churches provide ministers with health insurance. A smaller percentage of churches provide these benefits to lay staff members. Such discrimination by church employers ordinarily does not violate federal law.*

The cost of group term life insurance bought by an employer for its employees ordinarily is not taxable to the employees so long as the amount of coverage does not exceed $50,000 per employee. Generally, life insurance can qualify as group term life insurance only if it is available to at least ten full-time employees. However, there are some exceptions to this rule. For example, the ten full-time employee rule does not apply if (l) an employer provides the insurance to all full-time employees who provide satisfactory evidence of insurability, (2) insurance coverage is based on a uniform percentage of pay, and (3) evidence of insurability is limited to a medical questionnaire completed by the employee that does not require a physical examination.

Other kinds of insurance premiums paid by the church on behalf of a minister or lay church employee ordinarily represent taxable income. For example, the cost of premiums on a whole life or universal life insurance policy paid by a church on the life of its minister (and naming the minister's spouse and children as beneficiaries) ordinarily must be reported as income to the minister.

⬚ Recommended Resources.

For more detailed information about tax law and insurance,
see chapter 5 in the *Church & Clergy Tax Guide*.

9. RETIREMENT ACCOUNTS. Most ministers (and some lay staff members) participate in some form of retirement plan. Such plans often are sponsored either by the local church, or by a denomination or agency with which the church is affiliated. Church workers covered by certain kinds of plans can choose to have part of their pay set aside each year (through "salary reductions") in the retirement fund, rather than receiving it as income. Amounts set aside by the employing church under these plans may be excludable from gross income for tax purposes. These amounts are sometimes called "elective deferrals" because the employee elects to set aside the money, and tax on the money is deferred until it is taken out of the account. This option is available to ministers or lay workers who are covered by tax-sheltered annuities ("403(b) plans"), simplified employee pensions (SEPs), and certain other plans.

Payments made by an employing church toward an employee's tax-sheltered annuity, SEP, and certain other plans, and funded out of church funds rather than through a reduction in an employee's compensation, may also be excluded from the employee's gross income for tax purposes under certain circumstances. There are limits on how much an employee can elect to contribute into such plans, and on how much the employing church can contribute out of its own funds. Of course, ministers and lay workers (whether employees or self-employed for income tax purposes) can also contribute to an IRA.

Recommendation. *If a church has not established or contributed to a retirement plan for its staff members, then it should consider doing so or at least ensuring that staff members are participating in an adequate alternative (particularly in the case of ministers who have exempted themselves from Social Security coverage). Further, if staff members are participating in a retirement plan, then the end of the year is a good time to determine how contributions to the plan in 2010 and 2011 will be funded (i.e., through employee contributions, salary reductions, or church contributions) and in what amounts.*

>**Key point**< Churches that have not adequately contributed to their minister's retirement, or that would like to make contributions in excess of applicable limits, should consider the possible advantages of a "rabbi trust." A church's contributions to such a trust will not be included in a minister's current taxable income, and income generated by the trust is tax-deferred. Further, a church ordinarily can contribute more toward a rabbi trust than to most other kinds of retirement program. This is very attractive for churches whose minister is approaching retirement with inadequate retirement savings.

▯ Recommended Resources.
For more detailed information about tax law and retirement accounts,
see chapter 10 in the *Church & Clergy Tax Guide*

10. WORKS MADE FOR HIRE. It is common for church employees to compose music or write books or articles in their church office during office hours. What is often not understood is that such persons do not necessarily own the copyright to the works they create. While the one who creates a work generally is its author and the initial owner of the copyright in the work, section 201(b) of the Copyright Act specifies that "in the case of a work made for hire, the employer or other person for whom the work was prepared is considered the author ... and, unless the parties have expressly agreed otherwise in a written instrument signed by them, owns all of the rights comprised in the copyright."

The copyright law defines "work made for hire" as "a work prepared by an employee within the scope of his or her employment." There are two requirements that must be met: (1) the person creating the work is an employee, and (2) the employee created the work within the scope of his or her employment. Whether or not one is an employee will depend on the same factors used in determining whether one is an employee or self-employed for federal income tax reporting purposes (see chapter 2 of Richard Hammar's annual *Church & Clergy Tax Guide*). However, the courts have been very liberal in finding employee status in this context, so it is possible that a court would conclude that a work is a work made for hire even though the author reports federal income taxes as a self-employed person.

The second requirement is that the work must have been created within the scope of employment. This requirement generally means that the work was created during regular working hours, on the employer's premises, using the employer's staff and equipment. This is often a difficult standard to apply. As a result, it is desirable for church employees to discuss this issue with the church leadership to avoid any potential misunderstandings.

Section 201(b), quoted above, allows an employer and employee to agree in a signed, written instrument that copyright ownership in works created by the employee within the scope of employment does not belong to the employer. This should be a matter for consideration by any church having a minister or other staff member who creates literary or musical works during office hours, on church premises, using church staff and church equipment (e.g., computers, printers, paper, library, secretaries). The services of an attorney will be needed to draft an appropriate instrument, assuming that the church desires to divest itself of copyright ownership in a particular work made for hire. An attorney also will be able to explain the potential tax ramifications of such an instrument.

▯ Recommended Resources.
For more detailed information about tax law and works made for hire,
see Richard Hammar's *Church Guide to Copyright Law.*

THE 2010-2011 COMPENSATION HANDBOOK FOR CHURCH STAFF

11. QUALIFIED TUITION REDUCTIONS ("QTR"). Many churches operate elementary or secondary schools, and charge reduced tuition to certain school employees. For example, assume that a church operates an elementary school, charges annual tuition of $2,000, but only charges tuition of $500 for the children of school employees and charges no tuition at all for the child of Pastor Eric (the church's senior minister and president of the school). Such "tuition reductions" are perfectly appropriate. Further, section 117(d) of the federal tax code specifies that they will not result in taxable income to the school employees. In other words, a $500 annual tuition reduction awarded to a school employee whose child attends the school need not be reported as income (on the employee's W-2 or Form 1040). This obviously can be a significant benefit to school employees.

However, section 117(d) also provides that "highly compensated employees" cannot exclude qualified tuition reductions from their income unless the same benefit is available on substantially similar terms to other employees. The term "highly compensated employee" is defined to include any employee who was paid compensation for the previous year in excess of a specified amount. For 2009, the amount was $110,000. The amount for 2010 and 2011 was not available at the time of publication of this text.

If in the example cited above Pastor Eric was paid more than $110,000 for the previous year, then the church would have to include $2,000 (the entire amount of the tuition reduction) in Pastor Eric's reportable income since he is a highly compensated employee and the benefit available to him is not available on substantially similar terms to other employees. However, this will not affect other school employees who are not "highly compensated." They will be able to exclude tuition reductions from their income.

>**Key point**< The IRS has ruled that tuition reductions are tax-free only for school employees, and so if a church operates a private school only employees who perform duties on behalf of the school qualify for this benefit. If the school offers tuition reductions to church employees who perform no duties for the school, these reductions are a taxable fringe benefit.

▯ Recommended Resources.
For more derailed information about tax law and QTRs,
see chapter 5, section K.5, in the *Church & Clergy Tax Guide*

12. LOANS TO MINISTERS. Churches often make loans to ministers to enable a minister to pay for housing or some other major purchase. In some cases the church charges no interest or a low rate far below the prevailing market rate of interest. These loans can create problems for a number of reasons. Consider the following.

▪ Many state nonprofit corporation laws prohibit loans to officers and directors. No church should consider making any loan (even at a reasonable rate of interest) to a minister who is an officer or director of the church without first confirming that such loans are permissible under state law.

▪ No-interest or low-interest loans to ministers may be viewed as "inurement" of the church's income to a minister. As noted above, this can potentially jeopardize the church's tax-exempt status.

▪ For loans of $10,000 or more (or for loans of lower amounts where an intent to avoid taxes exists), a church must value the benefit to a minister of receiving a no-interest or low-interest loan and add this amount to the minister's reportable income. This is a complex calculation that is beyond the scope of this book. The point is this—even if loans to ministers are allowed under your state's nonprofit corporation law, the church must recognize that no-interest and low-interest loans of $10,000 or more will result in income to a minister that must be valued and reported (on the ministers W-2 or 1099-MISC, and Form 1040). Failure to do so could result in prohibited "inurement" of the church's income to a private individual, jeopardizing the church's tax-exempt status.

Observation. *Some ministers and lay workers never fully repay a loan made to them by their church. The forgiveness of debt ordinarily represents taxable income to the debtor. As a result, if a church makes a loan to a minister or other staff member and the debt is later forgiven by the church, taxable income is generated in the amount of the forgiven debt.*

◻ Recommended Resources.

For more detailed information about tax law and loans to ministers,
see chapter 4, section B.9, in the *Church & Clergy Tax Guide.*

13. VOLUNTARY WITHHOLDING. Ministers' compensation is exempt from income tax withholding whether a minister reports income taxes as an employee or as self-employed. While it is true that the tax code requires every employer, including churches and religious organizations, to withhold federal income taxes from employee wages, there are some exceptions to this rule. One exception is wages paid for "services performed by a duly ordained, commissioned, or licensed minister of a church in the exercise of his ministry." Therefore, a church need not withhold income taxes from the salary of a minister who is an employee for income tax reporting purposes. Further, since the withholding requirements only apply to the wages of employees, a church should not "withhold" taxes from the compensation of a minister (or any other worker, such as a part-time custodian) who reports his or her income taxes as a self-employed person.

The IRS maintains that a church and a minister-employee may agree voluntarily that federal income taxes be withheld from the minister's wages, but this is not required. Some ministers find voluntary withholding attractive since it eliminates the guesswork, quarterly reports, and penalties associated with the estimated tax procedure (which applies automatically if voluntary withholding is not elected). A minister-employee who elects to enter into a voluntary withholding arrangement with his or her church need only file a completed Form W-4 (employee's withholding allowance certificate) with the church. The filing of this form is deemed to be a request for voluntary withholding. Voluntary withholding arrangements can be terminated unilaterally by either a minister or the church, or by mutual consent. Alternatively, a minister can stipulate that the voluntary withholding arrangement will terminate on a specified date. In such a case, the minister must give the church a signed statement setting forth the date on which the voluntary withholding is to terminate; the minister's name and address; and a statement that he wishes to enter into a voluntary withholding arrangement with his or her employer. This statement must be attached to a completed Form W-4. The voluntary withholding arrangement will terminate automatically on the date specified. But what about a minister's self-employment taxes? Ministers who have not exempted themselves from Social Security coverage are required to pay the self-employment tax (Social Security tax for self-employed persons). Can a church "withhold" the self-employment tax from a minister-employee's wages? The answer is yes. IRS Publication 517 ("Social Security and Other Information for Members of the Clergy") states that "if you perform your services as an employee of the church (under the common law rules), you may be able to enter into a voluntary withholding agreement with your employer, the church, to cover any income and self-employment tax that may be due." A church whose minister has elected voluntary withholding (and who is not exempt from Social Security taxes) simply withholds an additional amount from each paycheck to cover the minister's estimated self-employment tax liability for the year. The additional amount withheld to cover self-employment taxes must be reported (on the minister's W-2 form and the church's 941 forms) as additional income tax withheld, and not as "Social Security taxes" (or "PICA" taxes). The minister should amend his or her W-4 (withholding allowance certificate) by inserting on line 6 the additional amount of tax to be withheld. The excess income tax withheld is a credit against tax that the minister claims on his or her federal income tax return, and it in effect is applied against the minister's self-employment tax liability. Further, it is considered to be a timely payment of the minister's self-employment tax obligation, and so no penalties for late payment of the quarterly estimates will apply.

Recommendation. *Churches should apprise ministers that they may enter into a voluntary withholding arrangement. For many ministers, such an arrangement will be preferable to the estimated tax procedure. This procedure requires ministers to estimate their income tax and self-employment tax liability for the year 2010 and 2011 prior to April 15, 2010 or April 15, 2011, and then to pay one-fourth of the total estimated tax liability on or by April 15, June 15, September 15, and the following January 15. These quarterly payments are accompanied by a "payment voucher" that is contained in IRS Form 1040-ES. Some ministers find the estimated tax procedure inconvenient and undesirable (it is often hard to budget for the quarterly payments).*

Recommended Resources.
For more detailed information about tax law and voluntary withholding,
see chapter 1, section D, in the *Church & Clergy Tax Guide.*

14. SPECIAL OCCASION GIFTS. It is common for ministers (and in some cases lay workers) to receive special occasion gifts during the course of the year. Examples include Christmas, birthday, and anniversary gifts. Churches and church staff members often do not understand how to report these payments for federal tax purposes. The general rule is this—if the "gifts" are funded through members' contributions to the church (i.e., the contributions are entered or recorded in the church's books as cash received and the members are given charitable contribution credit) then the distribution to the minister or lay worker should be reported as taxable compensation and included on his or her W-2 or 1099 and Form 1040. The same rule applies to special occasion "gifts" made to a minister or lay worker by the church out of the general fund. Members who contribute to special occasion offerings may deduct their contributions if (1) the contributions are to the church and are entered or recorded in the church's books as cash received, and (2) they are able to itemize deductions on Schedule A (Form 1040). Churches should be prepared to include such "gifts" to a minister or lay worker on his or her W-2 or 1099-MISC. Of course, members are free to make personal gifts to ministers and lay staff members, such as a card at Christmas accompanied by a check or cash. Such payments may be tax-free gifts to the recipient (though they are not deductible by the donor). These same rules apply to other kinds of special occasion gifts as well.

It is common for churches to make generous retirement gifts to retiring ministers (and in some cases lay workers). Do these gifts represent taxable income to the recipient? To the extent that the recipient is an employee (or would be classified as an employee by the IRS), there is little doubt that the "gift" would constitute taxable income since section 102(c) of the tax code specifies that "any amount transferred by or for an employer to or for the benefit of an employee" is not excludable from taxable income by the employee as a gift, other than certain employee achievement awards and insignificant holiday gifts. This conclusion is reinforced by the narrow definition of the term *gift*. The Supreme Court has noted that "a gift... proceeds from a detached and disinterested generosity... out of affection, respect, admiration, charity, or like impulses.... The most critical consideration ... is the transferor's intention." *Commissioner v. Duberstein*, 363 U.S. 278, 285 (1960). The Court also observed that "it doubtless is the exceptional payment by an employer to an employee that amounts to a gift," and that the church's characterization of the distribution as a "gift" is "not determinative—there must be an objective inquiry as to whether what is called a gift amounts to it in reality."

>**Key point**< Intermediate sanctions, discussed earlier in this chapter, may apply to a retirement gift that results in unreasonable compensation to the recipient, or that is not reported as taxable income regardless of the amount involved. Church leaders must be sure to consider this possibility before finalizing such a gift.

Recommended Resources.
For more detailed information about tax law and special occasion gifts,
see chapter 4, section B.2, in the *Church & Clergy Tax Guide.*

15. BARGAIN SALES. Occasionally, a church will sell property to a staff member at a price that is below market value. To illustrate, some churches "sell" a parsonage to a retiring minister at a price well below the property's fair market value. Other churches may sell a car or other church-owned vehicle to a minister at a below-market price. The important consideration with such "bargain sales" is this—the "bargain" element (*i.e.*, the difference between the sales price charged by the church and the property's market value) must be reported as income to the minister on his or her W-2 or 1099-MISC and Form 1040. Churches should consider thoroughly the tax consequences of such sales before approving them.

◻ Recommended Resources.

For more detailed information about tax law and bargain sales,
see chapter 4, section B.4, in the *Church & Clergy Tax Guide.*

16. DIRECTOR IMMUNITY. Most states have adopted laws that provide *uncompensated* officers and directors of most charitable organizations (including churches) with limited immunity from legal liability. The federal Volunteer Protection Act provides similar protection as a matter of federal law. The immunity provided under state and federal law only applies to uncompensated officers and directors. What does this have to do with compensation planning? Simply this—churches should consider adopting an appropriate resolution clarifying that a minister's annual compensation package is for ministerial duties rendered to the church, *and is not for any duties on the church board.* Like any other church officer or director, the minister serves without compensation. Such a provision, if adopted, might qualify the minister for protection under the legal immunity law. It is worth considering.

◻ Recommended Resources.

For more detailed information about tax law and director immunity,
see section 6-08 in *Pastor, Church & Law* (4th ed. 2008).

17. DISCRETIONARY FUNDS. It is a fairly common practice for a church to set aside a sum of money in a "discretionary fund" and give the senior minister the sole authority to distribute the money in the fund. In some cases, the minister has no instructions regarding permissible distributions. In other cases, the church establishes guidelines, but these often are oral and ambiguous. Many churches are unaware of the tax consequences of such arrangements. To the extent the minister has the authority to use any portion of the discretionary fund for his or her own personal use, then the entire fund must be reported as taxable income to the minister in the year it is funded. This is true even if the minister does not personally benefit from the fund. The mere fact that the minister *could* personally benefit from the fund is enough for the fund to constitute taxable income. The basis for this result is the "constructive receipt" rule, which is explained in the income tax regulations as follows:

Income although not actually reduced to a taxpayer's possession is constructively received by him in the taxable year during which it is credited to his account, set apart for him, or otherwise made available so that he may draw upon it at any time, or so that he could have drawn upon it during the taxable year if notice of intention to withdraw had been given. However, income is not constructively received if the taxpayer's control of its receipt is subject to substantial limitations or restrictions.

For a discretionary fund to constitute taxable income to a minister, it is essential that the minister have the authority to "draw upon it at any time" for his or her own personal use. This means that the fund was established without any express prohibition against personal distributions. On the other hand, if a discretionary fund is set up by a board resolution that absolutely prohibits any distribution of the fund for the minister's personal use, then the constructive receipt rule is avoided. In the words of the regulation, "income is not constructively received if the taxpayer's control of its receipt is subject to substantial limitations or restrictions." Accordingly, in order to avoid the reporting of the entire discretionary fund as taxable income to the minister, it is essential that the fund be established by means of a board or congregational resolution that absolutely prohibits any use of the fund by the minister for personal purposes. Further, the resolution should specify that the fund may be distributed by the minister only for needs or projects that are consistent with the church's exempt purposes (as set forth in the church's charter). For accountability purposes, a member of the church board should review all distributions from the discretionary fund to be sure that these requirements are met.

⬚ Recommended Resources.
For more detailed information about tax law and discretionary funds,
see chapter 4, section B.I 3, in the *Church & Clergy Tax Guide.*

18. SEVERANCE PAY. Many churches have entered into severance pay arrangements with a pastor or other staff member. Such arrangements can occur when a pastor or staff member is dismissed, retires, or voluntarily resigns. Church treasurers must determine whether severance pay is taxable so that it can be properly reported (on a W-2 and the church's 941 forms). Also, taxes must be withheld from severance pay that is paid to nonminister employees (and ministers who have elected voluntary withholding). Failure to properly report severance pay can result in substantial penalties for both a church and the recipient.

In most cases severance pay represents taxable income to the recipient. There is one exception that will apply in some cases. The tax code excludes from taxable income "the amount of any damages received (whether by suit or agreement and whether as lump sums or as periodic payments) *on account of personal injuries or sickness.*" According to this provision, severance pay that is intended to settle personal injury claims may be nontaxable. The words "personal injuries" are defined broadly by the IRS and the courts, and include potential or threatened lawsuits based on discrimination and harassment.

>**Key point**< The Tax Court has noted that "payments for terminating and canceling employment contracts are not payments for personal injuries."

>**Key point**< The tax code specifies that the term "personal injury" does not include emotional distress.
Here are some factors to consider (based on actual cases) in deciding whether a severance payment made to a former worker represents taxable compensation or nontaxable damages in settlement of a personal injury claim: (1) An amount paid to a former employee "to reward her for her past services and to make her severance as amicable as possible" is taxable compensation. (2) An amount paid to a former employee under a severance agreement that contains no reference to a specific discrimination or other personal injury claim is taxable compensation. (3) If an employer pays a former employee severance pay, and reports the severance pay on a W-2 (or 1099), this is strong evidence that the amount represents taxable compensation. (4) If an employer continues one or more employee benefits (such as health insurance) as part of a severance agreement, this suggests that any amount payable under the agreement represents taxable compensation. (5) If an employer withholds taxes from amounts paid under a severance agreement, this "is a significant factor" in classifying the payments as taxable income. Of course, this factor will not be relevant in the case of ministers whose wages are not subject to withholding (unless they elect voluntary withholding). (6) Referring to a payment as "severance pay" indicates that it is taxable compensation rather than nontaxable damages in settlement of a personal injury claim. (7) Severance pay based on a former employee's salary (such as one year's salary) is more likely to be viewed as taxable compensation rather than nontaxable damages in settlement of a personal injury claim. (8) To be nontaxable, severance pay must represent "damages" received in settlement of a personal injury claim. The IRS has noted that this language requires more than a settlement agreement in which a former employee "waives" any discrimination or other personal injury claims he or she may have against an employer. If the employee "never filed a lawsuit or any other type of claim against [the employer] ... the payment cannot be characterized as damages for personal injuries" since "there is no indication that personal injuries actually exist."

>**Key point**< Section 409A of the tax code imposes strict requirements on most nonqualified deferred compensation plans (NQDPs). In 2007 the IRS published final regulations interpreting section 409A. The final regulations define an NQDP broadly, to include any plan that provides for the deferral of compensation. This definition is broad enough to include severance agreements and many other kinds of church compensation arrangements. Any church or other organization that is considering a severance agreement with a current employee (or any other arrangement that defers compensation to a future year) should contact an attorney to have the arrangement reviewed to ensure compliance with both section 409A and the final regulations. Such a review will protect against the substantial penalties the IRS can assess for noncompliance. It also will help clarify whether a deferred compensation arrangement is a viable option in light of the limitations imposed by section 409A and the final regulations.

▢ Recommended Resources.

For more detailed information about tax law and severance pay,
see chapter 8, section B.17, in the *Church & Clergy Tax Guide.*

19. INCOME "SPLITTING." Some ministers have attempted to "split" their church income with their spouse. This often is done to qualify the spouse for Social Security or other benefits or to avoid the Social Security "annual earnings test" (which reduces Social Security benefits to retired workers who are under "full retirement age" who earn more than an amount prescribed by law). For income splitting arrangements to work, the courts have required proof that the spouse is in fact an employee of the church. This means that the spouse performs meaningful services on behalf of the church. The courts have pointed to a number of factors indicating that a spouse is not an employee: (1) The spouse did not receive a paycheck. (2) The spouse was not employed elsewhere. (3) The spouse's "compensation" was designed to provide a tax benefit (such as an IRA contribution), and lacked any economic reality. (4) Neither the church nor the minister documented any of the services the spouse performed. (5) Neither the church nor the minister could explain how the spouse's "salary" was determined. (6) There was no employment contract between the church and the minister's spouse. (7) No taxes were withheld from the spouse's "salary." (8) The spouse's income was not reported on the church's employment tax returns (Forms 941). (9) There was no evidence that wages were actually paid to the spouse, or that any employment contract existed, or that the spouse was treated as an employee.

The courts generally have been skeptical of attempts by taxpayers to shift income to a spouse. The message is clear— ministers should not attempt to obtain tax benefits by shifting income to a spouse unless there is economic reality to the arrangement.

▢ Recommended Resources.

For more detailed information about tax law and income "splitting,"
see chapter 4, section F, in the *Church & Clergy Tax Guide.*

COMPENSATION CHECKLIST FOR 2010-2011

ITEM	RECOMMENDATION
SALARY	■ avoid unreasonable compensation ■ avoid use of salary reductions that are not recognized by federal tax law
HOUSING ALLOWANCE	■ for ministers who own or rent their home, designate a portion of their compensation as a housing allowance prior to December 31 for the next year ■ for ministers who live in a church-owned parsonage, designate a portion of their compensation as a parsonage allowance (if they will incur any housing expenses) prior to December 31 for the next year
EQUITY ALLOWANCE	■ consider contributing to a tax-sheltered investment (such as a retirement fund) for ministers who live in church-owned parsonage, to compensate for their inability to accumulate equity
ACCOUNTABLE BUSINESS EXPENSE REIMBURSEMENT ARRANGEMENT	■ adopt an accountable business expense reimbursement arrangement by reimbursing only those business expenses that are adequately substantiated, and by requiring any excess reimbursements to be returned
TRAVEL EXPENSES OF A SPOUSE	■ reimburse a spouse's travel expenses incurred in accompanying a minister or lay employee on a business trip if the spouse's presence serves a legitimate business purpose and the expenses are duly substantiated (if these requirements are not met, then the church's reimbursements represent taxable income to the minister or lay employee)
CHURCH-OWNED VEHICLES	■ avoid allowing minister or lay employee unrestricted personal use of a church-owned car (such usage must be valued and reported as taxable income) ■ consider adopting a policy limiting the use of the car to business purposes and requiring it to be kept on church property (this avoids most recordkeeping requirements and does not result in any income to the minister) ■ an alternative is to limit use of the car to business purposes except for commuting to and from work (if the commuting is required for security reasons); each round trip commute represents $3 of reportable income
SELF-EMPLOYMENT TAX PAID BY CHURCH	■ all ministers are self-employed for Social Security purposes with respect to their church work; this means they pay the self-employment tax rather than FICA taxes ■ some churches pay a portion of a minister's self-employment tax (as they pay a portion of a nonminister employee's FICA taxes), such payments represent taxable income ■ nonminister employees of churches that waived payment of FICA taxes by filing a timely Form 8274 are treated as self-employed for Social Security purposes—churches may want to pay a portion of the self-employment taxes owed by these workers if they do so for ministers

COMPENSATION CHECKLIST FOR 2010-2011

ITEM	RECOMMENDATION
INSURANCE	■ consider paying health insurance premiums for ministers and lay employees (a tax-free fringe benefit for employees) ■ consider paying premiums for up to $50,000 of group term life insurance (a tax-free fringe benefit for employees)
RETIREMENT ACCOUNTS	■ consider contributing toward a tax-sheltered retirement plan
WORKS MADE FOR HIRE	■ urge staff members not to write books and articles in the scope of their employment
QUALIFIED TUITION REDUCTIONS	■ consider tuition discounts for ministers and lay employees whose children attend church-operated schools or preschools (they may be a tax-free fringe benefit)
LOANS TO MINISTERS	■ avoid making any low or no interest loan to ministers ■ avoid making any loan to ministers at market rates unless permitted by state nonprofit corporation law
VOLUNTARY WITHHOLDING	■ ministers and lay workers who report their income taxes as employees should consider entering into a voluntary withholding arrangement with the church (can avoid the quarterly estimated tax procedure); be sure to provide for the withholding of self-employment taxes too, but classify these extra withholdings as additional income taxes
SPECIAL OCCASION GIFTS	■ special occasion gifts to ministers and lay employees that are processed through the church's books, and for which contribution credit is given to donors, are taxable income to the minister or lay employee
BARGAIN SALES	■ any property sold to a minister or lay employee at less than fair market value will result in taxable income (the amount by which the fair market value exceeds the sales price)
DIRECTOR IMMUNITY	■ consider adopting a board resolution certifying that all church board members, including the senior minister, serve without compensation (this may qualify the minister for the limited immunity the law provides to uncompensated directors of nonprofit organizations)
DISCRETIONARY FUNDS	■ avoid them unless (1) the minister cannot use the fund for his or her own personal use, (2) the fund may be distributed only for purposes consistent with the church's exempt purposes, and (3) a board member reviews all distributions to ensure compliance with these limits
SEVERANCE PAY	■ severance pay is perfectly appropriate, but be sure that it is reported as additional taxable income unless it represents payment *on account of personal injuries or sickness*
INCOME "SPLITTING"	■ do not attempt to shift a portion of a minister's compensation to his or her spouse for tax savings purposes, unless there is "economic reality" to the arrangement (the spouse performs services that otherwise would be compensated, and receives a reasonable rate of compensation)

APPENDIX

Regions by State

PACIFIC
Alaska
California
Hawaii
Oregon
Washington

MOUNTAIN
Arizona
Colorado
Idaho
Montana
Nevada
New Mexico
Utah
Wyoming

WEST NORTH CENTRAL
Iowa
Kansas
Minnesota
Missouri
Nebraska
North Dakota
South Dakota

WEST SOUTH CENTRAL
Arkansas
Louisiana
Oklahoma
Texas

EAST NORTH CENTRAL
Illinois
Indiana
Michigan
Ohio
Wisconsin

EAST SOUTH CENTRAL
Alabama
Kentucky
Mississippi
Tennessee

MIDDLE ATLANTIC
New Jersey
New York
Pennsylvania

NEW ENGLAND
Connecticut
Maine
Massachusetts
New Hampshire
Rhode Island
Vermont

SOUTH ATLANTIC
Delaware
District of Columbia
Florida
Georgia
Maryland
North Carolina
South Carolina
Virginia
West Virginia

TEN YEAR COMPENSATION TREND
FOR FULL-TIME CHURCH STAFF*

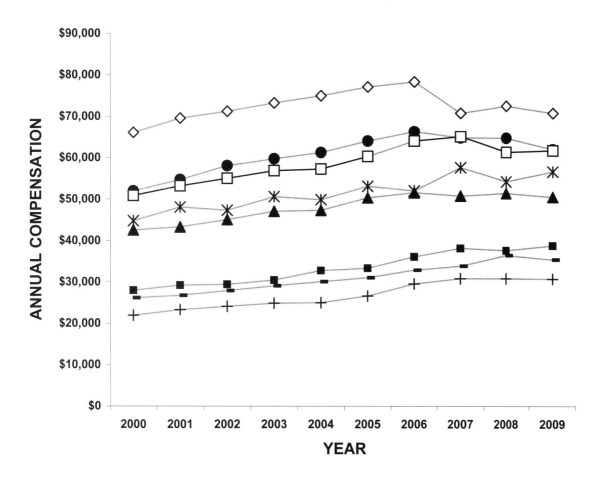

* Historical data is not available for Adult Ministry/Christian Education or Children's/Preschool Pastor/Director.

** Averages for Pastor include data for both Senior and Solo Pastors for comparison purposes.

*** The above trend is made available for your reference only. In addition to looking at this overall data, please refer to the detailed tables using your church's income, attendance, setting, region, and denomination as well as the person's education, gender, and years employed for guidance in compensating this position.

—◇— **Senior/Solo Pastor****

—●— **Associate Pastor**

—▲— **Youth Pastor/Director**

—□— **Music Pastor/Director**

—✳— **Administrator**

—■— **Bookkeeper/Accountant**

—+— **Secretary/Administrative Assistant**

—–— **Custodian**

Kathleen J. Turpin, JD, CPCU
Employment Law Expert

Ask the Expert

Wouldn't it be great to have access to a panel of experts who are recognized authorities in the problems that keep ministry leaders awake at night?

Guess what? You do.

Visit *www.churchsafety.com* where you'll find free safety articles, online assessments, and our exclusive Ask the Expert service.

! churchsafety.com℠

SIMPLE | SMART | STEP-BY-STEP